The contents of this book were previously published in
U.S. Marine Corps Aircraft 1914–1959, copyright © 1959
by William T. Larkins, and *U.S. Navy Aircraft 1921–1941*,
copyright © 1961 by William T. Larkins

This 1988 edition published by Orion Books, a division of
Crown Publishers, Inc., 201 East 50th Street, New York,
New York 10022

ORION and Colophon are trademarks of Crown Publishers, Inc.
Manufactured in the United States of America

Library of Congress Cataloging-in-Publication Data

Larkins, William T.
[U.S. Navy aircraft, 1921–1941]
U.S. Navy aircraft, 1921–1941; U.S. Marine Corps aircraft, 1914–1959
by William T. Larkins.
p. cm.
Includes bibliographies and indexes.
Contents: U.S. Navy aircraft, 1921–1941—U.S. Marine Corps aircraft, 1914–1959

1. Airplanes. Military—United States. 2. United States. Navy—
Aviation. 3. United States. Marine Corps—Aviation. 4. United
States. Coast Guard—Aviation. I. Larkins, William T., 1922–
U.S. Navy aircraft, 1921–1941. 1988. II. Larkins, William T.,
1922– U.S. Marine Corps aircraft, 1914–1959. 1988. III. Title.
IV. Title: U.S. Navy and Marine Corps, 1914–1959.
UG1243.L38 1988
358.4′ 1983—dc19
88-17753
CIP

ISBN 0-517-56920-5
10 9 8 7 6 5 4 3 2

U.S. NAVY

AIRCRAFT

1921-1941

ACKNOWLEDGEMENTS

This book is graphic evidence of the superior quality that can result from a combination of official photographs and information, and the work of civilian enthusiasts. Neither group could have produced this book alone; only through a merger of the resource material and talents of both can such a volume emerge.

Ironically the basic framework of the annual *Status of Naval Aircraft* reports, without which this book would have been impossible, came from the vast and priceless files of the Air Force Museum at Wright-Patterson Air Force Base, Dayton, Ohio. The necessary work of locating the material, having it declassified and then made available was started by the late Robert S. Houston, a devoted and sincere professional historian. Royal Frey, Director of the Reference Branch of the Air Force Museum, carried on with this work and made additional copies available.

The second most valuable contribution was made by Peter M. Bowers, who made his entire collection of photographs and negatives available, and in addition loaned a vast file of "Characteristics and Performance Charts" for Navy aircraft. Coupled with his file was the same generosity of total contribution by Gordon S. Williams and John C. Mitchell. Dozens of official Navy photographs, as well as old factory photos, which are included in the book were available only because of their outstanding cooperation. Many of these were old yellow, fading, prints; long since gone from official and factory files.

In like manner Lee Enich made an important contribution in the form of various photos from an album of the late Commander Earl Spencer, and Harry Gann contributed additional photos from an album of Commander George White. These photos have not been available from any other source and they constitute a valuable historical contribution.

The loan of several priceless documents by Adrian O. Van Wyen, head of the Aviation History Unit, Navy Department, contributed greatly to the accuracy and completeness of the appendixes. Elbert L. Huber, of the National Archives, located and made available some additional early Status reports, as well as certain previously missing photos as will be seen by the photo credits.

Adding to the material from the professional historians was the advice and information made available by the following members of the American Aviation Historical Society: Harold Andrews, Harvey Lippincott, William A. Riley, Jr., Richard K. Smith and Ray Wagner.

Several official photos were made available by Alexis Dawydoff, James C. Fahey, Deward B. Gresham and Chalmers A. Johnson. Many original photos were contributed by Howard Levy and Warren Shipp and they are individually credited.

A limited number of photographs was made available by the public relations departments of Convair, Grumman, Douglas, Vought and Pratt & Whitney Aircraft.

Commander H. Harold Bishop USNR, of the Bureau of Naval Personnel, provided the original impetus that got this work started as a part of the 50th anniversary of naval aviation. Lieutenant Commander F. A. Prehn USN, of the Office of Information, made a number of requested official photographs available and has followed the project from the beginning.

Lawrence S. Smalley spent endless hours of tedious work in connection with the appendixes, and William R. McIntyre demonstrated his enthusiasm and interest in drawing the squadron insignias.

In so far as possible the credit line below each photograph is for the person or agency that actually took the picture. This has been done specially in order to give credit to the aircraft photo collectors, several of whom are now deceased, whose work is now a permanent contribution to naval aviation history. Their efforts of thirty years ago, often preserved by additional collectors, are for the most part published here for the first time.

Naturally such a credit is not always possible, and where the photographer is completely unknown the name of the source of the photo is given in the credit line. In the case of private collectors this is usually an indication that the person named holds the original negative to the photograph. Official photos, particularly from the National Archives, are often copies of factory photos and this is sometimes pointed out in the captions.

As a matter of interest to the reader all Navy photographs taken prior to September 1945 were transferred from the Naval Photographic Center at NAS Anacostia to the National Archives in 1961, where they are now available for public use.

Photo credits for the Introduction are as follows: Page 1, U.S. Navy; page 2, Pratt & Whitney Aircraft; pages 3-8, U.S. Navy; page 9, Gordon S. Williams; page 10, insignia, Oliver R. Phillips, SOC-1 cowl, John C. Mitchell, Chief of Bureau insignia, U.S. Navy, remainder W. T. Larkins; page 11, William T. Larkins; page 12, U.S. Navy.

———————

The Landing Signal Officer bringing an F3B-1 of Bombing Two aboard the USS SARATOGA in 1929. In today's world of constant radio communication and complex mirror landing systems, Navy pilots tend to forget that carrier landings were once made with one man and two flags.

INTRODUCTION

This is a book about airplanes. It is not a history of naval aviation, nor is it a description of the personalities, command policies, or the pre-war development of carrier aviation. All of these subjects are adequately covered in books already published, described in Appendix G, and this book is intended to supplement them with additional information and photographs.

It is an attempt to present in an organized fashion all Heavier-than-air aircraft operated by the United States Navy from January 1, 1921 to December 31, 1941. For some unknown reason, probably because of its complexity and the lack of adequate information and photographs, a thorough description of Navy aircraft of this period has been non-existent. It is hoped that this volume, admittedly still incomplete, will help to fill this void until such time as the subject may be completely covered.

The text is presented in a manner different than any other book, i.e. chronologically by year, with the emphasis on the service duty of all types of planes. This style of presentation is the most difficult of all to produce because it requires a knowledge of the use of all aircraft for all of the years described, and in addition limits the use of photographs to the dates on which they were taken. If it can be achieved, however, it is the most singularly valuable method of historical presentation of this type of material that can be made.

With the passing of the battleships, and the emergence of the carrier as the symbol of naval aviation, one is likely to forget the majesty that was once theirs—and the fact that airplanes were carried as an integral part of both battleships and cruisers in the Fleet during the pre-war years. The O3U-3 shown here aboard the PENNSYLVANIA is being run-up in the top photo; launched in the bottom photo.

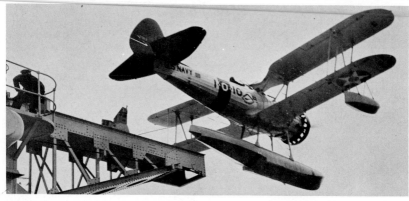

Pre-war carrier operations, in all its color and appeal, is shown in these two photos of carriers under way in bright, clear skies with a fresh sea breeze and a calm sea. Flight operations were not always carried out under such ideal conditions and rough weather landings on a pitching, rolling deck took its toll of lives and planes. The top photo shows the SARATOGA in the foreground, with VF-6B F4B-4's on deck, followed by the LEXINGTON and RANGER. The bottom photo shows Great Lakes BG-1's of Bombing Four taking off. Planes were launched one at a time and flown off under their own power.

A 3-place Loening OL-6 on the turret catapult of the CALIFORNIA. Note the ship name under the left wing. Battleship Observation squadrons moved about from one ship to another. Compare this photo of 1-O-10 with 2-O-2 on page 58, which was also aboard the CALIFORNIA.

For the most part each year of the book is arranged in the following manner: aircraft assignment tables; Fleet aircraft; Fleet auxiliary and utility types; new and experimental planes for the year; Naval Reserve information and photos (if any); and Coast Guard aircraft (if any).

The reader is asked to pardon certain liberties taken with the English language because of space limitations, or for the purpose of emphasis. As the author of *The Ford Story*, it is well realized that an entire book can be written about many individual aircraft types, but such information has of necessity been held to a minimum because of costs.

Since a picture contains far more information than can be written in words in the same space, photographs have been used wherever possible. Tables and abbreviated captions add to the total information presented, but the reader must contribute a certain amount of effort to gain the maximum amount from this book. A pencil and note-pad are indispensable to the use of this book for with them information on a given subject may be collated from various parts to form a very complete story. A reader interested in what planes and squadrons flew from the USS SARATOGA, for example, will find this information readily available in the annual Fleet Aircraft Assignment tables, together with the photo captions and appendixes.

More than 550 different model designations were used by the Navy during the period 1921-1941. Some of these were World War I types, such as the HS-2L, that carried on for several years. This disorganized mixture of company designations was joined by a new system in 1922, but it was reversed in 1923, resulting in three different types of aircraft designations being in service at the same time during the early 1920's. (See Appendix E and F for more detailed information.)

In addition, certain types such as the O3U-6, RC-1, etc., that were used solely, or almost entirely, by the Marine Corps are not included. An effort has been made to avoid as much duplication as possible between this book and its companion volume which complement each other, and both should be used jointly to present the complete story of Navy, Marine Corps and Coast Guard aircraft for the pre-war years. It is worth mentioning in passing that the complete assignment of Marine Corps aircraft for December 1941, which is contained in this book, is not included in the USMC volume.

The intent of this book from the beginning has been to illustrate every squadron number that was in commission between 1921 and 1941, and in addition to illustrate, if possible, every aircraft type flown in the markings of each of these squadrons.

Patrol Squadrons, however, have been particularly elusive, and most are not represented at all; only twelve squadrons are included. The two worst examples are VP-2 and VP-5. If one counts their continuous service through number changes both were in service for over fourteen years and yet not one single photograph of any plane of either squadron has been available from any source! The frightening conclusion one must draw from this is that unless the Navy Department files contain a great deal of unknown material their history from a photographic standpoint is already lost.

Another example, the Berliner-Joyce OJ-2, operated with VS-5B and VS-6B for three years aboard OMAHA Class cruisers, yet not one single photo of an OJ-2 on floats has been available. Incredible as it may seem, there appears to be no historical photographic record of these two squadron's daily operations from 1933 through 1935, except for photos taken by private collectors of the planes on wheels. The OJ-2's are the real orphans of the service, and their description on pages 126-127 of this book it the first time that they have been given proper credit. Even the exhaustive, official work *United States Naval Aviation 1910-60* does not acknowledge their existence in its aircraft appendix.

This Martin T3M-2 shore-based torpedo-bomber from a Naval District squadron shows the unique use of the squadron and plane designation on the under-side of both wings. It is the 6th plane of Torpedo Squadron Seven of the 14th Naval District at Pearl Harbor, Hawaii.

Coast Guard aviation has been another orphan and although it was under the Treasury Department in peace time it is included in this book for two reasons. First, because USCG aircraft used the Navy model designation system and many designations were reserved for Coast Guard use. The JRF-2 and JRF-3, for example, were Coast Guard designations in the middle of the navy JRF series. Secondly, the USCG is a branch of the Navy in wartime and all USCG pilots are Navy trained.

The individual aircraft assignment for every plane in the Navy is included for the years 1926, 1937 and 1941. For the remaining years, due to space limitations and considerable duplication, this has been reduced to those squadrons which may be considered as the tactical operating Fleet. This is an arbitrary decision made by the author and does not reflect any Navy policy on what constitutes such an organization. Much of the remaining material for experimental planes, training and reserve activities, has been included in the captions. Specific information on aircraft assignments for the years prior to 1926 has not been available. As a result the years 1921-1925 must be considered incomplete at this time.

While the assigned serial number of an aircraft was permanent, all other markings were temporary. As may be seen by various examples, such as the O3U-3 on page 177, squadron numbers and individual aircraft numbers within a squadron were often subject to considerable change. It is this very thing that gives the individual history to each plane, and in turn to the over-all picture of Navy aircraft use.

Many instances are to be found of aircraft being used by the Navy, transferring to the Marine Corps, and returning to the Navy again. Some examples of this are pointed out in the SU captions, and a check of the photos in *U. S. Marine Corps Aircraft 1914-1959* with those of the same type in this book will prove enlightening. In addition a comparison of serial numbers for photos in this book will prove quite informative. Quite a bit of individual aircraft history, for example, is contained on pages 74, 86 and 94 for those with the curiosity to seek it out. Photographic evidence is presented which shows that #7144 as 1-B-10 on floats with the Red Rippers, later modified to test a special engine cooling device, and finally as station plane No. 23 at NAS Hampton Roads.

The Boeing XF3B-1 shown here, and several other "Navy" aircraft, were individual company projects built as private ventures. The tail stripes shown were developed by Boeing, adopted by the Army Air Corps.

Bombing Squadron One, shown here, is the only unit to use the F3B-1 that is not illustrated in the body of the book. Note the large size of the national star insignia and chrome yellow top surface of wing.

It should be remembered that what is for the retired Admiral over-simplicity and incompleteness is at the same time incomprehensible to the present-day high school student who has never seen a bi-plane. This book is an attempt at a median approach to bridge this gap in the hope that this information will not be lost forever with the passing of those who knew it from personal experience. Even at this very recent date, historically speaking, it is extremely difficult to find the explanation for many things which were commonplace at the time of their occurrence.

This book is not complete, and yet it is far more complex than any similar work has been in the past. The Index, for example, should not be used as a list of U. S. Navy aircraft for the years 1921-1941 for it is simply a listing of the photographs in this book. It has not been possible to obtain a number of photographs so that certain types that were used by the Navy will not be found in the Index. 153 known model designations, for example, are not illustrated in this book. The most accurate listing for this purpose is Appendix B, the Assigned Serial Number List, but even this must be used with caution for it does not contain all of the model designations that were assigned to modifications of Navy planes.

Throughout this book the reader will find a constant emphasis on markings, painting schemes, colors and insignia. These are the things that create an individual personality for an otherwise inanimate machine. Without these distinctive additions each airplane in a production batch is indistinguishable from any other. The Navy went through several specific programs for color and markings during 1921-1941 and these will be readily seen by the arrangement of this book which portrays each in its proper chronological position.

A High Hat F4B-3 just about to catch the wire on the SARATOGA. Arresting cables were held off deck surface by retractable guides, as seen in the foreground. See an additional photo on page 113.

The slightest error in judgment while landing could lead to minor accidents; here SU-1 2-S-9 from the SARATOGA has skidded over the side on top of the port after gun gallery. Cables sometimes broke.

A Grumman Widgeon of 1941 banking away to show the underside markings of the Coast Guard used in the late 1930's. The leading edge of the wing and tail shows a rubber de-icer boot, not special markings.

The constant emphasis on squadron markings is not without purpose. It is felt that the only historical continuity that can be given to pre-war Naval aircraft history lies in the chronological lineage of its users. The re-numbering of squadrons, which has continued on through WW2 and since, leads to so many apparent contradictions that an explanation is meaningless without a reference to their former identity. The High Hat squadron illustrates this clearly, going from VF-1 to VB-2 to VB-3 to VB-4 to VS-41 prior to 1942. Realizing that this was only *one* squadron, always the High Hats, helps to dispel the illusion that there were more Navy squadrons in service than were actually in commission. There were only 20 carrier squadrons in 1937; 29 in late 1941. The average number of squadrons aboard carriers in the pre-war years was only 12.

Today we watch the Blue Angels performing aerobatics in six jets as a symbolic representation of naval aviation. What a contrast this is to the June 1934 Naval Pageant in New York City when 81 ships steamed into the harbor in line with 185 naval aircraft in formation

In the 1930's the Reserves adopted a shield insignia (left) for all of their planes. The name of the base was on the anchor. Some planes, as XR40-1 (right) had designation and serial on both sides of twin tail.

Pilots qualifying for the annual Individual Battle Practice could place an "E" on their plane; SOC on left has four. The wing chevron, in section colors, was applied on low-wing monoplanes as shown on right.

Four-plane Cruiser sections used a vertical cowl stripe on the fourth plane, see left photo. Right photo shows little-known insignia of the Chief of the Bureau on his Vought UO-1, in addition to his two stars.

In 1937 squadron tail colors were changed so that all squadrons from the same carrier had the same color. The rare Winged Turtle was for aircraft that had flown over the equator. Note section stripe detail.

This NRAB Oakland SBC-4 shows the continuation of the fuselage stripe on the under side of the fuselage, as well as the two stars on the lower surface of the bottom wing. Note new design, full-span flaps.

overhead. After review by President Roosevelt the ships continued up the Hudson River to anchor or berth themselves along the New York and New Jersey waterfronts. 500,000 people turned out for this event, and to visit the ships, an indication of public interest at that time.

Anyone who lived in the seaport cities of San Diego, Norfolk, San Francisco, Seattle, New York or Honolulu can never forget the peace time majesty of the freshly painted white ships and their colorful aircraft. The genuine pre-war Navy buff could name from memory every ship in the Navy, including such things as gun boats and yard craft. It is hoped that this volume will help to bring back some of that enthusiasm.

This book will mean many things to many people. To the pre-war Navy pilots and crews it will mean nostalgia at seeing again planes once flown and almost forgotten; to the photo collector it is like a giant stamp catalog—full of priceless oddities and curios, as well as the commonplace; to the professional historian the facts and tables speak for themselves without the additional value of photos; to the serious scale model builder it is a profuse source of authentic material on markings and color; to the youth and layman of today it is a fascinating look into the past, an organized tour of naval aircraft development.

Each should enjoy it in his own way.

WILLIAM T. LARKINS
September 3, 1961

All Fleet aircraft had been camouflaged with warpaint by December 1941. The horizontal tail stripes seen here were adopted January 5, 1942. Note machine gun inside rear canopy on the lead Vought OS2U-1.

13

Boeing C-1F (A-4347)   *Manufacturer*
*Typical of the wood-and-wire period of Navy aircraft, this one-only
plane was built in 1918. Metal construction became common by 1930's.*

Douglas AD-1 (09204) and Grumman F8F-1 (95318)   William T. Larkins
*The ultimate in the propeller-driven Navy combat plane; the F8F was
the last carrier prop fighter, the AD is still in use by Attack squadrons.*

Vought F8U-1P (144622)   *U. S. Navy*
*Photo-jet over the USS-FORRESTAL CVA-59; everything, including the
hook, retracts; speed and streamlining are today's design factors.*

Aeromarine 39-B (A-643)   *U. S. Navy*
Two-place trainer on skis about to land in the snow. This plane was
selected because of its stability as first type to land on a carrier.

The aircraft inventory for 1 July 1921, less experimental types, was
as follows: Class VF, 31 VE-7SF; Class VO, 47 Loening M-81 and M-80,
17 Vought VE-7, 17 Vought VE-7G and VE-7GF, 68 DH-4B, 37 JN-4H and
JN-6H, 122 N-9, 6 F Boat, 87 MF Boat, 38 Aeromarine 40; Class VP,
347 HS-1L and HS-2L, 106 H-16, 172 F-5L; Class VT, 25 R-6L, 2 MBT,
7 MT; Class VG, 5 NC Boat. The VE-7, DH-4B, JN-4H, JN-6H, MF and
Aeromarine 40 types were also classified as training planes. It can
readily be seen that Patrol planes were the foremost type used by the
Navy in 1921. The original HS-1L's, with 12 struts, became HS-2L's
with an additional 12-foot span and increase of six feet in rudder
area. The addition of one six-foot panel on each side of the fuselage
gave the HS-2L 16 struts. The 31 VE-7SF's were a big increase over
the 8 Nieuport 28's that constituted the entire Navy VF category in
July 1920. The following pages illustrate the aircraft types used by
the U. S. Navy from the founding of the Bureau of Aeronautics to the
entry of the United States into World War II. Congress authorized
the establishment of a Bureau of Aeronautics on July 12, 1921; a Navy
General Order of August 10th defined its duties under the Secretary
of the Navy, and the Bureau began operations under its first Chief,
Rear Admiral W. A. Moffett, on September 1st. During these twenty
years the Navy developed the aircraft designs and tactics that, together
with well trained men, formed the foundation of its WW-II operations.

Curtiss CR-1 (A-6080)   *U. S. Navy*
Winner of 1921 Pulitzer Race at Omaha, flown by Bert Acosta, with a
new world speed record of 176.7 mph. Note Lamblin cooling radiators.

Curtiss R-6L (A-976)   *U. S. Navy*

Beefed-up, converted trainer as our first torpedo plane. Compare with PT-2, page 29. First Fleet torpedo practice took place one year later.

Burgess N-9 (A-2351)   *U. S. Navy*

The first Burgess-built Curtiss "Jenny" on a contract for 300. Built in 1918 as the standard Navy floatplane for primary flight training.

Burgess N-9 (A-2449)   *U. S. Navy*

A later production model with Hispano-Suiza I in place of Hisso A. Note radiator extending above the wing. 122 N-9's were used in 1921.

Curtiss H-16 (A-4073)   *U. S. Navy*
One of several patrol planes of this type built by Curtiss and the
Naval Aircraft Factory in 1918-1919. 106 in 1921; 6 lasted to 1929.

Aeromarine 40-F (A-5086)   *U. S. Navy*
Small two-place OXX powered trainer, one of 50 built. Fifty additional
planes on the contract for A-5040 to A-5239 were cancelled. Class VA.

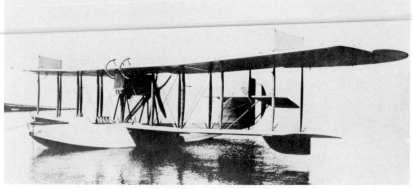

Curtiss HS-3 (A-5459)   *U. S. Navy*
Late WWI improved version of HS-2L with same engine, slightly better
performance. Curtiss built four; the Naval Aircraft Factory built two.

Vought VE-7GF (A-5683)   *The National Archives*
Pulling the prop through on the two-place Observation version of the
VE-7 trainer. Note fixed forward gun, rear gun, original flotation bags.

Loening M-81S (A-5791)   *U. S. Navy*
Designed as a fighter in 1919, 8 of these were used by the Navy for
Observation duty in 1921. By 1922 there were 47 M-81's and M-80's as VO.

Loening LS-1 (A-5606)   *U. S. Navy*
Rare photo of only LS-1 two-place floteplane with rear gun ring built,
A-5607 was cancelled. This and M-80, M-81 used 300 hp Hipsano-Suiza.

Nieuport 28 C.1 (A-5800)   *U. S. Navy*
One of 12 WW-I fighters obtained from the Army after the armistice and
used by Combat Squadron Three (VF-2) prior to delivery of VE-7F's.

Dornier CS-2 (A-6055)   *U. S. Navy*
A German designed and built six-passenger flying boat purchased by the
Navy to study its all-metal construction. Pilot sat behind engine.

J. L. Aircraft Corporation JL-6 (A-5867)   *U. S. Navy*
Junkers-built all-metal transport assembled in the U. S. Imported by
Larsen who promoted their sale to the Army, Navy and Post Office.

Donne-Denhaut (A-5652)   *U. S. Navy*
One of two French flying boats purchased abroad during the war and
returned to the U. S. in 1919. Had 200 hp Hispano-Suiza, 54-foot span.

Austrian Government K Boat (A-5806)   *U. S. Navy*
Believed to be the Hansa-Brandenburg W-13 flying boat. Gross weight
7500 pounds. One of two war-time procurements aboard; see below.

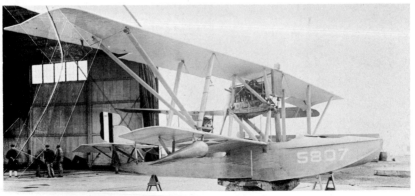

Austrian Government K Boat (A-5807)   *U. S. Navy*
The second of these two boats, this one was smaller and lighter at
4000 pounds. Has been listed as War. Eissler AG Wein XXII, K-248.

Sopwith 1½ Strutter (A-5740)   *U. S. Navy*
One of 22; A-5660 purchased overseas during WW-1, A-5725-5728 and
A-5734-5750 obtained from the U. S. Army. They were Class VO in 1920.

Davis-Douglas DT-1 (A-6031)   *U. S. Navy*
The first plane designed and built for the USN as a torpedo plane.
Single-place, Liberty powered. Note torpedo in place under fuselage.

Martin MBT (A-5711)   *U. S. Navy*
The first large bomber and torpedo plane used operationally by the
Navy. The engines were lowered to the bottom wing in later models.

Curtiss HS-2L (A-2076)   *U. S. Navy*

The most numerous type on hand in July 1922. The aircraft inventory, as of that date less experimental types, was as follows: Class VF, 5 VE-7S, 11 MB-3, 1 MB-7, 2 TS-1, 1 CR, 2 18-T, 4 Fokker D-7 and 2 Fokker C-1; Class VO, 200 DH-4B, 2 AS-2, 4 EM-2, 6 PT, 2 Parnall, 1 JL-6, 1 Viking IV; Class VP, 253 HS-2, 127 F-5L, 97 H-16, 4 NC Boat, 2 TF; Class VT,19 R-6L, 5 MBT, 3 MT, 6 PT-1, 13 PT-2, 1 CT-1, 2 ST-1, 1 DT-1, 1 DT-2, 2 Blackburn Swift; Class VA, 75 JN, 95 N-9, 23 F Boat, 73 MF Boat, 40 Model 40 Boat, 36 39-A, 6 39-B, 66 VE-7, 33 VE-7G, 1 VE-7H, 6 Morane-Saulnier AR-1. Effective 1 July 1922 all Fleet Air Squadrons were reorganized; Scouting Squadron 2 became VS-1, Torpedo Plane Squadron 1 became Torpedo and Bombing Plane Squadron 1 (VT-1), Seaplane Patrol Squadron 1 became VT-2, Spotting Squadron 4 became VO-1, Spotting Squadron 3 became VO-2, Spotting Squadron L1 became VO-3, Combat Squadron 4 became VF-1 and Combat Squadron 3 became VF-2. VF-3 was organized as a new unit to provide air protection to Train ships and to be a nucleus for Aircraft Squadrons, Base Force. VS-1, VT-1 and Kite Balloon Squadron 1 formed Aircraft Squadrons, Scouting Fleet (Atlantic); the remainder forming Aircraft Squadrons, Battle Fleet (Pacific). USS WRIGHT and USS AROOSTOOK were flagships.

War Department DH-4B1 (A-6377)   *U. S. Navy*

LT Ben Wyatt taking off from San Diego on October 14, 1922 for a two-plane 7,000 mile trip to Washington, D.C., and back. Returned Nov. 29.

Bee Line BR-2 (A-6430)   *U. S. Navy*
The Booth racer with wing skin radiators for engine cooling, note
large surface in photo. BR-1 had then standard Lamblin radiators.

Curtiss Triplane Racer   *Peter M. Bowers*
Al Williams standing in front of the Curtiss-Cox "Wildcat" racer
entered in the 1922 Pulitzer. Navy connection and serial unknown.

Curtis CR-1 (A-6081)   *Manufacturer*
LT H. J. Brow in the cockpit of the second Curtiss Racer, photo on
9-14-22 when it had wing radiators. He finished third at 193 mph.

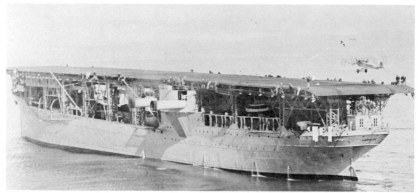

USS LANGLEY CV1   *U. S. Navy*
The first experimental carrier, commissioned March 20, 1922. First
T.O. by LT Griffin in VE-7SF on 10-17; first landing 10-26 in 39-B.

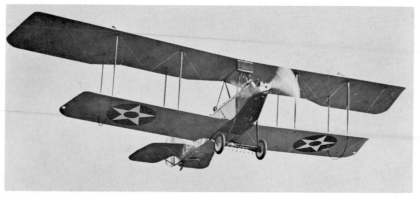

Aeromarine 39-B   *U. S. Navy*
First airplane to make a carrier landing in USN. LCDR Godfrey deC.
Chevalier made the landing on October 26th. Note early guide hooks.

Curtiss TS-1 (A-6248)   *Manufacturer*
The first post-war fighter designed and built for the Navy; at the
factory on July 11th. Curtiss production was supplemented by NAF.

Aeromarine AS-2 (A-5613)   *U. S. Navy*
One of three special "fighting ship machines" delivered and assigned
to Observation duty. Had a 300 hp Hispano, rear pit machine gun ring.

Morane-Saulnier AR-1 (A-5980)   *The National Archives*
One of six purchased after the war. An 80 hp trainer with a Le Rhone
rotary engine. Note the typical French World War I design features.

Dornier D-1 (A-6058)   *The National Archives*
A German all-metal cantilever biplane purchased for design study and
the possible advantages of metal construction. Note serial on aileron.

Naval Aircraft Factory TF (A-5576)   *U. S. Navy*
The rare Tandem Fighter powered by two Hispano-Suiza engines. Note
the tail booms, twin tails. A-5578 had Packard engines. Three were built.

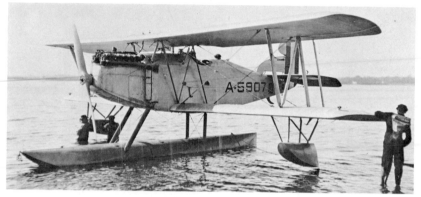

Elias EM-2 (A-5907)   *U. S. Navy*
One of six built to design specifications for a Marine Expeditionary
aircraft. See EM-1 (A-5905) and EM-2 (A-5906) in Marine Corps book.

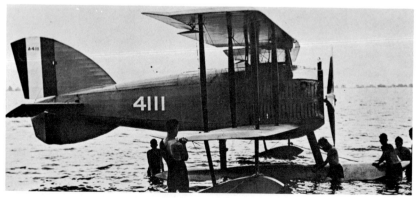

Curtiss HA (A-4111)   *U. S. Navy*
The late World War I "Dunkirk Fighter" changed to a two-place scout.
It had a big Liberty engine and was about the same size as a DH-4B.

Martin M2O-1 (A-6453)   *The National Archives*
Three-place observation plane also built by the Naval Aircraft Factory
as the model NO-1 (see page 38). Both types used the Curtiss D-12.

Martin M2O-1 (A-6453)   *U. S. Navy*
Note rear cockpit with machine gun ring. It was about the same size
as the DH-4 and typical of the post World War I period of design.

Naval Aircraft Factory DH-4B (A-6125)   *U. S. Navy*
Special ambulance modification with litter behind pilot. Note small
window for patient; wing crosses. Top surface of both wings was red.

Naval Aircraft Factory PT-2 (A-6330)　　　　　　　*U. S. Navy*
NAF designed and built torpedo bomber utilizing R-6 fuselages and HS
wings. Note unusual placement of squadron designation 1-T-15 on rudder.

Fokker FT-1 (A-6008)　　　　　　　　　　　　　*U. S. Navy*
Dutch-built torpedo bomber flying over Hampton Roads in April 1923.
Note typical Fokker ailerons, box fuselage and small vertical tail.

Curtiss CS-1 (A-6502)　　　　　　　　　　　　*Manufacturer*
Three-purpose type built to perform as a scout, bomber or torpedo
plane. Had folding wings, was convertible from landplane to seaplane.

Martin MS-1 (A-6521)   *Manufacturer*
The wood and fabric XS-1 submarine scout built in all-metal construction by Martin. Aluminum floats, wings quickly detachable for stowage.

Naval Aircraft Factory N2N-1 (A-6695)   *U. S. Navy*
Two-place trainer of conventional design for training in flying and gunnery. Three were built. Powered by a 200 hp Lawrence J-1 engine.

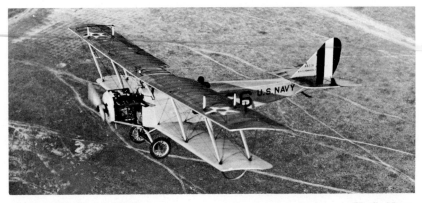

Curtiss JN-4H (A-6226)   *U. S. Navy*
From NAS Pensacola, note station name on fin. One of several obtained from the Army. Curtiss design, various manufacturers, lasted to 1927.

Huff-Daland HO-1 (A-6561)   *U. S. Navy*
Two-place observation type, three were built. Near duplicate HN-1
and HN-2 trainers were also built in 1923. Had a 180 hp Wright E-2.

Curtiss CR-3 (A-6080)   *U. S. Navy*
Original CR-1 converted to a seaplane for the Schneider Cup Race at
Cowes, England. Flown by LT Irvine, placed second at 173.46 m.p.h.

Curtiss CR-3 (A-6081)   *U. S. Navy*
LT Rittenhouse's first place winner at 177.38 mph. See earlier photo of
A-6081 as land racer on p. 22. The USN showing was widely acclaimed.

Wright NW-2 (A-6544)   *U. S. Navy*

The sesquiplane NW-1, flown by Lt. Sanderson (USMC) in 1922, was modified to this standard biplane configuration for the 1923 Schneider Cup Race. Unfortunately it did not get to fly in the race because a broken propeller blade tore one of its floats during flight trials in England. It was powered by the big Wright "Tornado" engine of 750 hp. Note the wing-skin cooling radiators on the top and bottom surfaces of both wings. LT Al Williams placed first in an R2C-1 in the 1923 Pulitzer Race, held in October as a part of the National Air Races at St. Louis, with a speed of 243.68 mph. The second R2C-1, flown by LT Brow, placed second at 241.77 mph. The two Wright F2W-1's placed third and fourth at 230 mph, with the Army Curtiss Racers finishing fifth and sixth. Following the St. Louis races the Navy withdrew from racing, except for the Schneider Cup Race, due to lack of funds. A great deal of useful information was gained from these races, particularly in regard to increased horse power, new types of fuels, engine cooling and high speed control problems. Although November 1926 marked the end of the Navy's participation in the Schneider Race one R3C-4 remained through 1928. From February 1928, until it was surveyed in November, it was designated XR3C-4.

Curtiss R2C-2 (A-6692)   *U. S. Navy*

The winner of the 1923 Pulitzer Race at St. Louis in 1923 after its conversion to a seaplane in preparation for 1924 Schneider Cup Race.

Wright F2W-1 (A-6743)   *Manufacturer*
The Wright Aeronautical Corporation racer with regulation Fighter
model designation. As flown in 1923 St. Louis races, see page 36.

Naval Aircraft Factory TR-3 (A-6447)   *The National Archives*
NAF TS-2 re-built into a seaplane racer. Flown by LT Rittenhouse in
the 1922 Curtiss Marine Trophy Race at Detroit, had forced landing.

Naval Aircraft Factory TR-3A (A-6447)   *U. S. Navy*
The same plane further modified, note lowering of upper wing, etc.
Scheduled third in the 1923 Schneider Race in England but didn't fly.

Vought UO-1 (A-6613)   *U. S. Navy*

Two-place battleship observation floatplane being catapulted from the
USS NEVADA. See next p. for additional information on Observation 6.

Vought UO-1 (A-6607)   *U. S. Navy*

Early model UO-1, with propeller spinner, from the USS TENNESSEE.
Note shape of early wing floats, compare with later UO-1 on page 55.

Vought UO-1 (A-6493)   *U. S. Navy*

Being hoisted aboard the cruiser USS RICHMOND. Observation Squadron
Three was assigned to the Light (Scout) Cruisers upon commissioning.

Martin MO-1   *U. S. Navy*

Three-place convertible land or sea observation plane. The huge all-metal wing shows the strong Junkers influence of its designer who had been an engineer with the German company. Observation Squadron Six was commissioned on January 1, 1924 at NAS Hampton Roads to service test six of these planes. Their weight, almost twice that of the UO-1, and twin floats, proved inadequate for ship-borne catapult operations and in December the Squadon replaced them with VE-7's and UO-1's. Note the 6-O-2 on this plane and its replacement below. The diagonal / was used on observation types to prevent confusion between the letter O and the numeral zero. See 1923 Aircraft Year Book for three-view plans of the Dayton-Wright WA-1 shipboard observation plane similar to the VE-7H. It had folding wings and a machine gun ring for the rear cockpit. The Vought UO-1 overcame all competition and was produced in large numbers to become the standard battleship and cruiser based observation type until replaced by yet another Vought—the O2U-1.

Naval Aircraft Factory VE-7H (A-5698)   *U. S. Navy*

6-O-2 replacing the MO-1 above. Note the VO-6 squadron insignia on both planes. VO-6 became VO-5S in 1927, was decommissioned in 1930.

Wright F2W-2 (A-6743)   *U. S. Navy*
The 1923 landplane converted with new wings, a Wright T-2 engine,
wing radiators and twin floats. Note similarity to R3C-1 design.

Douglas DT-2 (A-6580)   *U. S. Navy*
The two-place DT-2 torpedo plane became standard equipment for VT
operations for several years, replacing the previous interim R-6L's.

Curtiss F4C-1 (A-6689)   *U. S. Navy*
All-metal TS-1 type built under the direction of Charles Ward Hall to
furnish comparative data on costs, weights, performance & maintenance.

Longren (A-6747) *U. S. Navy*
Purchased to test service performance of molded fiber construction, a potential answer to faster and cheaper production. Built in Kansas.

Martin N2M-1 (A-6800) *U. S. Navy*
Two-place primary trainer similar in design to the NAF N2N-1 and the NB-1. One only for Navy; also offered as a mail plane by manufacturer.

Wright WP-1 (A-6748) *U. S. Navy*
Swiss Dornier all-metal cantilever monoplane as "Wright Pursuit" with Wright H-3 engine. Had amazing performance for its time, see Appendix.

Naval Aircraft Factory TG-2 (A-6345)   *U. S. Navy*

NAF designed and built gunnery trainer. The TG-1 and TG-2 were
Liberty powered; the TG-3 and TG-4 had an Aeromarine T-6, and TG-5
had a Wright E water cooled engine. TG-1, 3 and 5 had the fuel tank in
the fuselage; the TG-2 and TG-5 had the fuel tank in the main float.

Naval Aircraft Factory NO-1 (A-6431)   *U. S. Navy*

Similar to Martin M2O-1, powered by a Curtiss D-12 engine. Three were
built, the third was modified into the NO-2. For short range spotting.

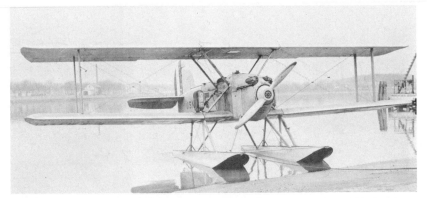

Naval Aircraft Factory DT-5   *U. S. Navy*
The DT-4 and DT-5 were DT-2 modifications with the Wright T-2 in
place of the regular Liberty. DT-5 had, in addition, a geared T-2 engine.

Wright SDW-1 (A-6596)   *U. S. Navy*
LWF DT-2 modified by Wright as a long range scout, note the added fuel
tanks on under side of fuselage. To VS-3 at Anacostia and USS PATOKA.

Blackburn Swift (A-6056)   *U. S. Navy*
One-place British torpedo bomber powered by a 450 h.p. Napier Lion.
It carried one 18-inch torpedo, had no guns. Two bought for testing.

Naval Aircraft Factory PN-9 (A-6878)   *U. S. Navy*

The famous PN-9 Number One flying off Hawaii after being repaired following its remarkable flight and sea voyage from San Francisco Bay on August 31. Forced down from lack of fuel CDR John Rodgers and his crew sailed the "boat" with fabric from the wings for ten days.

Naval Aircraft Factory PN-8 (A-6799)   *U. S. Navy*

Improved PN-7 with metal hull and tail to improve seaworthiness and reduce water soakage by the hull. Patrol bomber, Wright T-3 engines.

Curtiss CS-1   *U. S. Navy*

VT-1 operated mixed CS-1's and DT-2's in early 1925 as can be seen by this photo of the squadron leader and 1-T-5 below. Note the squadron insignia under pilots cockpit. Two CS-2's were built with Wright T-3 engines, one of these was modified to CS-3 by NAF. Of the eight CS's built all were gone by October 1928. See Martin SC duplicate model.

Douglas DT-2   *U. S. Navy*

Pearl Harbor based VT-1 torpedo bomber. Note squadron markings and bomb racks on underside of wings, photographer with camera in rear pit.

Curtiss TS-1's (A-6300, A-6301)   *U. S. Navy*
Upon formation in July 1922 VO-1 was given the additional duty to
carry on the development of small, single-seat planes on destroyers. No
catapults were intended, as may be seen by the top photo of a TS-1
aboard a four stack DD, the planes were hoisted over the side by a crane
as in lower photo of USS ALLEGHENY AT19—an ocean-going tug.

Curtiss TS-1 *U. S. Navy*

Fighting Squadron One, later the famed High Hats, was ordered to change from wheels to floats and go aboard 11 battleships in March 1925. The top photo shows 1-F-13 with its wire wheels and the lower photo shows 1-F-15 on twin floats, together with a UO-1, on the stern of a battleship. Note the diving bird insignia of VF-1 which was abandoned because of its similarity to the parrot used by the Ghirardelli Chocolate Company in their advertising. It was replaced by High Hat in 1927.

Douglas DT-2 (A-6421) *U. S. Navy*

19-T-4 with parachutist on wing and engine covers off in flight over Pearl Harbor, home station for Naval District assigned VT-14 and VT-19.

Martin SC-1 (A-6807)   *U. S. Navy*
Production version of CS-1. 35 SC-1's and 40 SC-2's built; two were
modified to SC-6, one to SC-7. Was later assigned T2M-1 designation.

Vought VE-7SF   *U. S. Navy*
Fighting Squadron Two was equipped with 18 of these single-place
fighters. Note WW-I type machine gun installation near pilot's hand.

Naval Aircraft Factory PN-7 (A-6616)   *U. S. Navy*
Modification of F-5L design with thick, high lift, airfoil allowing
shorter span and elimination of many struts and wires. Note insignia.

Loening OL-1 (A-6880)   *U. S. Navy*
Second of two three-place amphibians designed for operation from the
turret catapults of battleships. It used an inverted Packard engine.

Loening OL-2 (A-6981)   *U. S. Navy*
Five of these inverted Liberty powered models followed the OL-1.
After flight testing they were assigned to Marine Corps aviation units.

Boeing NB-2 (A-6770)   *U. S. Navy*
The last 30 airplanes on the NB-1 contract were delivered with the
Wright E-4 water-cooled engine. This plane assigned to NAS Anacostia.

War Department DH-4B1 Command (A-6371)   *U. S. Navy*
Blue and silver command plane of LCDR Millington B. McComb,
Commanding Officer of the NAS at Pearl Harbor. Note wheel colors.

Curtiss R3C-1   *U. S. Navy*
One of three land racers built for the Pulitzer Race. All were Class
VF, Fighter, on paper, including F3C-1 designation. Curtiss V-1400.

Curtiss R3C-2   *U. S. Navy*
All three R3C-1's were converted to float planes for the Schneider Cup
Races. One became R3C-3 with Packard 2A-1500; one became R3C-4.

Naval Aircraft Factory UO-2 (A-6546)   *Manufacturer*
A special UO-1 modified for racing with an Aeromarine U-873 engine.
Entered in 1922 Curtiss Marine Trophy Race but was damaged at start.

Naval Aircraft Factory UO-2 (A-6546)   *U. S. Navy*
At the Naval Aircraft Factory on 6-30-25 with the Lamblin radiators
moved up to the wings, the second cockpit replaced, two-blade prop.

Wright DT-6 (A-6581)   *U. S. Navy*
One DT-2 was modified by Wright Aeronautical with the installation of
a Wright P-1 air-cooled engine. See Appendix A for DT performances.

Curtiss F6C-2 (A-6974)   *U. S. Navy*
First model of the Hawk fighter for carrier use. The squadron leader's
red fuselage band matched its tail color. VF-2 became VF-6B in 1927.

STATUS OF NAVAL AIRCRAFT
August 1926

BATTLE FLEET
AIRCRAFT SQUADRONS, BATTLE FLEET

USS LANGLEY
    1 DT-2, 1 F6C-2, 2 OL-1, 2 OL-3, 2 UO-1,
    2 VE-7S, 2 VE-7SF, 1 VE-9, 1 39-A

Fighting Plane Squadron One
    1 F4C-1, 17 TS-1, 1 VE-9

Fighting Plane Squadron Two
    3 F6C-1, 3 F6C-2, 4 FB-1, 1 FB-3, 3 VE-7S

Transportation Squadron One (VJ-1)
    2 H-16, 2 MO-1, 1 NB-1, 1 PN-7

Torpedo and Bombing Plane Squadron Two (VT-2)
    4 SC-1, 12 SC-2

SHIP AIR UNITS, BATTLE FLEET

USS ARIZONA, 2 UO-1   USS NEW MEXICO, 2 UO-1
USS CALIFORNIA, 2 UO-1   USS OKLAHOMA, 3 UO-1
USS COLORADO, 2 UO-1   USS OMAHA, 2 UO-1
USS IDAHO, 2 UO-1   USS PENNSYLVANIA, 2 UO-1
USS MARYLAND, 2 UO-1   USS TENNESSEE, 2 UO-1
USS MISSISSIPPI, 2 UO-1   USS WEST VIRGINIA, 1 UO-1
USS NEVADA, 2 UO-1

SCOUTING FLEET
AIRCRAFT SQUADRONS, SCOUTING FLEET

Scouting Plane Squadron One
2 SC-1

Torpedo and Bombing Plane Squadron One (VT-1)
8 SC-1, 5 SC-2

Utility Detachment, Scouting Plane Squadron One
4 SC-2

SHIP AIR UNITS, SCOUTING FLEET

USS CINCINNATI, 3 UO1   USS NEW YORK, 3 UO-1
USS CONCORD, 2 UO-1   USS RALEIGH, 1 UO-1
USS DETROIT, 2 UO-1   USS RICHMOND, 2 UO-1
USS MARBLEHEAD, 2 UO-1   USS TRENTON, 2 UO-1
USS MEMPHIS, 2 UO-1   USS UTAH, 4 UO-1
USS MILWAUKEE, 3 UO-1   USS WYOMING, 2 UO-1

AIRCRAFT SQUADRONS, ASIATIC FLEET

Torpedo and Bombing Squadron Twenty (Cavite, P.I.)
8 DT-2

NAS ANACOSTIA
5 DH-4B2, 1 F-5L, 1 F6C-1, 1 F6C-4, 1 FB-3, 1 FB-6, 1 H-16, 1 MO-1, 1 NB-1, 1 NB-2, 2 O2B-1, 4 O2B-2, 1 R2C-2, 1 SC-2, 1 T3M-1, 1 OC-3, 5 UO-1, 1 VE-9, 1 VE-9H, 1 SC-6

NAS COCO SOLO
1 DT-2, 1 F-5L, 6 H-16, 1 N-9, 3 SC-2

NAS DAHLGREN
1 DH-4B1, 2 DH-4B2, 2 HS-2L, 1 SC-6, 1 VE-7H

NAVAL AIRCRAFT FACTORY PHILADELPHIA
1 CS-1, 5 DH-4B1, 1 DH-4B2, 1 DT-2, 1 EM-2, 17 F-5L, 23 H-16, 4 HS-2L, 1 M2O-1, 5 MO-1, 1 MS-1, 1 N-9, 1 NB-3, 1 NB-4, 1 NM-1, 1 NO-2, 3 OL-2, 2 PN-10, 1 R3C-2, 1 R3C-3, 1 SC-7, 3 UO-1, 1 VE-7, 2 VE-7H

NAS HAMPTON ROADS
1 CS-2, 1 DH-4B1, 1 DH-4B2, 2 DT-2, 2 DT-4, 1 FT-2, 2 F-5L, 1 H-16, 14 HS-2L, 1 MO-1, 2 N-9, 9 NB-2, 10 SC-1, 4 SC-2, 14 UO-1, 2 VE-7, 1 39-A, 1 T3M-1, 1 Viking

NAVAL SUPPLY STATION, HAMPTON ROADS
2 FT-1, 3 MO-1, 3 MS-1, 3 SC-2, 1 XS-1

NAS PEARL HARBOR
2 SC-1, 9 DT-2, 3 DH-4B1, 10 F-5L, 6 H-16, 1 N-9, 1 R-6L, 6 SC-2, 3 VE-7.

NAS PENSACOLA

    7 DH-4B1, 2 DH-4B2, 6 DT-2, 25 F-5L, 4 H-16, 3 HN-2, 23 HS-2L, 21 JN, 1 N2M-1, 68 N-9, 25 NB-1, 14 NB-2, 3 NO-1, 15 NY-1, 1 TS-1, 7 VE-7, 5 VE-9

NAS SAN DIEGO

    1 CS-1, 8 DH-4B1, 2 DT-2, 2 H-16, 14 MO-1, 6 NB-1, 1 NB-2, 1 PN-7, 2 SC-1, 3 SDW-1, 4 TS-1, 23 UO-1, 1 VE-7H, 15 VE-7S, 1 VE-9, 2 OL-3, 2 PN-9

NAVAL AIR DETAIL, NEWPORT

    1 DT-4, 1 N-9

MISCELLANEOUS

Massachusetts Institute of Technology
    1 JN

U. S. Naval Mission to Brazil (Rio de Janeiro)
    1 VE-9

Langley Field, N.A.C.A.
    1 CS-3, 1 F3W-1, 1 F4C-1, 1 TS-1, 2 VE-7

G.I.N.A., McCook Field, Dayton, Ohio
    1 UO-1

Curtiss Aeroplane and Motor Company
    1 R3C-4

Boeing Airplane Company
    2 FB-2

Wright Aeronautical Corporation
    1 DT-6

U. S. Naval Attache, Rome, Italy
    1 LePere

U. S. Naval Academy, Annapolis
    3 N2N-1, 3 XS-1, 1 UO-1

USS NIAGARA
    1 OL-4

Alaskan Aerial Survey
    1 OL-2, 2 OL-4

Commanding Officer, Submarine S-1
    1 XS-2

Loening OL-3 (A-7056)   *U. S. Navy*
One of three OL's used by LT Ben Wyatt and the Alaskan Aerial Survey Expedition in the summer of 1926. They did first aerial mapping of area.

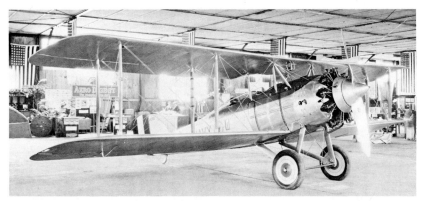

Vought UO-1 Command (A-6986)   *Manufacturer*

Special high-polished staff plane for the Chief of the Bureau of Aeronautics, Navy Department. Fuselage top is blue. See introduction.

Curtiss TS-1   *U. S. Navy*

VF-1 fighter at San Diego in July, with carrier hook added as well as
guide hooks between wheels for the fore and aft wires of LANGLEY.

Curtiss F6C-2 (A-6973)   *U. S. Navy*

LANGLEY No. 6 running up on the stern. Note guide hooks in place and
fore and aft wires on the deck. F6C-2 and DT-2 were used to test ship.

Boeing FB-3 (A-7089)   *Manufacturer*
The Curtiss D-12 powered FB-1 and FB-2 was modified to the FB-3 model
by installation of the Packard 1A-1500 engine. Three FB-3's were built.

Naval Aircraft Factory PN-10 (A-7028)   *U. S. Navy*
Service development of the all-metal PN-9 with two Packard 2A-1500
engines. A five-place patrol-boat seaplane. See PN-8, PN-9, page 40.

Martin T3M-1 (A-7065)   *Manufacturer*
First of the large Martin and Great Lakes torpedo planes. Note the
longer span in lower wing, radiator above fuselage; neither on T3M-2.

Boeing FB-6 (A-6896)   *U. S. Navy*
The single FB-4 with a Wright P-2 engine was further modified into the
FB-6 with the engine changed to the P&W R-1340 Wasp. Photo on 4-8-26.

Boeing F2B-1 (A-7385)   *Manufacturer*
The first test model on 10-7-26, note similarity to FB-6. The prefix
letter "X," for experimental planes was not adopted until 1927.

Wright F3W-1 (A-7223)   *U. S. Navy*
The Wright Aeronautical "Apache" designed as a single float battleship
fighter. Tested on both wheels and floats but not put in production.

USS S-1 and Cox-Klemin XS-2 (A-6519)   *U. S. Navy*

Although the XS-1 and MS-1 sub scouts had been built much earlier it was not until 1926 that full tests took place. The top photo shows the first trial on the Thames River at New London, Conn., on July 22. At this time the #3 main ballast tank was flooded and the assembled plane floated off the ship. The first full cycle of surfacing, plane assembling (lower photo), launching, return, disassembling and submerging took place on July 28. XS-2 had Kinner in place of Lawrence.

Boeing PB-1 (A-6881)   *Manufacturer*

Unique patrol plane with tandem Packard 1A-2500 engines. One PB-1 was scheduled to fly to Hawaii with the PN-9's. Later XPB-1 and XPB-2.

Vought UO-1 (A-7048)   *U. S. Navy*

The Naval Aviation Reserve Units at Squantum, Mass., and Fort Hamilton, N. Y., were founded on August 13, 1923. The early use of seaplanes by the naval reserve was changed by the 1930's so that the only water flying done was with a single assigned Loening or Grumman utility amphibian. The markings on both planes are rare and unusual.

NAVAL RESERVE AIRCRAFT
August 1926

NRAU ROCKAWAY BEACH, Long Island, New York
    2 UO-1, 4 NY-1

NRAU GREAT LAKES, Illinois
    3 N-9, 2 UO-1

NRAU SAND POINT, Seattle, Washington
    1 DH-4B2, 2 NB-1, 1 UO-1, 2 NY-1, 1 PB-1
    (PB-1 assigned during July and August 1926)

NRAU SQUANTUM, Massachusetts
    1 N-9, 1 TG-3, 1 TG-4, 2 TG-5, 4 UO-1
    (Plus 1 UO-1 assigned to Coast Guard)

Vought UO-1 (A-6992)   *U. S. Navy*

Great Lakes was commissioned on December 14, 1923 with six seaplanes. Note the markings which combine the squadron number and base name.

FLEET AIRCRAFT ASSIGNMENT
August 1927

BATTLE FLEET
AIRCRAFT SQUADRONS, BATTLE FLEET

USS LANGLEY
　　1 FU-1, 1 UO-1, 2 UO-1C, 2 VE-7S, 1 VE-7SF

VF-1B	12 FB-5
VF-2B	14 FU-1, 1 F6C-2, 1 UO-1
VF-6B	13 FB-5, 1 DT-2
VT-2B	16 T3M-2, 4 SC-1, 9 SC-2, 1 T2D-1
VJ-1B	1 F-5L, 5 FU-1, 2 H-16, 1 NB-1, 1 PN-7, 1 PN-10, 1 OL-1, 3 UO-1C, 1 TB-1

VO-1B	USS COLORADO	1 OL-3, 2 OL-6
	USS MARYLAND	1 OL-3, 3 UO-1C
	USS PENNSYLVANIA	1 UO-1C, 1 OL-6
	USS TENNESSEE	1 UO-1C, 1 OL-6
	USS WEST VIRGINIA	1 OL-6
VO-2B	USS ARIZONA	3 UO-1C
	USS CALIFORNIA	1 OL-6
	USS IDAHO	1 UO-1, 1 UO-1C
	USS MISSISSIPPI	1 UO-1, 1 UO-1C
	USS NEW MEXICO	1 OL-6, 2 UO-1C
VO-4B	USS OMAHA	1 UO-1, 1 UO-1C

SCOUTING FLEET
AIRCRAFT SQUADRONS, SCOUTING FLEET

USS LEXINGTON at Quincy, Mass.　　2 UO-1C

VJ-2S	1 T3M-1
VT-1S	16 T3M-2

USS SARATOGA & LEXINGTON DETACHMENT, Hampton Roads
　　1 DT-2, 3 F6C-3, 2 NB-2, 1 VE-7

VF-5S	18 F6C-3

USS SARATOGA
　　3 F6C-4, 2 OL-6, 1 FB-1, 3 T3M-2, 3 UO-1

VO-3S	USS CONCORD	1 UO-1, 1 UO-1C
	USS DETROIT	1 UO-1C
	USS MEMPHIS	1 UO-1, 1 UO-1C
	USS MILWAUKEE	2 UO-1, 1 UO-1C
	USS RALEIGH	1 UO-1, 1 UO-1C
	USS TRENTON	2 UO-1C
VO-5S	USS ARKANSAS	1 UO-1, 2 OL-6
	USS NEVADA	1 UO-1, 1 UO-1C
	USS OKLAHOMA	2 UO-1C
	USS UTAH	1 OL-6
	USS WYOMING	1 OL-6
	USS TEXAS	1 OL-6

ASIATIC FLEET

VT-5A	6 DT-2	
VO-11A	USS CINCINNATI	2 UO-1C
	USS MARBLEHEAD	2 UO-1C
	USS RICHMOND	2 UO-1C

Martin T3M-2's (A-7233 and A-7237)   *U. S. Navy*

1-Ts-11 in the foreground appears to be a radio-controlled drone, but it is simply an illusion caused by the pilot, in the center cockpit, being hidden by the wing in the photo. The small "s" after the "T" squadron designator was used for a short time to indicate that the squadron was attached to the Scouting Fleet. A still different use was made by VT-5A of the Asiatic Fleet, as may be seen on page 72. The T3M-2 became the backbone of all Navy torpedo squadrons, both carrier and shore based. The XT3M-3, with a Pratt & Whitney R-1700, and the NAF modified XT3M-4 with a Wright R-1750, introduced the air-cooled engine to this design and gave birth to the T4M-1. 1927 was an important year in naval aviation because it saw the commissioning of the first two service carriers, the SARATOGA and LEXINGTON. Although the USS LANGLEY was in use it was classified experimental carrier so that the USS LEXINGTON CV2 (12-14-27) and the USS SARATOGA CV3 (11-16-27) became the first two combat ships of this kind in the Fleet. Although these two carriers entered service in late 1927 the air units and squadrons were organizing earlier by training on the LANGLEY. Torpedo Squadrons One and Two became the first carrier VT units.

Martin T3M-2 Command (A-7320)   *U. S. Navy*

Rare photo of a twin-float torpedo bomber as a command plane. Note the two-star card and title "Commander Aircraft, Scouting Fleet."

Loening OL-6   *U. S. Navy*
Plane number two of Observation Squadron Two being catapulted from
USS CALIFORNIA. Note three-man crew and rear gun ring. See p. 4.

USS MARYLAND BB46   *Bear Photo Service*
With an OL-6 on the number three turret catapult and an FU-1 of VF-2,
and a UO-1, on the stern catapults. See page 56 for ship assignments.

Vought O2U-1 (A-7536)   *Manufacturer*
3-O-3 from the USS RALEIGH CL7. Note the Bat insignia of VO-3S. The
squadron number changed to VS-5S in mid-1928 but stayed on cruisers.

Boeing FB-5 (A-7102)   *Peter M. Bowers*
Red-tailed VF-1B fighter next to a white-tailed VF-6B FB-5. The large
number 21 was for the Spokane Air Races; VF-1B only had 12 fighters.

Boeing FB-5   *U. S. Navy*
1-F-4 with what must have been special markings for maneuvers as the
white fuselage band for number four plane had been well established.

Boeing FB-5 (A-7123)   *U. S. Navy*
Fighting Squadron Six was organized on January 1, 1927 for the Battle
Fleet; VF-5S was commissioned at the same time for the Scouting Fleet.

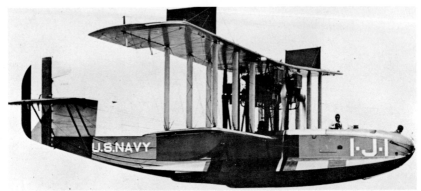

Curtiss F-5L Command (A-4281)   *U. S. Navy*
Blue command transport operated by VJ-1B for Aircraft Squadrons,
Battle Fleet. Rank card would be in holder on nose if Admiral aboard.

Vought VE-9 (A-6478)   *Peter M. Bowers*
Third plane of the 11th Naval District's Utility Squadron. The VE-9 had
a Wright E-3 water-cooled engine. The tail shapes varied on UO's.

Cox-Klemin XS-1 (A-6520)   *James C. Mathiesen*
At the Naval Air Base, Oakland Airport, in 1927. It was later given to
the University of California where it hung from ceiling of Hesse Hall.

Boeing NB-1   *U. S. Navy*

A radial-engine NB-1 from VN-1D8 at NAS Pensacola. Note starter crank, wind-driven electrical generator and rear cockpit gun ring. The NB-2, with a water-cooled E-4, was also used for gunnery training. At least one NB-3 modification was flown with the tail moved two feet aft and the engine moved ten inches forward; as well as one NB-4 in which the tail was moved three feet aft and the engine 26 inches forward. Both the NB-3 and NB-4 had the air-cooled Wright J-4 engine. The 220 planes on hand at Pensacola in March were: 4 DH-4B1, 5 DT-2, 3 F-5L, 3 HS-2L, 26 JN, 66 N-9, 22 NB-1, 13 NB-2, 37 NY-1, 9 SC-1, 3 SC-2, 3 UO-1, 2 UO-1C, 7 VE-7, 5 VE-9, 11 T3M-1, 1 CS-1. In November five squadron designations were introduced and the equipment had changed to: VN-1D8, 5 NB-1, 1 NB-2, 71 NY-2; VN-2D8, 33 NY-1; VN-3D8, 3 F-5L, 10 T3M-1, 15 SC-1, 15 SC-2; VN-4D8, 3 DT-2, 26 NB-1, 2 UO-1, 2 UO-1C; VN-5D8, 6 VE-7, 12 VE-7S, 5 VE-9, 15 F6C-4; and 2 N-9 and 16 TS-1 in storage. Two additional training squadrons existed: VN-6D5 at NAS Hampton Roads with 3 NB-2, 5 NY-1, 6 T3M-1, 2 NY-2; and VN-7D11 at NAS San Diego with 3 NB-1, 1 NB-2, 9 NY-1 and 7 NY-2.

Naval Aircraft Factory DH-4B (A-6133)   *U. S. Navy*

From NAS Pensacola in May 1927. This was the last use, and year, for the DH-4's in the Navy. NAF assembled these planes, did not build them.

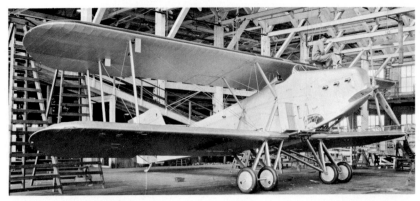

Boeing XTB-1 (A-7024)   *Manufacturer*
Competitor to the T3M-2, powered by one Packard 1A-2500 of 730 h.p.
Flew on twin floats. Had two .30 cal m.g.'s and one 1740 lb. torpedo.

Naval Aircraft Factory XTN-1 (A-7027)   *U. S. Navy*
Navy designed twin-engine torpedo bomber and scout. One built at
NAF; 3 built by Douglas as T2D-1. Wright R-1750 engines used in both.

Eberhart XFG-1 (A-7944)   *U. S. Navy*
Tested as XFG-1 on wheels in Nov. and Dec. 1927; tested as XF2G-1 with
lengthened wings, on single float, January to March 1928. One only.

Boeing XF3B-1 (A-7674)   *U. S. Navy*
Company, private venture, test model 74; later converted to model 77
and delivered as first F3B-1. Note flotation gear and wood floats.

Curtiss XF7C-1 (A-7653)   *U. S. Navy*
Both the XF3B-1 and the XF7C-1 were tested as single float battleship
fighters. Production F7C-1 turned over to Marine Corps as land plane.

Curtiss XF6C-5 (A-6968)   *Manufacturer*
The first F6C-1 was modified into the first F6C-4, with the air-cooled
P&W R-1340 Wasp engine, then into XF6C-5 with P&W R-1690 engine.

FLEET AIRCRAFT ASSIGNMENT
August 1928

BATTLE FLEET

Commander-in-Chief U. S. Fleet　　　　　1 O2U-1

AIRCRAFT SQUADRONS, BATTLE FLEET

USS SARATOGA
VF-1B	15 F2B-1
VB-2B	16 F2B-1, 1 UO-1C
VS-2B	No aircraft assigned
VT-2B	14 T3M-2, 10 T4M-1
Utility Unit	1 T3M-2, 2 UO-1C, 1 UO-5

USS LEXINGTON
VF-3B	12 FB-5, 1 UO-1
VB-1B	2 F6C-2, 17 F6C-3, 1 UO-1C
VS-3B	No aircraft assigned
VT-1B	9 T3M-2, 10 T4M-1
Utility Unit	3 O2U-1, 1 T3M-2

USS LANGLEY
VF-2B	4 F3B-1, 8 FU-1, 1 FU-2, 1 UO-5
VS-1B	6 O2U-1, 2 UO-1C, 1 UO-5
Utility Unit	4 FU-2, 1 UO-1C, 3 UO-5

USS AROOSTOOK
VJ-1B	2 NB-1, 2 OL-3, 1 OL-6, 5 OL-8, 2 T2D-1, 1 PN-12

Battleship Division Three
VO-3B	USS ARIZONA	2 O2U-1
	USS NEW YORK	4 O2U-1
	USS PENNSYLVANIA	2 O2U-1
	USS TEXAS	2 O2U-1

Battleship Division Four
VO-4B	USS CALIFORNIA	2 O2U-1
	USS IDAHO	3 O2U-1
	USS MISSISSIPPI	3 O2U-1
	USS NEW MEXICO	4 O2U-1

Battleship Division Five
VO-5B	USS COLORADO	3 O2U-1
	USS MARYLAND	3 O2U-1
	USS TENNESSEE	3 O2U-1
	USS WEST VIRGINIA	3 O2U-1

SCOUTING FLEET
AIRCRAFT SQUADRONS, SCOUTING FLEET

Comairons Flag Unit　　　　　　　　1 UO-1

USS WRIGHT
VT-9S	19 T3M-2
VJ-2S	5 T3M-2, 3 T4M-1

WEST INDIES SURVEY SHIP
VJ-3S	1 OL-3, 2 OL-8

AIRCRAFT IN BATTLESHIPS

Battleship Division Two

VO-2S	USS ARKANSAS	1 OL-8
	USS FLORIDA	1 OL-8
	USS UTAH	1 OL-8
	USS WYOMING	3 OL-6

AIRCRAFT IN LIGHT CRUISERS

Light Cruiser Divisions Two and Three

VS-5S	USS CONCORD	1 O2U-1
	USS CINCINNATI	2 O2U-1
	USS DETROIT	1 UO-1C
	USS MARBLEHEAD	2 O2U-1
	USS RICHMOND	2 O2U-1
	USS RALEIGH	1 O2U-1

ASIATIC FLEET

USS JASON

VT-5A	6 T3M-2, 2 UO-1C, 1 UO-1, 1 UO-5, 3 T3M-2	
VO-11A	USS MILWAUKEE	2 O2U-1
	USS MEMPHIS	2 O2U-1
	USS TRENTON	2 O2U-1

NAS PEARL HARBOR

VT-6D14	10 T3M-2
VT-7D14	1 SC-1, 4 SC-2
VP-1D14	No aircraft assigned
VP-4D14	1 F-5L, 3 H-16
Utility Unit	2 UO-1C, 2 UO-5

NAS COCO SOLO

VT-3D15	12 T3M-2
VP-2D15	2 H-16, 1 SC-2
Utility Unit	1 UO-1, 2 UO-1C, 1 UO-5

USS LEXINGTON CV2   *U. S. Navy*
Under way at sea with VT-1B T3M-2's and T4M-1's taking off from the
888-foot deck. Horizontal black stripe on stack indicated LEXINGTON.

Vought O2U-1 Command   *U. S. Navy*
Admiral Henry A. Wiley, Commander-in-Chief of the United States
Fleet, flying in his command plane from the USS TEXAS, Flagship of
the U.S. Fleet. The "Corsairs" were convertible from wheels to a single
float for operation aboard ship at sea or from a Naval Air Station
ashore while the ship was in port. Note the wind-driven generator on
the top wing for radio communications. See page 132 for a description
of command planes and colors. The carriers LEXINGTON and SARA-
TOGA, commissioned in late 1927, began operations in early 1928. LT
A. M. Pride made the first takeoff and landing on the LEX on January
5th, and CDR Marc Mitscher made the first takeoff and landing aboard
the SARA on January 11th. Both flights were made in Vought UO-1's.
The dirigible LOS ANGELES made a landing aboard the SARATOGA
at sea off Newport, R.I., on January 27th; remained on board one hour.

Boeing FB-5 (A-7125)   *U. S. Navy*
3-F-6 from the USS LANGLEY with a green tail. VF-3B received its new
F3B-1's in 1928, moved to the LEXINGTON where it stayed thru 1930.

Martin T3M-2   *U. S. Navy*
From the newly operating SARATOGA. Note the unusual placement of
red Gunnery Pennant in the middle of the section leader's black stripe.

Vought UO-1 (A-6994)   *William T. Larkins*
Number four utility plane of the LEXINGTON in April 1928. Note
the black and white Minuteman, official insignia of the ship itself.

Vought FU-1 (A-7370)   *U. S. Navy*
Originally ordered as single-place UO-3 training fighter. VF-2B left
the battleships in 1928 and went aboard the LANGLEY. Note insignia,

Curtiss F6C-3 (A-7143)   *U. S. Navy*
5-F-11 without propeller spinner and showing the center section bomb
racks added for dive bombing. VF-5S became VB-1B in July 1928.

Curtiss F6C-3 (A-7138)   *U. S. Navy*
The same squadron, The Red Rippers, after July 1928. They also flew
on twin floats, see page 74. In 1930 the squadron again became VF-5.

Loening OL-8 Command (A-7847)   *U. S. Navy*

1-J-3 on December 14, 1928 with Rear Admiral Butler aboard. Note his two-star placard on fuselage in addition to flag on outboard wing strut.

Loening OL-8   *U. S. Navy*

1-J-5 taking off and landing aboard LEXINGTON. 4 OL-8's of VJ-1B were aboard for annual cruise. Note raised fore and aft wires on deck.

Boeing F2B-1 (A-7429)   *U. S. Navy*
LT Daniel W. Tomlinson, leader of the famed "Three Sea Hawks" acro-
catic team, getting ready for the group's takeoff on September 16th
at Mines Field, Los Angeles, to perform during the National Air Races.
Note that the deck hook has been removed to lighten the plane for
maneuverability. VB-2B was previously VF-6B aboard the LANGLEY
with LCDR J. E. Ostrander as C.O. Soon after he left LT Tomlinson
took over, the squadron was re-designated VB-2B, and he formed the
Three Sea Hawks with LTjg Aaron P. Storrs and LTjg William V. Davis.
This trio gained lasting fame from their performance before 100,000
people at the 1928 NAR. Full details on the organization of this group,
as well as a description of their flying, is contained in "Tommy"
Tomlinson's book *The Sky's The Limit;* see page 385 for further details.

Curtiss F6C-3 (A-7140)   *U. S. Navy*
LT Stuart H. Ingersoll flying a Red Rippers "Hawk" in September 1928.
Note the 1-B-20 and forward position of stars on upper surface of wing.

Boeing F2B-1 (A-7440) *William T. Larkins*
Fighting Squadron One replaced its FB-5's (see page 59) with new
F2B-1's in 1928. Production version of FB-6 with the same engine.

Vought O2U-1 (A-7557) *U. S. Navy*
One of six O2U-1 amphibians of VS-1B aboard the LANGLEY. Note
the VF-1B F2B-1's on the deck of the mother ship in the background.

Vought O2U-1 (A-7572) *U. S. Navy*
USS LANGLEY-5, an additional amphibian attached to the carrier's
Utility Unit. This was first use of amphibian float; see page 102.

Martin T3M-2 (A-7305)   *U. S. Navy*
VT-9S was organized on Sept. 30, 1927. During the January to March
1928 maneuvers they operated at Guantanamo Bay; then to Annapolis.

Martin T3M-2 (A-7308)   *U. S. Navy*
The small letter "s" following the Torpedo designation indicated that
the squadron was assigned to the Scouting Fleet, was soon abandoned.

Martin T3M-2 (A-7259)   *U. S. Navy*
Still different, and unofficial, presentation by VT-5A of the Asiatic
Fleet; it should read 5-T-1. Battle Fleet did not paint B on planes.

Curtiss F6C-4 (A-7403)   *U. S. Navy*

At the same time that the Boeing FB-5 with its liquid-cooled engine was being changed to an air-cooled engine in the FB-6 and subsequent F2B-1 production model, the Curtiss F6C-3 underwent the same change. The new air-cooled model was the F6C-4 with the new Pratt & Whitney R-1300 engine. This period, beginning in 1927, marked the change from the use of liquid-cooled engines to air-cooled throughout the Fleet. Because the F6C-4 was an obsolescent type its only service use was with VF-2B aboard the LANGLEY in late 1929 and early 1930; they had 19 on hand in December 1929. The other major user was VN-4D8 at Pensacola, the advanced fighter training squadron, which had 20 on hand in August 1928. See page 95 for formation photo of three of these "trainers." One of the little-known facets of naval aircraft use involves Naval Attaches assigned to American Embassies overseas. In 1928 the U.S. Naval Attache at London, England, had a DeHavilland DH-60 "Moth" for his use, later trading it in for a DH-80 "Puss Moth." The USNA at Rome, Italy, flew the Ro.1, Romeo-built Fokker C.V.

Curtiss F7C-1 (A-7655)   *Manufacturer*

Showing the experimental Reed Tandem propeller mounted at the factory on December 19, 1928. An F7C-1 was also used to test full span slots.

Curtiss F6C-3 (A-7144)　　　　　　　　　　　*U. S. Navy*
Bombing Squadron One, the "Red Rippers," operated their F6C-3 fighters
on twin floats for a short time in 1928. See also HR-23 on page 94.

Curtiss OC-2 (A-7969)　　　　　　　　　　　*Manufacturer*
The last production OC-2 at the factory on 4-16-28. Redesignated from
F8C-3 two-place fighter. All went to Marine Corps VO-8M and VO-10M.

Martin XT3M-3 (A-7224)　　　　　　　　　　　*U. S. Navy*
T3M-2 with air-cooled P&W R-1700 engine, forerunner of production
T4M-1. NAF modified another T3M-2 to XT3M-4 with Wright R-1750.

Douglas T2D-1's   *J. M. F. Hasse*

Utility Squadron One lineup at NAS San Diego in October 1928.
This use of torpedo bombers by utility squadrons was not unusual.

Naval Aircraft Factory PN-12 (A-7383)   *U. S. Navy*

The squadron leader of VJ-1B in September 1928. Note crewman sitting
on fuselage between engines. A-7383 and 7384 were ordered as PN-10's.

Sikorsky XPS-1 (A-8005)   *U. S. Navy*

First of the twin-engine amphibians ordered as armed patrol planes
but soon relegated to transport and utility duty. Wright J-5 engines.

Curtiss XN2C-1 (A-7650)   *Manufacturer*
Winner of training plane competition; see photo on p. 170 of the same
plane in 1934. 3 XN2C-1's were purchased; one was with VN-5D8 in 1928.

Boeing XN2B-1 (A-8010)   *Manufacturer*
Entry in the 1928 competition, shown with its original Caminez 130
hp engine. This engine was later changed to a Wright R-540 of 165 hp.

Keystone XNK-1 (A-7942)   *Manufacturer*
Third entry, shown at the factory. Three of these experimental
models were built, one serving with VN-1D8 at Pensacola. See page 95.

Atlantic XJA-1 (A-8012) *U. S. Navy*
Rare photo of the Fokker "Super Universal" transport. It was delivered to the Navy but judged not acceptable for service. 450 hp Wasp.

Ford XJR-1 (A-7526) *U. S. Navy*
The first all-metal transport delivered to the Navy, at Anacostia in April 1928. Note serial number painted on tail in civil NC style.

Fairchild XJQ-1 (A-7978) *U. S. Navy*
Another April 1928 photo at Anacostia showing the little known FC-2 transport with a Wright J-5 engine. Civil version with Wasp was "71."

Curtiss TS-1 (A-6261)   *Peter M. Bowers*
One of two TS-1 fighters assigned to the Naval Reserve Air Base at
Sand Point (Seattle) in 1928. The reserves had 11 TS-1's in 1929.

Vought UO-1C (A-7007)   *Boardman C. Reed*
One of two UO-1C's on loan from San Diego to VN-13RD11 to start the
first reserve squadron for the Los Angeles area. Note rare markings.

Consolidated NY-1 (A-7175)   *Peter M. Bowers*
One of two reserve NY-1's at NRAB Sand Point in 1928. This unit
also had an NY-1B, the modified NY-1 with larger area NY-2 wings.

Consolidated NY-2 (A-7977)   *Peter M. Bowers*
The increased wing area of the NY-2 was for seaplane training. This
Seattle unit was one of few reserve bases to fly seaplanes. See p. 170.

NAVAL RESERVE AIRCRAFT
December 1928

NRAB ROCKAWAY BEACH, Long Island, New York
    1 NY-1B, 5 NY-2, 2 UO-1C

NRAB GREAT LAKES, Illinois
    1 NY-1B, 5 NY-2, 1 O2U-1, 3 TS-1

NRAB SEATTLE, Washington
    1 NY-1, 1 NY-1B, 3 NY-2, 1 O2U-1, 2 TS-1

NRAB SQUANTUM, Massachusetts
    1 NY-1, 3 NY-2, 2 UO-1C

NRAU OAKLAND, California
    1 NY-1B, 1 NY-2

HEADQUARTERS, Naval Training Station, Great Lakes, Illinois
    4 TS-1

Squadron VN-6R, NAS Anacostia
    1 O2U-1

Squadron VN-9RD9, Detroit, Michigan
    1 NY-1, 1 NY-2, 1 TS-1

Squadron VN-11RD9, Minneapolis, Minnesota
    1 NY-2, 1 TS-1

Squadron VN-13RD11, Long Beach, California
    2 UO-1C (Aircraft on loan from NAS San Diego)

NRAB Oakland, at Oakland Municipal Airport, and NRAB Minneapolis, at Wold-Chamberlain Airport, were commissioned in Fiscal
1928-29. Naval Reserve Aviation Bases for Miami, Florida and St.
Louis, Missouri, were authorized for Fiscal 1931. In addition to the
above squadrons VN-8RD8 at NAS Pensacola, with 9 NY-2, 5 SC-1 and
5 T3M-1, existed for active duty flight training of reserve officers. In
1929 1 NY-2 was assigned to VN-5RD4 at the Naval Aircraft Factory,
Philadelphia. The transition from reserve primary trainers to service
types flown on 15-day active duty periods was severe, called for newer
reserve types.

FLEET AIRCRAFT ASSIGNMENT
April 1929

UNITED STATES FLEET

Commander-in-Chief U. S. Fleet	1 O2U-1

BATTLE FLEET

Commander-in-Chief Battle Fleet	1 O2U-1

AIRCRAFT SQUADRONS, BATTLE FLEET

Comairons, Flag Unit	1 F2B-1

USS SARATOGA

VF-1B	19 F2B-1, 1 FU-2
VB-2B	18 F3B-1, 1 FU-2
VS-2B	12 O2U-2
VT-2B	27 T4M-1
Utility Unit	2 FU-2, 3 O2U-1, 1 O2U-2

USS LEXINGTON

VF-3B	12 F3B-1, 1 FU-2
VB-1B	15 F3B-1
VS-3B	12 O2U-2
VT-1B	28 T4M-1
Utility Unit	1 UO-1, 3 O2U-1

USS LANGLEY

VF-2B	18 F3B-1, 1 FU-2
VS-1B	6 O2U-2
Utility Unit	3 FU-2, 2 O2U-1

USS AROOSTOOK

VJ-1B	1 UO-1, 1 O2U-1, 2 FU-2, 6 T2D-1, 11 OL-8, 2 XPS-2

Battleship Division Three	VO-3B	10 O2U-1
Battleship Division Four	VO-4B	10 O2U-1
Battleship Division Five	VO-5B	11 O2U-1, 1 O2U-2
USS OMAHA	VS-4B	2 O2U-1
USS MEDUSA		1 O2U-1

SCOUTING FLEET
AIRCRAFT SQUADRONS, SCOUTING FLEET

Commander-in-Chief Scouting Fleet	1 OL-8

USS WRIGHT

VT-9S	17 T4M-1
VJ-2S	4 T4M-1
Ship Unit	1 OL-8

Battleship Division Two	VO-2S	9 O2U-1
Light Cruiser Divisions Two and Three and USS CONCORD	VS-5S	11 O2U-1
West Indies Survey	VJ-3S	2 OL-8

AIRCRAFT SQUADRONS, ASIATIC FLEET

USS JASON
>   VT-5A   10 T3M-2, 2 UO-1, 1 UO-5

NAS PEARL HARBOR
>   VT-6D14   No aircraft assigned
>   VT-7D14   7 T3M-2
>   VP-1D14   4 T2D-1
>   VP-4D14   2 H-16, 2 T2D-1

NAS COCO SOLO
>   VT-3D15   7 T3M-2
>   VT-4D15   7 T3M-2
>   VP-2D15   12 T3M-2

Vought O2U-2 (A-8118)   *John C. Mitchell*
The O2U-2 was the first type to be operated in squadron strength by
the new VS-2B organized in late 1928 for the USS SARATOGA.

Vought O2U-1 (A-7808)   *William T. Larkins*
Rare photo of one of only two aircraft that made up VS-4B in 1929-
1930 aboard the USS OMAHA. Formerly VO-4B. Note "E" in gunnery.

Flight Deck Scene   *U. S. Navy*
Pilots, plane handlers and crew abound in this photo of the flight deck
of the USS SARATOGA. In the background, behind the F2B-1, from
left to right are: O2U-1 2-S-3 (see previous page), O2U-1 2-S-9,
and T4M-1's 2-T-12 and 2-T-15 with their wings folded for storage.

Boeing F4B-1 (A-8153)   *U .S. Navy*
Section Three leader of the "Red Rippers" taking off from the LEX.
VB-1B was the first squadron to get the new F4B-1's; VF-2B was second.

Boeing F3B-1 (A-7720)   *U. S. Navy*
LCDR S. P. Ginder, Commanding Officer of Fighting Squadron Three,
flying 3-F-1 from the LEXINGTON. See photo of same plane on p. 114.

Boeing F3B-1 (A-7722)   *U. S. Navy*
3-F-2 posed for its photograph. Note the green tail, Diving Eagle
insignia and guide hooks on horizontal bar added to landing gear.

Boeing F3B-1 (A-7675)   *U. S. Navy*
2-F-19 used by CDR E. E. Wilson, on staff of ComAirBatFor, also aboard
the LANGLEY. VF-2, VF-3, VB-1 and VB-2 flew F3B-1's in January 1929.

Douglas T2D-1 (A-7591) *U. S. Navy*
VP-1D14's Pearl Harbor based T2D-1's operated on floats to avoid the mounting criticism by the Army of Navy-operated heavy land bombers.

Curtiss F7C-1 (A-7655) *U. S. Navy*
Showing one of several experimental cowlings tested on the F7C-1 by both the Navy and the National Advisory Committee for Aeronautics.

Sikorsky PS-3 (A-8284) *Manufacturer*
First of three, at the factory, with the nose gunners cockpit. This, and a rear gunners position on some, were removed shortly afterward.

Loening OL-8A (A-8072)   *U. S. Navy*

The Second Alaskan Survey took place in the summer of 1929. Note the special insignia designed for this expedition; plane name JUNEAU.

Vought FU-2 (A-7372)   *U. S. Navy*

All of the remaining 18 FU-1 fighters were converted to two-place FU-2 trainers in late 1928. Most then served as utility planes.

Martin T4M-1   *U. S. Navy*

Utility Squadron Two of the Scouting Fleet consisted of four T4M-1's in mid-1929. The leader is pictured here flying on twin floats.

Consolidated NY-2 (A-7521)   *U. S. Navy*
Number Ten airplane from the Naval Air Station at Hampton Roads.
The Navy had 108 NY-2's on hand in 1929, plus 35 assigned to reserves.

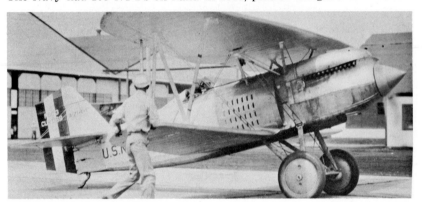

Curtiss F6C-3 (A-7144)   *U. S. Navy*
Experimental aircraft with special cooling radiator, probably used
during developmental stage which resulted in XF6C-6 racing plane.

Boeing XPB-2 (A-6881)   *U. S. Navy*
The XPB-1 as remodeled by the Naval Aircraft Factory. The original
Packard liquid-cooled engines were replaced by geared P&W R-1690's.

Boeing F4B-1 (A-8129) *Manufacturer*

The second company test plane, Model 83, in front of the factory on June 17th. It was later modified to company Model 99 and delivered as the second F4B-1 on the production contract. The 500 lb. bomb under the center section marked the beginning of the light bombers, single-place fighters converted for dive bombing. VB-1B and VB-2B operated in this capacity for a year and a half before returning to fighter status. During 1929 the familiar tail skid, shown here, was replaced by the first of the small, hard rubber carrier tail wheels. At the same time the fore and aft wires on the LANGLEY and SARATOGA were removed from those ships. On August 20th LT A. W. Gorton made the first hook-on landing aboard the USS LOS ANGELES ZR-2 with a modified UO-1. VJ-3S was organized and assigned to Aircraft Squadrons, Scouting Fleet, on February 1, 1929, for photographic survey duty with USS NOKOMIS and USS HANNIBAL along the coast of Cuba. Upon completion of this survey duty on April 20, 1929, the squadron was decommissioned and its personnel and material were distributed among other units. A third Utility Squadron did not appear again until 1940.

Curtiss XOC-3 (A-7672) *Manufacturer*

A further modification of the F8C-3 using the experimental Curtiss H-1640 engine. A sister ship was built for the Army as model XO-18.

Hall-Aluminum XFH-1 (A-8009)   *U. S. Navy*
Unique all-metal fighter that was designed with a water-tight
fuselage in lieu of flotation gear for emergency ditching at sea.

Vought XF2U-1 (A-7692)   *Manufacturer*
The experimental two-place fighter with its guns removed; original
version had wing guns as well as rear cockpit machine gun ring.

Curtiss XF8C-2 (A-7673)   *William T. Larkins*
Two-place carrier fighter and dive bomber. After refinement it was
produced as the F8C-4 and went aboard the SARATOGA with VF-1B.

Consolidated XN2Y-1 (A-8019)   *Manufacturer*
Civil sport trainer, the Fleet 1 with a 110 hp Warner Scarab engine,
built by the Fleet Aircraft Co. of New York, division of Consolidated.

Consolidated XN3Y-1 (A-7273)   *U. S. Navy*
Two-seat training plane with a Wright R-790-A engine. It was similar
to the NY-2 except that the NY-1 system of wing bracing was used.

Martin XT5M-1 (A-8051)   *U. S. Navy*
Tested as a two-place carrier dive bomber. The design was similar to
the Naval Aircraft Factory XT2N-1 (page 98). Produced as the BM-1.

FLEET AIRCRAFT ASSIGNMENT
June 1930

UNITED STATES FLEET

Commander-in-Chief U. S. Fleet	1 O2U-3

BATTLE FLEET

Commander-in-Chief Battle Fleet	1 O2U-2

AIRCRAFT SQUADRONS, BATTLE FLEET

Commander Aircraft Squadrons, Flag	1 O2U-3

USS SARATOGA

VF-1B	No aircraft assigned
VF-6B	20 F3B-1
VS-2B	14 O2U-2
VT-2B	9 T4M-1, 3 TG-1
Utility Unit	2 O2U-2, 2 FU-2, 1 O2U-1
VJ-1B Unit	5 OL-8

USS LEXINGTON

VF-3B	20 F3B-1
VF-5B	18 F4B-1
VS-3B	13 O2U-4
VT-1B	19 T4M-1
Utility Unit	1 OL-8, 2 O2U-1

USS LANGLEY

VF-2B	8 F2B-1, 8 F6C-4
VS-1B	7 O2U-4, 1 O2U-2
Utility Unit	3 O2U-1

USS AROOSTOOK

VJ-1B	1 UO-1, 3 FU-2, 1 PN-12
VP-7B	8 PD-1
VP-9B	No aircraft assigned
Ship Unit	1 FU-2, 1 PS-3

Battleship Division Three	VO-3B	3 O2U-3
Battleship Division Four	VO-4B	8 O2U-1
Battleship Division Five	VO-5B	6 O2U-1, 1 O2U-3
USS OMAHA	VS-4B	1 O2U-1, 1 O2U-3

SCOUTING FLEET

Commander Scouting Fleet, Flag Unit	1 PS-3, 1 OL-8

USS WRIGHT

VT-9S	13 T4M-1
VJ-2S	6 T4M-1
Ship Unit	4 O2U-3, 13 O2U-1, 3 O2U-4, 4 T4M-1

Battleship Division Two	VO-2S	8 O2U-4
Light Cruiser Division	VS-5S	7 O2U-1, 2 O2U-4
	VS-6S	8 O2U-1, 3 O2U-4
USS CONCORD	VS-7S	2 O2U-1
	VS-9S	No aircraft assigned

ASIATIC FLEET

USS JASON
    VT-5A   5 T3M-2
    VS-8A   10 O2U-3

NAS PEARL HARBOR
    VT-6D14   13 T3M-2
    VT-7D14   7 T3M-2
    VP-1D14   7 T2D-1
    VP-4D14   7 PD-1

NAS COCO SOLO
    VT-3D15   6 T3M-2
    VT-4D15   7 T3M-2
    VP-2D15   3 T3M-2, 1 XPS-2
                 (15 T3M-2 in storage)

USS LANGLEY CV1   *U. S. Navy*
On July 3, 1930 with its full complement of 24 aircraft aboard; 8
F6C-4's and 8 F2B-1's of VF-2B, and 7 O2U-4, 1 O2U-2 of VS-1B.

Douglas PD-1 (A-7987)   *U. S. Navy*
4-P-1 in flight with VP-4D14's rainbow circle insignia. This District
Patrol Squadron became VP-4B in 1931, operated PD-1's through 1935.

Vought O3U-1   *U. S. Navy*

4-O-11, 4-O-12 and one additional O3U-1 on the stern of the battleship
CALIFORNIA. The / mark for Observation was changed to O in 1930.

Vought O2U-1   *Peter M. Bowers*

5-O-3 from the USS WEST VIRGINIA. Photographs of planes with
these markings are rare as VO-5B (old VO-6) operated from 1927-30 only.

Martin T3M-2's   *U. S. Navy*

7-T-4 and 7-T-5 in formation on February 17, 1930. Note the use of
the "7-T-4" squadron designation on the top surface of the wing.

Boeing F4B-1A Command (A-8133)   *U. S. Navy*
Special command plane for the Assistant Secretary of the Navy for
Air. Note his insignia of anchor and four stars; blue cowl and wheels.

Loening XHL-1 (A-8276)   *U. S. Navy*
HR-42, a hospital-ambulance plane from VJ-4D5 at NAS Hampton Roads.
See USMC book, page 25, for photo of A-8275. Two only were built.

Boeing F4B-1's (A-8410+)   *U. S. Navy*
5-F-10, 5-F-19 and 5-F-11 in formation. Note mixture of tail colors, reverse
V chevron used on top wing. VF-5B was formerly numbered VB-1B.

Great Lakes TG-1 (A-8458) *U. S. Navy*
The first TG-1, delivered in 1930. Note torpedo under fuselage and the twin .30 calibre machine guns on the rear cockpit scarf ring.

Vought O2U-1 (A-7937) *N.A.C.A.*
Rare photo of a reserve O2U-1 from NAS Anacostia with a modified cowl under test by the NACA Laboratory at Langley Field, Virginia.

Curtiss F6C-3 (A-7144) *U. S. Navy*
Station-based utility plane; Number 23 from Hampton Roads, Virginia. Obsolescent fighters were popular with Navy pilots as fast transports.

New Standard NT-1 (A-8585) *Pete Sarkus*
Light weight primary trainer purchased at the same time as the N2Y-1 and NK-1 in an attempt to find a low-priced plane for flight training.

Keystone NK-1 (A-8053) *U. S. Navy*
Production of the NK-1 was held up by modifications necessary in the XNK-1 (see page 76); note change in shape of fin. Note wire wheels.

Curtiss F6C-4's *U. S. Navy*
Three from VN-5D8 at NAS Pensacola in acrobatic demonstration. There were 11 in service at Pensacola in 1930. Marines also used F6C-4's.

Curtiss XF8C-4 (A-8314)   *Manufacturer*
Factory photo on April 25, 1930. Heavier, strengthened version of
the XF8C-2 following its crash during a terminal velocity test dive.

Curtiss O2C-2 (N-983V)   *Manufacturer*
The original company prototype tested with a civil registration, at
the factory 12-5-30. To XF10C-1, then XS3C-1, then back to O2C-2.

Curtiss XF8C-7 Command (A-8845)   *R. R. Martin*
Special plane for David S. Ingalls, Assistant Secretary of the Navy
for Aeronautics. Note blue struts, tail wheel pant. Became XO2C-2.

Curtiss XF6C-6 (A-7147) *Manufacturer*
Special racer in which Capt. Page was killed during Thompson Trophy
Race at Chicago on 9-1-30. See photo as F6C-3 racer, USMC book, p. 30.

Boeing XF5B-1 (A-8640) *U. S. Navy*
Company owned test plane with civil registration NX-271V. Similar
to Army XP-15 except for carrier arresting gear. Note large ailerons.

Bristol Bulldog IIa (A-8607) *U .S. Navy*
Second "Bulldog" fighter purchased to replace A-8485 which crashed
during flight tests at Anacostia; gave comparative performance data.

Hall-Aluminum XPH-1 (A-8004)   *U. S. Navy*
A five-place patrol boat with two Wright R-1750 engines; a development
of the PN-11 with improved hull, wing and engine nacelle construction.

Naval Aircraft Factory XP4N-1 (A-8482)   *U. S. Navy*
A development of the earlier Naval Aircraft Factory PN-12 with twin
tails. XP4N-1 had the same engines as the PN-12 but they were geared.

Naval Aircraft Factory XT2N-1 (A-8052)   *U. S. Navy*
The fuselage of this carrier dive bomber was built of water-tight
metal monocoque construction to eliminate need for flotation gear.

FLEET AIRCRAFT ASSIGNMENT
June 1931

UNITED STATES FLEET

Commander-in-Chief U. S. Fleet + TEXAS   4 O3U-1

BATTLE FORCE

Commander Battle Force + CALIFORNIA   3 O3U-1

COMMANDER BATTLESHIPS, BATTLE FORCE

Battleship Division One	VO-1B
USS IDAHO	3 O2U-1
USS MARYLAND	1 O2U-1, 1 O3U-1
Battleship Division Three	VO-3B
USS ARIZONA	3 O3U-1
USS NEVADA	2 O3U-1
USS OKLAHOMA	3 O3U-1
USS PENNSYLVANIA	3 O3U-1
USS NEW YORK	3 O3U-1
Battleship Division Four	VO-4B
USS COLORADO	3 O3U-1
USS TENNESSEE	2 O2U-1, 1 O3U-1
USS WEST VIRGINIA	3 O3U-1

COMMANDER DESTROYERS, BATTLE FORCE

USS DETROIT   2 O2U-1

COMMANDER AIRCRAFT, BATTLE FORCE
CARRIER DIVISION TWO

ComAirBatFor Flag Unit   No aircraft

USS SARATOGA	
VF-1B	18 F8C-4
VF-6B	18 F4B-2, 1 F3B-1, 1 O2C-2, 1 FU-2
VS-2B	12 O2U-2, 1 O2U-3
VT-2B	14 T4M-1, 7 TG-1
Utility Unti	2 O2U-2, 1 O2U-3, 2 O3U-1
USS LEXINGTON	
VF-2B	18 F3B-1, 1 FU-2
VF-5B	11 F4B-1, 8 F4B-2, 1 O2C-2
VS-3B	4 O2U-2, 6 O2U-4
VT-1B	17 T4M-1
Utility Unit	2 O2U-1, 3 O2U-2

BASE FORCE
COMMANDER TRAIN SQUADRON TWO

USS ARGONNE	
VP-17F	6 PD-1, 1 P3M-1, 1 PN-12
VP-9F	6 PM-1
VJ-1F	6 OL-8, 1 RS-3, 1 XRS-2, 4 FU-2

COMMANDER MINECRAFT, BATTLE FORCE

Fleet Air Base, Pearl Harbor	
VP-1B	5 T2D-1
VP-4B	12 PD-1
VP-6B	7 T3M-2
VP-12B	No aircraft
Utility Unit	1 OL-8, 1 O2U-3

SCOUTING FORCE

Commander Scouting Force + AUGUSTA		4 O2U-3
Cruiser Division Two	VS-5S	8 O2U-1
Cruiser Division Three	VS-6S	5 O2U-1
Cruiser Division Four	VS-9S	11 O2U-3, 1 O2U-4
	VS-10S	4 O3U-1

COMMANDER DESTROYERS, SCOUTING FORCE

Flag Unit (CONCORD until relieved by RALEIGH)   2 O2U-1

COMMANDER AIRCRAFT, SCOUTING FORCE

Flag Unit   1 O2U-1

USS LANGLEY
VS-1S	7 O2U-4, 1 O2U-3
VF-3S	18 F3B-1
Utility Unit	3 O2U-1, 3 F6C-3

USS WRIGHT
VP-8S	6 PM-1
VP-10S	3 PM-1, 2 P3M-1
VJ-2S	5 T4M-1
Utility Unit	3 O2U-1, 1 O2U-3, 5 O2U-4, 11 O3U-1, 1 P3M-1

FLEET AIR BASE, COCO SOLO, CANAL ZONE
VP-2S	6 PM-1
VP-3S	5 T3M-2
VP-5S	No aircraft
Utility Unit	2 O2U-1, 1 XRS-2, 1 RS-3, 1 OL-8, 18 T3M-2

ASIATIC FLEET

Commander-in-Chief Asiatic Fleet, Flag Unit	1 O2U-3
VS-11A, USS HOUSTON	3 O2U-3

Martin PM-1 (8296)   *U. S. Navy*
VP-8S replaced its six T4M-1's in 1930 with PM-1's, these were in turn replaced by PH-1's in 1932. Note squadron insignia, wing bomb racks.

Vought O2U-2 (8108)   *J. M. F. Hasse*
3-S-5 from the LEXINGTON showing the early version of the Indian
Head insignia of VS-3B. See page 208 for later, modified version.

Boeing F4B-1 (8151)   *J. M. F. Hasse*
Beautiful flight photo of "Red Rippers" fighter by famed San Diego
photographer Joseph Malta F. Hasse. Tail color at this time was blue.

Curtiss F8C-4 (8433)   *J. M. F. Hasse*
1-F-13 with a modification of the High Hat squadron insignia; it is
superimposed upon a colored disc. Note tail wheel, skid on O2U-2.

Vought O2U-4 (8351)   *Grumman*

Experimentation with an amphibious Vought float for the O2U Corsair
began in 1928 (see page 71) in an effort to duplicate the land-water-
carrier performance of the OL-8. This early device was limited to a
method of folding the wheels upward, as on the Brewster float below,
which got them out of the way for water landings but left them exposed
to cause excessive drag. The first product of the new Grumman Aircraft
Engineering Corp., was the development of a fully enclosed retractable
gear amphibious float. The original model "A" float is shown above
on the test O2U-4. This model of float was built in 1930 and Fleet
tested aboard the LEXINGTON and TENNESSEE in 1931. Note the
step-down in the top of the wide float to allow propeller clearance.
At the same time Chance-Vought and Brewster were also building an
amphibious float, but a thinner, revised flat-topped Grumman "B" float
(see pages 128, 177) was given the production order that equipped
VO-3B and VO-4B O3U-1's for Fleet service. Brewster continued their
production of stainless steel non-amphibious floats and wing pontoons.

Vought O3U-1 (8582)   *U. S. Navy*

Mounted on the Brewster stainless steel amphibious float. The wheels
were pulled upward to form a V above the float. Note carrier hook.

Vought O2U-4   *U. S. Navy*
The Grumman "A" float, described on the previous page, being flight
tested aboard the LEX. Note hook trailing above the Number Six Wire.

Vought O2U-4 (8333)   *U. S. Navy*
Note insignia of VS-1S with amphibious floats, extra large "E" in
Bombing and Machine Gunnery. Bar on tail is rudder lock, not markings.

Douglas O-38C (USCG 9)   *Manufacturer*
Shown new at the factory on December 10, 1931. Purchased new by
Army as serial # AC 32-394, transferred to Coast Guard. See Appendix C.

Lineup at NAS Anacostia   *U. S. Navy*
Showing the station-based command planes and staff utility types such
as the F3B-1, XRO-1, SU's, O2U's and two Ford RR-5 transports.

Lockheed XRO-1 Command (9054)   *U. S. Navy*
Beautiful "Altair" for AsstSecNav Ingalls, replacing XO2C-2 below
in October. First Navy landplane with fully retractable landing gear.

Curtiss XO2C-2 Command (8845)   *U. S. Navy*
David Ingalls' XF8C-7 (page 96) in March re-designated as XO2C-2. It
went back to XF8C-7 later, see page 144. There were also 3 O2C-2's.

Curtiss XF9C-1 (8731)   *U. S. Navy*
Small carrier fighter tested at Anacostia in April. Short span with gull
wing was designed to permit carrier storage without folding wings.

Berliner-Joyce XFJ-1 (8288)   *Manufacturer*
Another proposed design built for the same characteristics. It was
neecssary to lower the bottom wing in order for prop to clear ground.

Vought XO4U-1 (8641)   *Manufacturer*
Small two-place observation type of similar design. Crashed during flight
tests. The XO4U-2 (page 122) bore little resemblance to this design.

Keystone XOK-1 (8357)   *Manufacturer*
Designed as light-weight observation type to replace the heavier
O2U's on air-type catapults aboard surface craft. Photo on 1-12-31.

Keystone XOK-1 (8357)   *Manufacturer*
As modified on April 8th, note addition of guns and carrier arresting
gear, new cowling. Was not purchased for either ship or carrier use.

Berliner-Joyce XOJ-1 (8359)   *U. S. Navy*
From Bureau Design No. 86, same as XOK-1. Shown here with full-span
Zap Flaps. Production model, OJ-2, was placed aboard light cruisers.

Keystone PK-1 (8507)   *U. S. Navy*
The first PK-1 under test in 1931. The production PK-1's and PM-2's,
both twin-tailed designs based on the XP4N-1, joined the Fleet in 1932.

Martin XP2M-1 (8358)   *U. S. Navy*
This 100-foot span monoplane, designed by Consolidated to Bureau
specifications, was built by Martin as lowest bidder on contract.

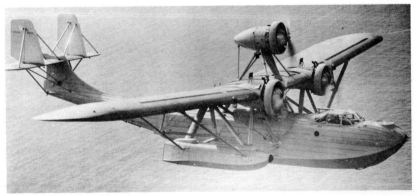

Martin XP2M-1 (8358)   *U. S. Navy*
Both the XPY-1 and the XP2M-1 tried the use of a third engine on
top of the wing but abandoned it in favor of twin-engine performance.

Martin P3M-1 (8412)   *The National Archives*
Refined, production version of the XP2M-1. Operated with VP-10S in
1931-1932; became P3M-2's with engine change. See Pensacola, 1941.

Curtiss F7C-1 (7653)   *U. S. Navy*
The only F7C-1 to have a carrier hook was this original XF7C-1 while
under test with VX-1D5 at Norfolk. Service use was with VF-5M, VF-9M.

Pitcairn Autogiro XOP-1 (8850)   *The National Archives*
Purchased to test suitability of carrier use. Landed on USS LANGLEY
September 23rd. Marines flew A-8976. See XOP-2. Note NT-1 in rear.

Martin XT6M-1 (8411)   *U. S. Navy*
Last of the biplane VT designs fully armed. Not produced. The T4M-1's
and sister TG-2's remained in service until the TBD-1's came in 1938.

Douglas XT3D-1 (8730)   *U. S. Navy*
Three-place torpedo bomber in the tradition of the T4M-1. It was not
accepted, was later modified into XT3D-2 with larger engine, hatches.

Loening XSL-1 (8696)   *U. S. Navy*
Small proposed sub scout. The large building in rear, that shows in
many photos, is Army War College across the river from NAS Anacostia.

FLEET AIRCRAFT ASSIGNMENT
October 1932

UNITED STATES FLEET

Commander-in-Chief U. S. Fleet	1 O3U-1
USS PENNSYLVANIA	4 O3U-1

BATTLE FORCE

ComBatFor Flag Unit	3 O3U-1

COMMANDER BATTLESHIPS, BATTLE FORCE

Battleship Division One	VO-1B	6 O2U-2, 3 O3U-1, 1 XO2L-2
Battleship Division Three	VO-3B	9 O3U-1
Battleship Division Four	VO-4B	9 O3U-1

COMMANDER CRUISERS, BATTLE FORCE

Cruiser Division Three	VS-6B	6 O2U-1, 4 O3U-1

COMMANDER DESTROYERS, BATTLE FORCE

USS DETROIT	2 O2U-1

COMMANDER AIRCRAFT, BATTLE FORCE

ComAirBatFor Flag Unit	1 F4B-3, 1 F3B-1, 1 O2U-3, 2 SU-1

USS SARATOGA

VF-1B	19 F4B-3, 1 SU-1
VF-6B	13 F3B-1, 9 F4B-4, 1 SU-1
VS-2B	15 SU-1, 2 OL-9, 1 XO2L-1
VT-2B	21 TG-2
VS-14M	5 SU-1
Utility Unit	1 O2U-1, 3 O2U-2, 1 OL-8, 1 OL-9

USS LANGLEY

VF-3B	6 F3B-1, 11 F4B-4, 1 SU-1
VS-1B	2 O2U-2, 4 O2U-3, 6 O2U-4
Utility Unit	2 O2U-1

BASE FORCE
COMMANDER TRAIN SQUADRON TWO

USS ARGONNE

VP-7F	6 PM-1
VP-9F	7 PM-1
VJ-1F	3 PM-2, 4 OL-8, 2 OL-9, 1 O2U-3, 1 RS-3, 1 XRS-2

COMMANDER MINECRAFT, BATTLE FORCE

FLEET AIR BASE, PEARL HARBOR

VP-1B	12 PK-1
VP-4B	12 PD-1
VP-6B	9 T4M-1, 3 T2D-1
Utility Unit	1 O2U-3, 2 OL-8, 1 RS-1

SCOUTING FORCE

ComScoFor, USS AUGUSTA	5 O3U-1
USS AKRON	6 F9C-2, 1 XF9C-1, 1 F6C-3, 3 N2Y-1

COMMANDER CRUISERS, SCOUTING FORCE

Cruiser Division Two	VS-5S	2 O2U-1, 2 O2U-4, 3 O3U-1
Cruiser Division Four	VS-9S	10 O2U-4, 4 O2U-3
Cruiser Division Five	VS-10S	17 O3U-1, 2 O2U-4

COMMANDER DESTROYERS, SCOUTING FORCE

USS RALEIGH, Ship Unit	3 O2U-1

COMMANDER AIRCRAFT, SCOUTING FORCE

ComAirScoFor Flag Unit	1 SU-2, 1 O3U-1

USS LEXINGTON

VF-2S	10 F4B-1, 8 F4B-2, 1 SU-2, 1 O2U-1
VF-5S	19 F4B-2, 1 SU-2
VS-3S	13 SU-2, 1 OL-8
VT-1S	15 BM-1
VS-15M	4 SU-2
Utility Unit	1 OL-8, 1 O2U-1, 2 O2U-2

USS WRIGHT

VP-8S	No aircraft assigned
VP-10S	No aircraft assigned
VJ-2S	4 PM-2, 1 RS-1, 4 OL-9, 1 T4M-1
Utility Unit	1 O2U-1, 1 O2U-3

FLEET AIR BASE, COCO SOLO

VP-2S	8 PM-2
VP-3S	12 P2D-1
VP-5S	1 P2D-1, 1 RS-3, 1 O2U-1, 1 OL-9, 1 PM-2
Utility Unit	9 PM-2

COMMANDER SPECIAL SERVICE SQUADRON

USS MEMPHIS Ship Unit	2 O2U-3

ASIATIC FLEET

USS HOUSTON	4 O2U-3
USS HERON	4 T4M-1

USS SARATOGA CV3   *U. S. Navy*
Beautiful aerial photo of the SARATOGA landing her planes off Maui,
Hawaii, on March 2nd, 1932. T4M-1's of VT-2B are landing; one is
taxiing forward, while the next in line takes a wave-off and enters
his climbing left turn. The forward group of T4M-1's are having their
wings folded by the deck handlers. Six SU's of VS-14M are aboard as
well as VF-6B's F4B-2's. Note the SU Command plane on the starboard
bow. Torpedo Two replaced their T4M-1's with new TG-2's in 1932.

Martin T4M-1 (7893)   *U. S. Navy*
2-T-15 circling for a landing five days later. Note name of ship,
SARA, on stern of flight deck; lowered deck hook, squadron insignia.

Boeing F4B-2 (8823)   *U. S. Navy*
Second section plane taking off on March 2nd. Note wing bomb racks
added to fighter for dive bombing duty; center section fuel tank.

Boeing F4B-3 (8898)   *U. S. Navy*
LCDR F. P. Sherman, C.O. of the High Hats, in his 1-F-1 catching the
wire aboard the SARATOGA 3-2-32. These action photos are very rare.

Boeing F4B-3 (8911)   *U. S. Navy*
Another VF-1B fighter, this one just leaving the deck on take-off.
Fuselage stripe, cowl, are Lemon Yellow; tail surfaces are all Red.

Boeing F3B-1 (7720)   *U. S. Navy*
The unusual horizontal tail stripe was used for war maneuvers. The
authority to designate tail colors was given to Force Commanders.

Boeing F4B-4 (8920)   *U .S. Navy*
LANGLEY-based VF-3B got its new F4B-4's in 1932. This 9-21-32 photo
shows one of their 11 F4B-4's and two of their 6 F3B-1's in left rear.

Boeing F4B-2 (8796)   *William Palmer*
One of 19 VF-5S fighters from the LEX at the old National Guard
Airport, Griffith Park, Los Angeles on August 14th. Tail color, Blue.

Douglas P2D-1 (8648)   *U. S. Navy*

Flying over the Panama Canal. VP-3S was based at Coco Solo, Canal
Zone from 1930 through 1937. Prior to 1930 the squadron number had
been used by the Marine Corps for VP-3M at Guam. VP-3S started with
six PM-1's in 1930, changed to five T3M-2's in 1931, and finally
standardized on P2D-1's in 1932—keeping them through 1936 until they
were replaced by PBY-1's in 1937. Note the Elephant insignia and the
horizontal tail stripes. In 1932 VP-1B was flying 12 PK-1's out of
Pearl Harbor; VP-2S had 8 PM-2's, also in the Canal Zone; VP-4B was
operating 12 PD-1's at Pearl Harbor; VP-5S had 9 PM-2's in the Canal
Zone; VP-6B operated mixed equipment of 3 T2D-1's and 9 T4M-1's at
Pearl Harbor; VP-7F and VP-9F operated 6 PM-1's each, were attached to
USS ARGONNE; VP-8S had 6 PH-1, VP-10S 6 P3M-2's, both on WRIGHT.

Hall-Aluminum PH-1 (8694)   *U. S. Navy*

Patrol Squadron Eight, with the winged 8-ball insignia, was the only
unit to fly the PH-1 operationally; from 1932 to 1937. Became VP-24.

Great Lakes TG-1 (8462)   *U. S. Navy*
Rare type with P&W R-1690 engine. Better known TG-2 had Wright
R-1820 of increased h.p. See App. A for comparative performance figures.

Vought O3U-1 Command (8870)   *U. S. Navy*
The Staff plane, which together with Rear Admiral Halligan's SU-2,
made up the Flag Unit of the Commander Aircraft, Scouting Force.

Ford RR-4 (8840)   *R. R. Moore*
Staff transport from NAS Pensacola. The only civil model 5-AT-C that
the Navy had as an RR-4. Went to Marine Corps, see USMC book p. 60.

Curtiss O2C-1 (8945)   *Manufacturer*
A special "Helldiver" with a "cabin installation" for LCDR Dillon
of the Bureau at Washington. Factory photo taken on January 4, 1932.

Curtiss XF6C-7 (7403)   *U. S. Navy*
Test-bed for early, experimental Ranger SGV-770 geared, air-cooled,
12-cylinder engine. Installation was made by Naval Aircraft Factory.

General Aviation FLB (USCG 51)   *Manufacturer*
The first rescue plane designed specifically for Coast Guard use, see
Appendix C for further details. Became PJ-1, later modified to PJ-2.

Curtiss XS3C-1 (8847)   *Manufacturer*
In flight near the factory at Buffalo, New York, on January 29, 1932.
It was given temporary, paper, designation of XF10C-1. See 02C-2.

Curtiss XF11C-2 (9213)   *Manufacturer*
Rare 4-13-32 photo with original tail wheel and no cut-out in bottom
of rudder. Note 500-pound bomb. #9213 was later redesigned XBFC-1.

Grumman XFF-1 (8878)   *Howard Eckert*
First of the all-metal Grumman fighters, with fully retractable landing
gear, a design destined to influence all naval aircraft in the 1930's.

Curtiss XF9C-1 (8731) *U. S. Navy*
The first Sparrowhawk carrier fighter was modified with a test hook for airship use following successful UO-1 flights aboard USS LOS ANGELES.

Atlantic XFA-1 (8732) *U. S. Navy*
The American-Fokker designed small carrier fighter. The XF9C-1, XFA-1 and XFJ-2 were all built to the specifications of Bureau Design 96.

Berliner-Joyce XFJ-2 (8288) *Gordon S. Williams*
The XFJ-1 (p. 105) was modified with an engine change, cowl and wheel pants added, to XFJ-2. It stayed on the Navy inventory until 1934.

Loening XO2L-1 (8525)   *The National Archives*
The final development of the OL-8 design resulted in the XO2L-1 for
combined battleship and carrier duty. Note similarity to later XJF-1.

Loening XO2L-1 (8525)   *U. S. Navy*
While under test at Anacostia small vertical fins were added to the
horizontal tail surfaces. Was tested on SARATOGA with VS-2B in 1932.

Loening XO2L-2 (8606)   *The National Archives*
Modified version, note different rudder than original XO2L-1. It was
Fleet tested with VO-1B aboard battleships; later served with VJ-1B.

Consolidated XP2Y-1 (8939)   *U. S. Navy*
As originally tested at Anacostia on May 6th with three engines. It
was essentially the XPY-1 with a half-wing added below. Note bow gun.

Consolidated XP2Y-1 (8939)   *U. S. Navy*
With the top engine removed on 5-23-32. Several of these were built as
civil Commodore transports for PAA use in Central and South America.

Consolidated XBY-1 (8921)   *U. S. Navy*
The reverse, a civil transport turned bomber, was the case of this
Fleetster offered to the Navy. Note bomb bay doors in the fuselage.

Vought XO4U-2 (8641)   *U. S. Navy*
Standard design, similar to O3U-3, not produced. Under the designation
system the XO4U-2 should have been a minor modification of XO4U-1.

Douglas XT3D-2 (8730)   *U. S. Navy*
The modified XT3D-1 with new engine, cowl and cockpit canopy. Note
bomb and machine gun. Assigned to Naval Proving Ground, Dahlgren.

Bellanca XSE-1 (9186)   *Manufacturer*
A unique new approach to carrier based scout planes was offered by the
Bellanca company in 1932 with this folding-wing monoplane. See XSE-2.

Bellanca XRE-1 (8938)   *U. S. Navy*
One of three (see below) civil CH-400 "Skyrocket" light transports
bought by Navy. Number 8938 was used for radio research at Anacostia.

Bellanca XRE-2 (9207)   *U. S. Navy*
Second CH-400. The third, XRE-3 #9341, was a two-litter ambulance
type delivered to the Marine Corps. All 3 had P&W R-1340 Wasp engines.

Douglas XRD-1 Command (8876)   *William T. Larkins*
Blue "Admiral's Barge" attached to NAS Anacostia. Note blue color
on retractable landing gear struts as well as wing struts and float.

FLEET AIRCRAFT ASSIGNMENT
June 1933

UNITED STATES FLEET

Commander-in-Chief U. S. Fleet	None assigned
USS PENNSYLVANIA	1 O3U-1, 3 O3U-3

BATTLE FORCE

ComBatFor Flag Unit	None assigned
USS CALIFORNIA	1 O3U-1, 3 O3U-3

COMMANDER BATTLESHIPS, BATTLE FORCE

Battleship Division One	VO-1B	4 O3U-1, 6 O3U-3
Battleship Division Three	VO-3B	7 O3U-1, 3 O3U-3
Battleship Division Four	VO-4B	7 O3U-1, 1 O2U-1

COMMANDER CRUISERS, BATTLE FORCE

Cruiser Division Two	VS-5B	6 OJ-2
Cruiser Division Three	VS-6B	8 OJ-2

COMMANDER DESTROYERS, BATTLE FORCE

USS DETROIT	2 OJ-2

COMMANDER AIRCRAFT, BATTLE FORCE

ComAirBatFor Flag Unit	1 O2U-3, 1 F3B-1, 1 SU-2

USS SARATOGA	
VF-1B	14 F11C-2, 19 F4B-3, 1 SU-3
VF-6B	20 F4B-4, 1 SU-3
VS-2B	5 SU-2, 2 SU-3, 5 SU-1, 2 OL-9
VT-2B	4 TG-1, 18 TG-2
VS-14M	6 SU-1, 1 SU-3
Utility Unit	1 OL-8, 1 OL-9, 1 O2U-1, 2 O2U-2

USS LEXINGTON	
VF-2B	14 F4B-2, 3 F4B-1, 1 SU-2
VF-5B	18 F4B-2, 1 XFF-1, 1 SU-2
VS-3B	3 SU-2, 8 SU-3
VT-1B	6 BM-1, 12 BM-2
VS-15M	6 SU-2
Utility Unit	2 OL-9, 1 O2U-1, 2 O2U-2

USS LANGLEY	
VF-3B	18 F4B-4, 1 SU-1
VS-1B	7 SU1-, 4 O2U-3, 1 O2U-4
Utility Unit	3 O2U-2

SCOUTING FORCE

ComScoFor, USS AUGUSTA	4 O3U-1

COMMANDER CRUISERS, SCOUTING FORCE

ComScoFor, Flag Unit		1 O2U-4
Cruiser Division Four	VS-9S	4 O2U-3, 7 O2U-4, 1 O3U-1
Cruiser Division Five	VS-10S	16 O3U-1, 4 O2U-4

COMMANDER DESTROYERS, SCOUTING FORCE

USS RALEIGH	2 O3U-1

COMMANDER AIRCRAFT, BASE FORCE

ComAirBaseFor, Flag Unit   1 OL-8 1 O3U-1

USS WRIGHT
VP-7F	6 PM-1
VP-9F	6 PM-1
VP-10F	6 P2Y-1
VJ-1F	1 RD-2, 1 RS-3, 1 XO2L-1, 1 XO2L-2, 3 PM-2, 3 OL-8, 1 OL-9, 1 XRS-2
VJ-2F	3 OL-9, 2 PM-2
Ship Utility	1 O3U-1

ALEUTIAN ISLAND SURVEY EXPEDITION   2 OL-9

FLEET AIR BASE, COCO SOLO
VP-2F	9 PM-2
VP-3F	12 P2D-1
VP-5F	8 P2Y-1
Utility Unit	1 RD-2, 1 RS-3, 2 O2U-1, 1 OL-9

FLEET AIR BASE, PEARL HARBOR
VP-1F	12 PK-1
VP-4F	12 PD-1
VP-6F	3 T4M-1, 6 PD-1
VP-8F	6 PH-1
Utility Unit	2 OL-8, 1 O2U-3, 1 RS-1

COMMANDER, SPECIAL SERVICE SQUADRON

USS RICHMOND   2 O2U-4

ASIATIC FLEET

USS HOUSTON   7 O2U-3
USS HERON   4 T4M-1

Vought SU-3 (9137)   *A. L. Whitmer*
LEXINGTON based VS-3B scout with the old Indian Head insignia. This
squadron operated with mixed SU-2's and SU-3's from 6-33 to 6-34.

Berliner-Joyce OJ-2 (9407)   *John C. Mitchell*
VS-5S squadron leader's plane from the four-stack light cruiser USS
TRENTON CL11. Production OJ-2's entered service in 1933 on the CL's.

Berliner-Joyce OJ-2 (9405)   *John C. Mitchell*
Second plane aboard the USS MARBLEHEAD CL12. These ships carried
two plane sections making aircraft 1, 3, 5, 7 and 9 the section leaders.

Berliner-Joyce OJ-2 (9193)   *Ed McCollon*
The USS MEMPHIS CL13 completed Cruiser Division Two, giving VS-5B
a total of six airplanes. Note E in machine gunnery. Tail stripe Blue.

Berliner-Joyce OJ-2 (9199)   *A. L. Whitmer*

VS-6B squadron leader, with red tail band, from the USS CONCORD.
VS-5B and VS-6B operated OJ-2's until 1935; replaced then by SOC-1's.

USS CINCINNATI CL6   *Bear Photo Service*

As far as is known this is the first photo ever published to show the
OJ-2's on floats aboard ship. 6-S-6 and 6-S-7 are on twin catapults.

Vought O2U-4 (8323)   *U. S. Navy*

Cruiser-based VS-9S and VS-10S still used Vought Corsairs of various
models at this time. See 1937 for complete renumbering of VS squadrons.

USS COLORADO BB45 *Bear Photo Service*

Showing O3U-1 amphibians 4-O-6, 4-O-4 and 4-O-5 aboard the second newest battleship at that time. The photos on this page are very rare.

Vought O3U-1 *U. S. Navy*

4-O-2 being catapulted from the USS WEST VIRGINIA. On 10-6-33, date of photo, COLO, WEST VA and TENN made up Battleship Division 4.

Vought O3U-1 (8551) *Gordon S. Williams*

Good photo showing the Grumman "B" float, carrier arresting hook, blue three-plane section leaders stripe. Tail color was solid Black.

Curtiss F11C-2 (9270) *Clark Scott*
VF-1B was the only Navy squadron to operate F11C-2's; in 1933 only, by 1934 they were redesignated BFC-2's. Correct tail color is Red.

Boeing F4B-2 (8628) *Don McCash*
By late 1933 The Red Rippers were operating mixed F4B-2's and new FF-1's. F4B-2's left the Fleet in 1935, went to Pensacola as trainers.

Grumman FF-1 (9357) *Charles W. Kossack*
VF-5B, the only unit to fly FF-1's, operated their blue-tailed planes aboard the LEXINGTON until 1935 when they went aboard RANGER.

Martin BM-2 (9178)   *U. S. Navy*
1-T-1 with a yellow tail from the LEXINGTON. VT-1S was the first
to get these new dive bombers, was re-designated VB-1B in 1934.

Vought SU-1 (9073)   *U. S. Navy*
Marine Corps squadrons VS-14M and VS-15M were stationed on board
SARATOGA & LEXINGTON 1931-1934. See USMC book for more photos.

USS SARATOGA CV3   *U. S. Navy*
With TG-2's, F4B-4's, F11C-2's and SU's aboard. Note Crowing Cock ship
insignia on stack contrary to statements that it was not used on ship.

SARATOGA Deck Scene   *U. S. Navy*
Great Lakes TG-2's, of VT-2B, are shown landing aboard. Note the short
distance between planes necessitating fast, precision handling on deck.

SARATOGA Deck Scene   *U. S. Navy*
On April 3, 1933, with 2-S-7 (SU-1 #9071) in the foreground and
14-S-1 and 14-S-2 next in line. Hazard of props is clearly shown.

Vought SU-2 Command (9095)   *U. S. Navy*

Rear Admiral John Halligan, Commander Aircraft, Battle Force, in his
blue command plane. He and his staff had three aircraft assigned to his
Flag Unit, the other two may be seen on the next page. In the early
1920's a system of painting command planes, adapted from the existing
method of painting boats aboard ship, was formulated and by 1933 was
well standardized. The Commanding Officer of the United States Fleet
(CinCUS) set the pattern with an all-blue fuselage and tail. Flag
planes for those of Admiral rank had blue fuselages and silver tails.
Planes for Commanding Officers of Captain rank were half blue and
half silver, and were used by C.O.'s of carriers and large Naval Air
Stations. Staff planes, not assigned to any individual commander as
his personal plane, were silver with the name of the Flag Unit on the
side of the fuselage. In all cases, except CinCUS and SecNav, the
wings and horizontal tail surfaces were silver. The wheel pants on land
planes had a distinctive horizontal silver bar. The use of red, white
and blue rudder stripes was optional. The blue F4B-1A (page 93),
which replaced the earlier silver UO-1 (page 51), started the blue
fuselage color for the Assistant Secretary of the Navy for Air. This
color continued through the use of the F8C-7, XRO-1, XR2O-1, R5O-1.

Vought O3U-3 Command (9224)   *William T. Larkins*

Flagplane for Admiral J. M. Reeves, Commander Battle Force, aboard
his flagship the USS CALIFORNIA. Note the oversize rear windshield.

Vought SU-3 Command (9138)   *William T. Larkins*
Second of the three planes assigned to the Flag Unit of Commander Aircraft, Battle Force, based aboard the USS SARATOGA.

Boeing F3B-1 Command (7743)   *William T. Larkins*
Third of the three assigned in 1933. Rear Admiral Halligan had 15 Staff Officers in his Flag Unit. Fighters were popular for this use.

Vought O3U-1 Command (8870)   *John C. Mitchell*
Plane assigned to Rear Admiral A. W. Johnson, Commander Aircraft Base Force, and his staff of 12—including CDR Mitscher and LT Pirie.

Vought SU-2 Command (9103)   *William T. Larkins*
An example of the half blue and half silver colors for Captain rank.
Personal plane of CAPT A. W. Fitch, C.O. NAS Norfolk, 5th Naval Dist.

Boeing F3B-1 (7741)   *William N. Fleming*
An example of the "staff transport" type of command plane which could
be used by any of a dozen or more junior staff officers of a NAS.

Douglas PD-1   *U. S. Navy*
Patrol Squadron Six-F got 6 PD-1's in 1933 and kept them through 1936,
operating them jointly with 6 Martin PM-1's. Note the anchor on bow.

Vought O2U-2 (8126)   *Gordon S. Williams*
The Number One plane of the SARATOGA's Utility Unit. Note that
these planes operated on both wheels and floats when carrier based.

Vought O2U-2 (8104)   *Warren D. Shipp*
SARATOGA-2 on wheels at Floyd Bennett Field, New York City. Note
the Crowing Cock insignia under the cockpit. Two OL's were #4 and #5.

Vought O2U-1 (7936)   *Gordon S. Williams*
SARATOGA-3, the third utility O2U. This page represents the ultimate
goal of the aircraft photo collector and is a rare presentation.

Curtiss F9C-2 (9057)   *U. S. Navy*
LT D. W. Harrigan, pioneer LTA plane pilot, hooking on the MACON's
number two fighter for the first time; over New Egypt, N. J., July 7th.

Curtiss F9C-2 (9059)   *A. U. Schmidt*
When the USS AKRON ZRS-4 went down off New Jersey on April 4th she
did not have any of her 'Sparrowhawks' aboard, thus all went to MACON.

USS MACON ZRS-5   *U. S. Navy*
Pride of the LTA fleet, commissioned March 11th. Left Lakehurst in
October for Sunnyvale. Lost off Point Sur, California, Feb. 12, 1935.

Curtiss F9C-2 (9056)   *U. S. Navy*
November photo showing first use of blue-black tail colors (see
1934). The Heavier-than-Air Unit insignia was created by LT Harrigan.

Consolidated N2Y-1 (8604)   *William T. Larkins*
AKRON trainer also used by the MACON. Standard Fleet 2 with airship
hook attachment added. These were replaced by the newer XJW-1's.

Sikorsky RS-1 (8842)   *The National Archives*
First of 3 S-41's, new at the factory. Went to VO-9M in the Marine
Corps and then to Haiti. See photo as 9-O-10 in USMC book, page 42.

Sikorsky RS-3 (8285)   *U. S. Navy*
Re-designated PS-3 as transport for Utility Squadron Five of the
Eleventh Naval District at San Diego. Rare markings as VJ-5D11-4.

Vought O2U-3 (8248)   *Warren D. Shipp*
Plane number one of Experimental Squadron One of the Fifth Naval
District at NAS Norfolk, Virginia. VX markings were rarely seen.

Grumman XSF-1 (8940) *George M. Smith*
Following the FF-1 fighter, in November 1933, the Scout model appeared which eventually equipped VS-3B and most of the reserve bases.

Vought XF3U-1 (9222) *Manufacturer*
A two-place fighter design, slow in development, which eventually was rebuilt into the XSBU-1 Scout Bomber. See photos, pages 139 and 291.

Hall-Aluminum XP2H-1 (8729) *U. S. Navy*
Unusual four engined patrol bomber with two tractor and two pusher props. In January 1935 it flew non-stop from Norfolk to Coco Solo.

Great Lakes XBG-1 (9220)   *The National Archives*
Original open cockpit model of the dive bomber widely used by both the
Navy and Marines. Became Marine command job, see USMC book, p. 68.

Consolidated XB2Y-1 (9221)   *Manufacturer*
Competitor in dive bomber competition, note similarity to XBG-1.
Was not put into production. See photo as later modified on page 165.

Curtiss XS2C-1 (9377)   *Manufacturer*
Rare photo of experimental scout similar to the one Air Corps YA-10.
Non-folding wings on 44-foot span created a carrier storage problem.

Grumman XJF-1 (9218)   *U. S. Navy*
First of a long line of bi-plane utility amphibians used by the
Navy, Marine Corps, Coast Guard and Army Air Forces for 15 years.

Great Lakes XSG-1 (8974)   *U. S. Navy*
A smaller, folding wing design intended for use on catapults aboard
cruisers. Experimental project only, and was not placed in production.

Curtiss XF11C-3 (9269)   *U. S. Navy*
In an attempt to improve the performance of the F11C-2 a hand operated
retractable landing gear was devised. Later became the XBF2C-1.

Sikorsky XP2S-1 (8642)   *U. S. Navy*
Little known tractor-pusher twin R-1340-88 Sikorsky patrol bomber
built in 1932. Note bow machine gun and 50 lb. bomb on wing rack.

Loening XSL-2 (8696)   *U. S. Navy*
The XSL-1, which had a Warner Scarab radial engine, was modified to
XSL-2 with a Menasco B-6 in-line engine. Flying boat, not amphibious.

Loening XS2L-1 (8971)   *U. S. Navy*
Small, compact folding-wing amphibian designed for submarine use.
Note pilot just above wheel, rear machine gun for enclosed gunner.

Sikorsky XSS-2 (8972)   *U. S. Navy*
The Sikorsky XP2S-1, XSS-2, and Loening XSL-1 and XS2L-1, were an attempt to design a new scout-observation type based on the flying boat concept instead of the usual single-float biplane. None of the designs proved practical and the standard for VO-VS aircraft remained the same through the end of the SOC's. The two-place XSS-2 had folding wings and a carrier arresting hook; mounted an R-1340 Wasp on struts.

Boeing XF6B-1 (8975)   *Manufacturer*
Last refinement of the F4B design. Had shorter, equal span wings, R-1535-44, 125 hp more than F4B-4. Revised as dive bomber XBFB-1.

Curtiss XF12C-1 (9225)   *Manufacturer*
Two-place parasol carrier fighter with folding wings, slots, flaps,
retractable gear. Radical change from previous Hawk bi-plane series.

Curtiss XF12C-1 (9225)   *Manufacturer*
Note cowling change in this November photo from above July shot. In
December re-designated XS4C-1; changed again to XSBC-1 with R-1820.

Curtiss XF8C-7 (8845)   *Fred E. Bamberger*
The XO2C-2 re-designed again, back to F8C-7, as an Anacostia staff
plane prior to going out of service in 1933. See pages 96 and 104.

Curtiss XF13C-2 (9343)   *Manufacturer*
December 1933 photo showing the monoplane XF13C-1 modified into the
bi-plane XF13C-2. Eventually went to USMC as XF13C-3, See USMC p. 77.

Curtiss XF11C-1 (9219)   *U. S. Navy*
Note long cowling on Twin Row R-1510. Not put into production, later
re-designated XBFC-1. Had P-6E fuselage, XP-23 wings. See page 164.

Boeing XF7B-1 (9378)   *Manufacturer*
9-14-33 factory photo as originally built with enclosed cockpit. Navy
objected to poor visibility for carrier landings, changed to open pit.

1934

FLEET AIRCRAFT ASSIGNMENT
June 1934

UNITED STATES FLEET

CinCUS, Flag Ship	1 O3U-3
USS PENNSYLVANIA, Ship Unit	3 O3U-3

BATTLE FORCE

ComBatFor Flag Unit	1 O3U-3
USS CALIFORNIA	2 O3U-3

COMMANDER BATTLESHIPS, BATTLE FORCE

Battleship Division One	VO-1B	8 O3U-3, 3 O3U-1
Battleship Division Three	VO-3B	8 O3U-3, 3 O3U-1
Battleship Division Four	VO-4B	12 O3U-1

COMMANDER CRUISERS, BATTLE FORCE

Cruiser Division Two	VS-5B	6 OJ-2
Cruiser Division Three	VS-6B	5 OJ-2

COMMANDER DESTROYERS, BATTLE FORCE

USS DETROIT	2 OJ-2

COMMANDER AIRCRAFT, BATTLE FORCE

ComAirBatFor Flag Unit	1 SU-2, 1 SU-3, 1 F3B-1

USS SARATOGA

VF-1B	18 BFC-2, 1 SF-1
VF-6B	20 F4B-4, 1 SF-1, 1 SU-3
VS-2B	7 SU-1, 4 SU-2, 3 SU-3
VS-14M	7 SU-1
VT-2B	18 TG-2
Utility Unit	2 BFC-2, 4 F4B-4, 1 O2U-1, 2 O2U-2, 2 OL-9

USS LEXINGTON

VF-2B	20 F4B-2, 1 SF-1, 1 SU-2
VF-5B	19 FF-1
VS-3B	8 SU-2, 6 SU-3
VT-1B	12 BM-1, 6 BM-2
VS-15M	5 SU-2, 2 SU-3
Utility Unit	2 O2U-2, 2 O3U-1

USS MACON

Macon Unit	4 F9C-2, 2 XJW-1, 1 OL-8, 2 N2Y-1

SCOUTING FORCE

ComScoFor, USS INDIANAPOLIS	4 O3U-1

COMMANDER CRUISERS, SCOUTING FORCE

ComCruScoFor Flag Unit		1 O3U-3
Cruiser Division Four	VS-9S	3 O3U-1, 4 O2U-3, 8 O2U-4
Cruiser Division Five	VS-10S	18 O3U-1
Cruiser Division Six	VS-11S	21 O3U-3

COMMANDER DESTROYERS, SCOUTING FORCE

USS RALEIGH, Ship Unit	2 O3U-1

COMMANDER AIRCRAFT, BASE FORCE

Flag Unit   1 O3U-1, 1 O3U-3

USS WRIGHT
VP-7F	6 PM-1
VP-9F	7 PM-1
VJ-1F	1 OL-8, 4 OL-9, 1 RD-2
VJ-2F	5 PM-2
Ship Utility	1 O3U-1

FLEET AIR BASE, COCO SOLO
VP-2F	7 PM-2
VP-3F	13 P2D-1
VP-5F	11 P2Y-1
Utility Unit	2 F4B-3, 2 O2U-1, 1 O2U-3, 1 OL-9, 1 OL-8, 1 RS-3, 1 RD-2

COMMANDER, SPECIAL SERVICE SQUADRON

USS RICHMOND   2 O2U-4

FLEET AIR BASE, PEARL HARBOR
VP-1F	11 PK-1
VP-4F	12 PD-1
VP-6F	6 PM-1, 6 PD-1
VP-8F	6 PH-1
VP-10F	6 P2Y-1
Utility Unit	2 F4B-3, 1 OL-8, 1 RS-1, 2 O2U-3

ASIATIC FLEET

USS AUGUSTA   4 O3U-1

Aircraft Detachment, USS HERON   2 T4M-1

Navy Yard, Cavite, P.I.   2 T4M-1, 3 O3U-1

Consolidated P2Y-1's   *U. S. Navy*
VP-10F broke three seaplane records on January 10-11, 1934, when
they flew six P2Y's in nonstop formation from San Francisco to Hawaii.

Curtiss BF2C-1 (9601)   *William T. Larkins*
From Bombing Five formed in 1934 for these new aircraft aboard the new
RANGER. Gear trouble caused their replacement by F4B-4's in mid-1935.

Boeing F4B-2 Modified (8619)   *Kipp Cooper*
Section Two leader with yellow tail from LEXINGTON. F4B-2's still
in use had fin and rudder replaced by F4B-4 type. Compare with p. 114.

Boeing F4B-4 (9246)   *Ed McCollon*
3-F-1, Squadron Leader of the Striking Eagles. VF-3 switched from
the LANGLEY to the RANGER in mid-1934. Cowl should be solid red.

Boeing F4B-4 (9042)   *John C. Mitchell*
2-F-1, Squadron Leader of the enlisted pilots squadron. Each section
leader was an officer, remainder of pilots CPO Aviation Pilot rank.

Boeing F4B-4 (8915)   *John C. Mitchell*
Section Three leader with True Blue fuselage band and cowling color.
This same color was applied to chevron on top wing enclosing "7."

Boeing F4B-2 Modified (8795)   *Ed McCollon*
Section Five leader with a Willow Green fuselage band and cowling.
Fighting Two operated mixed F4B-2's and F4B-4's in late 1934 only.

Vought SU-2 (9097)   *Don McCash*
Fighting Two's number 19 utility plane used since late 1932. It
was replaced by a new SF-1 in early 1934.

Martin BM-1 (9216)   *Howard Eckert*
Another new outfit formed for the LANGLEY. Operated mixed BM-1's
and BM-2's for a few months until replaced by 18 new BG-1's in 1935.

Martin BM-2 (9171)   *Gordon S. Williams*
Rare photo of BM with cowling. Probably used on an experimental
basis as service use was without cowl as shown in photo above.

Loening OL-9 (8983) *Gordon S. Williams*
Beautiful action photo of the SARATOGA-3 utility ship just entering the water near Seattle. Many OL-9's served the reserve air bases.

Grumman JF-1 (9444) *John C. Mitchell*
LEXINGTON-4 in pre-war smogless Los Angeles. These new Grumman's began replacing the OL-9's as carrier utility planes in late 1934.

Vought SU-3 (9125) *U. S. Navy*
The High Hat's utility plane at San Diego on January 25th, 1934. It carries the squadron's red tail but does not use section colors.

Curtiss F9C-2 (9058)   *U. S. Navy*
LT Harold B. Miller, who took over command of the Heavier-than-Air
Unit in June 1934, flying over Moffett Field. LCDR Herbert V. Wiley
became C.O. of the USS MACON in July 1934 and during this year
developed a highly imaginative and successful system of search tactics
for the airship-airplane combination. In spite of this she was
repeatedly "shot down" during maneuvers with the Fleet and became
the last of the heavy rigids with her loss in 1935. Each F9C-2 had
a section color assigned in 1932 and when fully painted it was used
on the cowl, wheel pants, wing chevron and fuselage band. 9056 was
Red, 9057 White, 9058 Blue, 9059 Black, 9060 Green and 9061 Yellow.

Curtiss XF9C-2 (9264)   *John C. Mitchell*
Original Curtiss carrier fighter proposal which had civil registration
NX-986M. Later purchased by Navy, never had airship hook installed.

Waco XJW-1 (9521) *John C. Mitchell*
MACON-5, first of the two Waco UBF sport planes modified for use as hook-on trainers. Also used to fly mail and passengers to airship.

Waco XJW-1 (9522) *John C. Mitchell*
Unique view of MACON-6. Each of the 9 F9C pilots was carefully checked out in these because of F9C's bad ground looping tendency.

Stinson XR3Q-1 (9718) *Robert McLarren*
Civil SR-5A "Reliant" assigned as utility transport to NAS Sunnyvale (Moffett Field). This was a station plane and not part of HTA Unit.

Vought O3U-1 (8562)   *Warren D. Shipp*

LANGLEY-2 utility plane showing its Covered Wagon insignia—grey
ship with white canvas superimposed on red, white and blue stripes.

USS WRIGHT AV1   *U. S. Navy*

8600-ton Seaplane Tender in use from 1921-1941 shown at Pearl Harbor
in Feb. 1934 with two PH-1's and one OL-8 aboard. See VP assignments.

Vought O3U-1 (8864)   *A. U. Schmidt*

The USS WRIGHT's ship utility plane. Note carrier hook as well
as flotation gear enabling transportation over water to carriers.

Vought O2U-4 (8352)   *Dave Russell*
Utility plane assigned to the Inspector of Naval Aircraft at the
Grumman factory, Farmingdale, Long Island, N.Y., in 1934-1935.

Loening OL-8A (8081)   *Warren D. Shipp*
Rare photo of OL-8A assigned in 1934 only to Torpedo Station, Newport,
R.I. Plane #2 of Experimental Squadron Two of First Naval District.

Loening OL-9 (8984)   *Warren D. Shipp*
Number seven aircraft of the U. S. Naval Academy at Annapolis, Md. It
replaced earlier OL-8 and was used 6-34 to 6-36, replaced by J2F-1.

Vought SU-1 (8872)   *U. S. Navy*

One of Anacostia's highly polished staff planes in flight 12-13-34 showing the photographer in position for oblique shots. The Navy had 936 servicable aircraft on hand, and 227 on order, as of June 30th. The USS RANGER CV4 was commissioned on June 4th and VB-3B, VB-5B, VF-3B and VS-1B went aboard later in the year. During her construction period Congress made no provision for her 114 planes, forcing the Navy to curtail other activities to provide the ship's complement.

Boeing F4B 4 (9018)   *U. S. Navy*

Green-tailed 3-F-9 parked on a RANGER outrigger boom in August 1934. These ingenious devices solved temporary deck handling problems.

Vought SU-4 (9430) *John C. Mitchell*
Leader of Section Six with Lemon Yellow stripe and cowl, green tail.
Note amphibious duck squadron insignia and rear cockpit machine gun.

Vought SU-3 *U. S. Navy*
Two-Sail-Five from the SARATOGA laying a smoke screen from one
of its two detachable tanks mounted on the under-wing bomb racks.

Vought O2U-3 (8229) *William T. Larkins*
VS-9S of Cruiser Division Four operated mixed O2U-3's, O2U-4's and
O3U-1's at this time. See page 159. Note E in both m.g. and bombing.

Vought O3U-1 (8856)   *Warren D. Shipp*
Orthochromatic film makes Yellow tail band of VS-10S appear darker
in this photo of the squadron leader's plane from the USS CHICAGO.

USS CHICAG0 CA29   *Bear Photo Service*
With Vice Admiral Laning's (Commander Cruisers, Scouting Force)
O3U-3 Flagplane aboard, together with O3U-1's 10-S-1, 2, 3 and 4.

Vought O3U-1 (8867)   *Warren D. Shipp*
10-S-2 from the CHICAGO. Although normally operated on single floats
cruiser-borne aircraft often flew on wheels from shore bases as above.

Vought O3U-1   *U. S. Navy*

This interesting series of action photos shows the system, and some
of its problems, for recovering aircraft aboard battleships and cruisers
while the ship was moving. The first operational test of this "plane
trap" was made on April 18, 1933 when LT G. A. Ott landed an O2U
alongside the USS MARYLAND and was taken aboard the ship under
way. The device consisted of a towed sea sled with a net on the top.
The plane was taxied onto the sled, the power was cut, and as the plane
slid backward a hook on the front underside of the float engaged the
coarse net. The rear seat radio operator then stood on the rear cockpit
and fastened the hoisting cable to the wires permanently mounted
on the top wing of such aircraft for this purpose. The "plane trap"
was reeled out as the plane was lifted to disengage the net, but as
can be seen by the lower photo this did not always happen. Note the
Commander pointing out the hooked net to the observer who in turn is
leaning over and telling the pilot. Note the other O3U-1 on catapult
in upper right. The float hook for engaging the net can be clearly
seen on the O3U-1 on page 177, and the Stearman XOSS-1 on page 239.

Vought O2U-4 (8349) *Warren D. Shipp*
10-S-6 from the USS CHESTER CA27, sister ship to the CHICAGO and part of Cruiser Division Five. These ships were commissioned in 1930-31.

Vought O3U-1 (8838) *John C. Mitchell*
Another CruDivFive plane, from USS HOUSTON CA30. Note insignia which later became VCS-5, rear pit machine gun ring and flotation gear.

Vought O3U-1 (8555) *John C. Mitchell*
9-S-10 with white tail stripe from USS PENSACOLA CA24, one of two sister ships launched in 1929. See p. 157 for 9-S-11, p. 175 for 9-S-9.

Douglas R2D-1 (9620)   *U. S. Navy*
First of five civilian transports purchased by the Navy. The fast
cross-country record set by TWA in DC-2 marked end of Ford Tri-Motor.

Martin T4M-1 (7649)   *U. S. Navy*
One of two T4M-1's assigned to the Aircraft Detachment, USS HERON,
with the Asiatic Fleet in 1932-1934. Replaced by JF-1's in 1935.

Curtiss R4C-1 (9584)   *U. S. Navy*
Rare photo with skis and markings of U. S. ANTARCTIC SERVICE.
Went to Marine Utility Seven in 1935, see photos pp. 59, 76 USMC book.

Vought XO3U-5 (9078)   *U. S. Navy*
An O3U-4 with experimental P&W cowling designed to force cooling
air onto rear bank of cylinders of R-1535 twin-row radial engine.

DeHavilland XDH-80 (8877)   *U. S. Navy*
Puss Moth for the U.S. Naval Attache, London. C/n 2187, impressed by
RAF in 1939 as HM534, sold surplus in 1946 as G-AHLO. Replaced DH-60.

Consolidated XN4Y-1 (9457)   *U. S. Navy*
One of three, shown with Pensacola markings. It had a Lycoming
R-680-6 engine and was similar to the Army Air Corps PT-11D.

Northrop XFT-1 (9400)   *Manufacturer*
On January 18, 1934. Another attempt at an all-metal low wing fighter.
Note life raft behind headrest. Modified to XFT-2 in 1935, see p. 197.

Curtiss XF13C-1 (9343)   *U. S. Navy*
As converted back to a monoplane, at NAS Anacostia on April 18,
1934. Note slots in leading edge of wing flaps, not used on XF13C-2.

Curtiss XSBC-1 (9225)   *Manufacturer*
At factory in February. Crashed in June, rebuilt and sent to Anacostia.
Crashed again at factory in September, total wreck. Rebuilt to XSBC-2.

1934

Berliner-Joyce XF2J-1 (8973)   *Manufacturer*
Unsuccessful two-place fighter development of XFJ-1 design. Flown with both open and enclosed cockpits. On Navy List in 1934 only.

Grumman XF2F-1 (9342)   *The National Archives*
With the change in fighter design philosophy moving away from two-place VF aircraft Grumman revised the FF-1 design to this classic.

Curtiss XBFC-1 (9219)   *N.A.C.A.*
#1 of 4 experimental "nose-slot cowlings." Used increased velocity of air to increase cooling during low-speed, high-power operation.

Bellanca XSE-2 (9186) *Manufacturer*
The XSE-1 of 1932 (page 122) with engine changed to R-1510-92.
Note beefed-up rear fuselage and enlarged vertical tail surfaces.

Consolidated XB2Y-1 (9221) *U. S. Navy*
At NAS Hampton Roads in March 1934 with a modified cowling and
an auxiliary, detachable belly tank in place of 500 pound bomb.

Douglas XFD-1 (9223) *Manufacturer*
New, at the factory January 11th. 1934 saw the last of the bi-plane
fixed-gear fighter designs; such was the impact of the Grumman FF-1.

Curtis XO3C-1 (9413)   *U. S. Navy*
First of the long line of "Seagull" scouts. The amphibious gear was abandoned, hatches added, and plane re-designed XSOC-1 in June 1935.

Berliner-Joyce XOJ-3 (9196)   *U. S. Navy*
Note canopy, wing and rear pit machine guns. After a crash in March it was re-built as OJ-2, sent to Seattle NRAB. See photo, page 276.

Pennsylvania Aircraft Syndicate XOZ-1 (8602)   *U. S. Navy*
Rare photo of the Consolidated XN2Y-2 rebuilt into a twin-float, monoplane autogiro, and was similar in appearance to Pitcairn XOP-1.

Douglas XO2D-1 (9412) *Manufacturer*
At the factory, March 1934. Note similarity in design between the
XO2D-1, XO5U-1 and XO3C-1. All were for battleship observation use.

Vought XO5U-1 (9399) *U. S. Navy*
All three of these planes had folding wings and retractable, amphibious
landing gear. The XO5U-1 was on hand from 1934 through 1937.

Vought XSBU-1 (9222) *Harry Thorell*
The unsuccessful XF3U-1 rebuilt as a dive bomber. Placed in production
for VS-1, 2 and 3. The X job stayed on through 1941, see page 291.

Curtiss O2C-1 (8948)   *Jack Canary*

1934 was the Year of The Helldiver for the reserves. 20 F8C-4's and 55 O2C-1's served every reserve air station. Note the Ram insignia.

Curtiss O2C-1 (8951)   *Warren D. Shipp*

9-N-4 from Grosse Isle, Michigan. Insignia of man on horse was known as "The Black Knight." Used by VN-9RD9 and VO-7MR; had Red tails.

Curtiss O2C-1 (8758)   *Corbett K. Bates*

Squadron leader with red cowl and band. Oakland used the R-W-B tail stripes which were optional. Markings were regular Navy at this time.

Curtiss O2C-1 (8784) *Warren D. Shipp*
Section Two leader from VN-5RD4 based at the Navy Yard, Philadelphia. Note the wing lights replacing earlier flares. See page 156.

Curtiss O2C-1 (8941) *F. C. Dickey, Jr., Collection*
Unusual photo showing both VN-11RD9 insignia and USMC insignia representing the newly formed VO-7MR squadron. Note station name.

Curtiss F8C-4 (8427) *John C. Mitchell*
Fighter version of the Helldiver serving with VN-13RD11 at Long Beach, California. Note modified Jiggs insignia with name of base.

Curtiss N2C-1 (7650)   *William N. Fleming*
The original XN2C-1 of 1928 (see page 76) now serving New York. Odd
Markings "VN3-4RD3" show combined use by both reserve squadrons.

Consolidated NY-2 (7463)   *Gordon S. Williams*
One of six flown by Seattle's VN-15RD13 and VO-8MR on both wheels
and floats. Seattle was one of few bases to operate reserve seaplanes.

Consolidated NY-2A (8017)   *William Pinnell*
13 out of 36 NY-2A's went to the reserves in June 1933, all were gone
by November 1936. This plane is from NRAB Floyd Bennett, N.Y.

Berliner-Joyce OJ-2 (9576)   *Gene Sommerich*
6-N-5 from the Naval Reserve Aviation Unit at NAS Anacostia. Note
insignia. 9572-9583 were built for reserves, ten in use by November.

Vought O2U-1 (7940)   *Gordon S. Williams*
Rare reserve type, only four in use from May 1928. The last one went
out of service in December 1935. Note the Mountain Goat insignia.

Martin T4M-1 (7893)   *William T. Larkins*
Oakland's reserve T4M-1. Most reserve bases had one as an overage
to assigned aircraft. Ten used 1932-1934, and one lasted until 1937.

FLEET AIRCRAFT ASSIGNMENT
June 1935

UNITED STATES FLEET

CinCUS Flag Unit	2 O3U-3
USS PENNSYLVANIA, Ship Unit	4 O3U-3

BATTLE FORCE

ComBatFor Flag Unit	1 O3U-3
USS CALIFORNIA, Ship Unit	4 O3U-3

COMMANDER BATTLESHIPS, BATTLE FORCE

Battleship Division One	VO-1B	9 O3U-1
Battleship Division Two	VO-2B	3 O3U-1, 7 O3U-3
Battleship Division Three	VO-3B	6 O3U-1, 1 O3U-3
Battleship Division Four	VO-4B	9 O3U-3

COMMANDER CRUISERS, BATTLE FORCE

Cruiser Division Two	VS-5B	6 OJ-2
Cruiser Division Three	VS-6B	10 OJ-2

COMMANDER DESTROYERS, BATTLE FORCE

USS DETROIT	2 O3U-1

COMMANDER AIRCRAFT, BATTLE FORCE

ComAirBatFor Flag Unit	1 F3B-1, 1 SU-2, 1 SU-3

USS SARATOGA

VB-2B	20 BFC-2, 1 O2U-2, 1 SF-1
VF-6B	17 F4B-4, 1 O2U-4, 1 SF-1
VS-2B	9 SU-2, 9 SU-3
VT-2B	18 TG-2
Utility Unit	4 O3U-1, 3 JF-1

USS LEXINGTON

VF-2B	21 F2F-1, 3 F4B-4, 1 O2U-4, 1 SU-1
VF-5B	21 FF-1, 1 O2U-4, 1 SF-1
VS-3B	18 SF-1
VB-1B	7 BM-1, 12 BM-2
Utility Unit	1 F3B-1, 2 JF-1, 3 O3U-1

USS RANGER

VF-3B	18 F2F-1, 19 F4B-4, 1 O3U-1, 1 SU-2, 1 SF-1
VB-3B	18 BG-1
VB-5B	15 BF2C-1, 1 O2U-2, 1 SF-1
VS-1B	20 SU-4
Utility Unit	3 O3U-3, 2 JF-1

USS LANGLEY

Utility Unit	2 OJ-2, 1 O2U-2, 2 O3U-1

USS TRENTON

Ship Unit	2 OJ-2

SCOUTING FORCE

USS INDIANAPOLIS	4 O3U-1

COMMANDER CRUISERS, SCOUTING FORCE

ComCruScoFor Flag Unit		1 O3U-1
Cruiser Division Four	VS-9S	7 O2U-3, 8 O2U-4
Cruiser Division Five	VS-10S	10 O3U-1
Cruiser Division Six	VS-11S	4 O2U-4, 10 O3U-3
Cruiser Division Seven	VS-12S	13 O3U-3

COMMANDER DESTROYERS, SCOUTING FORCE

USS RALEIGH	3 O2U-3, 1 O2U-4

COMMANDER AIRCRAFT, BASE FORCE

Flag Unit	1 O3U-1

USS WRIGHT

VP-7F	6 PM-1, 6 P2Y-3
VP-9F	6 PM-1
VJ-1F	6 JF-1, 1 O3U-1, 3 PM-2, 1 RD-2, 1 RD-3
VJ-2F	1 PM-1, 3 PM-2, 3 OL-9, 1 RD-3
Ship Utility	1 O3U-1, 1 O3U-3

FLEET AIR BASE, COCO SOLO

VP-2F	12 PM-2
VP-3F	12 P2D-1
VP-5F	11 P2Y-1
Utility Unit	2 F4B-3, 1 O2U-1, 1 RD-2, 1 RD-3

FLEET AIR BASE, PEARL HARBOR

VP-1F	13 PK-1
VP-4F	12 PD-1, 3 P2Y-3
VP-6F	6 PM-1, 6 PD-1
VP-8F	6 PH-1
VP-10F	6 P2Y-1
Utility Unit	2 F4B-3, 3 O2U-3, 1 OL-9, 1 RD-3

ASIATIC FLEET

USS AUGUSTA	4 O3U-1
Aircraft Detachment USS HERON	2 JF-1
Navy Yard, Cavite, P.I.	1 JF-1, 3 O3U-1

Grumman F2F-1 (9637)   *U. S. Navy*
Fighting Two (LEXINGTON) and Fighting Three (RANGER) got their new F2F-1's in 1935. Note camera gun on top wing, gunnery pennant.

Vought O3U-3 (9324)   *Gordon S. Williams*
Beautiful VS-11S job in full markings. Note E in machine gunnery,
Willow Green tail stripe and Flying Fish insignia (later VCS-6).

Vought O3U-3 (9308)   *Jack Canary*
Scout from the heavy cruiser MINNEAPOLIS CA36 of CruDivSeven.
Note how Black tail stripe is placed on top of horizontal tail surface.

Vought O3U-3 (9319)   *Gordon S. Williams*
O3U-3's served on 5 of the new ASTORIA Class cruisers (commissioned
in 1934) for a little over one year, were replaced by new SOC-1's.

Vought O3U-1 (8820)   *Gordon S. Williams*
Rare photo of two of the AUGUSTA's four O3U-1's. USS AUGUSTA
CA31 spent several years with the Asiatic Fleet out of Cavite, P.I.

Curtiss SOC-1 (9889)   *William T. Larkins*
18 were delivered by November 1935. Note folding turtle-deck for
rear gun. Blue fuselage stripe on #9 caused by four-plane sections.

Grumman SF-1 (9476)   *Wilford Ransom*
1935 was the only year that VS-3B operated SF-1's. They replaced
SU-2's and SU-3's and were in turn replaced by SBU-1's in 1936.

Boeing F4B-4 (9029)   *John C. Mitchell*
The white-tailed Squadron Leader of Fighting Six from the SARATOGA.
This Felix-the-Cat squadron flew F4B-4's from 1932 through 1936.

Boeing F4B-4 (9252)   *John C. Mitchell*
Leader of Section Six during a visit of the entire squadron, and its
utility plane, to Los Angeles in the summer of 1935. Note SF-1.

Grumman SF-1 (9463)   *John C. Mitchell*
LT Pickering warming up VF-6B's utility plane which can be seen in
the right rear of above photo. Each VF unit had one or more scouts.

Vought O3U-1 (8561)   *Oliver R. Phillips*
3-O-1 from the USS NEW MEXICO BB40, equipped with the Grumman B
float and carrier arresting hook. Note BB "plane trap" hook on float.

Vought O3U-3 (9285)   *Gordon S. Williams*
From 1933 to 1936 VO-3B operated with mixed O3U-1's and O3U-3's.
Note 3-O-4, an amphibian, on left; others in background. Blue tail.

Vought O3U-3 (9285)   *Gordon S. Williams*
3-O-5 from the USS MISSISSIPPI BB41, but the same plane #9285
as 3-O-14 above, illustrating aircraft movement within a squadron.

Martin PM-1 (8305)   *Gordon S. Williams*
7-P-5 with solid Blue tail and E in machine gunnery. VP-7F was
changing over to P2Y's at this time and operated mixed equipment.

Consolidated P2Y-3 (9570)   *Gordon S. Williams*
In 1934 VP-7F operated six PM-1's; in 1935 six PM-1's and six
P2Y-3's; in 1936 six P2Y-3's, which they kept through 1937.

Martin PM-1 (8300)   *John C. Mitchell*
VP-9F Squadron Leader with E in Bombing and gunnery pennant. Tail
color solid Red. Note four stack OMAHA Class cruiser in left rear.

Boeing F4B-3 (8911)   *William T. Larkins*
The only F4B-3 stationed at NAS Anacostia; there from June 1934
to June 1935 only. Note vertical alignment of model designation.

Boeing F4B-4 (9232)   *William T. Larkins*
One of four NAS Anacostia's dash fours used as staff aircraft for
VX-4D5. Note high polished aluminum used only by NAS Anacostia.

Boeing F4B-4 (9045)   *Roger Besecker*
Rare photo of F4B-4 with F4B-3 rudder. Serial Numbers 9012 and 9046
were the other two F4B-4's used by Experimental Squadron Four.

Berliner-Joyce XF3J-1 (9224)   *Manufacturer*
Built in March 1934, carried on the Navy List in November 1935 only.
Often "Navy" planes under test had not been officially accepted.

Boeing XBFB-1 (8975)   *Peter M. Bowers*
The XF6B-1 re-designated and tested as a dive bomber in 1935. It
and the single-place, fixed-gear XF3J-1 were already obsolescent.

Grumman XF3F-1 (9727)   *Manufacturer*
The new look. Crashed 3-22-35, entire new plane built to same serial
number; it crashed 5-17-35. Finally delivered to Anacostia in June.

Douglas XP3D-1 (9613)   *Manufacturer*
Flown a month ahead of the XP3Y-1, and in competition to it, these
were the first attempts to modernize the aging patrol plane fleet.

Consolidated XP3Y-1 (9459)   *John C. Mitchell*
The original "Catalina" with its triangular tail — later changed.
Note retractable wing floats used for the first time in VP design.

Curtiss SBC-2 (9225)   *Manufacturer*
The XSBC-1 completely rebuilt on November 29th. Engine changed to
Wright XR-1510-12. Design now resembled production, service SBC-3.

Grumman XSF-2 (9493)   *U. S. Navy*
SF-1 design with P&W R-1535-80 and controllable pitch propeller.
Note deck hook hanging down in this magnificent posed photograph.

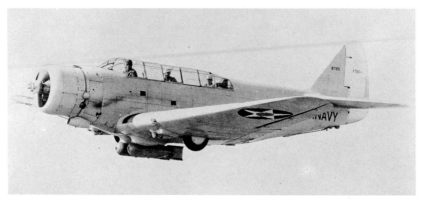

Douglas XTBD-1 (9720)   *The National Archives*
Rare photo of the original "Devastator" carrying two 500 pound bombs
in lieu of a torpedo. Compare canopy with production model, page 245.

Great Lakes XTBG-1 (9723)   *U. S. Navy*
A further enlarged version of the XB2G-1 as a three-place torpedo
bomber. Had XR-1830-60 engine, same as the competitive XPTBH-2.

Northrop RT-1 (382)   *Gordon S. Williams*

The only civil "Delta" in the Navy or USCG. It was used as a Command Transport for the Secretary of the Treasury, note his insignia.

Douglas RD-2 (129)   *William T. Larkins*

An early "Dolphin" delivered to the USCG. Named ADHARA. The designation on its tail, RD-129, is a concoction of model and serial.

Stinson RQ-1 (391)   *William T. Larkins*

SR-5A "Reliant" mis-painted as QR-1. In 1937 when it was re-numbered V149 designation was changed to R3Q-1. Used for USCG radio testing.

Consolidated P2Y-2   *U. S. Navy*
10-P-1 with Admiral King aboard off Oahu, Hawaii. Note unusual
use of lanyard at trailing edge of wing to hoist the Admiral's Flag.

FLEET AIRCRAFT ASSIGNMENT
June 1936

UNITED STATES FLEET

CinCUS Flag Unit	1 O3U-3
USS PENNSYLVANIA, Ship Unit	3 O3U-3

BATTLE FORCE

ComBatFor Flag Unit	2 O3U-3
USS CALIFORNIA, Ship Unit	3 O3U-3

COMMANDER BATTLESHIPS, BATTLE FORCE

Battleship Division One	VO-1B	9 O3U-1
Battleship Division Two	VO-2B	9 O3U-3
Battleship Division Three	VO-3B	7 O3U-1, 1 O3U-3
Battleship Division Four	VO-4B	8 O3U-3

COMMANDER CRUISERS, BATTLE FORCE

Cruiser Division Two	VS-5B	6 SOC-1
Cruiser Division Three	VS-6B	8 SOC-1

COMMANDER DESTROYERS, BATTLE FORCE

USS DETROIT	2 SOC-1

COMMANDER AIRCRAFT, BATTLE FORCE

Flag Unit   1 F2F-1, 2 F3F-1, 1 SBU-1

USS SARATOGA

VB-2B	18 BFC-2, 1 SBU-1
VF-6B	16 F3F-1, 13 F4B-4, 1 SBU-1, 1 O3U-1
VS-2B	19 SBU-1
VT-2B	18 TG-2
Utility Unit	2 O3U-1, 2 JF-1, 1 SOC-1

USS LEXINGTON

VB-3B	17 BG-1
VB-5B	10 F4B-4, 1 SBU-1, 1 SU-4
VF-2B	17 F2F-1, 1 SBU-1, 1 O3U-1
VS-3B	18 SBU-1
Utility Unit	1 F3B-1, 2 JF-1, 3 O3U-3

USS RANGER

VB-1B	12 BM-1, 8 BM-2
VF-3B	17 F2F-1, 1 SBU-1, 1 O3U-1
VF-5B	18 F3F-1, 1 SBU-1, 1 O3U-1
VS-1B	19 SBU-1
Utility Unit	2 F2F-1, 4 O3U-3, 2 JF-1, 1 N2Y-1

USS LANGLEY

VF-1B	18 F4B-4, 1 SU-4
VS-4B	11 SU-4
Utility Unit	1 OJ-2, 1 O3U-1, 3 O3U-3

USS YORKTOWN

Utility Unit	1 O2U-4, 1 O3U-3

COMMANDER, SPECIAL SERVICE SQUADRON

USS MEMPHIS   2 SOC-1

SCOUTING FORCE

USS INDIANAPOLIS   3 SOC-1

COMMANDER CRUISERS, SCOUTING FORCE

ComCruScoFor Flag Unit		1 SOC-1
Cruiser Division Four	VS-9S	17 SOC-1
Cruiser Division Five	VS-10S	12 SOC-1
Cruiser Division Six	VS-11S	13 SOC-1
Cruiser Division Seven	VS-12S	10 SOC-1, 8 O3U-3

COMMANDER DESTROYERS, SCOUTING FORCE

USS RALEIGH   2 SOC-1

COMMANDER AIRCRAFT, BASE FORCE

Flag Unit   1 O3U-1, 2 SOC-1

USS WRIGHT

VP-7F	6 P2Y-3
VP-9F	6 PM-1
VP-12F	6 PM-1
VP-14F	6 PM-2
VJ-1F	3 JF-1, 1 PM-1, 3 PM-2, 1 RD-3
VJ-2F	1 PM-1, 3 PM-2, 3 OL-9, 1 RD-3
Ship Utility	No aircraft assigned

FLEET AIR BASE, COCO SOLO
>
> VP-2F   9 PM-2
> VP-3F   13 P2D-1
> VP-5F   3 P2Y-1, 9 P2Y-2
> Utility Unit   1 F4B-3, 2 O2U-3, 1 RD-3,
>   1 RD2, 1 JF-1

FLEET AIR BASE, PEARL HARBOR
>
> VP-1F   9 PK-1
> VP-4F   12 P2Y-3
> VP-6F   4 PM-1, 5 PD-1
> VP-8F   7 PH-1
> VP-10F   1 P2Y-1, 5 P2Y-2
> Utility Unit   2 F4B-3, 1 JF-1, 1 O2U-3, 1 RD-3

ASIATIC FLEET

USS AUGUSTA   4 SOC-1

Aircraft Detachment USS HERON   2 JF-1

Navy Yard, Cavite, P.I.   2 SOC-1, 1 JF-1

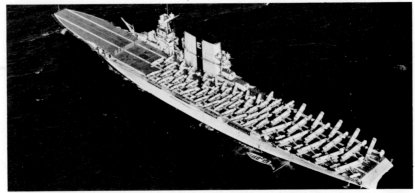

USS SARATOGA CV3   *U. S. Navy*
With 61 aircraft on deck; SU-4 Command, 15 SBU-1 VS-2, 15 F3F-1
of VF-6, 15 BFC-2 of VB-2, 15 TG-2 of VT-2. Note the E on the stack.

Consolidated N2Y-1 (8603)   *John C. Mitchell*
One of six purchased by the Navy from the Fleet Aircraft Company
division of Consolidated. Both SARATOGA and RANGER had N2Y-1's.

Lockheed XR2O-1 (0267) *John C. Mitchell*

The fifty-second "Electra" transport at the original Lockheed factory
in Burbank in February 1936. This plane, Lockheed serial number 1052
and Model 10-A, was delivered to the Navy on February 19th. It was
purchased as a command transport for the Secretary of the Navy and
retained its dark blue fuselage through 1941. After delivery it had
SecNav's Flag mounted on the outboard side of each engine nacelle as
with XR3O-1 below. Three 10-A's went to the Air Corps as Y1C-36's,
one to the National Guard Bureau as the Y1C-37. The 10-A was ATC-551,
powered by two P&W Wasp Jr. SB's of 450 hp each. A total of 148 were
built, serving many foreign airlines as well as US routes. XR2O-1 was
sold surplus after the war as N-57573 to Associated Transport, Mo.

Lockheed XR3O-1 (383) *William T. Larkins*

Serial Number 1053, a Model 10-B, was delivered to the U. S. Coast
Guard as a command transport for the Secretary of the Treasury on
April 9, 1936. Although officially listed as the XR3O-1 the X was not
painted on the plane and it soon became known as the R3O-1. When
delivered the Coast Guard three-digit serial system was in effect,
after October 13th it was V151. It replaced the earlier RT-1 (see page
185), was in turn replaced by Lockheed R5O-1 V188 in 1940. The 10-B
was licensed under ATC-584 with Wright R-975E-3's of 450 hp each.
USCG-383 was sold surplus after the war as N-44794 to Zigler Flying
Service of Louisana. A single Model 12A (1287, NC-33615) was bought
8-16-41 to become R3O-2 02947. It later went to England as G-AGTL.

Vought O3U-3 (9318)   *U. S. Navy*
USS RANGER-1, one of four O3U-3 utility planes assigned, with tail hook
engaged. Pre-war photos like this are rare, were heavily censored.

Vought O3U-3 (9283)   *U. S. Navy*
Three white-tailed NEVADA VO-2B floatplanes, in formation with
black-tailed 4-O-5, sisters from VO-4B on OKLAHOMA, over San Diego.

Vought SBU-1 (9773)   *William T. Larkins*
Fighting Six's scout, used for one year, replaced by SBC-3 in 1937.
Each VF outfit had a VS to tow aerial targets for gunnery practice.

Martin PM-2 *U. S. Navy*
A beautiful flight photograph of Utility One's PM-2 flying near San Diego. Note cameraman in bow with heavy 35mm motion picture camera.

Martin PM-2 (8676) *U. S. Navy*
The second of four PM-2's assigned to VJ-1F at this time. Note the solid Green tail color extending down to the top of the fuselage.

Grumman JF-1 (9434) *William T. Larkins*
The new Grumman utility amphibians were beginning to equip VJ units in 1936 replacing the former mixture of patrol and torpedo types.

Boeing F3B-1 Command (7738)   *John C. Mitchell*
A half silver and half blue (color scheme reserved for Captain rank)
executive transport for the Commanding Officer of the LEXINGTON.

Boeing F3B-1 Command (7743)   *John C. Mitchell*
VJ-5D11 command plane, probably for C.O. of NAS San Diego. Utility
Squadron markings unusual. #7743 was formerly ComAirBatFor Flag.

Vought O3U-3 Command (9289)   *Harry Thorell*
The air-borne "Captain's Gig" for the C.O. of the USS LANGLEY.
Red, white and blue tail stripes were ususual for command planes.

Kinner XRK-1 (9748)   *John C. Mitchell*
One of three civil "Envoy" four-passenger transports, assigned to
the Inspector of Naval Aircraft, Santa Monica, California (Douglas).

Kinner XRK-1 Command (9747)   *John C. Mitchell*
Another "Envoy" as a staff transport, probably a replacement for the
aging F3B-1. See photo with modified engine and cowl on page 223.

Fairchild XR2K-1 (9998)   *N.A.C.A.*
Civil 22 C-7F used by the National Advisory Committee for Aeronautics
to test full span Zap Flaps. Note official NACA insignia on rudder.

Douglas XP3D-2 (9613)   *Manufacturer*
The XP3D-1 one year later with the engines lowered into the wing
structure, and bow turret added and wing floats made retractable.

Bellanca XSOE-1 (9728)   *The National Archives*
Rare photo of a little known proposal for a cruiser based scout.
Shown at the factory on March 28th. Plane was not accepted by Navy.

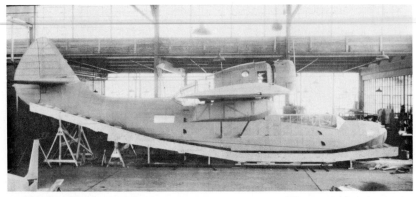

Fairchild XSOK-1 (9724)   *The National Archives*
A full size mockup of the proposed patrol bomber version of the
XA-942 eight-passenger transport built for Pan American Airways.

Curtiss XSBC-3 (9225) *U. S. Navy*
Old 9225 back again—in its final configuration. Shown at the plant
on April 10th with its new P&W R-1535-82 engine. See XF12C-1, etc.

Northrop XBT-1 (9745) *Manufacturer*
At the factory 12-4-36. Note the partially retractable wheels, as on
XTBD-1, designed for minimum damage in emergency wheels-up landing.

Great Lakes XB2G-1 (9722) *U. S. Navy*
BG-1 re-designed with enclosed bomb bay; note open doors in photo.
Not produced; plane went to Marines as command job, see USMC p. 78.

Pitcairn Autogiro XOP-2 (8850)   *The National Archives*
The XOP-1 converted by removal of fixed wings. Motion was supplied by
normal engine and prop, air turned powerless blades to provide lift.

Vought XSB2U-1 (9725)   *U. S. Navy*
The original "Vindicator," note aerial on center hatch, hook down.
It was accepted by the Navy on July 2nd, crashed on August 20th.

Vought XSB3U-1 (9834)   *Manufacturer*
A February 1936 project to modernize the SBU-1 bi-plane by adding a
retractable landing gear. In use by the Navy from 1936 through 1938.

Naval Aircraft Factory XN3N-2 (0265) *U. S. Navy*
Improvement on XN3N-1 with re-designed tail and variable pitch prop.
May have been model tested with Guiberson XR-918-2 Diesel engine.

Consolidated XPBY-1 (9459) *U. S. Navy*
VP-11F leader with three VP-9F PM-1's; formed late 1936 with XPBY-1,
XP3D-2 and 2 PM-1's. XP3Y-1 re-designated in May. Note tail change.

Northrop XFT-2 (9400) *Manufacturer*
XFT-1 modified with engine change and less fuel capacity; to Anacostia
in April 1936. Crashed in July, contract closed out in November.

Douglas "PROCYON" (V106)   *Donald F. Kauer*
The first production "Dolphin," delivered in February 1931. It was a
flying boat, wheels shown are beaching gear. No Navy duplicate built.

Douglas RD-4 (V128)   *William T. Larkins*
Production Coast Guard rescue version, compare with early model above.
All 13 RD's had Star names, see Appendix C for a complete listing.

General Aviation PJ-1 (V113)   *Gordon S. Williams*
In 1936 the former blue and silver colors for USCG aircraft changed
to all-over silver with chrome yellow on top of wing. See page 117.

Waco J2W-1 (V159)   *Howard Levy*
One of three civil EQC-6's attached to the Air Patrol Detachment at El
Paso. Designation follows USN XJW-1, was used only by Coast Guard.

Fairchild J2K-1 (V160)   *William T. Larkins*
V160-161 were J2K-1's assigned to St. Petersburg, Florida; V162-163
were J2K-2's assigned to Charleston, South Carolina. Ranger engines.

Viking OO-1 (V155)   *Howard Levy*
Five US-built versions of French Schreck FBA-17HT4 (USCG 8). Used
at St. Petersburg, Miami, Biloxi, Cape May and Charleston Air Stations.

STATUS OF NAVAL AIRCRAFT
June 1937

UNITED STATES FLEET

CinCUS Flag Unit	1 O3U-3
USS PENNSYLVANIA, Ship Unit	3 O3U-3

BATTLE FORCE

ComBatFor Flag Unit	1 O3U-3
USS CALIFORNIA, Ship Unit	3 O3U-3

COMMANDER BATTLESHIPS, BATTLE FORCE

Battleship Division One	VO-1B	3 O3U-3
Battleship Division Two	VO-2B	8 O3U-3, 1 SOC-1
Battleship Division Three	VO-3B	9 O3U-3
Battleship Division Four	VO-4B	9 O3U-3, 1 SOC-1

COMMANDER CRUISERS, BATTLE FORCE

Cruiser Division Two	VS-5B	6 SOC-1
Cruiser Division Three	VS-6B	6 SOC-1, 1 SOC-2

COMMANDER DESTROYERS, BATTLE FORCE

USS DETROIT	1 SOC-1, 1 SOC-2

COMMANDER AIRCRAFT, BATTLE FORCE

ComAirBatFor and ComCarDivOne
Flag Unit	2 SOC-1, 1 F3F-1, 2 SBU-1

CARRIER DIVISION ONE

USS SARATOGA
VF-6B	19 F3F-1, 1 SBU-1, 1 O3U-1
VB-2B	18 BFC-2, 1 SBU-1, 2 O3U-1
VS-2B	18 SBU-1
VS-4B	11 SU-4
VT-2B	17 TG-2
Utility Unit	2 J2F-1, 3 O3U-3, 1 N2Y-1

USS LEXINGTON
VF-2B	18 F2F-1, 1 SBU-1, 1 O3U-1
VB-3B	18 BG-1
VS-3B	18 SBU-1
VB-5B	19 F4B-4, 1 SBU-1, 2 O3U-1
Utility Unit	2 J2F-1, 3 O3U-3

CARRIER DIVISION TWO

ComCarDivTwo Flag Unit	(2 SBC-3 on order)

USS YORKTOWN
VF-7B	6 F2F-1
VB-7B	1 SU-3
VS-7B	2 SU-2
VT-7B	1 SU-2, 1 SU-3
Utility Unit	2 J2F-1, 3 O3U-3

USS ENTERPRISE
VF-8B	16 F4B-4
VS-8B	1 SU-4
Utility Unit	2 J2F-1, 2 O3U-3, 2 SU-2

USS RANGER
VB-1B	8 BM-1, 10 BM-2
VF-5B	17 F3F-1, 1 SBU-1
VS-1B	18 SBU-1
Utility Unit	3 O3U-3, 2 J2F-1, 1 N2Y-1

SPECIAL SERVICE SQUADRON

Flag Unit	(1 RD-2 on order)
USS OMAHA	2 SOC-1
USS ERIE	1 SOC-2
USS CHARLESTON	1 SOC-1

BATTLE FORCE POOL
(Overhaul, storage, awaiting action)

NAS SAN DIEGO
4 O3U-1, 12 O3U-3, 2 SOC-1, 12 F2F-1, 3 F3F-1,
3 F4B-4, 1 BFC-2, 5 SU-4, 12 SBU-1, 2 BG-1,
3 BM-1, 2 TG-2

NAS NORFOLK
2 O3U-1, 8 O3U-3, 1 SOC-1, 2 SU-4, 9 F2F-1,
2 F4B-4, 3 BM-1, 2 BM-2, 2 JF-1

SCOUTING FORCE

USS INDIANAPOLIS	4 SOC-1

COMMANDER CRUISERS, SCOUTING FORCE

ComCruScoFor Flag Unit		1 SOC-1
Cruiser Division Four	VS-9S	11 SOC-1, 6 SOC-2
Cruiser Division Five	VS-10S	13 SOC-1, 3 SOC-2
Cruiser Division Six	VS-11S	12 SOC-1, 1 SOC-2
Cruiser Division Seven	VS-12S	8 SOC-1, 4 SOC-2

COMMANDER DESTROYERS, SCOUTING FORCE

USS RALEIGH	4 SOC-1

SCOUTING FORCE POOL

NAS NORFOLK
18 SOC-1, 8 SOC-2 (4 for BOISE, 4 for BROOKLYN)

COMMANDER AIRCRAFT, BASE FORCE

Flag Unit	2 SOC-1

USS LANGLEY
VP-11F	3 PBY-1
VP-12F	12 PBY-1
Utility Unit	3 SOC-2

USS WRIGHT
VP-7F	7 P2Y-3
VP-9F	6 PBY-1
VJ-1F	5 JF-1, 1 RD-2, 6 PM-2
VJ-2F	3 JF-1, 3 J2F-1, 1 RD-3
Ship Unit	1 J2F-1, 1 SOC-2

USS OWL
VP-14F	5 PM-2
VP-15F	1 PM-2, 9 P3M-2

USS THRUSH
>   VP-16F   8 PM-1
>   VP-17F   6 PM-1

BASE FORCE POOL

NAS SAN DIEGO
>   1 O3U-1, 1 XPBY-1, 7 PH-1, 1 PM-1, 1 J2F-1, 1 RD-3

FLEET AIR BASE, COCO SOLO
>   VP-2F   No aircraft assigned
>   VP-3F   12 PBY-1, 1 PM-1
>   VP-5F   12 PBY-2
>   Utility Unit   1 F4B-3, 1 RD-2, 1 RD-3, 1 JF-1,
>   1 J2F-1, 2 O3U-1, 1 SOC-1
>   Repair and   1 F4B-4, 1 PM-2, 2 P2Y-2,
>   Storage   1 JF-1, 1 J2F-1

FLEET AIR BASE, PEARL HARBOR
>   VP-1F   10 PK-1
>   VP-4F   13 P2Y-3
>   VP-6F   12 PBY-1
>   VP-8F   12 PBY-1
>   VP-10F   7 P2Y-2, 2 P2Y-3
>   Utility Unit   2 F4B-3, 1 RD-3, 1 O2U-3, 2 O3U-1, 1 JF-1
>   Repair and   2 O3U-1, 4 PK-1, 2 P2Y-2,
>   Storage   3 J2F-1

ASIATIC FLEET

USS AUGUSTA   3 SOC-1

Aircraft Detachment, USS HERON   2 JF-1

Navy Yard, Cavite, P.I.   3 SOC-1, 1 JF-1

FIRST NAVAL DISTRICT

Torpedo Station   VX-2D1   3 O3U-1, 2 NY-2A
  Newport, R.I.   1 J2F-1, 1 T4M-1,
                                    1 XP2Y-2

FOURTH NAVAL DISTRICT

Naval Aircraft Factory VX-3D4   1 XRK-1, 2 O2U-3, 1 XO4U-2,
  Philadelphia, Pa.   1 XO5U-1, 1 SU-1, 2 SU-2,
                                  1 T4M-1, 1 NT-1

NAF Repair, Storage and Test
>   1 O2U-2; 4 SOC-2 for USS PHILADELPHIA; 1 XSOE-1;
>   1 XSO2C-1 for Anacostia; 1 XSBC-3 for catapult test; 2 SU-1
>   for NAF Operations; 1 FF-2 for vibration test and then
>   transfer to NRAB Kansas City; 1 XFD-1 for Norfolk; 2
>   BF2C-1, 1 for vibration test, 1 for disposition; 1 XF3F-2 for
>   Anacostia; 1 BG-1 for Norfolk; 1 BM-2 for NAF Operations;
>   1 TG-2 for Anacostia; 1 NS-1 for vibration tests; 4 NT-1;
>   2 N2Y-1; 1 XN3N-1 for special flight tests.

NAS Lakehurst, N.J.
1 O3U-1, 1 T4M-1, 1 XJW-1

FIFTH NAVAL DISTRICT
ACTIVITIES ON THE SEVERN AND POTOMAC RIVERS

NAS Anacostia, D.C.   VX-4D5
1 O3U-1, 2 SOC-1, 1 SOC-2, 1 F2F-1, 2 F3F-1, 1 XF2F-1,
1 XF3F-1, 3 SU-1, 6 SU-2, 1 SU-4, 1 XSF-1, 1 XSF-2, 2 SBU-1,
1 XSBF-1, 1 XSBU-1, 1 BM-2, 1 XBT-1, 1 XJW-1, 1 JB-1,
1 JK-1, 1 RD-2, 2 R2D-1, 1 XRE-1, 1 XRE-2, 1 XR3Q-1,
1 XR2O-1

NAS Anacostia, D.C.   Flight Test
1 SBC-3, 1 XOSU-1, 1 XSBA-1, 1 TBD-1, 1 XN3N-2

Naval Proving Ground, Dahlgren, Virginia
VX-5D5   1 BG-1, 2 TG-2, 1 J2F-1, 1 T4M-1

U. S. Naval Academy, Annapolis, Maryland
VN-8D5   1 J2F-1, 6 O3U-1

NAS Norfolk
VX-1D5   1 JRS-1, 1 XPTBH-2, 1 F3B-1, 1 T4M-1
VJ-4D5   2 O2U-3, 3 SU-1, 1 SU-3

NAS Norfolk, Repair and Storage
1 OJ-2, 1 XSOC-1, 2 SOC-2, 1 SU-2, 1 BG-1, 1 XSB3U-1,
2 JF-1, 1 OL-9, 1 RD-3, 1 XRD-1

EIGHTH NAVAL DISTRICT

NAS Pensacola, Florida
VN-1D8   47 N3N-1, 9 NY-2, 5 NY-2A
VN-2D8   19 N3N-1, 31 NY-1, 1 NY-1B, 40 NS-1,
                     3 XN4Y-1, 1 RR-5, 1 Glider
VN-3D8   17 O2U-3, 10 O2U-4, 6 O3U-1, 4 SU-1,
                     8 SU-2, 7 SU-3, 5 SBU-2
VN-4D8   8 O3U-1, 10 TG-1, 11 PD-1, 5 PM-1,
                     1 XP2M-1
VN-5D8   21 F4B-2, 4 F4B-3, 8 F4B-4, 9 O2U-3,
                     3 O2U-4, 2 O3U-1, 1 SU-2, 1 RR-5, 7 NS-1

NAS Pensacola, Overhaul and Storage
4 O2U-3, 2 O2U-4, 4 O3U-1, 6 F4B-2, 6 F4B-3, 1 F4B-4, 3 SU-1,
2 SU-2, 3 SU-3, 5 SBU-2, 1 TG-1, 1 PD-1, 4 PM-1, 7 PM-2,
8 NS-1, 5 N3N-1, 1 JF-1

ELEVENTH NAVAL DISTRICT

NAS San Diego, California
VJ-5D11   1 OJ-2, 1 F3B-1, 2 SU-1, 1 SU-2, 1 SU-3,
                     1 R2D-1, 1 XRK-1, 1 PBY-2, 1 TG-1

THIRTEENTH NAVAL DISTRICT

NAS Seattle, Washington   1 O3U-1

MISCELLANEOUS GROUP

INA, Chance Vought, East Hartford, Conn.
1 SBU-1

INA, Curtiss-Wright Corp., Buffalo, N.Y.
1 O3U-1

INA, Douglas Aircraft Co., Santa Monica, Calif.
1 XRK-1

INA, Grumman, Bethpage, L.I., N.Y.
1 O3U-1, 2 J2F-1

INA, New York
1 O3U-1

INA, Pratt & Whitney, East Hartford, Conn.
1 XF3U-1, 1 XTBD-1, 1 O3U-1

INA, Wright Field, Dayton, Ohio
1 O3U-1

INA, Wright Corporation, Paterson, N.J.
1 XT3D-2, 1 O3U-1

NACA, Langley Field, Virginia
1 O2U-4, 1 XF13C-3, 1 XBM-1, 1 XBFC-1,
1 XOP-2, 1 XR2K-1, 1 XN2Y-1, 2 Gliders

Pennsylvania Air. Syndicate, Philadelphia, Pa.
1 XOZ-1

Naval Attache, Berlin, Germany
1 Me-108b

Naval Attache, Bogota, Colombia
1 J2F-1

Naval Attache, London, England
1 XDH-80

Naval Attache, Paris, France
1 LeSimoun

Naval Attache, Rio de Janeiro, Brazil
1 J2F-1, 1 SF-1

NAVAL RESERVE

NOTE: The following aircraft were used jointly by Navy and Marine
Corps Reserve squadrons. In both cases the suffix letter R indicates a reserve squadron. The letter D and the number following
it, on Navy squadrons, indicates the Naval District within which
the squadron was located; for example VN-15RD13 is heavier-
than-air training squadron 15, reserve, of the 13th Naval District.
MR denotes Marine Reserve. SS was used by Marine Reserve
Service Squadrons.

NRAB SQUANTUM, Massachusetts

VN-1RD1	3 OJ-2, 6 SBU-2, 1 O2C-1,
VN-2RD1	1 OL-9, 1 T4M-1, 2 NY-3,
VO-1MR	1 N2C-2
SS-1MR	

NRAB BROOKLYN, New York

VN-3RD3	3 OJ-2, 4 SF-1, 1 O2C-1,
VN-4RD3	1 JF-3, 3 NY-3, 1 N2C-2
VO-2MR	

NRAB NAVY YARD PHILADELPHIA, Pennsylvania
    VN-5RD4   2 OJ-2, 3 SBU-2, 1 FF-2, 3 NY-3

NRAB OPA-LOCKA, Florida
    VN-8RD7   3 OJ-2, 5 SBU-2, 1 JF-3,
    VO-4MR   2 NY-3, 2 N2C-2

NRAB GLENVIEW, Illinois
    VN-10RD9   5 FF-2, 3 OJ-2, 1 F8C4,
                     2 O2C-1, 1 OL-9, 3 N2C-1

NRAB ANACOSTIA, D.C.
    VN-6R   3 OJ-2, 4 SF-1, 4 N2C-2
    VO-3MR

NRAB GROSSE ISLE, Michigan
    VN-9RD9   3 OJ-2, 4 FF-2, 1 OL-9,
    VO-5MR   1 NY-3, 3 N2C-2
    SS-2MR

NRAB MINNEAPOLIS, Minnesota
    VN-11RD9   3 OJ-2, 3 FF-2, 2 O2C-1,
    VO-6MR   1 OL-9, 4 N2C-1

NRAB ROBERTSON, Missouri
    VN-12RD9   1 OJ-2, 3 FF-2, 2 O2C-1, 4 N2C-2

NRAB KANSAS CITY, Kansas
    VN-17RD9   3 OJ-2, 6 FF-2, 4 NY-3
    VO-10MR

NRAB LONG BEACH, California
    VN-13RD11   2 OJ-2, 6 SF-1, 1 JF-3,
    VN-16RD11   4 N2C-1, 2 N2C-2
    VO-7MR

NRAB OAKLAND, California
    VN-14RD12   3 OJ-2, 7 SF-1, 1 OL-9,
    VO-8MR   4 N2C-1, 1 N2C-2

NRAB SEATTLE, Washington
    VN-15RD13   3 OJ-2, 5 SF-1, 1 JF-3, 3 N2C-1
    VO-9MR
    SS-3MR

Vought SBU-1 Command (9815)   *William T. Larkins*
Special executive plane delivered new to Commander Aircraft, Battle
Force. Note modified canopy. Flag Unit had two, see photo page 248.

FLEET SQUADRON RE-ORGANIZATION 7-1-37

INSIGNIA	OLD NUMBER	SHIP	TAIL COLOR	NEW NUMBER	SHIP	TAIL COLOR
Bellerophon on Pegasus	VB-5B	LEXINGTON	Green	VB-2	LEXINGTON	Yellow
CPO Chevron	VF-2B	LEXINGTON	Yellow	VF-2	LEXINGTON	Yellow
Indian Head in Circle	VS-3B	LEXINGTON	Yellow	VS-2	LEXINGTON	Yellow
Bombman on Torpedo	VB-1B	RANGER	Yellow	VT-2	LEXINGTON	Yellow
High Hat	VB-2B	SARATOGA	Red	VB-3	SARATOGA	White
Felix the Cat	VF-6B	SARATOGA	White	VF-3	SARATOGA	White
Pointer Dog	VS-2B	SARATOGA	White	VS-3	SARATOGA	White
Dragon on Torpedo	VT-2B	SARATOGA	Red	VT-3	SARATOGA	White
Black Panther	VB-3B	LEXINGTON	Green	VB-4	RANGER	Green
The Red Rippers	VF-5B	RANGER	Blue	VF-4	RANGER	Green
Duck on Pontoons	VS-1B	RANGER	Green	VS-41	RANGER	Green
The Dodo Bird	VS-4B	SARATOGA	White	VS-42	RANGER	Green
Winged Satan's Head	VB-7B	YORKTOWN	Red	VB-5	YORKTOWN	Red
Eagle on Star (1)	VF-7B	YORKTOWN	Red	VF-5	YORKTOWN	Red
Man-o-War Bird	VS-7B	YORKTOWN	Red	VS-5	YORKTOWN	Red
Valkyrie	VT-7B	YORKTOWN	Red	VT-5	YORKTOWN	Red
Mountain Goat	VB-8B	ENTERPRISE	Blue	VB-6	ENTERPRISE	Blue
Shooting Star	VF-8B	ENTERPRISE	Blue	VF-6	ENTERPRISE	Blue
Aztec Headdress	VS-8B	ENTERPRISE	Blue	VS-6	ENTERPRISE	Blue
Great White Albatross	VT-8B	ENTERPRISE	Blue	VT-6	ENTERPRISE	Blue
Bat on S in Circle (2)	VS-5B	————	Blue	VCS-2	————	Blue
Winged Seahorse	VS-6B	————	Red	VCS-3	————	Red
(Unknown)	VS-9S	————	White	VCS-4	————	White
Duck on Catapult	VS-10S	————	Yellow	VCS-5	————	Yellow
Flying Fish	VS-11S	————	Black	VCS-6	————	Black
Wing and Binoculars	VS-12S	————	Green	VCS-7	————	Green
Four Dolphins	VS-14S	————	Black	VCS-8	————	Black

(1) Was VF-3 on RANGER with Green tail. For a few months, during the formation of the ENTERPRISE Air Group, it became VF-7B.

(2) Cruiser Scouting Squadrons added a "C" for Cruiser to their squadron designation. The four VO, Battleship Observation, squadrons remained the same, dropped the B suffix letter.

Boeing F4B-4 (9015)   *Harold G. Martin*

Boeing F4B-4 (9012)   *William T. Larkins*
These matched photos, and those on the following ten pages, are
arranged in this special manner to visually emphasize the squadron
re-designations that took place in July 1937 as shown on the table
on page 206. Here is seen Bombing Five becoming Bombing Two.

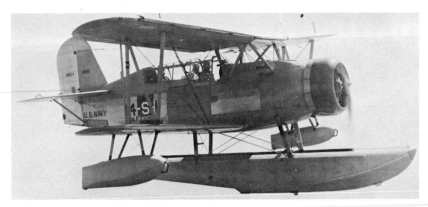

Curtiss SOC-1 (9921)   *U. S. Navy*
Rare photo showing short-lived VS-14S of CruDivEight formed in late
1936; became VCS-8. VS-15S of CruDivNine had 3 SOC-2, was disbanded.

Vought SBU-1 (9752)   *William T. Larkins*

Vought SBU-1 (9789)   *S. E. Savella*
VS-3B became VS-2 at the start of Fiscal 1938. Many organizational
changes were made in July 1937, including the dropping of the suffix
letter from the squadron designation. This letter, denoting the Force
to which it was assigned, was used for ten years; 1927 to 1937.

Grumman F2F-1 (9630)   *William L. Swisher*
Only carrier squadron not to change number was Fighting Two which
stayed aboard the LEXINGTON CV2. Note CPO insignia, rare on F2F-1's.

Martin BM-1 (8882) *John C. Mitchell*

Martin BM-2 (9170) *William T. Larkins*

In the change-over of squadron numbers, to conform to the hull
number of the carrier to which they were now assigned, Bombing One
also had its mission changed from bombing to torpedo squadron, thus
becoming Torpedo Two. Note rare Shellback insignia under pilot's cockpit.

Grumman J2F-1 (0177) *Howard Levy*

Reserve squadrons and Naval District units, such as this VX-2D1,
were the only units authorized to keep suffix letters on designation.

Curtiss BFC-2 (9332)   *John C. Mitchell*

Curtiss BFC-2 (9277)   *William T. Larkins*
These two photos graphically illustrate the changes being described.
When VB-2B stayed aboard the SARATOGA it had to change its tail
color from red to white, to conform to the ship color, and its squadron
number from 2 to CV3's "3." Note High Hat insignia remains unchanged.

Consolidated PBY-2   *Manufacturer*
At the factory ready for delivery on May 15th. VP-11, first to operate
the "Catalina," was also the first to get the new PBY-2 model.

Grumman F3F-1 (0231)   *Manufacturer*

Grumman F3F-1 (0259)   *William T. Larkins*

Felix-the-Cat got a new number in 1937 when Fighting Squadron Six was re-designated Fighting Squadron Three. The unit stayed aboard the SARATOGA and kept their all-white tail colors. Note thin black line outlining fuselage stripe and cowl color used by some units.

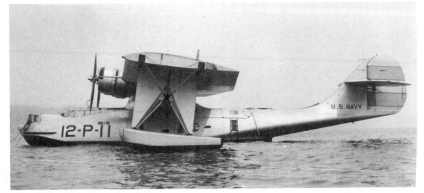

Consolidated PBY-1 (0135)   *Gordon S. Williams*

Patrol Squadron Twelve replaced its PM-1's with PBY-1's, changed from the USS THRUSH to the "new" seaplane tender LANGLEY, now AV3

Vought SBU-1 (9789)   *U. S. Navy*

Curtiss SBC-3 (0512)   *William T. Larkins*
Scouting Two not only received a new number, but replaced its old
SBU-1's with new SBC-3 dive-bombers. It too stayed aboard the SARA
and retained the same tail color. Just ahead of the Pointer Dog insignia is a unique Gunnery E with the "M" encircled in solid color.

Stearman-Hammond JH-1 (0908)   *William T. Larkins*
Civil Y-1S safety plane used as pioneer radio-controlled drone; first
flew December 23rd at CGAS Cape May. Two built; painted all-yellow.

Great Lakes TG-2 (8708)   *U. S. Navy*

Great Lakes TG-2 (8712)   *William T. Larkins*
Torpedo Squadron Two became Torpedo Squadron Three, retaining its
colorful Red Dragon astride a bomb insignia and white tail. Note the
torpedo rack under the fuselage between the landing gear in the top
photograph, also rear pit machine gun. Both planes have E in Bombing.

Douglas P2D-1 (8661)   *U. S. Navy*
VP-3 replaced its aging bi-planes with twelve PBY-1's in early 1937.
Number 8661 is the last production P2D, has double red tail stripes.

Great Lakes BG-1 (9495)   *Warren D. Shipp*

Great Lakes BG-1 (9507)   *William T. Larkins*
Green-tailed Bombing Three moved from the LEXINGTON to the
RANGER, changed its squadron number to Four, kept its original tail
color. Note Panther insignia on both planes. Pilot of 3-B-14 was LT
W. G. Michelet, note name painted on side of fuselage beneath cockpit.

Great Lakes BG-1 (9504)   *William L. Swisher*
A collector's oddity—the leader of Section Six with a half-striped
replacement cowl from another airplane. Note the Shellback insignia.

Grumman F3F-1 (0213) *Harold Andrews*

Grumman F3F-1 (0215) *William T. Larkins*

5-F-2 running up in front of the old Grumman factory on Long Island. Note the "pilot" with overcoat and felt hat in the cockpit. VF-5B, the Red Rippers, changed to VF-4 as seen in the lower photos. The tail color changed from Blue to Green. Squadron stayed aboard the RANGER.

Grumman F3F-1 (0220) *William L. Swisher*

Outstanding photo on panchromatic film. Compare with 4-F-4 above and note how type of film effects color rendition in squadron insignia.

Vought SBU-1 (9797)   *John C. Mitchell*

Vought SBU-1 (9787)   *U. S. Navy*

Consolidated P2Y-3 (9570)   *Gordon S. Williams*
Number Two plane of VP-7 taxiing in Puget Sound. By November their
seven P2Y's had been replaced by PBY-1's; in late 1938 by PBY-3's.

Grumman F2F-1 *William F. Yeager*

Grumman F2F-1 (9672) *U. S. Navy*

Fighting Three, The Striking Eagles, changed to VF-5 after a short tour as VF-7B. When the YORKTOWN's Air Group was forming the four squadrons were allotted "7." Soon thereafter the change to ship number policy changed all to "5." Tail color changed from Green to Red.

Douglas RD-3 (9530) *Fred Blanchard*

VJ-2's yellow-tailed "Dolphin" anchored in the Los Angeles harbor. These amphibians were used by the Army, Navy, Marines, Coast Guard.

Martin BM-2 (9185)   *Howard Levy*
6-T-3 in November 1937 during organization of the ENTERPRISE Air
Group ashore prior to commissioning. Also had 2 BM-1's, and 2 SU's.

Vought SU-2 (9094)   *Warren D. Shipp*
With SU-4 tail. This page, and 6-F-19, show provisional equipment
used for a few months only. VB-6 had 1 SU-2, 1 O3U-3, 2 SU-4's.

Vought SU-4 (9428)   *William T. Larkins*
By 1938 VB-6 was equipped with new BT-1's. The ENTERPRISE squadrons were briefly "8." VF-6 was VF-1B on LEXINGTON, then VF-8B.

Curtiss SBC-3 (0525)   *Howard Levy*
Utility scout for the new VF-6's sixteen F4B-4's. It was replaced by an
SBC-4 in November 1939. Note the Blue tail color for ENTERPRISE.

Vought O3U-1 (8855)   *William T. Larkins*
Old O3U-1's were still doing duty with VF-2 and VF-3 but were soon to
be replaced by other types. Note three-foot wide Red fuselage band.

Vought O3U-1 (8862)   *William L. Swisher*
Red fuselage and wing bands denoted plane used for instrument training
as air safety measure. Color was changed to Light Green in April 1943.

Vought SU-1 Command (9065)   *Harry Thorell*
Note special cockpit covers. The SU series was very popular, lasting
through 1941. In 1937 there were 21 SU-1, 33 SU-2, 17 SU-3, 21 SU-4.

Grumman J2F-1 (0168)   *William T. Larkins*
One of three serving Utility Squadron Two in 1937. Compare with VJ-2
JF-1 on page 191. VJ-2 insignia is under center section of the wing.

North American NJ-1 (0910)   *Manufacturer*
AC BT-9 type with power upped to 600 hp P&W R-1340. #0949 was tested
with Ranger XV-770-4 as NJ-2 but changed back and delivered as NJ-1.

Vought SU-2 (9107)   *Harry Thorell*
One of six on hand in VX-4D5 at NAS Anacostia in 1937, together with
three SU-1's and one SU-4. Compare special finish with SU-1 below.

Vought SU-1 (8875)   *Harry Thorell*
Rare photo of unusual squadron markings. For a short period Norfolk
used designation VM-4 (Miscellaneous Squadron) in place of VJ-4D5.

Vought O2U-3 (8271)   *William T. Larkins*
Another plane from VM-4. Note that station name does not appear under
squadron and class designation as above. Note change to balloon tires.

Lockheed JO-1 (1053)   *William T. Larkins*
Single 5-passenger 12A delivered 8-9-37. Sold surplus as N-1108. Note
two-star flag on engine nacelle. Photos of 1049-1051 in USMC book, p. 80.

Lockheed JO-2 (1048)   *Harry Thorell*
Six-passenger 12A delivered 9-8-37. Eight 12A's were used; one JO-1,
five JO-2's, one XJO-3 and one R3O-2. 14 in pre-war Army C-40 series.

Vought SU-3 (9123)   *William T. Larkins*
San Diego based Utility Five's SU-3. See page 203 for an example
of the mixture of aircraft types that such a squadron operated.

Fairchild JK-1 Command (0800) *Richard J. Illing*
The only such civil model 45 purchased by the Navy. Note two-star
placard on side. At NAS Anacostia in 1937, to NAS San Diego in 1938.

Douglas RD-2 (9348) *Henry W. Arnold*
1-J-11 taxiing out of the water at San Diego. Note Admiral's Flag on
bow when he is aboard. Note "En Gardé" Lion insignia, soon to change.

Kinner XRK-1 Modified (9747) *John C. Mitchell*
The Kinner R-1044-2 with which this plane was delivered (see p. 193)
has been changed to 400 hp P&W Wasp Junior. Note change in cowling.

Sikorsky XPBS-1 (9995)   *U. S. Navy*
Start of a new era with the first of the four-engine patrol boats flown
in August. Had fascinating career, finally sank in S. F. Bay in 1942.

Consolidated XPB2Y-1 (0453)   *Manufacturer*
In front of the factory before its first flight in December. Note the
retractable wing floats. Single tail was later changed to twin fins.

Hall-Aluminum XPTBH-2 (9721)   *Manufacturer*
Originally ordered as XPTBH-1, delivered in April as dash two. Only
example of a pre-war Navy plane with a three-mission model designation.

Grumman XSBF-1 (9996)   *Norman Budoff*
Enlarged scout-bomber version of XSF-2 built for competition with
the XSB2U-1, XSBC-3, XSBA-1, XB2G-1 and XBT-1. Was not purchased.

Curtiss XSO2C-1 (0950)   *Manufacturer*
Improved SOC-3 with flaps on both wings (SOC was upper wing only)
and fuselage lengthened five feet. All SOC's had folding wings.

Grumman XF3F-2 (0452)   *The National Archives*
Installation of the larger Wright XR-1820-22 of 950 hp flattened the
nose of the F3F-1 design. Tail shape was changed on production model.

Vought SBU-2 (0824)   *Gordon S. Williams*
Reserves had 24 delivered new in late 1937. Note aircraft number on
cowl of this NRAB New York ship. All were sent to Pensacola in 1941.

Consolidated NY-3 (8499)   *Pete Sarkus*
15 in use in 1937, the only model left in the Reserves. One lasted to
end of 1939. Reserves flew the NY-1, NY-1B, NY-2, NY-2A and NY-3.

Berliner-Joyce OJ-2 (9190)   *William T. Larkins*
1937 and 1938 were the high years for OJ-2 use in the reserves with 35
on hand. Most were used as instrument trainers. One lasted to 1941.

Loening OL-9 (8983) *William T. Larkins*
NRAB Oakland's OL-9 with its Golden Gater insignia (winged alligator on wheels, named for the Golden Gate entrance to San Francisco Bay).

Grumman SF-1 (9473) *William T. Larkins*
Anacostia's Four Spot. Note optional use of solid colored tails or stripes by reserve bases, in this case the NRA *unit* at a N.A.S.

Curtiss N2C-2 (8543) *John C. Mitchell*
NRAB Long Beach #19 with new Reserve Insignia. 8543 was formerly in Marine Utility Squadron Seven; see 7-J-4 in USMC book, page 40.

Vought SB2U-1's   *U. S. Navy*
3-B-13 (0739), 3-B-14 (0740) and 3-B-15 (0741) in what is probably
the most beautiful flight photograph taken during the pre-war years.
Note how wing chevron and plane number is painted on low-wing planes.

FLEET AIRCRAFT ASSIGNMENT
June 1938

UNITED STATES FLEET

CinCUS Flag Ship	1 SOC-3
USS PENNSYLVANIA, Ship Unit	3 SOC-3

BATTLE FORCE

ComBatFor Flag Unit	1 SOC-3
USS CALIFORNIA, Ship Unit	3 SOC-3

COMMANDER BATTLESHIPS, BATTLE FORCE

Battleship Division One	VO-1	6 SOC-3
Battleship Division Two	VO-2	6 SOC-3
Battleship Division Three	VO-3	9 SOC-3
Battleship Division Four	VO-4	6 SOC-1, 3 SOC-3

COMMANDER CRUISERS, BATTLE FORCE

Cruiser Division Two	VCS-2	6 SOC-1
Cruiser Division Three	VCS-3	8 SOC-1
Cruiser Division Eight	VCS-8	2 SOC-2, 8 SOC-3
Cruiser Division Nine	VCS-9	4 SOC-3
USS MEDUSA (Repair Ship)		2 SOC-1

COMMANDER DESTROYERS, BATTLE FORCE

COMMANDER FLOTILLA ONE

USS RALEIGH   2 SOC-1

COMMANDER FLOTILLA TWO

USS DETROIT   2 SOC-1

COMMANDER AIRCRAFT, BATTLE FORCE

Flag Unit   1 F3F-2, 1 SOC-1, 1 SOC-3, 1 SBU-1

CARRIER DIVISION ONE

USS SARATOGA
VB-3	21 SB2U-1, 1 XSBA-1, 1 SBC-3, 1 N2Y-1
VF-3	16 F3F-1, 1 SBC-3, 2 O3U-3
VS-3	21 SBC-3
VT-3	21 TBD-1
Utility Unit	2 J2F-1, 2 O3U-3

USS LEXINGTON
VB-2	22 SB2U-1
VF-2	20 F2F-1, 1 SBU-1, 2 O3U-3
VS-2	20 SBU-1
VT-2	21 TBD-1
Utility Unit	2 J2F-1, 3 O3U-3

USS RANGER
VB-4	19 BG-1
VF-4	19 F3F-1, 1 SBU-1, 2 O3U-3
VS-41	22 SBU-1
VS-42	19 SBU-1
Utility Unit	2 J2F-1, 2 O3U-3

CARRIER DIVISION TWO

Flag Unit   1 SBC-3, 1 SOC-1, 1 NJ-1, 1 N3N-1

USS YORKTOWN
VB-5	17 BT-1, 1 O3U-3
VF-5	19 F2F-1, 1 O3U-3
VS-5	10 SBC-3
VT-5	20 TBD-1
Utility Unit	2 J2F-1, 3 O3U-3

USS ENTERPRISE
VB-6	13 BT-1
VF-6	20 F3F-2, 2 O3U-3, 1 SBC-3
VS-6	20 SBC-3
VT-6	20 TBD-1
Utility Unit	2 J2F-1, 2 O3U-3, 1 TBD-1

SCOUTING FORCE

ComScoFor Flag Unit   1 SOC-2

COMMANDER CRUISERS, SCOUTING FORCE

Flag Unit   1 SOC-1

USS INDIANAPOLIS   4 SOC-1

Cruiser Division Four	VCS-4	12 SOC-1, 2 SOC-2
Cruiser Division Five	VCS-5	16 SOC-1
Cruiser Division Six	VCS-6	10 SOC-1, 1 SOC-2
Cruiser Division Seven	VCS-7	13 SOC-1, 3 SOC-2

COMMANDER AIRCRAFT, SCOUTING FORCE

Flag Unit   1 SOC-1, 1 SOC-2

PATROL WING ONE

VP-7	1 PBY-1, 12 PBY-3
VP-9	12 PBY-3
VP-11	13 PBY-2
VP-12	13 PBY-1

USS WRIGHT
  Utility Unit   1 SOC-2, 1 J2F-1
USS LANGLEY
  Utility Unit   3 SOC-2
USS SANDPIPER and USS LAPWING also assigned

PATROL WING TWO

FLEET AIR BASE, PEARL HARBOR

USS SWAN	VP-1	12 PK-1
USS PELICAN	VP-4	5 PBY-1, 4 PBY-2, 12 PBY-3
USS AVOCET	VP-6	10 PBY-1
	VP-8	11 PBY-1
	VP-10	12 PBY-2
	VP-18	12 PBY-3
	Utility Unit	2 F4B-3, 3 O3U-1, 1 RD-3, 3 J2F-1, 4 BFC-2

PATROL WING THREE

FLEET AIR BASE, COCO SOLO

USS GANNET	VP-2	10 PBY-2
USS THRUSH	VP-3	13 PBY-1
	VP-5	11 PBY-3
	Utility Unit	1 F4B-3, 1 F4B-4, 1 RD-2, 1 RD-3, 2 O3U-1, 1 J2F-1

PATROL WING FOUR

USS TEAL	VP-16	6 PBY-3
	VP-17	7 PBY-2
	VP-19	6 P2Y-3

PATROL WING FIVE

USS OWL	VP-14	10 P2Y-2, 1 XP2Y-2
	VP-15	11 P2Y-2, 1 PM-1

COMMANDER UTILITY WING, BASE FORCE

USS RIGEL

VJ-1	6 JF-1, 6 JRS-1, 1 RD-3, 1 O3U-1, 3 PM-2, 2 N2C-2, 2 TG-2
VJ-2	2 JF-1, 3 J2F-1, 1 RD-3, 5 PH-1

FLEET AIR BASE, SAN PEDRO

Commander Base Force   1 SOC-2

ASIATIC FLEET

USS AUGUSTA	5 SOC-1
Aircraft Detachment, USS HERON	2 JF-1

SUBMARINE FORCE

USS RICHMOND   2 SOC-1

Douglas TBD-1 (0302)   *William T. Larkins*
VT-2, VT-3, VT-5 and VT-6 all had new TBD-1's in early 1938. VT-3 was the first to get them, on 10-5-37. Note VT-2 Bombman insignia.

Douglas TBD-1 (0286)   *William T. Larkins*
Carrier storage problem of low-wing monoplanes was solved by folding the wings upward. BT-1 retained fixed wings as did all 1938 fighters.

Vought SB2U-1 (0772)   *William T. Larkins*
VB-3 had 22 SB2U-1's in November, this plane belonging to Aviation Cadet Carter. Note that no section colors were used on planes above 18.

Northrop BT-1   *William T. Larkins*
5-B-5 landing. Note slotted flaps which became famous on later SBD.
During dive top flaps, seen just under star, went up in addition.

Vought SU-3 (9129)   *Warren D. Shipp*
One of two SU-3's used during the forming of this new YORKTOWN
squadron, was kept on as a utility hack until replaced by an O3U-3.

Beechcraft JB-1 Command (0801)   *Donald F. Kauer*
The only one of its kind, a civil C-17R with R-975-26. In use from
1937 to 1939 only. Note Captain's four-stripe Epaulette rank card.

Curtiss SOC-1 Command (9985)   *Gordon S. Williams*
From the Commander, Carrier Division Two Flag Unit which at this
time consisted of 1 SBC-3, 1 SOC-1, 1 NJ-1 (see below) and 1 N3N-1.

North American NJ-1 Command (0937)   *Donald F. Kauer*
Presence of the two-star Rear Admiral aboard the plane is indicated by
insertion of card in front of windshield; is to rear on SOC-1 above.

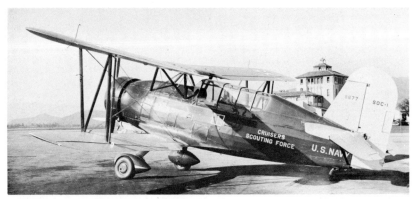

Curtiss SOC-1 Command (9877)   *John C. Mitchell*
Flagplane of Commander Cruisers, Scouting Force, based aboard the
INDIANAPOLIS CA35—giving that ship five aircraft rather than four.

1938

Curtiss SOC-1 (9858)   *William T. Larkins*
3-CS-7 and 3-CS-8 (9954) on their catapults aboard USS CINCINNATI.
Canvas on canopies and engines protected against corrosive salt water.

Curtiss SOC-1 (9858)   *William L. Swisher*
The same plane on wheels. Battleship and Cruiser based aircraft
often changed to wheels for shore operation from Naval Air Stations.

USS HOUSTON CA30   *George Winstead*
The sleek heavy cruiser HOUSTON with 4-CS-15 and two other aircraft
aboard. A nine-thousand tonner, six hundred feet long, with 4 planes.

Curtiss SOC-2 (0402)   *Arthur B. Geen*
On the heavy cruisers with four-plane sections, Numbers 1 (red), 5 (white), 9 (blue), 13 (black) and 17 (green) were section leaders.

Curtiss SOC-1 (9875)   *John C. Mitchell*
Note the different markings on this plane which is assigned to a ship rather than a squadron; the Flagship of Commander, Flotilla Two.

Curtiss SOC-2 (0387)   *Harry Thorell*
7-CS-13 from the USS TUSCALOOSA of Cruiser Division Seven. Note green tail stripe, squadron insignia. Leader of four-plane Section Four.

Vought O3U-3 (9300)   *William T. Larkins*

With Black tail color, from USS COLORADO BB45. All four battleship observation squadrons replaced their O3U-3's with SOC's in 1938.

Vought O3U-3 (9311)   *LeRoy McCallum*

Number 3 plane of the ENTERPRISE Utility Unit. Note the ship's insignia, blue in black circle, based on the original square-rigger.

USS RANGER CV4   *U. S. Navy*

With PBY-3 7-P-11 taking off alongside. The six stacks of RANGER folded downward to horizontal position during flight operations.

Consolidated PBY-2 *U. S. Navy*
VP-17 "Catalina" on Alaskan patrol replacing earlier PM-1's. VP-20
and VP-21 were commissioned 1 Sept and joined them in PatWingFour.

Consolidated P2Y-2 (8988) *Donald F. Kauer*
Patrol Fifteen was the only squadron to have P2Y-2's in 1938, but
newly commissioned VP-18 and VP-19 had P2Y-3's. Tail color Blue.

Consolidated PBY-3 (0858) *Gordon S. Williams*
VP-9 replaced its PBY-1's with PBY-3's in 1938. Early PBY's did not
have large waist gun blisters so familiar to World War Two veterans.

Grumman XF4F-2 (0383)   *Manufacturer*
Ordered as XF4F-1 bi-plane, re-designed and delivered as dash two mid-
wing monoplane. Note machine guns are in cowl rather than wings.

Brewster XF2A-1 (0451)   *U. S. Navy*
Competitor to the XF4F-2 and similar in design. Delivered in December
1938 it was modified to the XF2A-2 in 1939. Same engine as F3F-2.

Brewster XSBA-1 (9726)   *William T. Larkins*
Originally test flown in 1936, this photo shows it as modified with
XR-1820-22 engine, new cowl, prop. Produced as NAF SBN-1, see p. 284.

Stearman XOSS-1 (1052)   *Manufacturer*
Designed, along with NAF XOSN-1 below, as a replacement for the
SOC as a battleship observation type. Neither was put into production.

Stearman XOSS-1 (1052)   *U. S. Navy*
Both types were tested on floats as well as wheels. Note similarity to
XSO2C-1 configuration in this view and upper wing full span flaps.

Naval Aircraft Factory XOSN-1 (0385)   *U. S. Navy*
Shown on wheels at Anacostia 5-23-38. XOSN-1, XOSS-1 and XOSU-1 all
had P&W R-1340 engines. Note leading edge slots, unique strut system.

Northrop BT-1 Modified (0643)   *Manufacturer*
Experimental installation of tri-cycle landing gear in order to test
its suitability for carrier use. Shown at the factory on 10-19-38.

Northrop BT-1 Modified (0643)   *Gordon S. Williams*
The test gear was non-retractable. It is believed to be the first time
that a tri-cycle gear plane was landed aboard a carrier in the U. S.

Lockheed XJO-3 (1267)   *U. S. Navy*
The XJO-3 was delivered 10-15-38 to test twin-engine, tri-cycle gear,
carrier performance. Note tail hook in photo. See take-off, page 252.

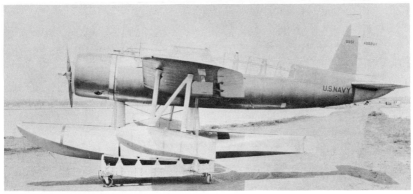

Vought XOS2U-1 (0951)   *The National Archives*

Shown at the factory 5-20-38 on beaching dolly. Note absence of wide strut between fuselage and float that was added on production model.

Curtiss XSBC-4 (0582)   *The National Archives*

The last production SBC-3 at the factory 4-4-38. The former 825 hp P&W R-1535-94 was changed to a Wright Cyclone R-1820-22 of 950 hp.

Bellanca JE-1 (0795)   *The National Archives*

A single, modified nine-place civil 31-42 "Senior Pacemaker" was delivered to the Navy in 1938. It was also stationed at NAS Lakehurst.

Grumman JF-3 (9835)   *William T. Larkins*
The JF-3 was a model produced for the reserves only, just as the
JF-2 was built for Coast Guard use only. Six bases operated the JF-3.

Vought SBU-2 (0816)   *William T. Larkins*
NRAB Squantum (Boston) reserve job with rarely seen revised Witch
and Moon base insignia. Reserves had 23 SBU-2's assigned in 1938.

Grumman FF-2 (9364)   *Jack McNulty*
NRAB Grosse Isle two-place fighter-trainer on 7-31-38. Installation
of dual controls in FF-1 fighter converted all remaining to FF-2's.

FLEET AIRCRAFT ASSIGNMENT
June 1939

UNITED STATES FLEET

CinCUS Flag Unit	1 SOC-3
USS PENNSYLVANIA, Ship Unit	3 SOC-3

BATTLE FORCE

ComBatFor Flag Unit	1 SOC-3
USS CALIFORNIA, Ship Unit	3 SOC-3

COMMANDER BATTLESHIPS, BATTLE FORCE

Battleship Division One	VO-1	6 SOC-3
Battleship Division Two	VO-2	6 SOC-3
Battleship Division Three	VO-3	6 SOC-3, 3 SON-1
Battleship Division Four	VO-4	7 SOC-3, 2 SON-1

COMMANDER CRUISERS, BATTLE FORCE

USS ST. LOUIS		4 SON-1
Cruiser Division Two	VCS-2	1 SOC-1, 2 SOC-2
Cruiser Division Eight	VCS-8	7 SOC-1, 9 SOC-3
Cruiser Division Nine	VCS-9	9 SOC-1, 6 SOC-2, 1 SOC-3, 4 SON-1

COMMANDER DESTROYERS, BATTLE FORCE

USS RALEIGH	2 SOC-1

COMMANDER FLOTILLA TWO

USS DETROIT	2 SOC-1

COMMANDER AIRCRAFT, BATTLE FORCE

Flag Unit	1 SOC-1, 2 SOC-3, 1 SBU-1

CARRIER DIVISION ONE

USS SARATOGA
VB-4	18 SB2U-2, 1 N2Y-1
VF-2	17 F2F-1, 1 SB2U-2, 2 SU-2, 1 SU-1, 1 O3U-3
VS-2	1 SBU-1, 1 SBC-4
VT-3	16 TBD-1, 1 SB2U-2
Utility Unit	2 J2F-1, 2 O3U-3, 1 SB2U-2(AGC)

USS LEXINGTON
VB-2	17 SB2U-1, 2 SB2U-2
VF-3	18 F3F-1, 1 SB2U-1, 2 SU-3
VS-3	18 SBC-3
VT-2	18 TBD-1
Utility Unit	2 J2F-1, 2 O3U-3, 1 N2Y-1, 1 SB2U-1(AGC)

USS RANGER
VB-3	2 SB2U-1
VF-4	20 F3F-1, 1 SBU-1, 2 SU-3
VS-41	18 SBU-1
VS-42	18 SBU-1
Utility Unit	2 J2F-1, 3 O3U-3

CARRIER DIVISION TWO

Flag Unit	1 SBC-3, 1 SOC-1, 1 NJ-1, 1 N3N-1

USS YORKTOWN
      VB-5   18 BT-1
      VF-5   18 F3F-3, 1 F2F-1, 1 SU-3
      VS-5   18 SBC-3
      VT-5   18 TBD-1
      Utility Unit   2 J2F-2, 3 O3U-3, 1 SBC-3(AGC)

USS ENTERPRISE
      VB-6   18 BT-1
      VF-6   16 F3F-2, 2 SBC-3, 2 SU-2
      VS-6   17 SBC-3
      VT-6   17 TBD-1
      Utility Unit   1 J2F-1, 1 J2F-3, 3 O3U-3

USS WASP
      Utility Unit   1 O3U-3, 3 SON-1
      (Operates from NRAB Squantum)

SCOUTING FORCE

ComScoFor Flag Unit	1 SOC-3
USS INDIANAPOLIS	2 SOC-1, 2 SOC-2

COMMANDER CRUISERS, SCOUTING FORCE

Flag Unit		1 SOC-1
USS WICHITA		4 SOC-1
Cruiser Division Four	VCS-4	12 SOC-1, 4 SOC-2
Cruiser Division Five	VCS-5	11 SOC-1, 1 SOC-2
Cruiser Division Six	VCS-6	11 SOC-1, 2 SOC-2
Cruiser Division Seven	VCS-7	13 SOC-1, 3 SOC-2

COMMANDER AIRCRAFT, SCOUTING FORCE

Flag Unit	2 SOC-3

PATROL WING ONE

ComPatWingOne		1 SOC-2
VP-7	13 PBY-3, 1 PBY-4	
VP-9	14 PBY-3	
VP-18	16 PBY-4, 1 PBY-2, 2 O3U-3	

USS WRIGHT
      Utility Unit   1 SOC-1, 1 J2F-1
USS LANGLEY
      Utility Unit   1 SOC-1, 1 SOC-2, 1 SON-1
USS SANDPIPER and USS LAPWING also assigned

PATROL WING TWO

FLEET AIR BASE, PEARL HARBOR

USS SWAN	VP-1*	15 PBY-4
USS PELICAN	VP-4	15 PBY-3
USS AVOCET	VP-6	12 PBY-1
	VP-8	13 PBY-1
	VP-10	13 PBY-2
	Utility Unit	1 F4B-3, 1 JRS-1, 3 J2F-1, 2 O3U-1, 1 SOC-2, 1 RD-3

PATROL WING THREE

FLEET AIR BASE, COCO SOLO

USS GANNET	VP-2	11 PBY-2
USS THRUSH	VP-3	13 PBY-1

*Temporarily based at NAS San Diego

VP-5   14 PBY-3
Utility Unit   1 RD-3, 2 F2F-1, 1 F4B-4, 2 O3U-1, 1 Glider

PATROL WING FOUR

USS TEAL
    VP-16   7 PBY-3
    VP-17   7 PBY-2
    VP-19   5 P2Y-3
    VP-20   6 P2Y-3
    VP-21   6 P2Y-3, 2 O3U-3
Fleet Air Base, Sitka, Alaska   1 SOC-1

PATROL WING FIVE

Commander PatWingFive, NAS Norfolk   1 SON-1
USS OWL
    VP-11   12 PBY-2
    VP-12   13 PBY-1, 1 O3U-3
    VP-14   8 P2Y-2, 1 XP2Y-2, 1 O3U-3
    VP-15   9 P2Y-2

COMMANDER, UTILITY WING, BASE FORCE

USS RIGEL
    VJ-1   8 J2F-2, 3 J2F-3, 8 JRS-1
    VJ-2   3 J2F-1, 2 J2F-2, 4 J2F-3, 1 JRS-1,
                  1 RD-3, 7 PH-1
Utility Detachment Dog   1 N2C-2, 1 TG-2

FLEET AIR BASE, SAN PEDRO

Commander Base Force   1 SOC-1

ASIATIC FLEET

USS AUGUSTA   4 SOC-1
USS MARBLEHEAD   2 SOC-1
USS HERON   2 JF-1, 2 J2F-2

SUBMARINE FORCE

USS RICHMOND   2 SOC-2

Douglas TBD-1 (0370)   *Manufacturer*
Section Four leader with hatches open and crew posed for the camera.
TBD was only VTB type in use with the fleet until arrival of TBF-1's.

Curtiss SOC-3 (1082)   *John C. Mitchell*
These two pages illustrate the four Battleship Observation Squadrons
in service in 1939. All VO and VCS Squadrons had SOC type in 1939.

Curtiss SOC-3 (1077)   *William T. Larkins*
From the PENNSYLVANIA, Flagship of the United States Fleet. 1-0-6
above is from NEVADA; ARIZONA completed Battleship Division One.

Curtiss SOC-3 (1065)   *Manufacturer*
VO-2 (note insignia) was aboard the TENNESSEE, OKLAHOMA and
CALIFORNIA at this time. Note VO squadrons have 3-plane sections.

Naval Aircraft Factory SON-1 (1166)   *William T. Larkins*
NAF-built SOC-3 from MISSISSIPPI. Note E in m.g., insignia. The two additional ships making up BatDivThree were IDAHO, NEW MEXICO.

Curtiss SOC-1 (9904)   *William T. Larkins*
WEST VIRGINIA SOC, note flaps on upper wing. Battleship name was to the rear of squadron number; Cruiser name under CS, see page 234.

Curtiss SOC-3 (1103)   *William T. Larkins*
VO-4 was on WEST VIRGINIA, COLORADO and MARYLAND. Note turtledeck. Tail colors: VO-1 Red, VO-2 White, VO-3 Blue, VO-4 Black.

Curtiss SOC-3 Command (1079)   *William T. Larkins*
Flagplane of the Commander-in-Chief of the United States Fleet, the
only command plane with blue fuselage, tail. Based on PENNSYLVANIA.

Vought SBU-1 Command (9830)   *Arthur B. Geen*
Second of two SBU-1's for the Flag Unit of Commander Aircraft, Battle
Force. Compare with earlier, modified version shown on page 205.

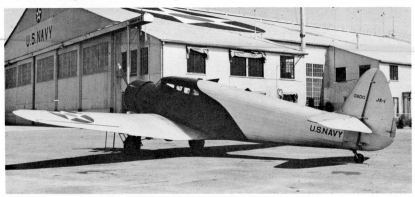

Fairchild JK-1 Command (0800)   *Harold Nolen*
With command colors revised (see page 223). Assigned as first plane to
newly forming NAS Alameda, Nov 1939. NRAB Oakland hangar in rear.

Consolidated PBY-4 (1241)   *U. S. Navy*

The PBY-4 was the first model of the "Catalina" to have the large waist machine gun blisters. The new R-1830-72 engines added 300 hp and the performance was improved over the PBY-3. On July 1, 1939, a new system of numbering Patrol Squadrons was introduced which resulted in the re-numbering of all squadrons then operating. Under the new system the first digit of the squadron "number" was the number of the newly formed Patrol Wing. Thus 13-P-12, above, was the third squadron of Patrol Wing One, *not* Patrol Squadron Thirteen. See page 278 for a second, almost complete, re-numbering of VP squadrons that took place in 1941. The squadron insignia remains as the only key to the squadron histories, thus is included in both of these tables.

1939 PATROL SQUADRON RE-ORGANIZATION

INSIGNIA	OLD NUMBER	NEW NUMBER
Great White Albatross	VP-7	VP-11
Goose Flying Under the Sun	VP-9	VP-12
	—	VP-13*
Sitka Spruce Tree	VP-21	VP-14
Elephant Standing on Cloud	VP-1	VP-21
Griffin and Numeral 4	VP-4	VP-22
Pegasus in Circle	VP-6	VP-23
Winged 8-Ball	VP-8	VP-24
Bomb in Compass Rose	VP-10	VP-25
Wings Over the Globe	VP-18	VP-26
Keystone Cop	VP-2	VP-31
Standing Elephant with Spyglass	VP-3	VP-32
Wings Over Panama	VP-5	VP-33
Husky Dog	VP-16	VP-41
Seal Balancing Bomb on Nose	VP-17	VP-42
Polar Bear on Mountain	VP-19	VP-43
Mine in Horseshoe	VP-20	VP-44
	—	VP-45*
Totem Pole and Mt. Rainier	VP-12	VP-51
Six Geese in Flight	VP-14	VP-52
Indian Scout Kneeling	VP-15	VP-53
Head of Odin	VP-11	VP-54

* Operated in late 1939 only, both were new units.

Martin BM-2 (9172)   *Howard Levy*
The last BM left in 1939, out in 1940. Assigned to VX-3D4 at the
Naval Aircraft Factory, Philadelphia. Note unpainted metal finish.

Grumman J2F-3 Command (1569)   *The National Archives*
Personal plane of Rear Admiral Wilson Brown, Superintendent of the
U.S. Naval Academy at Annapolis. Note silver trim line on wing float.

North American NJ-1 (0944)   *George Goodhead*
N.A.S. Pensacola staff airplane in all-silver finish. NJ-1's for flight
training at Pensacola carried large side numbers only.

Brewster F2A-1 (1386) *The National Archives*
The first production aircraft at the factory 6-20-39. Production was
slow and the first Navy squadron to use it had only ten a year later.

Grumman J2F-3 (1572) *Marvin J. Border*
Twenty built, had R-1820-36 engine change. #19 is a reserve job, one
of 3 operated by NRAB Chicago, NRAB Grosse Isle, NRAB Minneapolis.

Beechcraft GB-1 (1595) *Howard Levy*
The more powerful D-17S version which was later used in large numbers
in WW2. Note accidental reversal of serial and model designation.

Lockheed XJO-3 (1267)   *U. S. Navy*
Flight tests of the XJO-3 were carried out in 1939, here it is taking
off from the deck of the LEXINGTON on August 29th. See also p. 240.

Douglas TBD-1A (0268)   *U. S. Navy*
The first production airplane, delivered in 1937, modified in late 1939
for twin floats. Tested at Naval Torpedo Station, Newport, Rhode Island.

Curtiss N2C-2 Modified (8539)   *U. S. Navy*
Two radio-controlled Drones at San Diego in February. Simulated dive-
bombing attack on battleship UTAH was made by one in September test.

Naval Aircraft Factory XN3N-2 (0265)   *U. S. Navy*
The earlier open cockpit version was covered with an elaborate system of sliding hatches in later life. Used by Navy from Nov 1936 to 1941.

North American SNJ-1 (1552)   *Manufacturer*
Development of Army's BC-1 with a metal covered fuselage; it was more or less a re-engined NJ-1 with retractable landing gear. 16 were built.

Vought XSB2U-3 (0779)   *U. S. Navy*
Tested on wheels and twin floats in 1939, note large stabilizing fin added to float model. Production model went to Marine Corps in 1941.

Douglas XBT-2 (0627)   *Manufacturer*
Modified BT-1 by Douglas-El Segundo, prototype SBD-1. Canopy
raised, fully retractable gear, wing tip slots, constant speed propeller.

Brewster XF2A-2 (0451)   *The National Archives*
The XF2A-1 (see p. 238) was modified in mid-1939 with a more powerful
engine and longer span, greatly increasing performance. See Appendix A.

Lockheed XR4O-1 (1441)   *William T. Larkins*
The only example of the civil model 14 airline transport used by the
Navy. It was assigned to Anacostia as a high-speed staff transport.

Grumman XF4F-3 (0383) *Manufacturer*
Like the Brewster XF2A-1, the Grumman XF4F-2 (p. 238) was modified
a year later with changes in the engine, tail shape and wing span.

Grumman XF3F-3 (1031) *Manufacturer*
At the same time that experimentation was going on with the new F4F
monoplane improvements continued with F3F. Note bomb on wing rack.

Grumman XJ3F-1 (1384) *U. S. Navy*
First of a long line of "Goose" amphibians used by the Navy, culminat-
ing in the JRF-6B. Designation changed to JRF Utility Transport.

FLEET AIRCRAFT ASSIGNMENT
June 1940

UNITED STATES FLEET

CinCUS Flag Unit	1 SOC-3
USS PENNSYLVANIA, Ship Unit	3 SOC-3

BATTLE FORCE

ComBatFor Flag Unit	1 SOC-3
USS CALIFORNIA, Ship Unit	3 SOC-3

COMMANDER BATTLESHIPS, BATTLE FORCE

Battleship Division One	VO-1	6 SOC-3
Battleship Division Two	VO-2	5 SOC-3
Battleship Division Three	VO-3	6 SOC-3, 3 SON-1
Battleship Division Four	VO-4	7 SOC-3, 2 SON-1

COMMANDER CRUISERS, BATTLE FORCE

Cruiser Division Three	VCS-3	3 SOC-1, 4 SOC-2, 1 SOC-3, 1 SON-1
Cruiser Division Eight	VCS-8	6 SOC-1, 5 SOC-3, 6 SON-1
Cruiser Division Nine	VCS-9	1 SOC-1, 5 SOC-3, 11 SON-1

COMMANDER DESTROYERS, BATTLE FORCE

COMMANDER FLOTILLA ONE

USS RALEIGH	2 SOC-3

COMMANDER FLOTILLA TWO

USS DETROIT	2 SOC-1

COMMANDER AIRCRAFT, BATTLE FORCE

Flag Unit	2 SOC-3, 1 SBU-1, 1 SNJ-2

CARRIER DIVISION ONE

ComCarDivOne Flag Unit	1 SBU-1, 1 SOC-1

USS SARATOGA

VB-3	19 SB2U-2
VF-3	10 F2A-1, 9 F3F-1, 1 SB2U-2
VS-3	21 SBC-3
VT-3	22 TBD-1
Utility Unit	2 SOC-3, 2 J2F-1, 1 SB2U-2 (AGC)

USS LEXINGTON

VB-2	15 SB2U-1, 4 SB2U-2
VF-2	21 F2F-1, 1 SB2U-1
VS-2	21 SBC-4
VT-2	21 TBD-1
Utility Unit	3 SOC-1, 2 J2F-1, 1 SB2U-2(AGC)

CARRIER DIVISION TWO

USS YORKTOWN

VB-5	22 BT-1, 1 SBC-3
VF-5	22 F3F-3, 1 SBC-3
VS-5	19 SBC-3
VT-5	23 TBD-1
Utility Unit	2 O3U-3, 2 J2F-4, 2 SOC-2, 1 SBC-3, 1 SB2U-2(AGC)

```
USS ENTERPRISE
    VB-6          17 BT-1, 1 SBC-3, 2 SU-3
    VF-6          17 F3F-2, 1 SBC-4, 2 SU-2
    VS-6          17 SBC-3, 2 SU-2
    VT-6          18 TBD-1, 1 SU-2, 1 SU-3
    Utility Unit   1 SOC-3, 1 J2F-1, 1 SBC-4(AGC)
```

SCOUTING FORCE

```
ComScoFor Flag Unit                         1 SOC-3
USS INDIANAPOLIS                     3 SOC-1, 1 SOC-2
Cruiser Division Four    VCS-4      13 SOC-1, 3 SOC-2
Cruiser Division Five    VCS-5      14 SOC-1, 2 SOC-2
Cruiser Division Six     VCS-6      13 SOC-1, 5 SOC-2
```

COMMANDER AIRCRAFT, SCOUTING FORCE

```
Flag Unit                           1 XPB2Y-1, 1 SBC-4
USS MEMPHIS                          1 SOC-1, 1 SOC-3
```

PATROL WING ONE

```
ComPatWingOne, San Diego                    1 SOC-1
USS PELICAN       VP-11     12 PBY-3, 2 PBY-4
USS AVOCET        VP-12     12 PBY-3, 1 PBY-4
                  VP-14      6 P2Y-3
```

PATROL WING TWO

```
ComPatWingTwo  Flag  Unit          1 XPBS-1, 1 SOC-1
  (Pearl Harbor)                    1 SOC-2, 1 J2F-1
Utility Unit                                1 SOC-1
USS WRIGHT        VP-22     12 PBY-3
USS CHILDS        VP-23     12 PBY-1
USS SWAN          VP-24     14 PBY-1
                  VP-25     10 PBY-2
                  VP-26     15 PBY-4
```

PATROL WING THREE

```
Coco Solo         VP-31     11 PBY-2
USS LAPWING       VP-32*    10 PBY-1, 1 PBY-2
USS SANDPIPER     VP-33     12 PBY-3
*Temporarily at Guantanamo and Key West
```

PATROL WING FOUR

```
Seattle           VP-41      6 PBY-3
USS WILLIAMSON    VP-42      7 PBY-2
USS TEAL          VP-43      5 P2Y-3
                  VP-44      6 P2Y-3
```

PATROL WING FIVE

```
Norfolk
USS PATOKA                          2 SOC-1, 1 SON-1
Utility Unit      VP-51     12 PBY-1
USS GANNET        VP-52      7 P2Y-2
USS THRUSH        VP-53      3 PBY-1, 3 PBY-2, 3 PBY-3
USS OWL           VP-54     12 PBY-2
USS GEO. BADGER
(VP-51 temporarily at San Juan, Puerto Rico)
(VP-52 temporarily at Navy Yard, Charleston, S.C.)
(VP-53 temporarily at Key West, Florida)
```

COMMANDER, UTILITY UNIT
UTILITY WING

USS RIGEL	VJ-1	2 J2F-1, 5 J2F-2, 3 J2F-3, 8 JRS-1, 1 JRF-1A
	VJ-2	1 J2F-1, 5 J2F-2, 4 J2F-3, 2 JRS-1, 8 PH-1
	VJ-3	2 J2F-4, 1 JRF-1A, 7 O3U 6

SUBMARINE FORCE

USS RICHMOND	2 SOC-3

ATLANTIC SQUADRON

Battleship Division Five	VO-5	4 SOC-3, 5 SON-1
Cruiser Division Seven	VCS-7	9 SOC-1, 7 SOC-2
Aviation Unit, USS NOA		1 XSOC-1, 1 SON-1

USS RANGER

VB-4	13 SB2U-1, 3 SB2U-2, 3 SBC-3
VF-4	9 F3F-1, 2 F3F-3, 2 SU-3, 1 SBC-3
VS-41	16 SBU-1
VS-42	18 SBU-1
Utility Unit	2 SOC-1, 2 J2F-1

USS WASP

VB-7	17 BG-1
VF-7	15 F3F-1, 2 F2F-1, 1 SB2U-2, 2 SU-2
VS-71	17 SBU-1, 1 J2F-1, 1 NY-3
VS-72	19 SB2U-2
Utility Unit	1 SOC-1, 2 SON-1, 2 J2F-3, 1 O3U-3, 1 SB2U-2(AGC)

SPECIAL SERVICE SQUADRON

USS CHARLESTON	1 SOC-1
USS ERIE	1 SOC-1

ASIATIC FLEET

USS AUGUSTA		3 SOC-1, 1 SOC-2
USS MARBLEHEAD		2 SOC-1
USS HERON		2 J2F-2, 1 J2F-4
	VP-21	12 PBY-4
USS LANGLEY		2 SOC-1, 1 SOC-2, 1 SON-1

NOTE: Cruiser Division Three consisted of CONCORD, CINCINNATI, MILWAUKEE, OMAHA and TRENTON; Cruiser Division Eight PHILADELPHIA, BROOKLYN, NASHVILLE and SAVANNAH; Cruiser Division Nine HONOLULU, BOISE, PHOENIX and ST. LOUIS; Cruiser Division Four NORTHAMPTON, HOUSTON, PENSACOLA and SALT LAKE CITY; Cruiser Division Five CHICAGO, CHESTER, LOUISVILLE and PORTLAND; Cruiser Division Six MINNEAPOLIS, ASTORIA, NEW ORLEANS and SAN FRANCISCO; Cruiser Division Seven QUINCY, TUSCALOOSA, WICHITA, and VINCENNES; Battleship Division Five ARKANSAS, NEW YORK and TEXAS.

Consolidated XPB2Y-1 Command (0453) *U. S. Navy*
Flagplane of Commander Aircraft, Scouting Force; it flew Secretary of
Navy Knox to Hawaii on September 7th. Note change in tail, see p. 224.

Brewster F2A-2 (1398) *The National Archives*
Fighting Squadron Three aboard the SARATOGA was the first to
operate the F2A fighter; had 15 by Nov. Note modified tail configuration.

Vought SB2U-1 (0749) *Frank Shertzer*
Section Two leader with Lemon Yellow Tail and Bellerophon squadron
insignia. See Appendix D for full description of this insignia.

USS RANGER CV4   *U. S. Navy*
First U. S. ship designed from the keel up as an aircraft carrier.
Because of her short deck she did not operate a torpedo squadron.

Grumman F3F-1 (0235)   *U. S. Navy*
4-F-13, a Red Rippers fighter, taking off from the USS RANGER. These
two pages illustrate the units comprising the RANGER AIR GROUP.

Vought SB2U-2 (1383)   *James C. Fahey*
Rare photo of the High Hat squadron as VB-4. VB-3 became VB-4 in July
1939, changed again to VS-41 in July 1940. Note Neutrality Patrol Star.

Vought SBU-1 (9828)   *U. S. Navy*
Aircraft operating with the new Neutrality Patrol were authorized on
March 19, 1940 to place the National Star Insignia on the fuselage.

Vought SBU-1 (9764)   *William T. Larkins*
Both the RANGER and the new WASP had an extra scouting squadron
to replace the usual torpedo squadron. VS-42 was formerly VS-4B.

Vought SB2U-1 Command (0773)   *James C. Fahey*
Individual plane of COMMANDER RANGER AIR GROUP. The assigned
tail color of Willow Green for RANGER, used on diagonal fuselage stripe.

USS YORKTOWN CV5   *U. S. Navy*
19,900 ton carrier with 809' deck. She carried 85 aircraft, seen here
on deck. Note Y on stack; O3U-3 utility floatplane taking off water.

Grumman F3F-3 (1445)   *Manufacturer*
Fighting Squadron Five was the only unit to operate all F3F-3's, VF-4
and VF-6 had two each mixed in with their F3F-1's and F3F-2's.

Douglas TBD-1 (0335)   *William T. Larkins*
All squadrons operating from the YORKTOWN were numbered 5 to
conform to ship number. Assigned tail color for the 4 squadrons: Red.

Curtiss SBC-3 (0563) *Harold Nolen*
This photo clearly shows the seldom seen squadron insignia of Scouting Five, a black Man-of-War Bird superimposed on a red diamond.

Northrop BT-1 (0637) *William T. Larkins*
The rear seat gunner of 5-B-10 is standing on the wing next to the pilot to assist him in taxiing through parked planes at Oakland Airport.

Curtiss SBC-3 Command (0527) *Donald F. Kauer*
Air Group Commander's. Vought SB2U-2's became the AGC's equipment in 1940 for SARATOGA, LEXINGTON, YORKTOWN and RANGER.

USS ENTERPRISE CV6   *U. S. Navy*
With deck loaded, under way on February 12, 1940. Photo could not be
found of VS-6 SBC-3 to complete these ENTERPRISE Air Group pages.

Grumman F3F-2 (1003)   *William T. Larkins*
VF-6 flew the F3F-2 from early 1938 until they were replaced by new
F4F-3A's in May 1941. Note Fighting Six "Shooting Star" insignia.

Northrop BT-1 (0615)   *Manufacturer*
This photo of the squadron leader of Bombing Six shows the semi-
retractable landing gear of the BT-1. Note Wild Goat insignia.

Douglas TBD-1 (0324) *William T. Larkins*
Torpedo Squadron Six flew the TBD-1 from the time it was formed for
the new carrier ENTERPRISE in 1938 through 1941. Tail color: Blue.

Curtiss SBC-3 Command (1295) *Peter M. Bowers*
The ENTERPRISE Air Group Commander's plane, note additional
blue stripe on cowl as well as fuselage and use of ship's insignia.

Curtiss SBC-4 Command (1291) *Peter M. Bowers*
Plane number 2 of the U. S. Fleet Aircraft Tactical Unit, a part of
the Flag Unit for the Commander, Carrier Division Two in late 1940.

Vought SB2U-2 (1362)   *Howard Levy*
The USS WASP CV7, commissioned 4-25-40, had a 739' deck—even short*ı*
than RANGER's; thus no VT sqdn, instead **VS-71 SBU-1, VS-72 SB2U-2.**

Grumman F3F-1 (0262)   *U. S. Navy*
Beautiful photo of 7-F-1 on 4-16-40 in full markings with its newly
designed Blue Burglar Wasp squadron insignia and Neutrality Star.

Vought SB2U-2 Command (1379)   *Howard Levy*
WASP Air Group Commander's airplane. Assigned tail color for VB-7
(BG-1), VF-7 (F3F-1), VS-71 (SBU-1) and VS-72 (SB2U-2) was Black.

USS YORKTOWN CV5   *U. S. Navy*
Rare May 1940 photo showing 94 aircraft on deck; L to R F3F-3's,
SBC-3's, 16 J2F-s, 3 SB2U folded, 6 JRS-1, 2 JRF, BT-1's, TBD-1's.

Grumman J2F-2 (0792)   *Chester W. Phillips*
One of ten J2F's operated by Utility Squadron One at Pearl Harbor.
Tail color is solid Willow Green; see also 1-J-2 in photograph below.

Sikorsky JRS-1 (1193)   *U. S. Navy*
Magnificent flight photo of one of VJ-1's eight S-43 amphibians. Note
new squadron insignia next to front window; changed from earlier Lion.

Curtiss SBC-4 (1269) *Henry Clark*
NRAB NY SBC-4 painted as 2-S-1 hanging at 1940 New York World's
Fair. The Navy had a BF2C-1 on exhibit at 1936 San Diego Exposition.

Vought O3U-3 (9147) *U. S. Navy*
One of WASP's Utility Unit planes taking off. O3U-3 entered service in
June 1933; 74 in use during high year Fiscal 1935; 35 on hand 12-31-41.

Naval Aircraft Factory N3N-1 Modified (0680) *Harry Thorell*
NAS Anacostia staff plane with cockpit canopies added. The XN3N-1 and
XN3N-2 also had the same hatches added during their later years.

Vought O3U-3 (9324)   *James C. Fahey*
About to be hoisted out of the water by land crane. Number Three plane
of the Naval Academy at Annapolis. All Midshipmen were given flights.

Waco XJW-1 (9522)   *Howard Levy*
The last remaining XJW-1 hook-on trainer of the MACON HTA Unit
went to Anacostia in June 1938 where it stayed through September 1941.

Grumman J2F-4 (1651)   *William T. Larkins*
First plane of the new Utility Squadron Six (VJ-6D12) formed for
NAS Alameda. Soon changed to Station markings; see page 286.

Vought SU-2 (9106)   *Harry Thorell*
One of NAS Anacostia's highly polished staff planes with cockpit
covers added. Note extra wide cowling; compare with SU-2 below.

Vought SU-2 (9095)   *Howard Levy*
NAS Lakehurst station utility plane with SU-4 tail and controllable
pitch prop. Originally built as a command plane, see photo page 132.

Vought SU-3 (9139)   *Joe Williams*
Another station utility plane, this one from NAS Norfolk. The
SU-3 was originally built as a photographic version of the SU-2.

Vought SU-2 (9114)   *Harry Thorell*
This plane operated with the Marine Corps aboard the LEXINGTON
during 1932-1934. See photo as 15-S-6 on page 46 of the USMC book.

Vought SU-4 (9414)   *William T. Larkins*
For Inspector of Naval Aircraft, San Diego. Also a former USMC plane,
see USMC book for photos as 8-O-12 (page 64), and 1-MJ-10 (page 84).

Vought SU-4 (9109)   *William T. Larkins*
The original XSU-4 which was built with cockpit covers and wheel
pants. Changed to SU-4 in late 1933 and added to Anacostia's SU fleet.

Curtiss XSO3C-1 (1385)   *Manufacturer*
First of two "High Speed Scout" designs to replace SOC's aboard
the cruisers. Delivered in January with new Ranger XV-770-6 engine.

Vought XSO2U-1 (1440)   *Manufacturer*
Delivered in February with Ranger XV-770-4. Photo taken at factory
on July 26, 1939. Both planes operated on a single catapult float.

Grumman JRF-1A (1671)   *Manufacturer*
The first of five modified G-21A's for target towing and photography.
Seven-place, powered by R-985-48's, delivered late 1939 and early 1940.

Curtiss XSB2C-1 (1758)   *Manufacturer*
At the factory December 13, 1940. It was destroyed in a crash shortly
thereafter and the next SB2C was not delivered to the Navy until 1942.

Consolidated XPBY-5A (1245)   *James C. Fahey*
Demonstrating its new retractable tri-cycle landing gear at an air
show at Bolling Field, across from Anacostia, on May 29, 1940.

Martin XPBM-1 (0796)   *The National Archives*
First of the "Mariner" twin-engine patrol boats at the factory on May
8th. Martin Design Number 162 with inward retracting wing floats.

Curtiss SBC-4 (1819)   *Chester W. Phillips*
A VS-10R dive bomber running up. All reserve squadron numbers
changed in July 1937 along with the fleet, note new numbers on p. 275.

Grumman JF-3 (9839)   *Gordon S. Williams*
From NRAB Seattle with green tail. Seattle, Oakland and Long Beach
were the only bases with JF-3's in 1940; others had J2F-2, 3 and 4.

Curtiss SBC-4 (1816)   *William T. Larkins*
With new markings adopted in December 1940. These SBC-4's replaced
an earlier batch which were destined for France, ended at Martinique.

RESERVE AIRCRAFT ASSIGNMENT
June 1940

NRAB BOSTON VS-1R, VS-2R VMS-1R	3 SBC-4, 2 SBU-2, 3 SF-1, 2 OJ-2, 1 J2F-2, 5 N3N-1, 1 N3N-3, 1 SNJ-2
NRAB NEW YORK VS-3R, VS-4R VMS-2R	4 SBC-4, 4 SF-1, 3 SBU-2, 2 OJ-2, 1 J2F-2, 6 N3N-1, 2 N3N-3, 1 SNJ-2
NRAB, NAVY YARD, PHILADELPHIA VS-5R	2 OJ-2, 1 SF-1, 1 J2F-2, 5 SBU-2, 3 N3N-1, 4 N3N-3, 1 SNJ-2
NRAB MIAMI VS-7R VMS-4R	11 SBU-2, 3 SF-1, 1 OJ-2, 1 J2F-2, 7 N3N-1, 2 N3N-3, 1 SNJ-2
NRAB CHICAGO VS-9R	4 SBC-4, 3 FF-2, 1 J2F-3, 2 OJ-2, 5 N3N-1, 1 N3N-3, 1 SU-2, 1 SNJ-2
NRAB DETROIT VS-8R VMS-5R	3 SBC-4, 3 FF-2, 1 J2F-4, 4 N3N-1, 2 N3N-3, 1 SNJ-2
NRAB MINNEAPOLIS VS-10R VMS-6R	3 SBC-4, 3 FF-2, 1 OJ-2, 1 J2F-3, 4 N3N-1, 1 N3N-3, 1 SNJ-2
NRAB ST. LOUIS VS-11R	3 SBC-4, 3 FF-2, 1 OJ-2, 4 N3N-1, 1 N3N-3, 1 SNJ-2
NRAB KANSAS CITY VS-12R VMS-10R	4 SBC-4, 3 FF-2, 2 OJ-2, 4 N3N-1, 1 N3N-3, 1 SNJ-2
NRAB LONG BEACH VS-13R, VS-14R VMS-7R	4 SBC-4, 3 OJ-2, 3 SF-1, 1 JF-3, 6 N3N-1, 1 SNJ-2
NRAB OAKLAND VS-15R VMS-8R	4 SBC-4, 3 SF-1, 1 JF-3, 5 N3N-1, 1 N3N-3, 1 SNJ-2
NRAB SEATTLE VS-16R VMS-9R	4 SBC-4, 3 SF-1, 1 JF-3, 4 N3N-1, 1 N3N-3, 1 SNJ-2
NRAB WASHINGTON VS-6R VMS-3R	3 SBC-4, 2 SF-1, 4 N3N-1, 1 N3N-3, 1 SNJ-2

Berliner-Joyce OJ-2 (9196) *Oliver R. Phillips*
The XOJ-3 re-built and re-designated OJ-2 ended its days at NRAB
Seattle in early 1940. Note that it kept its hatches and cowling.

Grumman SF-1 (9485) *William T. Larkins*
NRAB Oakland's Ten Spot coming in for a landing. The 22 in use by the
reserves in June dropped to 9 in November, all were gone by 1941.

North American SNJ-2 (2025) *Art Sutter*
Each reserve base was given a new SNJ-2 as may be seen by the chart
on page 275. SNJ-1's were originally assigned but were not delivered.

Naval Aircraft Factory N3N-1 (0692)   *William T. Larkins*
OAKLAND-17 taking off through a mud puddle in September 1940; note
United Air Lines Boeing 247-D above pilots head. Painted all-yellow.

Naval Aircraft Factory N3N-1 (0695)   *Howard Levy*
Rare photo of a reserve trainer on skis. One of six assigned to the
three reserve squadrons at NRAB New York flying from Floyd Bennett.

Curtiss SBC-4 (1306)   *William T. Larkins*
Simulated carrier landing being made during annual inspection. Note
white flags representing deck, tail wheel on ground, elevator angle.

1941 PATROL SQUADRON RE-ORGANIZATION

In 1941 several squadrons were re-numbered and about nine new squadrons were forming.

INSIGNIA	OLD NUMBER	NEW NUMBER	EQUIPMENT	NOTES
Pegasus in Circle (Winged 8-Ball)	VP-23	VP-11	PBY-1	At Kaneohe, Hawaii
	VP-24	VP-12	PBY-1	At Kaneohe, Hawaii
	—	VP-13	PBY-4, PBY-5	At TTU-Pacific
Sitka Spruce Tree	VP-14	VP-14	PBY-5	At Kaneohe, Hawaii
Great White Albatross (Griffin)	VP-11	VP-21	PBY-3	At Pearl Harbor
Bomb in Compass Rose	VP-22	VP-22	PBY-3	At Pearl Harbor
Goose Under the Sun	VP-25	VP-23	PBY-2	At Pearl Harbor
Keystone Cop	VP-12	VP-24	PBY-5	At Pearl Harbor
Wings Over Panama	VP-31	VP-31	PBY-5	At Coco Solo and San Juan
Husky Dog	VP-33	VP-32	PBY-3	At Coco Solo
Seal Balancing Bomb	VP-41	VP-41	PBY-5	Alaska
	VP-42	VP-42	PBY-5	Alaska
	—	VP-43	PBY-5	New squadron, Alaska
	—	VP-44	PBY-5	New squadron, Alaska
Head of Odin	VP-54	VP-51	PBY-5	Norfolk and Bermuda
Standing Elephant	VP-32	VP-52	PBY-5	Norfolk
Totem Pole and Mt. Rainier	VP-51	VP-71	PBY-5	Support Force
Six Geese in Flight	VP-52	VP-72	PBY-5	Support Force
Indian Scout Kneeling	VP-53	VP-73	PBY-5	Support Force
Eagle Over North America	VP-56 VP-55	VP-74	PBM-1	VP-55 and VP-56 merged to form VP-74
Polar Bear on Mountain	VP-43	VP-81	PBY-5	Support Force
Mine in Horseshoe	VP-44	VP-82	PBY-5	Support Force
	—	VP-83	PBY-5A	Org 9-15-41 at Norfolk
	—	VP-84	PBY-5A	Org 10-1-41 at Norfolk
	—	VP-91	PBY-5A	New, at Quonset Point
	—	VP-92	PBY-5A	New, at Quonset Point
	—	VP-93	PBY-5A	New, at Quonset Point
	—	VP-94	PBY-5A	New, at Quonset Point
Elephant Standing on Cloud	VP-21	VP-101	PBY-4	At Cavite, P.I.
Wings Over the Globe	VP-26	VP-102	PBY-4	At Cavite, P.I.

Consolidated PB2Y-2 (1633) *Manufacturer*
VP-13 used 1 PBY-4 and 2 PB2Y-2's for Project Baker for VP radio-
instrument landing training. The vertical tail stripe is painted Blue.

Consolidated PBY-3 *E. F. Stewart*
VP-21 (old VP-1) was the first combat unit to extend the Neutrality
Patrol west to the Philippines. Squadron became VP-101 while there.

Consolidated PBY-3 *E. F. Stewart*
Quick on-the-spot camouflage added in November. PatWingTen evacuated
from the Philippines on December 14th; to East Indies, then Australia.

Curtiss SOC-3's   *U. S. Navy*
The USS HONOLULU Aviation Section. 9-CS-1 is SOC-3 1087; 9-CS-2
is SON-1 1175; 9-CS-3 is SOC-3 1077 and 9-CS-4 is SOC-3 1076.

Curtiss SOC-3 (1095)   *Gordon S. Williams*
The movement of ships within the fleet organization is graphically
shown by this page; note change in aircraft number as well as ship.

Curtiss SOC-3 (1134)   *Peter M. Bowers*
VCS-9 on the PHOENIX in November; see 9-CS-9 HONOLULU above.
E in machine gunnery with one hash mark. Tail stripes are Green.

Curtiss SOC-2 (0423)   *William T. Larkins*

Curtiss SOC-1 (9908)   *Peter M. Bowers*

Curtiss SOC-1 (9866)   *William T. Larkins*
VCS-5 aboard LOUISVILLE CA28 with yellow tail band, black fuselage
stripe as four-plane section leader. VCS-6 above has black tail band.

Northrop BT-1 Command (0633)   *William F. Yeager*
YORKTOWN Air Group Commander's plane which was replaced by an
SBD-3 in mid-1941 at the same time that VB-5 and VS-5 got their SBD-3's.

North American SNJ-2 Command (2549)   *Peter M. Bowers*
The land based half of the Flag Unit for the Commander of Carrier
Division One. The additional SBD-3 was used for carrier duty at sea.

North American SNJ-2 Command (2016)   *Art Sutter*
Assigned to the Flag Unit of Commander Aircraft, Scouting Force. Two
SOC-3's also used were replaced by OS2U-2's + 1 JRB-2 in December.

Vought OS2U-2 (1714)   *Manufacturer*
3-O-4 from the MISSISSIPPI with solid blue tail. CinCUS on the USS
PENNSYLVANIA had an all-blue OS2U-1. All VO units now had OS2U's.

Vought OS2U-2 (2216)   *Frank Shertzer*
Several seaplane tenders, such as the USS TANGIER AV8 with Partol
Wing Two at Pearl, had OS2U's assigned. TANGIER had three in 1941.

Vought OS2U-2 (2190)   *Manufacturer*
VS-5D4 (Fourth Naval District), one of new Inshore Patrol Squadrons.
Nine new VS-1D units were formed for 1942 delivery of NAF OS2N-1's.

Grumman F4F-3   *Manufacturer*
VS-41 became VF-42 in 1941 giving the RANGER two fighting squadrons.
New "Wildcat" shown here awaiting delivery to either VF-41 or VF-42.

Douglas SBD-2 (2102)   *Manufacturer*
The first SBD-2 at the factory. All SBD-1's went to the Marine Corps,
SBD-2 model started Navy deliveries. Had one more gun and more fuel.

Naval Aircraft Factory SBN-1 (1522)   *U. S. Navy*
Navy-built version of the Brewster XSBA-1. First production was
used in training Torpedo Eight formed for the new USS HORNET CV8.

Grumman F2F-1 (9623) *Chester W. Phillips*
One of several fighters assigned to Naval Air Stations to provide
gunnery exercises for Patrol Squadrons. See also on page 292.

North American SNJ-2 (2035) *Frank Shertzer*
Number Two staff utility plane from NAS Seattle. Insignia on plane
is for the Naval Air Station, not for the reserve unit at Seattle.

Lockheed R5O-1 Command (4250) *William T. Larkins*
Larger model 18 transport replacing the older XR2O-1 for the Secretary
of the Navy. A second R5O was obtained for the Assistant SecNav.

Grumman J2F-4 (1651)   *William T. Larkins*
Former 6-J-1 (see page 269) with new station markings of NAS
ALAMEDA. J2F-4's used by 4 USMC squadrons, all 4 Navy VJ squadrons.

Grumman JRF-4 (3854)   *Frank Shertzer*
NAS Alameda's number five station plane. Serial numbers 3846-3855 were
ordered as JRF-1's, delivered as JRF-4's. See USCG for JRF-2 and 3.

Beechcraft GB-2 (01628)   *Clayton L. Jansson*
At NAS Pensacola in December 1941; note the official air station
insignia of short-winged goose landing in the water. See Appendix D.

Douglas R4D-2 (4707)   *William T. Larkins*
Rarest of all the R4D's, only two of these airline transports were
bought by the Navy. Note the small door, curtains on the windows.

Douglas R3D-1 (1902)   *Frank Shertzer*
One of 3 DC-5 transports bought by the Navy; the first crashed and
burned near the factory 6-1-40. See Marine Corps for R3D-2 model.

Lockheed R5O-3 Command (01006)   *Howard Levy*
Two "Lodestar" 18-10 executive models were delivered to the Navy
in 1941, this one was for the Chief of the Bureau of Aeronautics.

Stearman N2S-2 (3644)   *Manufacturer*
Production of the Boeing-Wichita plant, designed to utilize Lycoming
R-680-8 production in place of the Continental used on the N2S-1.

Beech JRB-1 (2544)   *Manufacturer*
Development of civil model C-18S and Air Corps F-2 for photography.
Note center section of door, removable to enable use of large cameras.

Beech JRB-2 (4725)   *Manufacturer*
Light transport, the basic model of which has lasted twenty years. In
1941 two used as Flag planes for ComAirScoFor and Patrol Wing One.

Naval Aircraft Factory—1941   *U. S. Navy*
Fascinating interior photograph showing XSB2U-3, XBT-2, XF4F-3,
O3U-4, O3U-6, SBN-1, SOC or SON, T4M-1, JRB and eight N3N-3's.

Naval Aircraft Factory XN5N-1 (1521)   *The National Archives*
Two-place primary trainer designed and built by the NAF. It had
a Wright R-760-6 engine, and a canopy was added in later years.

Naval Aircraft Factory N3N-3 (1759)   *U. S. Navy*
First production dash three. Serial Number 0020 was changed from an
N3N-1 to the XN3N-3 by a 7-31-39 directive. 0426-0450 N3N-1 cancelled.

Curtiss SNC-1 (6291)   *Manufacturer*
The Curtiss-Wright (St. Louis plant) design CW-22, a light weight
advanced trainer used to complement the SNJ and the new SNV-1.

Spartan NP-1 (3645)   *Gene Sommerich*
First of 201 ordered in 1940 for naval reserve primary flight training.
NRAB Atlanta, NRAB Dallas and NRAB New Orleans opened in 1941.

Ryan NR-1 (4197)   *Manufacturer*
ST-3KR trainer also used in large numbers by the AAF as PT-22. XNR-1
designation was used by two Maxson twin-engine trainers (1756-1757).

Boeing F4B-4 (9029)   *U. S. Navy*
A radio-controlled drone used by VJ-3 at San Diego in 1941; director
plane was a BT-1. 23 F4B-4A's were transferred from the Army in 1940.

Vought O3U-3 (9287)   *Clayton L. Jansson*
One of 19 being operated by VN-2D8 at NAS Pensacola in late 1941.
Note instrument hood on rear pit, red wing and fuselage bands.

Vought XSBU-1 (9222)   *Clayton L. Jansson*
Assigned to Naval Air Detachment, NAS Pensacola. During 1941 NAS
Miami, NAS Jacksonville, NAS Corpus Christi added to primary fields.

Grumman F2F-1 (9662)   *Oliver R. Phillips*
Patrol Wing Four's fighter. Each VP Wing was assigned a fighter in
1941 for training in gunnery. 21 were used at Miami, 9 at Pensacola.

Consolidated P2Y-2 (8997)   *Clayton J. Jansson*
Number 33 of VN-4D8 at Pensacola. Note that all of the planes used
for fight training carry only a large number, and no other markings.

Martin XPBM-2 (1247)   *The National Archives*
At the factory 4-15-41. Designed for extended range and experimental
catapult launching. See photo XPBM-1, one year earlier, on page 273.

Vought XTBU-1 (2542) *Manufacturer*
Three-place torpedo bomber developed simultaneously with the TBF-1.
Shown here at the factory on December 20, 1941; to Anacostia 3-30-42.

Vought XTBU-1 (2542) *U. S. Navy*
Rare flight view showing unusual sliding canopy around rear turret.
Turned over to Consolidated for 1944 production as TBY-2 "Sea Wolf."

Grumman XTBF-1 Mockup *The National Archives*
Full size mockup in front of the factory. Note absence of dorsal fin.
Serial 2539 crashed and burned 10-28-41; 2540 was delivered in December.

Brewster XSB2A-1 (1632)   *Manufacturer*

The prototype in August 1941. Note dummy power turret in rear, solid fuselage between it and cockpit; both were removed in production model.

Grumman XF4F-5 (1846)   *U. S. Navy*

An F4F-3 with its Pratt & Whitney engine replaced by a Wright Cyclone R-1820-40. None to USN but 150 were ordered for England as F4F-4B.

Grumman XF4F-6 (7031)   *The National Archives*

Powered by a Pratt & Whitney R-1830-90. Note the difference in the shape of the cowling between this plane and the XF4F-5 above.

Grumman XF5F-1 (1442)   *Manufacturer*

This page shows three new 1941 fighters, only one of which went into production. The twin-engined XF5F-1 was a carrier fighter, note hook.

Bell XFL-1 (1588)   *The National Archives*

Modification of the Army's P-39C named the "Airabonita." Tail wheel added in place of tri-cycle gear; note carrier deck hook. One only.

Vought XF4U-1 (1443)   *U. S. Navy*

Prototype of the "Corsair" fighter that was to become so famous in World War II. Note difference in canopy and fuselage from later models.

COAST GUARD AIRCRAFT ASSIGNMENT
31 December 1941

CG AIR STATION	AIRCRAFT TYPE	AIRCRAFT SERIAL
Salem,	JRF-2	V185
Massachusetts	J4F-1	V197
	RD-4	V129
Brooklyn,	PH-3	V177, V179
New York	JRF-3	V190, V191
	J4F-1	V198
	N3N-3	V196
	R3O-1	V151
	R5O-1	V188
Elizabeth City,	PH-3	V182, V183
North Carolina	JRF-2	V175, V186
	J4F-1	V199
	N3N-3	V193
	J2K-1, 2	V161, V163
	N4Y-1	V110
	R3Q-1	V149
Miami,	PH-2	V167, V169
Florida	RD-4	V132
	SOC-4	V171, 172, 173
Saint Petersburg,	J4F-1	V200
Florida	RD-4	V125, V134
	N3N-3	V194, V195
Biloxi,	PH-2	V168, V170
Mississippi	JRF-2	V184
	J4F-1	V202
	JF-2	V137, V143
San Diego,	PH-2	V166
California	PH-3	V178
	RD-4	V127
	JF-2	V139
San Francisco,	PBY-5	V189
California	PH-3	V180, V181
	J4F-1	V201
	RD-4	V128, V133
	JF-2	V140
Port Angeles,	JRF-2	V176
Washington	J4F-1	V203
	JF-2	V148
Air Patrol Detachment,		
Traverse City,	JRF-3	V192
Michigan	J4F-1	V204
Senior CG Officer,		
14th Naval District	JRF-2	V187
Senior CG Officer,		
7th Naval District	JRF-2	V174

Hall-Aluminum PH-2 (V169)   *Gordon S. Williams*
Air-sea rescue version of the Navy PH-1 patrol bomber manufactured in
1938 for USCG only. Seven served Coast Guard Air Stations through 1941.

Hall-Aluminum PH-3 (V180)   *William T. Larkins*
1940 version with same Wright GR-1820-F51 engines of 750 hp each. Both
had a cruising range of 1,250 miles. V180 shown at CGAS San Francisco.

Grumman J4F-1 (V203)   *Gordon S. Williams*
New "Widgeon" light amphibians were added in 1941; V197-V204 delivered 1941, V205-V221 delivered 1942. All had wing bomb racks by 1942.

Curtiss SOC-4 (V173)   *Gordon S. Williams*
Three served the USCG from 1938 through 1941. V172 was attached to
Coast Guard Cutter BIBB in 1938-1939. V173 above at Pt. Angeles CGAS.

Grumman JF-2 (V140)   *William T. Larkins*
Used 1934-1941. V135 was carried on the stern of Coast Guard Cutter
TANEY at Honolulu; V144 was used aboard SPENCER, Cordova, Alaska.

Grumman JRF-2 (V176)   *Gordon S. Williams*
Seven JRF-2's and three similar JRF-3's were used from 1939. Both had
189 mph speed and P&W R-985 engines; JRF-3 had 240 miles less range.

Consolidated N4Y-1 (V110)   *Gordon S. Williams*
Originally the 10th airplane in the Coast Guard; became 310 and later
V110, lasted through 1941. First three USCG planes were Loening OL-5's.

Naval Aircraft Factory N3N-3 (V196)   *Howard Levy*
In 1941 the USCG traded the Navy JF-2's V135, V141, V144 and V146 for
four N3N-3's needed for the accelerated CG pilot training program.

Consolidated PBY-5 (V189)   *William T. Larkins*
The only one of its kind in the CG; a flying boat delivered in 1941.
Was former Navy Serial Number 2290. Shown at San Francisco 6-3-42.

LOCATION OF NAVAL AIRCRAFT
31 December 1941

The following table accounts for the assigned location of every airplane in the Navy as of 31 December 1941. It is arranged alphabetically by Class and by Model Designation.

CLASS VB

BD-1

NPG Dahlgren	1
Total	**1**

BG-1

VJ-5, Cape May	7
NAF (1 for Proj. F)	4
San Diego, Base Force	11
Total	**22**

BT-1

NAS Miami	33
VJ-3, RIGEL	2
VJ-5, Cape May	2
NAS San Diego	1
Total	**38**

XBT-2

NAF, Naval Instrument Development Section	1
Total	**1**

CLASS VF

F2A-1

NAS Norfolk	1
Total	**1**

XF2A-2

NAS Norfolk	1
Total	**1**

F2A-2

Brewster Corporation	1
NAS Anacostia	1
NAS Norfolk, Lant	1
San Diego, Battle Force	3
NAF	1
ACTG, Pacific	1

FAPU Pacific	1
NAS Miami	7
Total	**49**

F2A-3

INA Brewster (test)	1
NAS Anacostia (test)	1
San Diego, BatFor	5
NAS New York	37
NAF (test)	1
VF-2, LEXINGTON	19
LEXINGTON	2
VMF-221	14
Pearl Harbor BatFor	7
VJ-5, Cape May	3
VS-201, LONG ISLAND	7
ACTG Pacific	1
NAS Norfolk, Lant	1
NAS Miami	8
Total	**107**

F4B-3

VJ-3, Base Force	3
Total	**3**

F4B-4

NAF (test)	14
VJ-3, Base Force	3
VJ-5, Cape May	1
Total	**18**

F4B-4A

NAF	9
VJ-3, Base Force	2
VJ-5, Cape May	2
Total	**13**

FF-2

NAS Norfolk	3
NAF Operations	1
BAD-1, Quantico	

GINA, Dayton, Ohio   1
INA, New York   1
                         —
              Total   7

F2F-1

NAS Miami   16
NAS Pensacola   7
                         —
              Total   23

XF3F-1

NAS Norfolk   1
                         —
              Total   1

F3F-1

NAS Miami   28
NAS Norfolk   11
                         —
              Total   39

F3F-2

NAS Miami   18
NAS Pearl Harbor   1
NAS Norfolk   7
NAS Corpus Christi   14
BAD-2, San Diego   4
San Diego, BatFor   10
                         —
              Total   54

XF3F-3

NAS Corpus Christi   1
                         —
              Total   1

F3F-3

NAS Seattle   1
NAS Miami   4
NAS Corpus Christi   16
NAS Norfolk   1
                         —
              Total   22

F4F-3

NAS Anacostia   2
ENTERPRISE   3
VMF-211, Pearl Harbor   24
BAD-1, Quantico   2
VMF-121   21
VF-42, YORKTOWN   18
Pearl Harbor, BatFor   1
VF-5, RANGER   18
VF-71, WASP   18
ACTG, Norfolk   1

NAS Norfolk, Lant   12
VF-8, HORNET   19
VF-41, RANGER   17
Aircraft Armament
  Unit, Norfolk   1
San Diego, BatFor   1
VF-3, SARATOGA   8
VF-72, WASP   17
NAF   2
VF-6, ENTERPRISE   1
INA, P&W Aircraft   1
                         ———
              Total   176

F4F-3A

NAS Norfolk   4
VMF-111   16
San Diego, BatFor   3
VF-6, ENTERPRISE   17
ACTG, Atlantic   11
Pearl Harbor, BatFor   2
VF-5, RANGER   1
VF-8, HORNET   2
VF-3, SARATOGA   2
                         —
              Total   61

XF4F-4

VF-3, SARATOGA   1
                         —
              Total   1

F4F-4

NAS Anacostia (test)   1
NAS Norfolk, Lant   4
                         —
              Total   5

XF4F-5

Wright Corporation   2
                         —
              Total   2

XF4F-6

NAS Anacostia   1
                         —
              Total   1

XF5F-1

NAF (test)   1
                         —
              Total   1

XFL-1

Bell Aircraft Corp.   1
                         —
              Total   1

XF4U-1

INA, Stratford, Conn.		1
	Total	1

CLASS VG

GB-1

GINA, New York (at NRAB Brooklyn)		1
NAF (overhaul)		1
NAS Norfolk		1
NAS Pensacola		1
NAS Corpus Christi		1
Naval Attache, Madrid, Spain		1
Naval Attache, Mexico City, Mexico		1
NAS San Diego		1
NAS New York		1
NAF Air Detachment		1
	Total	10

GB-2

NAS Anacostia		2
GINA, Wright Field		1
NAD, Pensacola		1
Commander, Support Force, Atlantic		1
NAS New York		1
	Total	6

GB-2 (Reserves)

NRAB Anacostia		1
NRAB Detroit		1
NRAB New Orleans		1
NRAB Boston		1
NRAB Long Beach		1
NRAB New York		1
NRAB Chicago		1
NRAB Kansas City		1
NRAB Seattle		1
NRAB Oakland		1
NRAB Atlanta		1
	Total	11

GH-1

NAF		1
	Total	1

GH-1 (Reserves)

NRAB Chicago		5
	Total	5

GK-1

NAS Anacostia		1
NAS Pensacola		2
	Total	3

JE-1

NAS New York		1
	Total	1

JK-1

NAS San Diego		1
	Total	1

XJW-1

NAS Anacostia		1
	Total	1

XDH-80

Naval Attache, London, England		1
	Total	1

LeSimoun

Naval Attache, Paris, France		1
	Total	1

Me-108b

Naval Attache, Berlin, Germany		1
	Total	1

S-2

Naval Attache, Rome, Italy		1
	Total	1

CLASS VJ

JF-1

BAD-1, Quantico	1
Air Detachment, Parris Island	1
NAS Coco Solo	1
NAS Pensacola	1
NAS Miami	1
San Diego NAD	1

NTS Newport	1
NAS Key West	1
NAS Quonset Point	1
NAS Banana River	1
NAS Tongue Point	1
Norfolk (overhaul)	1
NAS Squantum	1
Total	**13**

JF-3 (Reserves)

NRAB Long Beach	1
NRAB Oakland	1
NRAB Seattle	1
Total	**3**

J2F-1

TTS San Diego	1
NA, Annapolis	1
BAD-1, Quantico	1
NPG, Dahlgren	1
VMJ-152	1
VJ-1, Base Force	1
Pearl Harbor Base Force	1
NAS Kaneohe Bay	1
NAS Coco Solo	2
NAS Kodiak	1
LEXINGTON	2
Seattle, Base Force	2
VJ-2, Hawaiian Det.	2
NAS Alameda	1
Navairdet, Newport	1
Norfolk, Lant	4
Total	**23**

J2F-2

NAS New York	1
Pearl Harbor Utility	1
ENTERPRISE	2
VJ-1, Base Force	4
VJ-2, Base Force	1
VJ-4, Squantum	1
WASP Utility Unit	1
NAS Palmyra Island	1
NAS Midway Island	1
NAS Johnston Island	1
VJ-5, Cape May	2
VJ-2, Hawaiian Det.	1
HERON Utility Unit	1
Total	**18**

J2F-2 (Reserves)

NRAB Boston	1
Total	**1**

J2F-2A

VMS-3, St. Thomas	9
Total	**9**

J2F-3

VJ-2, Base Force	3
Naval Mission, Rio de Janeiro, Brazil	1
NAS Jacksonville	1
NA, Annapolis	1
VJ-1, Base Force	1
VJ-2, Hawaiian Det.	1
VJ-4, Squantum	1
NAS Norfolk, Lant	2
Pearl Harbor, BaseFor	3
WASP	1
NRAB Squantum (for Coast Guard)	1
Total	**16**

J2F-3 (Reserves)

NRAB Minneapolis	1
Total	**1**

J2F-4

NAS Norfolk, Lant	2
NAD, Pensacola	1
VJ-1, Base Force	3
VJ-2, Hawaiian Det.	4
VJ-3, Base Force	1
VJ-4, Squantum	2
Pearl Harbor Operations	3
NAS Seattle	1
VMO-151	2
VMO-251	1
HERON	3
VJ-5, Cape May	1
VMJ-152	1
VMJ-252	2
NAS Alameda	1
NRAB Squantum (for Coast Guard)	2
NAS Norfolk	1
Naval Attache, Guatemala City, Guatemala	1
Total	**32**

J2F-5

SARATOGA	3
SARATOGA Utility Unit	2
NAS Norfolk, Lant	4
VJ-5, Cape May	2
NAS Anacostia (test)	3
NAS New York (1 for Navy Yard, Cavite, P.I.; 14 for San Diego Base Force, 5 for Norfolk Atlantic Pool)	20
RANGER	2
FAPU, Norfolk	2
Navy Yard, Cavite	2
HORNET Utility Unit	2
VJ-4, Squantum	12
San Diego Base Force	7
San Diego, Battle Force	4
ACTG, Norfolk	1
YORKTOWN	2
Total	68

XJ3F-1

NAS Lakehurst	1
Total	1

CLASS VJR

JRB-1

VJ-3, Base Force	4
NAF	2
VJ-5, Cape May	5
Total	11

JRB-2

Navairdet, Corpus Christi	1
NAS Norfolk	3
Navairdet, Miami	1
Naval Attache, Bogota, Colombia	1
Wing HQ, FMF, Quantico	1
Naval Research Lab, Anacostia	2
BAD-2, San Diego	1
Naval Attache, Lima, Peru	1
Commander Aircraft Scouting Force (Flag)	1
Navairdet, Jacksonville	1
NAF	2
Total	15

JRF-1

Naval Attache, Havana, Cuba	1
Naval Attache, Caracas, Venezuela	1
San Diego Operations	1
NAS Seattle	1
Total	4

JRF-1A

VMS-3, St. Thomas	1
NAS Coco Solo	1
Pearl Harbor Operations	1
VJ-3, Base Force	2
Total	5

JRF-4

NAS Alameda	1
NAS San Juan	1
NAS Anacostia	2
NAS Pensacola	1
NAS Miami	1
NAS Corpus Christi	1
Wing HQ, FMF, S.D.	1
Commander-in-Chief, Atlantic Fleet, Flag Unit	1
NAS Norfolk	1
Total	10

JRF-5

NAS New York (for USCG)	1
Commander, Support Force	1
Commander, Patrol Wing Seven	1
Commander, Aircraft Atlantic Fleet	1
NAS Jacksonville	1
NAS Trindad	1
NAS Guantanamo	1
NAS Sitka	1
NAS Kodiak	1
NAS San Diego	3
NAS Quonset Point	2
NAS Anacostia	1
Total	15

JRS-1

VMJ-252	1
Total	1

CLASS VN

NJ-1

NAS Pensacola	39
	Total 39

XN3N-1

Navairdet, NAF	1
	Total 1

N3N-1

NAS Anacostia	1
NTS Newport	3
NAS Corpus Christi	1
NAS Pensacola	84
ACTG, Pacific	1
	Total 90

N3N-1 (Reserves)

NRAB Anacostia	4
NRAB Boston	5
NRAB Chicago	5
NRAB Detroit	4
NRAB Kansas City	4
NRAB Long Beach	6
NRAB Miami	6
NRAB Minneapolis	4
NRAB New York	6
NRAB Oakland	5
NRAB Philadelphia	4
NRAB St. Louis	3
NRAB Seattle	4
	Total 60

XN3N-2

NAS Anacostia	1
	Total 1

XN3N-3

NAS Pensacola	1
	Total 1

N3N-3

NA, Annapolis	2
NPG, Dahlgren	2
NAS Jacksonville	33
NAS Pensacola	325
NAS Guantanamo	1
NAS Corpus Christi	184
NAS Miami	10

NAF (test)	2
	Total 559

N3N-3 (Reserves)

NRAB Anacostia	11
NRAB Dallas	22
NRAB Atlanta	22
NRAB Boston	17
NRAB Chicago	17
NRAB Detroit	22
NRAB Kansas City	7
NRAB Long Beach	18
NRAB Miami	7
NRAB Minneapolis	10
NRAB New York	16
NRAB Oakland	10
NRAB Philadelphia	10
NRAB St. Louis	11
NRAB Seattle	10
NRAB New Orleans	21
	Total 231

XN5N-1

NAF	1
	Total 1

NP-1 (Reserves)

NRAB St. Louis	9
NRAB Kansas City	13
NRAB Dallas	18
NRAB Chicago	14
NRAB Detroit	10
INA, Spartan	12
	Total 76

NR-1

NAS Jacksonville	99
	Total 99

NS-1

NAS Pensacola	42
	Total 42

NS2-1

NAS Pensacola	86
NAS Corpus Christi	39
NAS Jacksonville	114
	Total 239

N2S-2

NAS Corpus Christi	124

NAF	1

Total 125

N2S-3

NAS Jacksonville	94
NAS Corpus Christi	116
NAS Pensacola	1

Total 211

N2Y-1

SARATOGA Utility Unit	1

Total 1

CLASS VOS

XOSN-1

NA, Annapolis	1

Total 1

XOS2U-1

NA, Annapolis	1

Total 1

OS2U-1

NAS Seattle	1
NAS Norfolk, Lant	3
San Diego, BatFor	3
Commander-in-Chief, Pacific Fleet	1
CASCO, Seattle	1
NAS Pensacola	3
Commander, Patrol Wing Four	1
SARATOGA	2
IDAHO	1
MISSISSIPPI	1
NAS Pensacola	12
BARNEGAT	1
WASP	1
NAS Dutch Harbor	1
Pearl Harbor BatFor	6
Commander, Patrol Wing One	1
Hardman Aircraft Co.	1
NAS Alameda, BatFor	12

Total 52

OS2U-2

ACTG, Pacific	1
INA, Douglas	1
Norfolk, Lant	5
HORNET Utility Unit	2
ALBEMARLE	2
NAS Jacksonville	53
NAS Quonset Point	6
NAS Cape May	2
NAS Pearl Harbor	5
NAS Sitka	1
NAS Pensacola	46
Commander, Aircraft Battle Force (Flag)	1
NAS Roosevelt Base	1
Patrol Wing Five, Utility Unit	4
WRIGHT	2
CURTISS	2
NAS Anacostia	1
NAF	1
TANGIER	3
HERON Utility Unit	5
NAS Bermuda	1
BISCAYNE	1
Commander, Aircraft Scouting Force (Flag)	2
NRAB Squantum, for HUMBOLDT	1
POCOMOKE	2

Total 151

OS2U-3

WEST VIRGINIA	1
NAS New York (for delivery to fleet)	90
SARATOGA	3
VMO-251	2
NEW YORK	3
MARYLAND	3
INA, Vought	2
San Diego, BatFor	1
Norfolk, Lant	4
TEXAS	3
IDAHO	3
Pearl Harbor, BatFor	17
NAS Jacksonville	42
VS-1D3, New York	12
NAS Corpus Christi	89
PENNSYLVANIA	3

TTS, Atlantic	1
TENNESSEE	3
COLORADO	3
NEW MEXICO	3
CALIFORNIA	2
ARKANSAS	3
WASHINGTON	3
NORTH CAROLINA	3
NAS Pensacola	26
NAF	1
NAS Alameda, BatFor	1
ARIZONA	2
MISSISSIPPI	3
Total	332

O3U-1

NAS Pensacola	33
Total	33

O3U-3

Navairdet, NAF	3
NTS Newport	2
NAS Pensacola	22
NAF (overhaul)	3
NAS Norfolk, Lant	1
Navairdet, Annapolis	3
VJ-3, Base Force	1
Total	35

O3U-6

NAF	3
Pearl Harbor, Base Force	1
VJ-3, Base Force	2
Total	6

CLASS VPB

PBM-1

TTS, Atlantic	6
VP-74	13
NAF	1
Total	20

XPBM-1A

Aircraft Armament Unit, Norfolk	1
Total	1

XPBM-2

NAF	1
Total	1

PBO-1

VP-82	14
TTS, Norfolk	2
NAS Norfolk, Lant	2
Total	18

XPBS-1

Commander, Patrol Wings, Atlantic	1
Total	1

XPBY-1

NAF	1
Total	1

PBY-1

NAS Norfolk, for VJ-4	2
San Diego, Base Force	1
VJ-2, Hawaiian Det.	4
VJ-4, Squantum	3
NAS Seattle	1
NAS Coco Solo	2
NAS Jacksonville	21
NAS Corpus Christi	19
NAS Alameda	1
Total	54

PBY-2

NAS Seattle	2
NAS Corpus Christi	13
NAS Coco Solo	2
VP-51	1
NAS Jacksonville	10
NAS Pensacola	12
NAS Alameda	6
Total	46

PBY-3

VP-21	12
NAS Alameda	2
VP-22	13
NAS Corpus Christi	19
NAS Pearl Harbor, for Scouting Force	2
VP-32	13

NAS Coco Solo	1
NTS Newport	1
	Total 63

PBY-4

Navy Yard, Cavite, for overhaul	2
VP-41	1
Project Baker (Transitional Training Squadron Pacific)	2
VP-101	12
VP-102	14
	Total 31

PBY-5

NAS Seattle, for Scouting Force	1
TTS, Pacific	3
Aircraft Armament Unit, Norfolk	1
VP-23	12
NAF	1
VP-11	12
VP-12	12
VP-14	12
VP-31	11
VP-41	5
VP-42	6
VP-43	6
VP-44	6
VP-51	11
VP-52	12
VP-71	11
VP-72	12
VP-73	13
VP-81	8
VP-24 (new)	6
Norfolk, Lant	3
	Total 164

XPBY-5A

Commander, Patrol Wings, Atlantic	1
	Total 1

PBY-5A

INA, Consolidated (flight test)	6

VP-91	6
Patrol Wing Seven	1
TTS, Pacific	22
VP-83	10
	Total 45

XPB2Y-1

NAS Norfolk, Lant	1
	Total 1

PB2Y-2

NAS Norfolk, Lant	1
TTS, Pacific (VP-13)	4
	Total 5

XPB2Y-3

NAS San Diego (test)	1
	Total 1

P3M-2

NAS Pensacola	3
	Total 3

P2Y-2

NAS Pensacola	21
	Total 21

P2Y-3

NAS Pensacola	20
	Total 20

CLASS VR

RD-3

NAS Pearl Harbor	1
NAS Coco Solo	1
	Total 2

R2D-1

BAD-2, San Diego	1
NAS Pensacola	2
	Total 3

R3D-1

NAS New York	1
NAS San Diego	1
	Total 2

R3D-2

NAS Pearl Harbor, Battle Force	1
VMJ-152	2
VMJ-252	1
Total	4

R4D-2

NAS Pensacola	1
NAS Anacostia	1
Total	2

XR2O-1

NAS Anacostia	1
Total	1

R3O-2

NAS Quonset Point, For Naval Attache, London, England	1
Total	1

XR4O-1

NAS Anacostia	1
Total	1

R5O-1

NAS Anacostia	2
Total	2

R5O-2

NAS Pensacola	1
Total	1

R5O-3

NAS Anacostia	2
Total	2

JO-1

Naval Attache, Rio de Janeiro, Brazil	1
Total	1

JO-2

NAS Anacostia (1 for USMC HQ)	2
VMJ-152	1
VMJ-252	1
Total	4

XJO-3

NAS Norfolk	1
Total	1

CLASS VS

SF-1

NAS Alameda	1
San Diego, BatFor	2
Navairdet, NAF	3
NAS Norfolk	1
NAS San Diego	1
INA, Consolidated	1
INA, Baltimore	1
INA, Vought	1
Total	11

SU-1

NAS Pensacola	16
Total	16

SU-2

BAD-1, Quantico	2
NAS Pensacola	19
Total	21

SU-2 (Reserves)

NRAB Chicago	1
Total	1

SU-3

Patrol Wing Two	1
NAS Pensacola	14
Total	15

SU-4

NAS Cape May	1
NAS Norfolk	1
NAF	10
NAS Seattle	2
Total	14

CLASS VSB

XSBA-1

NACA Langley Field	1
Total	1

XSBC-3

NAF	1
Total	1

SBC-3

NAF (test)	1
NAS Miami	55
NAS Norfolk (for Miami)	2
NAS Norfolk (for Support Force)	2
San Diego, BatFor	6
NAS San Diego	3
Total	69

XSBC-4

BAD-1, Quantico	1
Total	1

SBC-4

NAS Norfolk	3
Aircraft Armament Unit, Norfolk	1
Wing HQ, FMF, San Diego	1
Norfolk, Lant	1
Naval Mission, Lima, Peru	1
Air Detachment, Parris Island	1
BAD-1, Quantico	3
VMO-151	12
BAD-2, San Diego, (overhaul)	4
NAS Corpus Christi	34
San Diego BatFor	7
VB-8, HORNET	19
VS-8, HORNET	20
NAS San Diego	4
ACTG, Norfolk	5
Wing HQ, FMF, Quantico	1
Total	117

SBD-1

SARATOGA	2
San Diego, BatFor	1
VMSB-132	19
VMJ-152	2
NAF	1
BAD-1, Quantico	4
VMSB-232	19
VMJ-252	1
BAD-2, San Diego	1
NAS Norfolk	2

NACA Moffett Field	1
Total	53

SBD-2

VB-6, ENTERPRISE	18
VS-6, ENTERPRISE	10
VS-2, LEXINGTON	2
ENTERPRISE	3
Air Group Commander, ENTERPRISE	1
ACTG, Pacific	5
VMSB-232	3
Air Group Commander, LEXINGTON	1
Pearl Harbor, Battle Force	8
Navairdet, NAS Anacostia	2
Commander, Aircraft Battle Force	2
San Diego BatFor	5
VB-2, LEXINGTON	16
Total	76

SBD-3

San Diego, BatFor	11
VS-2, LEXINGTON	14
VS-6, ENTERPRISE	8
VB-5, YORKTOWN	19
VB-3, SARATOGA	21
ACTU, Pacific	16
Norfolk, Lant	13
Commander, Carrier Division One	1
Pearl Harbor BatFor	9
ENTERPRISE	2
VS-3, SARATOGA	22
Fleet Air Tactical Unit	1
VS-5, YORKTOWN	19
Air Group Commander, YORKTOWN	1
Air Group Commander, SARATOGA	1
FAPU, Norfolk	1
LEXINGTON	1
NAS Anacostia	2
Aircraft Armament Unit, Norfolk	1
ACTG Norfolk	2
Total	162

SBN-1

NAS Anacostia	1
NAF	2
Advanced Carrier Training Group, Atlantic	3
Norfolk, Lant	8
VT-8, HORNET	7
Total	21

XSBU-1

NAS Pensacola	1
Total	1

SBU-1

NAS Corpus Christi	10
NAS Pensacola	49
Total	59

SBU-2

NAF	1
NAS Pensacola	24
INA, P&W	1
Total	26

SB2U-1

Vought-Sikorsky	1
Norfolk, Lant	16
ACTG, Atlantic	3
VS-42, RANGER	9
VS-71, WASP	4
VS-41, RANGER	8
Total	41

SB2U-2

VS-41, RANGER	2
VS-42, RANGER	6
VS-71, WASP	13
VS-72, WASP	18
VF-72, WASP	2
WASP	1
ACTG, Atlantic	3
Norfolk, Lant	7
Total	52

XSB2U-3

NAF	1
Total	1

SB2U-3

BAD-1, Quantico	2
BAD-2, San Diego	2
VMJ-252	1
VMSB-131	23
VMSB-231	24
VMJ-152	1
Total	53

CLASS VSN

SNC-1

NAS Jacksonville	19
NAS Corpus Christi	128
NAF	1
Total	148

SNJ-1

NAS Pensacola	14
Total	14

SNJ-2

NAS Anacostia	15
BAD-1, Quantico	3
Commander, Aircraft Atlantic Fleet	1
Commander, Aircraft Scouting Force	1
NAS Norfolk	1
Commander, Aircraft Battle Force	1
Commander, Carrier Division One	1
Navairdet, NAF	1
NAS Norfolk	1
Naval Attache, Buenos Aires, Argentina	1
NAS Pensacola	19
NAS New York	1
NAS Jacksonville	5
NAS Miami	1
NAS Seattle	1
ACTG, Pacific	2
ACTG, Atlantic	1
NAS San Diego	1
Total	57

SNJ-3

Fleet Tactical Unit	1
NAS Corpus Christi	39
NAS Jacksonville	85
VS-5, YORKTOWN	2
FAPU, Pacific	1
VMF-221	1
NAS Quonset Point	1
NAS Lakehurst	1
BAD-1, Quantico	2
Norfolk, Lant	3
VMO-251	2
NAS Pensacola	29
NAS Miami	95
NAS Norfolk	1
VF-72, WASP	1
NAS Anacostia	5
VMF-111	2
NAS Alameda	1
ACTG, Pacific	8
VMF-121	2
VMF-211	1
ACTG, Atlantic	5
VT-6, ENTERPRISE	2
Commander, Aircraft Atlantic Fleet	1
VF-8, HORNET	2
VF-41, RANGER	2
Total	**295**

SNV-1

NAS Anacostia	1
NAS Corpus Christi	35
NAS Pensacola	35
Total	**171**

ASTORIA	4
NAS Bermuda	1
ERIE	1
Alameda, for BatFor	4
HOUSTON	1
SARATOGA	4
NAS Quonset Point	1
AUGUSTA	3
CHARLESTON	1
CHESTER	2
CHICAGO	1
LOUISVILLE	3
RANGER	2
NOA	1
YORKTOWN	1
MINNEAPOLIS	4
NEW ORLEANS	2
NORTHAPMTON	4
PENSACOLA	4
PORTLAND	3
INDIANAPOLIS	4
SALT LAKE CITY	4
SAN FRANCISCO	2
OMAHA	1
QUINCY	3
LANGLEY	1
CINCINNATI	1
MARBLEHEAD	2
Patrol Wing Two, Utility Unit	1
Navy Yard, Cavite	2
Total	**103**

SOC-1A

VS-201, LONG ISLAND	1
Total	**1**

CLASS VSO

SOC-1

NAS Alameda	5
NAS Anacostia	2
NAS Pensacola	8
Norfolk, Lant	8
San Diego, Scouting Force	3
NAS San Diego	1
Pearl Harbor, for Battle Force	7
NAS Seattle, for BARNEGAT	1

SOC-2

LOUISVILLE	1
SARATOGA	1
Commander, Scouting Force	1
NAS Anacostia	2
NAS Pensacola	1
Norfolk, Lant	4
Pearl Harbor, BatFor	4
Commander, Aircraft Atlantic Fleet	1
NAS Alameda	2

CHESTER	2
NEW ORLEANS	2
PORTLAND	1
QUINCY	1
WICHITA	2
AUGUSTA	1
CHICAGO	3
SAN FRANCISCO	3
NASHVILLE	1
LANGLEY	1
VINCENNES	1
Navy Yard, Cavite	1
Total	36

SOC-3

Alameda, BatFor	5
NAS Norfolk	1
Norfolk, Lant	4
MILWAUKEE	1
BOISE	3
CONCORD	1
ENTERPRISE	2
DETROIT	1
HONOLULU	3
HELENA	3
OMAHA	1
NAS San Juan, P. R.	1
PHILADELPHIA	3
NAS San Diego	1
PHOENIX	4
RALEIGH	2
SAVANNAH	1
ST. LOUIS	3
Pearl Harbor, BatFor	4
TRENTON	2
TUSCALOOSA	1
Commander, Aircraft Atlantic Fleet	1
BROOKLYN	1
WICHITA	1
VINCENNES	3
LEXINGTON	1
HOUSTON	2
Navy Yard, Cavite	3
Total	59

SOC-3A

Norfolk, Lant	1
VS-201, LONG ISLAND	12
ACTG, Norfolk	1
Total	14

XSO3C-1

NAS Anacostia (test)	1
Total	1

SON-1

SARATOGA	3
HONOLULU	1
NAS Anacostia	2
Norfolk, Lant	4
NAS Alameda	2
BROOKLYN	3
BOISE	1
CINCINNATI	1
DETROIT	1
PHILADELPHIA	1
HOUSTON	1
NASHVILLE	3
Pearl Harbor, BatFor	1
HELENA	1
SAVANNAH	3
RICHMOND	2
TUSCALOOSA	3
WASP	1
WICHITA	1
MEMPHIS	1
ST. LOUIS	1
CONCORD	1
Total	38

XSO2U-1

NAF	1
Total	1

CLASS VTB

XTBD-1

NAS Pensacola	1
Total	1

TBD-1

VT-2, LEXINGTON	12
VT-3, SARATOGA	12
VT-4, RANGER	3
VT-5, YORKTOWN	14
VT-6, ENTERPRISE	18
VS-17, WASP	2
VT-8, HORNET	8
Pearl Harbor, BatFor	2
NPG Dahlgren	3
NAF	1

LEXINGTON	2	**TG-1**	
Norfolk, Lant	8		
ACTG, Atlantic	2	NAF	1
San Diego, BatFor	6		—
INA, Bethpage	1	Total	1
ENTERPRISE	4		
NAS San Diego	1	**TG-2**	
	—		
Total	99	NPG Dahlgren	1
		Norfolk (overhaul)	1
TBD-1A		NAF (test)	2
		NAS San Diego	1
NTS Newport	1		—
	—	Total	5
Total	1		
		T4M-1	
XTBF-1			
		NAF (test)	1
NAS Anacostia	1		—
	—	Total	1
Total	1		

NOTE: The above table includes both Navy and Marine Corps aircraft but does not include Coast Guard assignments.

Abbreviations used:

ACTG	Advanced Carrier Training Group.
BAD	Base Air Detachment (One and Two, used by Marine Corps only).
BatFor	Battle Force. Refers to planes being held in the Battle Force Pool.
FAPU	Fleet Air Photographic Unit.
FMF	Fleet Marine Force.
GINA	General Inspector of Naval Aircraft.
INA	Inspector of Naval Aircraft.
Lant	Atlantic. Refers to Atlantic Pool.
NA	Naval Academy, Annapolis, Maryland.
NACA	National Advisory Committee for Aeronautics.
NAF	Naval Aircraft Factory, Philadelphia.
NAS	Naval Air Station.
Navairdet	Naval Air Detachment. Also NAD & Det.
NPG	Naval Proving Ground, Dahlgren, Va.
NRAB	Naval Reserve Air Base.
NTS	Naval Torpedo Station, Newport, R. I.
TTS	Transition Training Squadron, formerly known as Transition Training Unit.

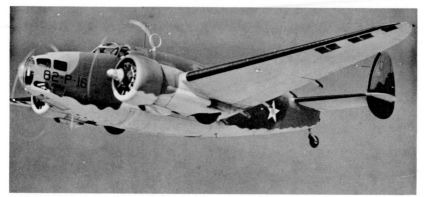

Lockheed PBO-1 *U. S. Navy*
82-P-16 flying out of Argentina. VP-82 sank first enemy subs in March
1942. 20 taken from British Defense Aid in October; note camouflage.

USS WASP CV7 *U. S. Navy*
Commissioned April 25, 1940; shown under way in March 1942 with three
SB2U-2's of VS-71 on deck. Entered war with two VF and two VS units.

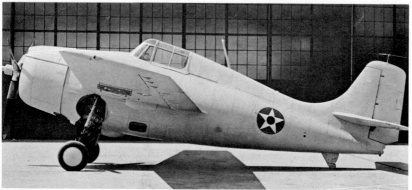

Grumman F4F-3A (3905) *Manufacturer*
95 F4F-3's (3875-3969) were delivered as fighter-bombers with wing
bomb racks (see photo) and designated F4F-3A. Had same engine as -3.

Douglas SBD-3 (4628)   *Peter M. Bowers*
Shown in September 1941 with special light green camouflage, differing from standard all-over grey as seen below and also to the right.

Vought SB2U-2   *Peter M. Bowers*
TACTICAL UNIT ONE, rare marking of March 1941 for three VM aircraft assigned to the Commander Aircraft, Battle Force, Pacific Fleet.

Douglas SBD-3   *Art Sutter*
A second plane from the same unit with markings changed to U. S.
FLEET AIRCRAFT TACTICAL UNIT. An F4F-3, SNJ-3 also assigned.

Grumman J2F-1   *Art Sutter*

Plane Number Five of the SARATOGA's Utility Unit in the new war-paint adopted by Fleet aircraft in mid-1941; serial, model one inch high.

Curtiss SOC-3   *Peter M. Bowers*

9-CS-13 from the late 1939 USS HELENA CL50. 9-CS-14 is ready to follow on the right. Note removal of star from lower left wing.

Curtiss SOC-2 (0405)   *Frank Shertzer*

Both battleship and cruiser squadron markings were changed to white characters on the grey background; all section colors were removed.

Consolidated PBY-5B (RCAF 9726)   *Clayton L. Jansson*
One of 150 boats ordered for Britain on 6-30-41; assigned a Royal
Canadian Air Force serial, returned to US and used at NAS Pensacola.

Vultee SNV-1 (03154)   *Clayton L. Jansson*
175 of the batch of 200 (02983-03182) ordered on 8-28-40 were delivered
by the end of 1941. They duplicated the Army model BT-13A.

Grumman F3F-2 (0995)   *Fred Bamberger*
Rare photo of the bi-plane fighter in warpaint; all had been replaced
by F2A's or F4F's by May 1941. See USMC book for many F3F-2 photos.

Grumman JRF-5   *Howard Levy*
With two-tone camouflage and small national star insignia on nose.
It had a crew of two plus four passengers; photographic capability.

Grumman J2F-5   *U. S. Navy*
Plane No. 3 of the FLEET AIR PHOTOGRAPHIC UNIT ATLANTIC,
a new unit established 5-3-41. FAPU-Pacific was founded at same time.

Consolidated XPB2Y-3 (1638)   *Manufacturer*
Ordered in March 1939, delivered for test in late December 1941. It
was heavier than PB2Y-2 with 2 more guns, but had smaller bomb load.

Brewster F2A-3   *U. S. Navy*
201-S-13 from the Escort Carrier USS LONG ISLAND AVG-1. The only
other Navy combat squadron to operate F2A's in late 1941 was VF-2.

Curtiss SOC-3A   *U. S. Navy*
LCDR Black making 2000th landing aboard LONG ISLAND 4-20-42.
VS-201 became VGS-1. SOC's, SON's with deck hook added, given A suffix.

USS LONG ISLAND AVG-1   *U. S. Navy*
Ex MORMACMAIL converted as first escort carrier; commissioned 6-2-41.
Her single squadron VS-201 operated mixed F2A's and SOC's. 360' deck.

Grumman F4F-4 *U. S. Navy*

F4F-3's with manually operated folding wings, no flotation gear. Oversize star and horizontal tail stripes were instituted 1-5-42.

Douglas SBD-3's *U. S. Navy*

6-S-14 and others from the ENTERPRISE on combat patrol. VS-6 was the first Navy squadron to engage in combat, at Pearl Harbor on 12-7-41.

USS HORNET CV8 *U. S. Navy*

Last carrier commissioned before the war; on 10-20-41. She carried VB-8 SBC-4's, VF-8 F4F-3's, VS-8 SBC-4's, VT-8 SBN-1's and TBD-1's.

APPENDIX A

CHARACTERISTICS AND PERFORMANCE OF U. S. NAVY AIRCRAFT 1921-1941

One of the most difficult problems involved in the preparation of this book has been the compilation of a meaningful and accurate statistical table listing the characteristics and performance for each type of Navy aircraft.

Although all of the material on the following pages has been taken from official records, primarily the annual *Characteristics, Weights and Performance of U. S. Navy Airplanes,* extensive contradictions have arisen. In some cases the dimensions for the same type change from year to year, in other cases the service ceiling may vary as much as ten thousand feet from one year to the next.

It is felt that some of this disparity is the result of actual performance changes over the years as an experimental type enters service and becomes a production model. In other cases, however, it seems likely that it simply reflects an error somewhere along the line in the continuous transcription of such material from one report to another and from one office to another.

It has been necessary, therefore, to make arbitrary decisions for each plane as it is presented here. In some cases as many as seven different listings for the same airplane have been reduced to one reasonable compromise.

It should be remembered when comparing performance figures that the factory publicity released for a new model is usually always above that which the type will record when in service. Often later production planes will have considerable armament and military equipment added during successive years so that it is not unlikely that the performance for a given type may actually be less than when it was first tested.

On the other hand, with the advent of larger engines with more horse power, many service models will have their performance increased considerably by the installation of a new engine.

A word of caution is necessary in regard to engine dash numbers. These were first assigned for military use in 1932, replacing the earlier letters, and it is a popular misconception that the higher the dash number for a given engine, the higher the horse power. This is not true, and the dash number of an engine is not an indication of its performance. These numbers refer to modifications, parts changes, etc., and correspond to the change in model designation of an airplane. Navy engines were assigned digits ending in even numbers from 0 through 8; Army Air Corps engines ended in odd numbers. Starting in late 1941 there were some exceptions to this rule when airplanes such as the SNV-1 were bought on Army contracts and then delivered to the Navy. Such types soon had a new engine model, the R-985-*AN*-1, for joint Army-Navy use.

For the CS-1, CS-2, CS-3, SC-1, SC-2, SC-6, SC-7 and T3M-1 the span given is for the lower wing which was the longest.

MODEL	ENGINE	H.P.	GROSS WEIGHT	MAX. SPEED	SERVICE CEILING	SPAN	LENGTH	HEIGHT	
AR-1	Le Rhone	80	1380	82	11000	34'7	22'2	11'1	
AS-2	Hispano-Suiza	300	3597	116.5	16000	37'6	30'6	10'8	Float
XB-1A	Hispano-Suiza	300	2910	114	21000	39'4	25'5	9'9	
XBFB-1	P&W R-1535-44	625	3705	189.1	20600	28'6	22'2	10'6	
XBFC-1	Wright R-1510-98	600	4368	203	23800	31'6	23'1	10'0	
BFC-2	Wright R-1820-78	700	4601	198.1	21200	31'6	25'0	10'7	Bomber
BFC-2	Wright R-1820-78	700	4083	205.0	22800	31'6	25'0	10'7	Fighter
XBF2C-1	Wright R-1820-80	700	4495	229	26000	31'6	23'0	10'7	
BF2C-1	Wright R-1820-04	700	5089	219.8	22400	31'6	23'0	10'10	Bomber
BF2C-1	Wright R-1820-04	700	4560	228.8	25700	31'6	23'0	10'10	Fighter
XBG-1	P&W R-1535-64	700	5880	193.5	19800	36'0	28'9	11'0	Bomber
BG-1	P&W R-1535-66	700	6279	188.1	19000	36'0	28'9	11'0	Bomber
BG-1	P&W R-1535-66	700	6055	188.3	19400	36'0	28'9	11'0	Scout
XB2G-1	P&W R-1535-66	700	6802	208.3	19300	36'0	28'9	11'1	Bomber
XB2G-1	P&W R-1535-66	700	6394	209.1	20800	36'0	28'9	11'1	Scout
BM-1	P&W R-1690-44	600	6183	144.9	14900	41'0	28'5	12'4	Bomber
BM-1	P&W R-1690-44	600	5634	145.3	16800	41'0	28'5	12'4	Scout
BM-2	P&W R-1690-44	600	6101	145.1	15200	41'0	28'5	12'4	Bomber
BM-2	P&W R-1690-44	600	5551	145.5	17200	41'0	28'5	12'4	Scout
XBN-1	Wright R-1820E	525	6730	123	13500	46'0	32'7	11'7	
BR-1	Wright H-3	390	2056	188.5	24600	28'1	21'5	6'11	
BR-2	Wright H-3	390	2026	177.1	24500	30'1	21'5	6'11	
BS-1	Wright E-2	220	2300	120.2	17200	32'0	26'10	10'10	Boat
XBT-1	P&W XR-1535-64	700	6192	213.2	25000	41'6	31'3	12'3	Bomber
XBT-1	P&W XR-1535-64	700	5636	223.2	27700	41'6	31'3	12'3	Scout
BT-1	P&W R-1535-94	750	6978	214.7	23300	41'6	31'8	13'0	
XBT-2	Wright XR-1820-32	800	7348	256.1	28100	41'6	31'9	12'10	
XBY-1	Wright R-1820E	575	6477	175.5	17100	50'0	33'8	12'4	

MODEL	ENGINE	H.P.	GROSS WEIGHT	MAX. SPEED	SERVICE CEILING	SPAN	LENGTH	HEIGHT	
XB2Y-1	P&W R-1535-82	700	6394	197.9	19400	36' 0	28' 9	11' 1	
XB2Y-2	P&W XR-1535-64	700	6255	206	22800	36' 6	27' 11	10' 10	Bomber
XB2Y-2	P&W XR-1535-64	700	5927	206.6	23900	36' 6	27' 11	10' 10	Scout
C-1F	Curtiss OXX	100	2395	72.7	6400	43' 10	27' 2	12' 9	Float
CR-1	Curtiss D-12	400	2095	185	24000	22' 8	21' 1	8' 11	
CR-3	Curtiss D-12	450	2593	193.7	23400	22' 8	25' 0	10' 8	
CS-1	Wright T-2	525	8668	100.2	6900	56' 6	40' 3	16' 0	Float
CS-1	Wright T-2	525	7934	101.5	9000	56' 6	38' 6	15' 2	
CS-2	Wright T-3	585	11333	102.5	2020	56' 6	40' 3	16' 0	Float
CS-2	Wright T-3	585	10361	104.5	4670	56' 6	38' 6	15' 2	
CT-1	2 Curtiss D-12	350	11208	107	5200	65' 0	52' 0	15' 5	
DH.4B	Liberty 12	400	3876	123.7	15800	42' 5	30' 1	10' 6	
DT-1	Liberty 12	400	6182	105	8700	50' 0	37' 8	15' 1	Float
DT-2	Liberty 12	400	7293	99	7400	50' 0	37' 8	15' 1	Float
DT-2	Liberty 12	400	6502	101	7800	50' 0	34' 1	13' 7	
DT-4	Wright T-2	525	6989	108	11075	50' 0	34' 5	13' 5	
DT-6	Wright P-1	400	6439	102	9500	50' 0	34' 1	13' 7	
E-1	Le Rhone	89	1144	100	13500	24' 0	18' 10	7' 10	
EM-1	Hispano-Suiza	300	4539	90	14500	39' 8	33' 9	12' 1	
EM-2	Liberty 12	400	3916	111	19300	39' 8	28' 6	10' 9	
EO-1	Liberty 12	400	4620	104	9200	39' 8	32' 10	13' 4	
F Boat	Curtiss OXX	100	2460	64	3500	45' 1	27' 10	11' 4	Float
F-5L	2 Liberty 12A	420	13256	89.7	5500	103' 9	49' 3	18'9	
XFA-1	P&W R-1340C	450	2508	170.2	20200	25' 6	22' 2	9' 3	
XF2A-1	Wright XR-1820-22	850	4832	280.1	29800	35' 0	25' 6	11' 9	
F2A-1	Wright R-1820-34	950	5043	301	32500	35' 0	26' 0	11'11	
XF2A-2	Wright XR-1820-40	1200	5397	325.2	35000	35' 0	25' 8	13' 0	
F2A-2	Wright R-1820-40	1200	5942	323	34000	35' 0	25' 7	12' 0	Float

MODEL	ENGINE	H.P.	GROSS WEIGHT	MAX. SPEED	SERVICE CEILING	SPAN	LENGTH	HEIGHT	
F2A-3	Wright R-1820-40	1200	6321	321.2	33200	35' 0	26' 4	12' 1	
FB-1	Curtiss D-12	400	2949	167	21200	32' 0	23' 6	8' 9	
FB-2	Curtiss D-12	410	3145	164	20350	32' 0	23' 6	8' 9	
FB-3	Packard 1A-1500	510	3204	170	23100	32' 0	22'11	8' 9	
FB-4	Wright P-2	440	2817	160	22500	32' 0	22' 10	8' 9	
FB-5	Packard 2A-1500	520	3581	165.1	21000	32' 0	26' 10	10' 2	Float
FB-5	Packard 2A-1500	525	3196	168.6	20200	32' 0	23' 3	9' 11	
XF2B-1	P&W R-1300	425	2670	154.8	21300	30' 1	23' 0	9' 1	
F2B-1	P&W R-1340B	450	2874	158.4	21500	30' 1	22' 11	9' 1	
XF3B-1	P&W R-1300	425	2867	156.7	21300	33' 0	25' 1	9' 2	
F3B-1	P&W R-1340-80	450	2950	156	20900	33' 0	24' 10	10' 1	
XF4B-1	P&W R-1340B	500	2557	169	26900	30' 0	20' 7	9' 3	
F4B-1	P&W R-1340-8	500	2750	176.4	27700	30' 0	20' 1	9' 4	
F4B-2	P&W R-1340-8	500	2799	186	26900	30' 0	20' 1	9' 1	
F4B-3	P&W R-1340-10	500	2918	187	27500	30' 0	20' 5	9' 9	
F4B-4	P&W R-1340-16	550	3124	188.4	25200	30' 0	20' 5	9' 9	
XF5B-1	P&W R-1340D	500	2848	183	27100	30' 6	21' 0	9' 4	
XF6B-1	P&W R-1535-44	625	3705	195	20700	28' 6	22' 2	10' 6	
XF7B-1	P&W XR-1340-30	550	3857	230.8	26900	32' 0	22' 7	10' 10	
F4C-1	Wright J-4	200	1707	125	17400	25' 0	18' 4	8' 9	
F6C-1	Curtiss D-12	400	2802	163.5	21700	31' 6	22' 7	10' 0	
F6C-2	Curtiss D-12	400	2868	159	22700	31' 6	22' 7	10' 7	
F6C-3	Curtiss D-12	400	2963	153.6	20300	31' 6	22' 10	10' 8	
F6C-4	P&W R-1340	410	2785	155	22900	31' 6	22' 6	10' 11	
XF6C-5	P&W R-1690	525	3415	158	19300	31' 6	25' 5	11' 8	Float
XF6C-5	P&W R-1690	525	2960	159.4	21900	31' 6	22' 6	9' 8	
XF7C-1	P&W R-1300	425	2892	155.5	22100	30' 8	20' 11	9' 0	
F7C-1	P&W R-1340B	450	2782	150.7	23350	32' 8	22' 2	10' 4	

MODEL	ENGINE	H.P.	GROSS WEIGHT	MAX. SPEED	SERVICE CEILING	SPAN	LENGTH	HEIGHT	
XF8C-1	P&W R-1300	425	4234	141	14450	38'0	29'5	10'4	Float
XF8C-1	P&W R-1300	425	3934	144.4	17200	38'0	28'0	10'6	
F8C-1	P&W R-1340	432	3918	137.5	17300	32'0	25'11	10'6	Bomber
XF8C-2	P&W R-1340B	450	3819	148	18500	32'8	25'11	10'6	
XF8C-2	P&W R-1340B	450	3353	144.9	20800	32'8	25'11	10'4	
XF8C-3	P&W R-1340	432	4191	136	16450	38'0	28'0	11'8	
F8C-3	P&W R-1340	432	4191	136.2	17100	38'0	27'11	10'10	
F8C-4	P&W R-1340-88	450	3783	137	15000	32'0	25'11	10'2	
F8C-5	P&W R-1340C	450	3957	147.5	18200	32'0	25'11	10'6	
XF8C-6	P&W R-1340C	450	3886	153	20500	32'0	25'11	11'0	
XF8C-7	Wright R-1820-64	575	4274	179	20800	32'0	26'0	10'3	
XF8C-8	Wright R-1820E	575	4554	174.1	20000	25'6	19'9	7'1	
XF9C-1	Wright R-975C	400	2357	177	24200	25'6	20'1	10'11	
XF9C-2	Wright R-975-22	400	2776	176.5	19200	25'6	20'1	10'11	
F9C-2	Wright R-975-22	420	2784	172.8	19200	31'6	23'1	10'0	
XF11C-1	Wright R-1510-98	600	4368	203	23800	31'6	25'0	10'7	
XF11C-2	Wright R-1820-78	700	4132	202.3	25200	31'6	25'0	10'7	
F11C-2	Wright R-1820-78	700	4120	205.1	24300	31'6	25'0	10'7	
XF11C-3	Wright R-1820-80	700	4495	229	26000	31'6	23'0	12'11	
XF12C-1	Wright R-1510-92	625	5461	217	22500	41'6	29'1	12'9	
XF13C-1	Wright XR-1510-94	600	4409	235.7	23800	35'0	25'8	12'9	Monoplane
XF13C-2	Wright XR-1510-94	600	4352	218	23900	35'0	25'8	12'0	Biplane
XF13C-3	Wright XR-1510-12	700	4721	232.3	24100	35'0	26'3	11'1	Monoplane
XFD-1	P&W XR-1535-64	700	5000	200.4	22000	31'6	25'4	11'1	Bomber
XFD-1	P&W XR-1535-64	700	4745	204.2	23700	31'6	25'4	9'8	Fighter
XFF-1	Wright R-1820E	600	3933	195	23600	34'6	24'6	11'1	
FF-1	Wright R-1820-78	700	4677	207.4	22100	34'6	24'6	11'1	
FF-2	Wright R-1820-78	700	4828	206.8	21100	34'6	24'6		

MODEL	ENGINE	H.P.	GROSS WEIGHT	MAX. SPEED	SERVICE CEILING	SPAN	LENGTH	HEIGHT	
XF2F-1	P&W XR-1535-44	625	3490	229	29800	28' 6	21' 1	8' 6	
F2F-1	P&W R-1535-72	650	3847	230.8	27100	28' 6	21' 5	10' 6	Fighter
XF3F-1	P&W R-1535-72	650	4079	225	29500	32' 0	22' 0	10' 6	Bomber
XF3F-1	P&W R-1535-72	650	4327	220	28000	32' 0	22' 0	10' 6	
F3F-1	P&W R-1535-84	650	4170	230.8	28400	32' 0	23' 3	10' 6	
F3F-2	Wright R-1820-22	850	4453	254.9	30900	32' 0	23' 0	10' 6	
XF3F-3	Wright R-1820-22	950	4495	267	33700	32' 0	23' 2	10' 6	
F3F-3	Wright R-1820-22	950	4535	264	33200	32' 0	23' 2	10' 6	
XF4F-1	Wright XR-1670-22	800	4594	264	29400	27' 0	23' 3	10' 10	Biplane
XF4F-1	P&W XR-1830-92	800	4631	258.2	27400	27' 0	23' 3	10' 10	Biplane
XF4F-2	P&W R-1830-66	900	5414	282.6	27400	34' 0	26' 5	11' 0	
XF4F-3	P&W R-1830-76	1200	5990	334	33800	38' 0	28' 0	11' 8	
F4F-3	P&W R-1830-76	1200	6206	350	33400	38' 0	28' 9	11' 11	
F4F-4	P&W R-1830-86	1200	7406	318	34900	38' 0	28' 9	11' 10	
XF4F-5	Wright R-1820-40	1200	6134	312	34000	38' 0	28' 9	11' 10	
XF5F-1	2 Wright XR-1820-40/42	1200	8671	350	32000	40' 0	27' 0	11' 4	
XFG-1	P&W R-1340C	425	2938	155.5	18700	28' 9	27' 3	9' 10	
XF2G-1	P&W R-1340D	400	8620			69' 8	46' 0		Float
XFH-1	P&W R-1340B	450	2518	152.6	25300	32' 0	22' 6	11' 0	
XFJ-1	P&W R-1340C	450	2835	172	23800	28' 0	19' 11	8' 4	
XFJ-2	P&W R-1340-92	500	2847	193	24700	28' 0	20' 10	9' 10	
XF2J-1	Wright R-1510-92	625	4539	193	21500	36' 0	28' 10		
XF3J-1	Wright XR-1510-26	625	4016	209.3	24500	29' 0	22' 11	10' 9	Fighter
XF3J-1	Wright XR-1510-26	625	4264	204.3	23000	29' 0	22' 11	10' 9	Bomber
XFL-1 Bell	Allison XV-1710-6	1150	6244	339	31900	35' 0	29' 9	11' 5	
XFN-1	Wright R-1820-22	950	5231	267	30700	36' 0	25' 2	9' 1	
FT-1 Fkr.	Liberty	450	3142	153.1		32' 0			Float
XFT-1	Wright XR-1510-26	625	3749	235	27000	32' 0	21' 1	9' 5	Fighter

MODEL	ENGINE	H.P.	GROSS WEIGHT	MAX. SPEED	SERVICE CEILING	SPAN	LENGTH	HEIGHT	
XFT-1	Wright XR-1510-26	625	3996	227.8	25600	32' 0	21' 1	9' 5	Bomber
XFT-2	P&W R-1535-72	650	3643	244	27500	32' 0	21' 1	9' 5	Fighter
XFT-2	P&W R-1535-72	650	3890	236.2	25600	32' 0	21' 1	9' 5	Bomber
FU-1	Wright R-790	220	2774	122	26500	34' 4	28' 4	10' 2	Float
FU-1	Wright R-790	220	2409	125	29300	34' 4	24' 4	8' 10	
FU-2	Wright R-790	220				34' 4	24' 4	8' 10	
XF2U-1	P&W R-1340C	450	3886	146.1	18700	36' 0	27' 0	10' 0	
XF3U-1	P&W R-1535-64	700	4616	214	24600	31' 6	26' 6	10' 11	
XF4U-1	P&W XR-2800-2	1800	8758	354	35200	41' 0	31' 11	15' 2	
F2W-1	Wright T-3	780	2858	247.7	36300	22' 6	21' 4	7' 11	
F3W-1	P&W R-1300	375	2128	162	33000	27' 4	22' 0	8' 6	
XF3W-1	P&W R-1340B	450	2180	161.4	33400	27' 4	22' 1	8' 6	
GB-1	P&W R-985-48	400	4250	189	21800	32' 0	26' 0	10' 7	
GB-2	P&W R-985-50	450	4250	199	21800	32' 0	26' 0	10' 7	
GH-1	P&W R-985-AN-6	400	4350	183	21700	38' 0	26' 2	11' 9	
GK-1	Warner R-500-4	145	2550	127	12000	36' 4	23' 9	8' 0	
H-16	2 Liberty 12	400	10900	95	9950	95' 0	46' 1	17' 8	
H-16-2	2 Liberty 12	330	11875	93.5	7400	109' 7	46' 1	17' 8	
HA-2	Liberty	360	3907	118	18000	42' 0	30' 9	11' 5	Float
XHL-1	P&W R-1690	525	5641	124	10000	46' 10	34' 9	12' 9	
HN-1	Wright E-2	180	2626	114.1	13700	33' 0	28' 6	10' 7	Float
HN-2	Lawrence J-1	200	2152	104.5	18150	33' 0	25' 5	9' 8	
HO-1	Wright E-2	180	2316	102	14800	33' 0	26' 3	9' 4	
HPS-1	Bentley BR-2	300	1885	120	16500	29' 3	21' 5	9' 7	
HS-1L	Liberty 12	360	5910	87	2500	62' 1	38' 6	14' 7	
HS-2L	Liberty 12	360	6432	82.5	5200	74' 1	39' 0	14' 7	
HS-3	Liberty 12	360	6432	89	6500	75' 6	38' 7	14' 7	
XJA-1	P&W R-1340B	450	5140	133.5	16900	50' 7	36' 7	11' 0	

MODEL	ENGINE	H.P.	GROSS WEIGHT	MAX. SPEED	SERVICE CEILING	SPAN	LENGTH	HEIGHT	
JB-1	Wright R-975-26	420	3888	204.5	22600	32' 0	24' 8	10' 4	
JE-1	P&W R-1340-27	570	5595	185	24000	50' 6	28' 6	13' 5	
XJF-1	P&W R-1830	700	4831	164	21500	39' 0	32' 7		
JF-1	P&W R-1830-62	700	5399	168.4	18000	39' 0	33' 0	14' 6	
JF-3	Wright R-1820-08	750	5591	174.9	16600	39' 0	33' 0	14' 6	
J2F-1	Wright R-1820-08	750	5902	173.0	16400	39' 0	34' 0	14' 6	
J2F-2	Wright R-1820-30	750	6180	168.5	17500	39' 0	34' 0	14' 6	
J2F-3	Wright R-1820-30	750	6279	179	21600	39' 0	34' 0	14' 6	
J2F-4	Wright R-1820-30	750	6311	179	20800	39' 0	34' 0	14' 6	
J2F-5	Wright R-1820-50	850	6711	188	27000	39' 0	34' 0	15' 1	
XJ3F-1	P&W R-985-48	400	8000	187	21300	49' 0	38' 6	16' 2	
JH-1	S-H XL-395-2	150	2150	130	18500	40' 0	26' 11	7' 11	
JK-1	Wright XR-760-6	320	4000	167.5	19500	39' 6	30' 0	12' 0	
JL-6	B.M.W.	185	3644	101	16600	48' 7	31' 7	19' 9	Float
JN	Hispano-Suiza	150	2165	93	15000	43' 7	27' 1	9' 11	
JN-4	Hispano-Suiza	150	2017	93	18000	43' 7	27' 1	9' 11	
JN-4H	Hispano-Suiza	150	2145	93	15000	43' 7	27' 1	9' 11	
JN-6H	Hispano-Suiza	150	2687	79	5700	43' 7	26' 11	9' 10	
JO-1	2 P&W R-985-48	400	8400	217	23500	49' 6	36' 4	13' 7	
JO-2	2 P&W R-985-48	400	8400	217	23500	49' 6	36' 4	13' 7	
XJO-3	2 P&W R-985-48	450	8650	176	19400	49' 6	36' 4	13' 10	
XJQ-1	Wright R-790	220	3648	114.8	12200	44' 0	30' 11	11' 2	
XJQ-2	P&W R-1340C	450	5423	134					
XJ2Q-1	P&W R-1340C	450	5325	134	14900	50' 0	32' 10	9' 4	
XJR-1	2 Wright R-790, 1 P&W R-1340B	200 450	10700	116.1	14500	68' 0	49' 10	18' 10	
JR-2	3 Wright R-790A	300	10441	130.2	17000	74' 0	49' 10	12' 8	
JR-3	3 P&W R-1340C	450	12686	135.2	18600	77' 10	49' 10	13' 6	

MODEL	ENGINE	H.P.	GROSS WEIGHT	MAX. SPEED	SERVICE CEILING	SPAN	LENGTH	HEIGHT	
JRB-1	2 P&W R-985-50	400	7850	210	24900	47' 8	34' 3	9' 5	
JRB-2	2 P&W R-985-AN-4	450	7850	213	24900	47' 8	34' 3	9' 5	
JRF-1	2 P&W R-985-AN-6	450	8000	192	21300	49' 0	38' 6	16' 2	
JRF-1A	2 P&W R-985-48	400	8000	187	21300	49' 0	38' 6	16' 2	
JRF-4	2 P&W R-985-50	450	8000	192	21300	49' 0	38' 6	16' 2	
JRF-5	2 P&W R-985-AN-6	450	8000	192	21300	49' 0	38' 6	16' 2	
JRS-1	2 P&W R-1690-52	750	19096	189.6	20700	86' 0	51' 1	20' 2	
XJW-1	Continental R-670-98	210	2355	128.5	14800	29' 6	20' 8		Float
LS-1	Hispano-Suiza	300	2530	122	15500	34' 10	28' 8	10' 5	
M-80	Hispano-Suiza	300	2068	145	22000	32' 9	24' 0	6' 7	
M-81	Hispano-Suiza	300	2742	125	13750	37' 10	24' 2	6' 10	
MB-3	Hispano-Suiza	300	1818	152	23700	26' 0	20' 0	8' 6	
MB-7	Hispano-Suiza	400	2000	180	25000	24' 0	18' 6	7' 3	
MBT	2 Liberty 12	400	10250	110	8400	71' 5	46' 4	14' 0	
MF	Curtiss OXX	100	2488	69	3500	49' 9	28' 10	10' 7	
MO-1	Curtiss D-12	350	4642	104.5	10600	53' 1	38' 1	12' 2	
M2O-1	Curtiss D-12	350	4173	104.1	11750	43' 6	31' 10	12' 4	
MS-1	Lawrence L-4	60	1007	100	8500	18' 0	18' 1	8' 0	Float
MT-1	2 Liberty 12	400	12076	105	8500	71' 5	46' 6	15' 1	
N-1	Liberty	360	5900	94	7800	51' 0	37' 7	15' 4	Float
N-9	Hispano-Suiza	150	2750	74	6600	53' 4	30' 10	10' 1	Float
N-9H	Hispano-Suiza	150	2799	80	9850	53' 3	30' 10	10' 8	Float
NB-1	Wright J-4	200	2569	99.4	15500	36' 10	25' 5	10' 9	
NB-2	Wright E-4	180	3031	96.2	9775	36' 10	28' 9	11' 8	
XN2B-1	Caminez	130	2221	103.9	12100	35' 0	25' 8	9' 10	
XN2B-1	Wright R-540	165	2246	113	13350	35' 0	25' 8	9' 10	
NC	3 Liberty 12	400	23000	85	4500	126' 0	68' 3	24' 5	Float
NC-TA	4 Liberty 12	400	27386	85	4500	126' 0	68' 3	24' 5	

MODEL	ENGINE	H.P.	GROSS WEIGHT	MAX. SPEED	SERVICE CEILING	SPAN	LENGTH	HEIGHT	
XN2C-1	Wright J-5A	200	2599	102	13500	39'0	26'10	10'8	
N2C-1	Wright R-790-8	200	2832	108.7	15100	39'1	27'4	10'11	
N2C-2	Wright R-760-94	240	2860	116.2	17800	39'1	27'4	10'8	
NJ-1	P&W R-1340-6	500	4441	167	24900	42'0	27'2	13'3	
NK-1	Wright R-790A	220	2950	114.8	13200	37'0	28'7	12'1	Float
NK-1	Wright R-790-8	220	2658	109.9	15600	37'0	27'0	10'3	
NM-1	Packard	325	4190	108	14300	42'0	31'0	13'6	
N2N-1	Lawrence J-1	200	2331	106.4	16900	33'8	26'11	10'2	Float
XN3N-1	Wright R-790-8	220	2661	122.3	14500	34'0	24'5	10'6	
N3N-1	Wright R-790-8	220	2850	114.1	11500	34'0	28'4	13'4	Float
XN3N-2	Wright R-760-96	240	2649	126	15500	34'0	24'10	11'10	
N3N-3	Wright R-760-2	235	2792	126.1	15200	34'0	25'6	10'10	
XN5N-1	Wright R-760-6	350	3286	137.3	17000	42'0	30'5	11'9	
NO-1	Curtiss D-12	350	4378	104.3	13900	43'6	37'7	12'6	
NO-2	Packard 1A-1500	425	4467	111	15650	43'6	30'0	12'6	
NP-1	Lycoming R-680-8	220	3006	108	9700	33'9	24'3	10'5	
NR-1	Kinner R-440-3	132	1825	115	10100	30'1	22'5	6'10	
NS-1	Wright R-790-8	220	2699	118.2	12200	32'2	25'1	9'7	
N2S-1	Continental R-670-4	220	2709	125	13400	32'2	25'0	9'10	
N2S-2	Lycoming R-680-8	220	2725	125	13400	32'2	25'0	9'10	
N2S-3	Continental R-670-4	220	2709	125	13400	32'2	25'0	9'10	
NT-1	Kinner K-5	115	1799	98.5	10800	30'0	24'7	9'7	
NW-2	Wright T-2	650	4448	176.5	21900	27'11	28'4	11'3	Float
NY-1	Wright R-790	220	2607	103.5	14400	34'6	27'9	9'8	
NY-1	Wright R-790	220	2746	101	9300	34'6	31'0	11'9	Float
NY-2	Wright R-790	220	2627	98	15200	40'0	27'9	9'10	
NY-2	Wright R-790	220	2934	95.2	12300	40'0	31'0	11'10	Float
NY-3	Wright R-760-94	240	2599	106.7	15150	40'0	31'0	10'10	Float

MODEL	ENGINE	H.P.	GROSS WEIGHT	MAX. SPEED	SERVICE CEILING	SPAN	LENGTH	HEIGHT	
NY-3	Wright R-760-94	240	2906	100.7	11750	40' 0	31' 0	11' 10	Float
XN2Y-1	Warner Scarab	110	1587	108.6	12900	28' 0	21' 0	7' 10	
N2Y-1	Kinner K-5	115	1637	108.4	11800	28' 0	21' 5	7' 10	
XN3Y-1	Wright R-790	220	2658	96.2	14000	40' 0	27' 10	10' 6	
XN4Y-1	Lycoming R-680-6	200	2544	117.8	13700	31' 6	26' 11		
O2B-1	Liberty 12	400	4214	122.5	14000	42' 5	30' 1	10' 6	
OC-1	P&W R-1340	410	3932	137.5	17300	38' 0	27' 11	11' 8	
OC-2	P&W R-1340	410	4021	137.2	16850	38' 0	27' 11	11' 8	
XOC-3	Curtiss H-1640-1	600	4315	146.1	18850	38' 0	28' 0	10' 10	
O2C-1	P&W R-1340C	450	4127	147.1	16300	32' 0	26' 0	10' 10	
XO2C-2	Wright R-1820-E	575	4274	176.6	20800	32' 0	26' 0	10' 3	
O2C-2	Wright R-1820-E	575	4554	174.1	20000	32' 0	26' 0	10' 3	
XO3C-1	P&W R-1340-12	550	5177	162.2	16500	36' 0	30' 3		
OD-1	Packard 1A-1500	500	4253	150	21200	39' 8	28' 8	11' 2	
OD-1	Liberty 12	400	4253	137.2	16900	39' 8	28' 8	11' 2	
XOJ-1	Wright R-975A	300	3241	128.9	15500	34' 0	30' 9	9' 10	Float
XOJ-1	P&W R-985-A	400	3160	153.6	20900	33' 8	25' 8	10' 10	
OJ-2	P&W R-985-A	400	3629	151.3	17400	33' 8	25' 8	10' 10	
XOK-1	Wright R-975A	300	3297	125	14200	34' 8	28' 9	11' 4	Float
XOK-1	Wright R-975C	400	3176	143	22500	34' 8	24' 10	9' 9	
OL-1	Packard 1A-1500	440	5208	125	12750	45' 0	35' 4	12' 8	
OL-2	Liberty 12	400	5016	121.3	12100	45' 0	33' 10	12' 1	
OL-3	Packard 1A-1500	475	5316	122	13000	45' 0	35' 1	12' 9	
OL-4	Liberty 12	400	5448	117	11000	45' 0	35' 1	12' 9	
OL-6	Packard 2A-1500	475	5350	122	13000	45' 0	35' 4	12' 9	
XOL-7	Packard 2A-1500	475	5623	117.5	9750	45' 8	35' 3	12' 9	
OL-7	Packard 2A-1500	475	5623	117.5	10100	46' 4	36' 1	12' 9	
OL-8	P&W R-1340B	450	4832	121.5	14300	45' 0	34' 9	13' 0	

MODEL	ENGINE	H.P.	GROSS WEIGHT	MAX. SPEED	SERVICE CEILING	SPAN	LENGTH	HEIGHT	
OL-9	P&W R-1340C	450	5125	121.9	14300	45' 0	34' 9	12' 9	
XO2L-1	P&W R-1340C	450	4053	132.2	16200	37' 0	29' 10	11' 7	
XO2L-2	P&W R-1340D1	550	4829	141.8	15600	37' 0	33' 3	13' 5	
XOSN-1	P&W R-1340-36	550	5093	172	18500	36' 0	27' 11	13' 10	45' rotor
XOP-1	Wright R-975	300	2807	123.4	16400	30' 0	23' 1	13' 0	
OP-1	Wright R-975	300	3057	114.5	12000	30' 4	23' 1	13' 2	
XOSS-1	P&W R-1340-36	550	4791	167.7	18500	36' 0	30' 0	13' 0	
O2U-1	P&W R-1340B	450	3893	146.9	18700	34' 6	28' 7	11' 7	Float
O2U-1	P&W R-1340B	450	3635	149.6	18700	34' 6	24' 6	10' 1	
O2U-2	P&W R-1340B	450	3887	147.3	17750	36' 0	28' 7	12' 7	Float
O2U-2	P&W R-1340B	450	3830	147	20100	36' 0	25' 4	11' 0	
O2U-2	P&W R-1340B	450	4060	136.1	15200	36' 0		13' 4	Amphib.
O2U-2	P&W R-1340B	450	3953	137	16900	36' 0	24' 6	10' 7	Bomber
O2U-3	P&W R-1340C	450	3991	135.8	16900	36' 0	28' 10	13' 2	Float
O2U-3	P&W R-1340C	450	3967	137.8	17900	36' 0	25' 1	11' 6	
O2U-3	P&W R-1340C	450	4327	120.2	12700	36' 0	30' 0		Amphib.
O2U-4	P&W R-1340C	450	4004	135.8	16900	36' 0	28' 10	13' 2	Float
O2U-4	P&W R-1340C	450	3995	137.8	17900	36' 0	25' 1	11' 6	
O2U-4	P&W R-1340C	450	4342	120.2	12700	36' 0	30' 0		Amphib.
O2U-4	P&W R-1340C	450	4158	140.6	16100	36' 0	26' 1	11' 6	
O3U-1	P&W R-1340C	450	4135	137.1	15100	36' 0	29' 11	13' 6	Float
O3U-1	P&W R-1340-96	450	4389	131.5	15000	36' 0	30' 3	15' 0	Amphib.
O3U-1	P&W R-1340C	450	4402	164.0	19000	36' 0	27' 3	11' 6	
O3U-3	P&W R-1340D1	550	4600	156.4	16600	36' 0	31' 0	13' 2	Float
O3U-3	P&W R-1340-12	550	4808	149.7	15900	36' 0			Amphib.
O3U-3	P&W R-1340D1	550	4739	164.2	17800	36' 0	27' 3	11' 5	
O3U-6	P&W R-1340-12	550	4917	160.1	16300	36' 0	32' 6	13' 6	Float
O3U-6	P&W R-1340-12	550							
XO4U-1	P&W R-1340D	500	3696	143	21200	37' 0	27' 9	9' 7	

MODEL	ENGINE	H.P.	GROSS WEIGHT	MAX. SPEED	SERVICE CEILING	SPAN	LENGTH	HEIGHT	
XO4U-2	P&W R-1535-64	625	4669	172.1	18750	36' 0		11' 6	
XO5U-1	P&W R-1340-12	550	4921	155.4	15100	36' 0	32' 6		
XOSU-1	P&W R-1340-18	550	5580	149	12300	36' 0	33' 2	12' 7	
XOS2U-1	P&W R-985-4	450	4611	177	20300	36' 0	30' 1	12' 11	
OS2U-1	P&W R-985-48	450	4542	184.2	19500	36' 0	30' 1	12' 11	
OS2U-2	P&W R-985-50	450	4542	182	20000	36' 0	30' 1	12' 11	
OS2U-3	P&W R-985-AN-2	450	4560	183.7	20100	36' 0	30' 1	12' 11	
P	Liberty 12	400	5245	94	10500	62' 0	34' 5	16' 8	Float
PB-1	2 Packard 1A-2500 Grd	800	26822	125	3300	87' 6	59' 4	22' 2	
XPB-2	2 P&W R-1690 Grd	475	24374	112	4470	87' 6	59' 4	20' 10	
PD-1	2 Wright R-1750	575	14837	120.8	11600	72' 10	49' 1	16' 1	
PD-1	2 Wright R-1820-64	575	14988	123	11600	72' 0	49' 2	16' 1	
P2D-1	2 Wright R-1820E	575	12656	129	10000	57' 0	43' 5	15' 3	Float
P2D-1	2 Wright R-1820E	575	11916	130	12100	57' 0	40' 8	13' 9	
XP3D-1	2 P&W R-1830-58	825	21346	160.8	15000	95' 0	69' 10	22' 5	
XP3D-2	2 P&W R-1830-64	850	22772	184.4	19300	95' 0	69' 7	22' 5	
XPH-1	2 Wright R-1750 Grd	500	12845	125.6	14700	72' 10	50' 11	17' 5	
PH-1	2 Wright R-1820-86	620	15447	134.5	11400	72' 0	51' 10	17' 6	
PH-2	2 Wright R-1820F-51	750	15411	145	21000	72' 10	51' 10	17' 10	
PH-3	2 Wright R-1820F-51	750	16152	159	21350	72' 10	51' 10	19' 10	
XP2H-1	4 Curtiss V-1570-54	600	35402	138.8	10900	112' 0	70' 10	25' 6	
XPTBH-2	2 P&W XR-1830-60	800	21397	182.3	16000	79' 4	55' 4	21' 11	Patrol
XPTBH-2	2 P&W XR-1830-60	800	17913	186.2	20400	79' 4	55' 4	21' 11	Torpedo
PK-1	2 Wright R-1820-64	575	16413	120	9700	72' 0	48' 11	16' 9	
PM-1	2 Wright R-1750D	525	15339	117.5	10100	72' 10	49' 5	16' 4	
PM-2	2 Wright R-1820-64	575	16964	115.9	8800	72' 0	49' 0	16' 9	
XP2M-1	3 Wright R-1820-64	575	17185	138.9	16900	100' 0	63' 0	17' 9	
P3M-1	2 P&W R-1340C	450	13991	118	13800	100' 0	61' 9	19' 8	

MODEL	ENGINE	H.P.	GROSS WEIGHT	MAX. SPEED	SERVICE CEILING	SPAN	LENGTH	HEIGHT	
P3M-2	2 P&W R-1690-32	525	17848	114.7	12050	100' 0	61' 9	16' 8	
XPBM-1	2 Wright R-2600-6	1200	37036	221	21900	118' 0	77' 2	21' 2	
PBM-1	2 Wright R-2600-6	1200	41139	197	22400	118' 0	77' 2	21' 2	
XPBM-2	2 Wright R-2600-6	1600	39857	225	22000	118' 0	77' 2	21' 2	
XPB2M-1	4 Wright XR-3350-4	2000	132250	240	18400	200' 0	117' 3	36' 1	
PN-7	2 Wright T-2	525	14203	104.5	9200	72' 10	49' 1	15' 4	
PN-8	2 Wright T-2	525	13928	106	9300	72' 10	49' 2	15' 11	
PN-9	2 Packard 1A-2500	475	19610	114.5	3080	72' 10	49' 2	16' 6	
PN-10	2 Packard 1A-2500	500	18994	114	4500	72' 10	49' 2	16' 8	
PN-11	2 Wright R-1750 Grd	500	17000	128.3	12800	72' 10	53' 6	17' 6	
XPN-11	2 P&W R-1690	525	16870	120	7700	72' 10	53' 6	17' 4	
PN-12	2 Wright R-1750	525	14142	114	10900	72' 10	49' 2	16' 9	
XP4N-1	2 Wright R-1750 Grd	525	16927	119	8000	72' 10	53' 9	17' 6	
XP4N-2	2 Wright R-1750 Grd	525	17145	119	7000	72' 10	53' 9	17' 6	
XPS-1	2 Wright R-790	220	8160	110	9000	71' 0	36' 8	14' 6	
XPS-2	2 P&W R-1340B	450	9885	124.5	19400	71' 8	40' 3	16' 4	
PS-3	2 P&W R-1340C	450	10323	123.5	14800	71' 8	40' 3	13' 10	
XP2S-1	2 P&W R-985A	400	9380	127	13900	56' 0	44' 1	16' 4	
XPBS-1	4 P&W XR-1830-68	900	47455	214.3	21200	124' 0	76' 3	26' 11	Patrol
XPBS-1	4 P&W XR-1830-68	900	45535	214.9	22100	124' 0	76' 3	26' 11	Bomber
PT-1	Liberty 12	400	6798	85	4500	74' 0	34' 5	16' 8	Float
PT-2	Liberty 12	400	7075	92	7250	74' 0	34' 5	16' 8	Float
XPY-1	2 P&W R-1340B Grd	450	13696	118.3	15300	100' 0	61' 9	17' 4	
XP2Y-1	2 Wright R-1820E	575	20047	126	11000	100' 0	61' 9	16' 8	
XP2Y-2	2 Wright R-1820-88	700	20251	135	10800	100' 0	61' 9	17' 3	
P2Y-2	2 Wright R-1820-90	700	20545	138.5	16500	100' 0	61' 9	17' 3	
P2Y-3	2 Wright R-1820-90	700	20613	138.5	16500	100' 0	61' 9	17' 3	Patrol
P2Y-3	2 Wright R-1820-90	700	20842	135.6	15900	100' 0	61' 9	17' 3	Bomber

MODEL	ENGINE	H.P.	GROSS WEIGHT	MAX. SPEED	SERVICE CEILING	SPAN	LENGTH	HEIGHT	
XP3Y-1	2 P&W XR-1830-58	825	19793	169.2	18600	104'0	63'6	18'6	
XPBY-1	2 P&W R-1830-64	850	20226	184.0	24000	104'0	63'6	18'6	
PBY-1	2 P&W R-1830-64	850	20671	183.8	23600	104'0	63'6	18'6	Patrol
PBY-1	2 P&W R-1830-64	850	21041	179.8	23300	104'0	63'6	18'6	Bomber
PBY-2	2 P&W R-1830-64	850	21779	175.5	20900	104'0	67'10	18'6	
PBY-3	2 P&W R-1830-66	900	22078	184.6	23100	104'0	67'10	18'6	
PBY-4	2 P&W R-1830-72	1050	22295	198	25400	104'0	65'2	18'6	
PBY-5	2 P&W R-1830-82	1050	26200	189.7	21600	104'0	63'10	18'11	
XPBY-5A	2 P&W R-1830-72	1050	24817	192	20200	104'0	65'2	18'6	
PBY-5A	2 P&W R-1830-92	1050	33975	179	14700	104'0	65'2	20'2	
XPB2Y-1	4 P&W XR-1830-72	900	49754	226.3	21500	115'0	79'3	27'4	
PB2Y-2	4 P&W R-1830-78	1000	60441	255	24100	115'0	79'0	27'6	
R-6	Curtiss V-2	200	3942	82	7300	57'1	33'5	14'2	Float
R-6L	Liberty 12	400	5440	92	6800	57'1	33'5	14'2	Float
RA-3	3 Wright R-975	300	9090	128.5	17100	63'4	49'1	13'4	
RA-4	3 P&W R-1340C	450	12850	150		79'3	50'7	12'9	
RC-1	2 Wright R-975	300	6115	137.2	16500	54'6	34'10	10'0	
R2C-1	Curtiss D-12A	488	2150	266.6	31800	22'0	19'8	8'1	
R2C-2	Curtiss D-12A	500	2640	226.9	24300	23'0	22'7	10'3	Float
R3C-1	Curtiss V-1440	565	2176	265	26400	22'0	20'0	8'1	
R3C-2	Curtiss V-1440	565	2733	238	21200	22'0	22'7	8'8	Float
R3C-3	Packard 2A-1500 Grd	685				22'0	22'7	8'8	Float
R3C-4	Curtiss V-1500	685				22'0	22'7	8'8	Float
R4C-1	2 Wright R-1820-12	700	17500	181.1	22800	82'0	49'1	20'5	
XRD-1	2 Wright R-975-E	400	8000	144.8	18000	60'0	43'3	14'7	
RD-2	2 P&W R-1340-96	450	9387	153.3	15900	60'0	45'3	15'2	
RD-3	2 P&W R-1340-96	450	9734	149.2	15100	60'0	45'3	15'2	
R2D-1	2 Wright R-1820-12	710	18200	209.6	23200	85'0	61'9	16'3	

MODEL	ENGINE	H.P.	GROSS WEIGHT	MAX. SPEED	SERVICE CEILING	SPAN	LENGTH	HEIGHT	
R3D-1	2 Wright R-1820-44	1000	19582	221	23800	78' 0	62' 2	20' 4	
R4D-1	2 P&W R-1830-82	1050	29000	226	22300	95' 0	64' 5	16' 2	
R4D-2	2 Wright R-1820-G202A	1050				95' 0	64' 5	16' 2	
XRE-1	P&W R-1340C	450	4600	148	17300	46' 4	27' 10		
XRE-2	P&W R-1340D1	500	4706	161	21300	46' 4	27' 10	6' 7	
XRE-3	P&W R-1340-96	450	4710	154.6	15600	46' 4	27' 10		
XRK-1	P&W R-985-38	400	4000	171	18500	39' 8	29' 0	12' 3	
XRO-1	Wright R-1820E	575	5193	208.4	22100	42' 10	27' 6	9' 2	
XR2O-1	2 P&W R-985-48	400	10100	204.6	17700	55'0	38' 7	12' 11	
XR4O-1	2 P&W R-1690-54	850	17500	231	21700	65' 6	44' 4		
XRQ-2	P&W R-1340C	450	5325	134	14900	50' 0	32' 10	9' 4	
XR3Q-1	Lycoming R-680-6	225	3550	133	13200	41' 0	27' 3	11' 8	
RR-4	3 P&W R-1340C	450	13500	152.5	18600	77' 11	50' 4	12' 8	
RR-5	3 P&W R-1340-96	450	14000	147	16200	77' 11	50' 4		
SA-1	Lawrence	55	695	65	18900	27' 8	21' 8	7' 6	
SA-2	Lawrence	55	810	70	15500	30' 2	20' 3	7' 3	
XSBA-1	Wright R-1820-04	700	5351	229.7	26800	39' 0	28' 3	11' 1	Scout
XSBA-1	Wright R-1820-04	700	5587	229.3	25900	39' 0	28' 3	11' 1	Bomber
XSB2A-1	Wright XR-2600-8	1400	10114	314	27100	47' 0	37' 4	15' 9	
SC-1	Wright T-2	525	9025	100	5850	56' 6	40' 3	16' 0	Float
SC-1	Wright T-2	525	8310	101	7950	56' 6	38' 6	15' 2	
SC-2	Wright T-3	540	9323	101	5430	56' 6	41' 9	16' 0	Float
SC-2	Wright T-3	540	8422	102	7470	56' 6	37' 9	14' 8	
XSC-6	Packard 1A-2500	730	8484	113	12400	56' 6	38' 5	15' 2	
XSC-7	Wright T-3 Grd/SC	640	9343	108		56' 6	41' 9	16' 0	Float
XSC-7	Wright T-3 Grd/SC	640	8609	109		56' 6	37' 9	14' 8	
XS2C-1	Wright R-1510-28	625	4822	186	18900	44' 0	31' 3	12' 2	
XSBC-2	Wright XR-1510-12	700	5453	217.0	24900	34' 0	28' 4	12' 7	Scout

MODEL	ENGINE	H.P.	GROSS WEIGHT	MAX. SPEED	SERVICE CEILING	SPAN	LENGTH	HEIGHT	
XSBC-2	Wright XR-1510-12	700	5790	210.3	23000	34' 0	28' 4	12' 7	Bomber
XSBC-3	P&W XR-1535-82	700	5675	221.1	25500	34' 0	28' 4	12' 7	Scout
XSBC-3	P&W XR-1535-82	700	6527	211.1	21700	34' 0	28' 4	12' 7	Bomber
SBC-3	P&W R-1535-94	750	6023	220	23800	34' 0	28' 1	13' 2	
SBC-4	Wright R-1820-34	950	6243	237	27300	34' 0	28' 2	12' 7	
SOC-1	P&W R-1340-18	550	5282	158.8	14500	36' 0		14' 1	Float
SOC-1	P&W R-1340-18	550	5000	162.2	17600	36' 0	26' 10	13' 2	
SOC-2	P&W R-1340-22	550	5146	162.9	16100	36' 0	26' 10	13' 2	
SOC-3	P&W R-1340-22	550	5366	162.9	15600	36' 0	26' 10	13' 2	
XSO2C-1	P&W R-1340-36	550	5479	165.7	13900	36' 0	31' 11	14' 8	
XSO3C-1	Ranger XV-770-4	550	5489	198	18200	38' 0	34' 3	15' 0	
SBD-1	Wright R-1820-32	1000	7943	251	25500	41' 6	31' 9	13' 9	
SBD-2	Wright R-1820-32	1000	9061	252	26000	41' 6	32' 2	13' 7	
SBD-3	Wright R-1820-52	1000	9407	250	27100	41' 6	32' 8	13' 7	
XSE-1	Wright R-1820F	650	5526	171.7	21200	49' 9	29' 11		
XSOE-1	Wright R-1820-84	725	5529	172.8	21400	41' 0	34' 11	15' 10	Float
XSF-1	P&W R-1690C	600	4599	193.1	21600	33' 0	24' 10	11' 2	
SF-1	Wright R-1820-84	725	5073	206.4	23100	34' 6	24' 11	11' 1	
XSF-2	P&W R-1535-72	650	4783	215.0	24100	34' 6	24' 8	10' 11	
XSBF-1	P&W R-1535-72	650	5001	214.3	22900	34' 6	25' 9	11' 3	Scout
XSBF-1	P&W R-1535-72	650	5441	209.4	21900	34' 6	25' 9	11' 3	Bomber
XSG-1	P&W R-985A	400	4218	136.0	14700	35' 0	32' 7	13' 0	
XSL-1	Warner Scarab	110	1512	101	14000	31' 0	27' 2	8' 11	
XSL-2	Menasco B-6	160	1684	116.4	15300	31' 0	27' 2	7' 10	
XS2L-1	P&W R-985A	400	3737	136.6	16900	34' 6	29' 5	14' 3	
SBN-1	Wright R-1820-38	950	5972	260	30500	39' 0	27' 10	10' 11	
XSS-2	P&W R-1340D1	550	4133	158.8	22600	42' 0	32' 0	13' 3	
ST-1	2 Packard V-1237	300	9817	110	10000	60' 0	37' 0	14' 0	Float

MODEL	ENGINE	H.P.	GROSS WEIGHT	MAX. SPEED	SERVICE CEILING	SPAN	LENGTH	HEIGHT	
SU-1	P&W R-1690C	600	4502	170.4	19900	36' 0	26' 3	11' 6	
SU-2	P&W R-1690-40	600	4481	170.7	19500	36' 0	26' 3	11' 6	
SU-3	P&W R-1690-40	600	4522	171.0	19500	36' 0	26' 3	11' 6	
SU-4	P&W R-1690-42	600	4765	167.5	18600	36' 0	27' 11	11' 4	
XSBU-1	P&W R-1535-80	700	5297	208	25300	33' 3	27' 10	11' 11	Bomber
SBU-1	P&W R-1535-80	700	5520	200.9	23700	33' 3	27' 10	11' 11	
SBU-2	P&W R-1535-98	700	5352	203	24900	33' 3	27' 9	11' 11	
XSB2U-1	P&W XR-1535-78	700	5916	229.6	26600	42' 0	33' 2	15' 10	Scout
XSB2U-1	P&W XR-1535-78	700	6706	219.2	23100	42' 0	33' 2	15' 10	Bomber
SB2U-1	P&W R-1535-96	750	6203	249.3	27500	42' 0	33' 11	14' 2	Scout
SB2U-1	P&W R-1535-96	750	6656	241.8	25400	42' 0	33' 11	14' 2	Bomber
SB2U-2	P&W R-1535-96	750	6379	241	27100	42' 0	33' 11	14' 2	
XSB2U-3	P&W R-1535-96	825	6683	246	27000	42' 0	36' 9	16' 1	
SB2U-3	P&W R-1535-02	825	7474	243	23600	42' 0	33' 11	10' 3	
XSB3U-1	P&W R-1535-66	700	5476	215.5	25000	33' 3	27' 10	10' 11	Scout
XSB3U-1	P&W R-1535-66	700	5711	210.9	23600	33' 3	27' 10	10' 11	Bomber
XSO2U-1	Ranger XV-770-4	550	5186	201	22200	38' 2	34' 2	15' 1	
SNV-1	P&W R-985-AN-1	450	4360	166	16500	42' 2	28' 8	12' 4	
SDW-1	Wright T-3	585	10410	105	3600	50' 0	34' 3	13' 7	
TA-1	3 Wright R-790	220	9060	116	12050	63' 4	49' 1	13' 4	
TA-2	2 Wright R-790, 1 P&W R-1340B	220 450	10440	115	16800	72' 10	48' 7	13' 6	
TB-1	Packard 1A-2500	730	10015	121	11750	55' 0	40' 9	14' 4	
T2D-1	2 Wright R-1750	525	11040	124	11400	57' 0	44' 4	16' 11	Float
T2D-1	2 Wright R-1750	525	10523	125	14400	57' 0	42' 0	15' 6	
XT3D-1	P&W R-1860 Grd	575	8049	122	13200	50' 0	35' 4	14' 8	Torpedo
XT3D-1	P&W R-1860 Grd	575	7852	123.1	14000	50' 0	35' 4	14' 8	Bomber
XT3D-2	P&W XR-1830-54	800	8543	142	13800	50' 0	35' 6	14' 0	

MODEL	ENGINE	H.P.	GROSS WEIGHT	MAX. SPEED	SERVICE CEILING	SPAN	LENGTH	HEIGHT	
XTBD-1	P&W XR-1830-60	800	8679	194.1	19000	50' 0	35' 0	14' 2	Torpedo
XTBD-1	P&W XR-1830-60	800	8374	198	20700	50' 0	35' 0	14' 2	Bomber
TBD-1	P&W R-1830-64	850	9251	207.4	19500	50' 0	35' 0	15' 1	
TF	2 Hispano-Suiza	300	8846	107	8000	60' 0	44' 5	17' 0	
TG-1	P&W R-1690	525	8265	108	5500	53' 0	36' 10	15' 9	Float
TG-1	P&W R-1690	525	7836	108	6900	53' 0	34' 8	14' 10	
TG-2	Wright R-1820E Grd	575	8271	128	13500	53' 0	35' 0	15' 2	
TG-2	Wright R-1820E Grd	575	8798	127	11400	53' 0	37' 0	16' 3	
TG-1 NAF	Liberty	200	2780	97	13850	36' 0	30' 0	11' 9	Float
TG-2 NAF	Liberty	200	2800	97	13140	36' 0	30' 0	11' 9	Float
TG-3 NAF	Aeromarine T-6	200	2957	98.5	11925	36' 0	30' 0	11' 8	Float
TG-4 NAF	Aeromarine T-6	200	2750	97	13850	36' 0	30' 0	11' 9	Float
TG-5 NAF	Wright E-4	180	2953	98.5	11050	36' 0	30' 0	11' 9	Float
XTBG-1	P&W XR-1830-60	800	9313	184.7	15600	42' 0	35' 1	15' 1	Torpedo
XTBG-1	P&W XR-1830-60	800	8924	185	16400	42' 0	35' 1	15' 1	Bomber
T3M-1	Wright T-3B	575	9840	107	3500	56' 7	42' 9	16' 0	Float
T3M-1	Wright T-3B	575	9879	108	5700	56' 7	41' 9	15' 1	
T3M-2	Packard 3A-2500	770	10209	107	5950	56' 7	42' 6	15' 11	Float
T3M-2	Packard 3A-2500	770	9503	109.4	7900	56' 7	41' 4	15' 1	
T3M-3	P&W R-1690	525	9081	100	5550	56' 7	42' 6	15' 11	Float
T3M-3	P&W R-1690	525	8304	102	8000	56' 7	41' 4	15' 1	
XT4M-1	P&W R-1690	525	6781	120	12500	53' 0	35' 7	13' 5	
T4M-1	P&W R-1690	525	7897	111	8400	53' 0	37' 8	16' 0	Float
T4M-1	P&W R-1690	525	7387	114	10150	53' 0	35' 7	14' 9	
XT5M-1	P&W R-1690	525	5623	134.1	13250	44' 0	28' 5	12' 4	
XT6M-1	P&W R-1860	575	6841	124	11600	42' 3	33' 8	13' 10	
XTN-1	2 Wright R-1750	525	10413	121.3	11300	57' 0	44' 10	15' 7	Float
XTN-1	2 Wright R-1750	525	9721	122.9	12600	57' 0	44' 10	15' 3	

MODEL	ENGINE	H.P.	GROSS WEIGHT	MAX. SPEED	SERVICE CEILING	SPAN	LENGTH	HEIGHT	
XT2N-1	Wright R-1750	525	5282	143.1	16750	41' 0	27' 9	12' 2	
TR-1	Lawrence J-1	200	1720	127	23100	25' 0	21' 6	9' 0	
TR-3	Wright E-2	180	1656	122	22100	25' 0	21' 6	9' 0	
TR-3A	Wright E-4	275	2129	159	20700	23' 0	26' 0	9' 3	Float
TS-1	Wright J-4	200	2123	122.8	14450	25' 0	24' 10	9' 7	Float
TS-1	Wright J-4	200	1920	125.3	16250	25' 0	22' 1	9' 0	
TS-2	Aeromarine U-8-D	210	2460			25' 0	24' 10	9' 6	Float
TS-3	Wright E-2	180	1667	110.5	22000	25' 0	21' 6	9' 0	
XTBU-1	P&W XR-2800-6	1850	16247	312	27800	57' 2	39' 0	18' 7	
TW-3	Lawrence J-1	220	2466	106	18150	34' 9	30' 7	10' 7	
UF-1	Lawrence J-1	220	1992	131.7	21700	26' 0	20' 1	7' 8	
UO-1	Lawrence J-1	200	2500	122	16550	34' 1	28' 6	9' 11	Float
UO-1	Lawrence J-1	200	2230	122	18200	34' 1	22' 1	8' 7	
UO-5	Wright R-790	220	2904	118		34' 4	28' 4	10' 2	Float
UO-5	Wright R-790	220	2500	120		34' 4	24' 4	8' 10	
VE-7	Wright E-3	180	2175	118.5	19200	34' 1	24' 5	8' 7	
VE-7G	Hispano-Suiza	180	2305	116	15000	34' 1	24' 5	8' 7	
VE-7H	Hispano-Suiza	180	2300	110	14800	34' 1	31' 1	10' 2	Float
VE-7S	Hispano-Suiza	180	2098	118	17500	34' 1	24' 5	8' 7	
VE-7SF	Wright E-2	180	2100	117	15000	34' 1	24' 5	8' 7	
VE-9	Wright E-3	180	2192	118.5	18850	34' 1	24' 2	8' 7	
VE-9H	Wright E-3	180	2328	116.5	14200	34' 1	30' 1	10' 2	Float
WA-1	Wright H-3	325	4296	98		40' 9	35' 0	12' 9	Float
WP-1	Wright H-3	325	2765	142	19400	32' 11	24' 9	9' 4	
WS-1	Wright H-3	325	4118	105.3	13450	40' 9	35' 0	12' 9	Float
XS-1	Lawrence L-4	60	1030	103	7820	18' 0	18' 2	8' 0	Float
XS-2	Kinner 5RA	84	1050	114.5	11300	18' 0	18' 2	8' 0	Float

MODEL	ENGINE	H.P.	GROSS WEIGHT	MAX. SPEED	SERVICE CEILING	SPAN	LENGTH	HEIGHT	
Aeromarine 39-A	Hall-Scott	100	2575	72	7500	47' 0	30' 4	13' 2	Float
Aeromarine 39-B	Curtiss OXX	100	2520	68	7000	47' 0	30' 5	13' 2	Float
Aeromarine 40	Curtiss OXX	100	2578	71	3500	48' 6	28' 11	12' 7	Boat
Blackburn Swift	Napier Lion	450	6000	115	13600	46' 0	35' 6	12' 0	
Bristol Bulldog IIa	Bristol Jupiter VII	515	3264	173	27300	33' 10	24' 10	9' 7	
Caspar U1	Siemens	60	1125	90	6250	23' 7	20' 4	7' 0	Float
Caudron C.620	Renault "Bengali-Six"	220	2970	191.3	23000	34' 1	28' 6	7' 4	
Curtiss 18-T-1	Curtiss D-12	400	3050	160	23000	31' 10	23' 4	9' 10	
Curtiss 18-T-2	Curtiss D-12	400	3572	139	21000	40' 7	28' 3	12' 0	Float
De Havilland XDH-80	D. H. Gipsy III	120	2100	126.3	16800	36' 9	25' 0	6' 10	
Donne-Denhaut	Hispano-Suiza	200	3860	72	6200	53' 7	35' 5	12' 4	
Dornier CS-2	B.M.W.	185	4400	93	7900	55' 10	33' 7	9' 10	Boat
Dornier D-1	B.M.W.	180	1503	122.4	17500	25' 7	21' 0	8' 6	
Dornier "Libelle"	Siemens	80	1652	98		28' 2	23' 6	7' 10	Boat
Fokker C-1	B.M.W.	243	2576	112	17000	37' 10	23' 8	9' 5	
Fokker D-7	Packard	350	2462	115	19750	27' 6	23' 0	9' 3	
Hanriot HD-1	Le Rhone	110	1521	100		28' 6	19' 2		

MODEL	ENGINE	H.P.	GROSS WEIGHT	MAX. SPEED	SERVICE CEILING	SPAN	LENGTH	HEIGHT	
Le Pere	2 Liberty	360	7750	126	22000	54' 6	38' 2	13. 6	
Levi-LePen	Renault	280	5180	82	8000	60' 0	40' 7	12' 8	
Longren	Lawrence	60	1195	87	9050	27' 11	19' 7	7' 8	
Macchi M-16	Anzani	30	572	82.5	8000	19' 8	13' 10	5' 8	Float
J. V. Martin K-4	Lawrence	60	980	82	11400	24' 2	17' 0	7' 1	Float
Messerschmitt Me.108B	Argus As.10C	240	2940	187	21000	34' 5	27' 2	7' 6	
Nieuport 28 C.1	Gnome	165	1625	122	17000	26' 3	20' 4	7' 2	
Parnall N.2a	Bentley BR.2	230	2595	112	14500	29' 6	24' 11	10' 6	
Sopwith 1½ Strutter	Clerget	130	2061	95	8000	33' 6	25' 4	10' 3	
Tellier	Hispano-Suiza	200	3745	75	6200	51' 3	38' 10	12' 0	Boat
Vickers Viking IV	Napier Lion	450	5600	111.2	10400	50' 0	33' 6	15' 1	

APPENDIX B

ASSIGNED SERIAL NUMBER LIST
1917-1941

In addition to being of the utmost historical importance in identifying photographs of old aircraft, the individual serial number is important because it is the only identification by which the life history of an individual Navy plane can be traced. It is for this reason that they have been included wherever known in the photo captions of this book.

While it is true that each plane carried a manufacturers serial number (termed c/n or constructors number by the British) on its required metal nameplate, and that this is the most useful item in historical research dealing with civil aircraft, it is of little or no importance in regard to Navy aircraft as all official records and correspondence uses the Assigned Serial Number.

The terminology of this number has varied over the years. Described as the "Building Number" in the original 1917 orders, it soon became known officially as the "Designating Number," a term used up until 1937. From that time on they were termed "Assigned Serial Numbers." In the post-war years these have become known as "Bureau Numbers," because of their assignment by the Bureau of Aeronautics, but this is a popularization not applicable to the pre-war years.

This number was assigned to the fuselage, or airframe, and was stamped on the nameplate fixed in the cockpit. It was not re-assigned and stayed with the fuselage of the aircraft until it was surveyed. The engine, wings and tail could be, and often were, changed without affecting the serial number, but the Aircraft Log and the aircraft's accountability began and ended with this serial number. It was at first painted in large figures on the side of the fuselage (see page 17). This was soon changed to the pre-war regulation three-inch high characters on both sides of the vertical fin.

Assigned serial numbers that were cancelled in the pre-war years were not re-assigned, although this was done with late World War II numbers. Since serial numbers are arbitrarily assigned when the contract is awarded by the Navy to the manufacturer it is obvious that contract cancellations will leave blocks of numbers essentially unused. This information has been included in the following list, wherever known, but the reader is cautioned against drawing the conclusion that all of the aircraft listed were built and delivered. Production totals cannot be accurately determined from serial number blocks.

The serial number system, as we know it today, began officially with the assignment of Number A-51, indicating the fifty-first aircraft procured by the Navy Department. At least 27 known aircraft had been delivered prior to that time, but official records do not indicate any serial number assignments prior to A-51.

The prefix letter "A" was applied to contract assignments until the end of Fiscal 1930 (OJ-2, A-9204). The first aircraft on the first Fiscal 1931 contract (RR-5, 9205) dropped the A prefix. Several manufacturers had ceased to paint the letter A on the aircraft just prior to this time.

Starting in World War I all types of "air"-craft were assigned serial numbers including LTA (balloons and dirigibles). With the advent of the large rigids they became known as Air*ships,* with a USS (United States Ship) prefix, and had their own serial number system assigned.

Thus the USS SHENANDOAH became ZR-1, the USS LOS ANGELES ZR-2, the USS AKRON ZRS-3 and the USS MACON ZRS-4 (Lighter-than-air, rigid, scout, number four). About July 1930 all LTA types were dropped from the Assigned Serial Number List. Gliders remained on the list throughout the pre-war years and into World War II.

The continued Navy use of blocks of four digits probably resulted from the established standard size for markings, these in turn being caused by the limited space available to paint these numbers on the majority of aircraft once they had been moved from the fuselage to the fin.

It was found necessary in 1940 to adopt a five digit system to avoid duplication. So many aircraft were being ordered and built, as a result of President Roosevelt's production program, that the serial numbers from 7304 to 9999 were not assigned to prevent two aircraft from being in service at the same time with the same number.

Long lasting types, such as the SOC-3's, were in service at the same time that new SB2C-1's were flying. Thus, without the added fifth digit, there would have been an SOC-3 number 1144 and an SB2C-1 number 1144 (01144) in service at the same time. Several aircraft, such as the SNV-1 #03410 on page 318, were delivered in 1941.

It is easy to understand why no one in the 1920's, when the four digit system was progressing, could possibly have foreseen the unbelievable numbers of aircraft that were to come when one stops to realize that we are now approaching the 167,000th Naval serial number assignment.

As an aid to better understanding of the serial system the following brief description of the complex beginning of U. S. Navy aircraft procurement is presented.

In 1911, with the purchase of its first three aircraft, the Navy Department developed a system of designators (model designations) for aircraft which combined the type of airplane with a serial number. It appears certain that the original prefix letters were assigned by the Navy for the pattern of letter assignment shows a degree of control over class and sequence that would not have been possible for an individual manufacturer to instigate.

During the summer of 1917 a new system was devised for assigning serial numbers to individual aircraft, completely independent of any designating system. Included in the May 1917 order establishing the adoption of a National insignia for all types of aircraft, was a directive for the placement of the "building number" (assigned serial number) on each aircraft. This was to be displayed as the letter "A" followed by the serial number, separated by a hyphen. Prior to, and in some cases subsequent to this order, the serial had a suffix A without a hyphen, as for example the Gallaudet D-1 "59A" and the Washington Navy Yard "82A."

The use of the letter A may have been intended to indicate "Aircraft," but it probably was simply to avoid conflict with the accounting systems of other Bureaus. During this period the Aeronautics Section was only a minor segment of the Navy Department.

Although the 1911-1916 aircraft "serial numbers" do not constitute a proper part of this system an understanding of them is necessary in order to follow the historical sequence of events.

Beginning in 1911 with the first procurement from Curtiss the letter A was assigned to Curtiss aircraft, to be followed by a number in sequence for additional purchases, as A-1, A-2, etc. The letter A probably had no other significance apart from its alphabetical position and its logical choice as the beginning of a record system.

Together with the Curtiss order for two aircraft the Navy ordered one Wright machine and assigned the letter B to designate Wright, also to be followed by progressive numbers for additional procurement.

This designating system was simple and efficient and, with the aviation industry at its then existing level, provided for an unlimited number of aircraft to be procured from at least 26 manufacturers if only single designator letters were assigned.

At this time, however, only hydroaeroplanes and landplanes had been contracted for and all of the landplanes had been converted for water operation to advance the utility of naval aircraft. The advent of the flying boat provided a new class of aircraft and with the purchase of the first Curtiss boat the system of assigning chronological procurement numbers to the previously established A for Curtiss would have resulted in the designator A-5 as this was the fifth aircraft purchased from Curtiss.

The assignment of A-5 would, of course, conform to the operating system, but there would have been no method of differentiating between a Curtiss Hydroaeroplane and a Curtiss flying boat as the Navy inventory increased. Thus, in order to clarify the situation, the letter "C" was assigned to Curtiss flying boats, to be followed by the standard practice of a numerical sequence number.

By this time a contract had been placed with a new manufacturer, Burgess, for a flying boat design. Burgess was thus systematically assigned "D."

The latter part of 1913 saw a Curtiss development which established yet another class of aircraft—the amphibian. This machine was actually the converted A-2, and was primarily an experimental development that appears to have had no immediate fleet use. But in order to distinguish the type from other classes the letter "E" was assigned to Curtiss for this variant.

By March 1941 the letter-number designators had progressed to Curtiss A-4, Wright B-3, Curtiss C-5, Burgess D-2 and Curtiss E-1. In review, the following prefix designators had been assigned prior to March 1914:

Curtiss	A, C and E
Wright	B
Burgess and Curtiss	D

This was further broken down to:

Curtiss	Land and Hydro	as A
Wright	Land and Hydro	as B
Curtiss	Flying boats	as C
Burgess and Curtiss	Flying boats	as D
Curtiss	Amphibian	as E

At this time a review of the designating system must have indicated a progression toward confusion as more aircraft were being purchased and an increasing number of companies were proposing more designs which would eventually lead to an increase in classes as new duty types were developed.

In view of this it must have been decided that a complete revision of the system was necessary. It was also found, at this time, that the aircraft system, which itself had been a logical outgrowth of the ship nomenclature system, was beginning to foreshadow a duplication of submarine numbers. Therefore on March 27, 1914, a complete revision was made which established four new classes and five types within the aircraft class as follows:

A   Heavier-than-air
B   Balloons
D   Dirigibles
K   Kite balloons

Within the A Class the following suffix letters were assigned:

B   Flying boats
C   Convertible aeroplanes
H   Hydroaeroplanes
L   Landplanes
X   Amphibians

Under the new system designations were assigned by class, in a numerical sequence within the class. The relationship to the original designators appears to have been made in alphabetical sequence to the original prefix letter assignment, and not in the order of procurement or delivery, as shown by the following table:

HYDRO CLASS	Curtiss A-1	re-assigned as	AH-1
	Curtiss A-3	"	AH-3*
	Curtiss A-4	"	AH-2*
	Wright B-1	"	AH-4
	Wright B-2	"	AH-5
	Wright B-3	"	AH-6
FLYING BOAT CLASS	Curtiss C-1	"	AB-1
	Curtiss C-2	"	AB-2
	Curtiss C-3	"	AB-3
	Curtiss C-4	"	AB-4
	Curtiss C-5	"	AB-5
	Burgess D-1	"	AB-6
	Burgess D-2	"	AB-7
AMPHIBIAN CLASS	Curtiss E-1	"	AX-1

---

* These two aircraft are out of sequence. Although this is probably an original error, it may be an error in transcription through the years.

As may be seen the new system employed two letters and a number, in which the first letter indicated the class of aircraft, the second letter the type within the class, and the number following the order in which aircraft of that type and class were acquired. The latter was not strictly adhered to, as is common with system changes.

The original A-2 had been converted and re-designated as E-1 prior to the new system and is therefore not included in the hydroaeroplane class re-assigments.

Note that prior to the new system all landplanes had been converted to hydroaeroplanes and were designated as such. The revised system made provisions for designating landplanes as "AL," but on the effective date none existed.

It appears that the first procurement subsequent to the March 1914 revision was the Burgess and Curtiss AH-7. With the limited amount of factual information available at this time it appears that the probable sequence of assignment for the first 27 "aeroplanes" in the Navy was as follows:

Curtiss A-1
Curtiss A-2 (E-1)
Wright B-1 (AH-4)

Curtiss A-3 (AH-3)
Wright B-2 (AH-5)
Curtiss A-4 (AH-2)
Curtiss C-1 (AB-1)
Wright B-3 (AH-6)
Burgess and Curtiss D-1 (AB-6)
Curtiss C-2 (AB-2)
Curtiss E-1 (AX-1)
Curtiss C-3 (AB-3)
Curtiss C-4 (AB-4)
Curtiss C-5 (AB-5)
Burgess and Curtiss D-2 (AB-7)
Burgess and Curtiss AH-7
Curtiss AH-8
Curtiss AH-9
Burgess and Curtiss AH-10
Curtiss AH-11
Curtiss AH-12
Curtiss AH-13
Curtiss AH-14
Curtiss AH-15
Curtiss AH-16
Curtiss AH-17
Curtiss AH-18

Three years later this whole system of combination aircraft type and serial number identification was abandoned in favor of the simplified numerical system still in use today. An attempt may have been made to re-assign consecutive serial numbers beginning with the first aircraft purchased, as the Coast Guard did in their 1936 serial revision, but no evidence has been found to support this popular theory.

A-51	Wright Seaplane
A-52	Paul Schmitt Seaplane
A-53	D. W. F. Seaplane (cancelled)
A-54-56	Burgess Seaplane
A-57-58	Thomas Brothers Seaplane
A-59	Gallaudet D-1
A-60-65	Curtiss N-9
A-66-67	Curtiss R-3
A-68-69	Martin Seaplane
A-70-75	Burgess Seaplane
A-76-81	Sturtevant Seaplane
A-82-84	Washington Navy Yard Seaplane (2 cancelled)
A-85-90	Curtiss N-9
A-91	Standard Seaplane
A-92	Standard (cancelled)
A-93	Curtiss JN-TW
A-94-95	Goodyear Kite Balloon
A-96-125	Curtiss N-9
A-126	Farman Seaplane
A-127	Connecticut Aircraft Corp. DN-1 Dirigible
A-128-133	Sturtevant Seaplane
A-134-136	Thomas-Morse SH-4
A-137-141	Standard H-4-H (140-141 cancelled)
A-142-146	Aeromarine Seaplane (145-146 cancelled)
A-147-148	Boeing C Seaplane
A-149-150	Curtiss JN-4
A-151	Goodyear Kite Balloon
A-152	Curtiss H-12
A-153-154	NAS Pensacola Seaplane (154 cancelled)
A-155-156	Burgess HT-B
A-157-159	Curtiss JN-4B
A-160-161	Goodyear Kite Balloon

A-162-197	Curtiss R-6
A-198-200	Curtiss JN-1
A-201-234	Curtiss N-9
A-235-243	Goodyear B Class Dirigible
A-244-248	Goodrich B Class Dirigible
A-249-250	Connecticut Aircraft B Class Dirigible
A-251	Connecticut Aircraft Free Balloon
A-252-275	Connecticut Aircraft Free Balloon (cancelled)
A-276-287	Goodyear Kite Balloon
A-288-290	Wright-Martin Seaplane
A-291-293	Curtiss L-2
A-294-301	Curtiss N-9
A-302-341	Curtiss R-6 (R-6L)
A-342-373	Curtiss N-9
A-374-379	Burgess HT-2T
A-380-385	Burgess U-2
A-386-387	Curtiss F Boat
A-388-389	Curtiss JN-4
A-390-393	Curtiss F Boat
A-394	Sopwith Baby
A-395-406	Thomas-Morse SH-4
A-407	Sopwith Baby
A-408	Curtiss F Boat
A-409-438	Burgess N-9
A-439-441	Aeromarine Seaplane
A-442-444	Loening M-2
A-445-449	Curtiss GS-2
A-450-499	Aeromarine 39-A
A-500-649	Aeromarine 39-B
A-650-699	Boeing C
A-700	Goodyear Kite Balloon
A-701	Goodrich Kite Balloon
A-702-726	Goodyear Kite Balloon
A-727-751	Goodrich Kite Balloon
A-752-756	Thompson F Boat
A-757-762	Thomas-Morse S-5
A-763-764	British Government M Kite Balloon
A-765-783	Curtiss H-12
A-784-799	Curtiss H-16
A-800-815	Curtiss HS-2
A-816-817	French Government P Kite Balloon
A-818-867	Curtiss H-16
A-868	Curtiss GS-2
A-869-872	Sopwith Baby
A-873-994	Curtiss R6L
A-995-997	Curtiss JN-4
A-998	Goodrich Kite Balloon
A-999-1028	Burgess N-9
A-1029	British Government O-SS Dirigible
A-1030-1048	Curtiss H-16
A-1049-1098	Naval Aircraft Factory (NAF) H-16
A-1099-1398	Lowe-Willard-Fowler HS-2 (HS-2L)
A-1399-1478	Standard HS-2 (HS-2L)
A-1479-1548	Standard HS-2 (cancelled)
A-1549-2207	Curtiss HS-2 (HS-2L)
A-2208-2214	Goodyear Kite Balloon
A-2215-2216	Connecticut Aircraft Free Balloon
A-2217-2276	Gallaudet HS-2 (HS-2L)
A-2277	Curtiss Triplane Flying Boat
A-2278	Curtiss HA
A-2279-2281	Curtiss F Boat
A-2282-2284	N.A.F. N-1 (2284 cancelled)
A-2285-2290	Curtiss N-9
A-2291	Curtiss-NAF NC-1
A-2292	Curtiss-NAF NC-2

A-2293	Curtiss-NAF NC-3
A-2294	Curtiss-NAF NC-4
A-2295-2344	Curtiss F Boat
A-2345-2350	Curtiss MF Boat
A-2351-2572	Burgess N-9
A-2573	Burgess N-10
A-2574-2650	Burgess N-9
A-2651-2652	Alexandria F Boat
A-2653-2654	Gallaudet D-4
A-2655-2844	Goodyear Kite Balloon
A-2845-2929	N.A.F. N-1 (cancelled)
A-2930-3020	Goodrich Kite Balloon
A-3021-3204	Balloons (cancelled)
A-3205-3234	Curtiss JN-4H
A-3235-3244	Thomas-Morse S-4B
A-3245-3324	Dayton-Wright DH-4
A-3325-3326	Curtiss 18-T
A-3327	Briggs F Boat
A-3328-3332	American Trans-Oceanic F Boat
A-3333-3362	Canadian Aeroplane F-5L
A-3363-3382	Canadian Aeroplane F-5L (cancelled)
A-3383	Goodrich Kite Balloon
A-3384-3458	Dayton-Wright DH-4
A-3459-3558	N.A.F. H-16
A-3559-4035	N.A.F. F-5L (343 cancelled)
A-4036-4038	N.A.F. F-5L (F-6L) (4038 cancelled)
A-4039-4078	Curtiss H-16
A-4079-4108	Curtiss F Boat
A-4109	Goodyear E-1 Dirigible
A-4110-4111	Curtiss HA
A-4112-4117	Curtiss JN-4B
A-4118-4127	Goodrich C Dirigible
A-4128-4217	Curtiss JN-4HG
A-4218-4227	Standard E-1
A-4228-4229	Loughead HS-2L
A-4230	Tellier Flying Boat
A-4231-4255	Boeing HS-2L
A-4256-4280	Boeing HS-2L (cancelled)
A-4281-4340	Curtiss F-5L
A-4341-4342	N.A.F. N-1
A-4343	Carolina Aircraft Corp. F Boat
A-4344-4346	Carolina Aircraft Corp. F Boat (cancelled)
A-4347	Boeing C-1F
A-4348	Goodyear F Dirigible
A-4349-4402	Curtiss F and MF Boats
A-4403-4449	Curtiss F and MF Boats (cancelled)
A-4450-4454	Goodrich Dirigible
A-4455-5019	Goodyear and Goodrich Dirigibles (cancelled)
A-5020-5021	Goodyear Kite Balloon
A-5022-5023	Goodrich Kite Balloon
A-5024	Alexandria F Boat
A-5025-5028	Goodyear Kite Balloon
A-5029-5039	Goodyear Kite Balloon (5030-5039 cancelled)
A-5040-5089	Aeromarine 40-F
A-5090-5239	Aeromarine 40-F (cancelled)
A-5240	British Government Kite Balloon
A-5241-5242	Italian Government Kite Balloon
A-5243	Sperry Flying Boat
A-5244-5246	Sperry Flying Boat (cancelled)
A-5247-5256	Alexandria F Boat
A-5257	Goodyear B Dirigible
A-5258	Curtiss F Boat
A-5259-5458	Boeing HS-2L (cancelled)
A-5459-5462	Curtiss HS-3
A-5463	Goodyear Kite Balloon

A-5464-5468	Goodyear B Dirigible (5468 cancelled)
A-5469	Loening M-3
A-5470-5471	Curtiss JN-6HG-1
A-5472	French Government AT-1 Dirigible
A-5473-5482	British Government Kite Balloon
A-5483-5562	N.A.F. MF Boat
A-5563	British Government Z-2 Dirigible
A-5564-5569	NAS Miami HS-2L
A-5570-5571	N.A.F. SA-1
A-5572-5573	N.A.F. SA-2
A-5574-5575	Macchi Seaplane
A-5576-5579	N.A.F. TF (5579 cancelled)
A-5580	British Government NS-1 Dirigible
A-5581-5586	Curtiss JN-6HG-1
A-5587	Italian Government O-1 Dirigible
A-5588-5589	Curtiss SE-5
A-5590-5591	N.A.F. HS-3
A-5592-5593	French Government VZ Dirigible
A-5594-5605	Connecticut Aircraft Kite Balloon
A-5606-5607	Loening LS-1
A-5608	Austrian Government KF Flying Boat
A-5609-5611	Austrian Government LB Flying Boat (cancelled)
A-5612-5614	Aeromarine AS-1 (AS-2)
A-5615-5619	NAS Hampton Roads HS-2L (one cancelled)
A-5620-5629	Hanriot Seaplane (to Landplane)
A-5630	Lowe-Willard-Fowler HS-2L
A-5631	Loening M-8
A-5632	N.A.F. NC-5
A-5633	N.A.F. NC-6
A-5634	N.A.F. NC-7
A-5635	N.A.F. NC-8
A-5636	Paul Schmitt Seaplane
A-5637-5646	Loening M-80
A-5647-5649	Tellier TB (one cancelled)
A-5650-5651	Le Pen Seaplane
A-5652-5653	Donne-Denhaut Seaplane
A-5654	Caproni Triplane
A-5655-5656	Sopwith Pup
A-5657	Le Pen Seaplane
A-5658-5659	Sopwith Camel
A-5660	Sopwith 1½ Strutter
A-5661-5680	Lewis and Vought VE-7
A-5681-5700	N.A.F. VE-7G and VE-7GF
A-5701-5710	N.A.F. M-81
A-5711-5712	Martin MBT
A-5713-5720	Martin MT
A-5721-5722	Sopwith Camel
A-5723-5724	Sopwith Camel (cancelled)
A-5725-5728	Sopwith 1½ Strutter
A-5729-5730	Sopwith Camel
A-5731-5733	Sopwith Camel (cancelled)
A-5734-5750	Sopwith 1½ Strutter
A-5751-5752	Parnall Panther
A-5753-5755	Connecticut Aircraft Kite Balloon
A-5756-5760	Connecticut Aircraft Kite Balloon (cancelled)
A-5761-5786	N.A.F. M-81
A-5787	NAS Key West HS-2L
A-5788-5793	Loening M-81S
A-5794-5805	Nieuport 28 C.1
A-5806-5807	Austrian Government K Flying Boat
A-5808	NAS Anacostia HS-2L
A-5809-5814	War Department DH-4B
A-5815-5829	War Department DH-4B (cancelled)
A-5830-5833	War Department JN-6H
A-5834-5839	War Department DH-4B

A-5840-5842	J. V. Martin K-4
A-5843-5848	Fokker D-7
A-5849-5854	Fokker D-7 (cancelled)
A-5855-5858	Thomas-Morse S-4C
A-5859	Curtiss JN-6H
A-5860-5866	Goodyear Free Balloon
A-5867-5869	J. L. Aircraft Corporation JL-6
A-5870-5884	War Department DH-4B
A-5885	N.A.F. NC-9
A-5886	N.A.F. NC-10
A-5887-5889	Fokker C-1
A-5890	Curtiss CT-1
A-5891-5898	Curtiss CT-1 (cancelled)
A-5899-5901	Stout ST-1 (ST-2)
A-5902-5904	Stout ST-1 (cancelled)
A-5905	Elias EM-1
A-5906-5911	Elias EM-2
A-5912-5941	Lewis and Vought VE-7SF
A-5942	N.A.F. VE-7SF
A-5943-5971	N.A.F. VE-7F
A-5972	Goodyear C Dirigible
A-5973	Goodyear H Dirigible
A-5974-5975	Dayton-Wright XB-1A
A-5976-5981	Morane-Saulnier AR-1
A-5982-6001	War Department DH-4B
A-6002-6004	War Department DH-4B (cancelled)
A-6005-6007	Macchi M-16
A-6008-6010	Fokker FT-1 (FT-2)
A-6011-6020	N.A.F. VE-7SF
A-6021-6030	Lewis and Vought VE-7SF
A-6031	Davis-Douglas DT-1
A-6032-6033	Davis-Douglas DT-2
A-6034-6048	N.A.F. PT-1
A-6049-6054	Austrian Government Seaplane
A-6055	Dornier CS-2
A-6056-6057	Blackburn Swift
A-6058	Dornier D-1
A-6059	N.A.F. "Giant Boat" (cancelled)
A-6060-6070	Thomas-Morse MB-3
A-6071	Thomas-Morse MB-7
A-6072	Stout SV-1
A-6073	Vickers Viking IV
A-6074-6076	Connecticut Aircraft Free Balloon
A-6077-6079	Connecticut Aircraft Free Balloon (cancelled)
A-6080	Curtiss CR-1 (CR-3)
A-6081	Curtiss CR-2 (CR-3)
A-6082	Dayton-Wright WA-1
A-6083	Dayton-Wright WS-1
A-6084-6102	Dayton-Wright WA/WD (cancelled)
A-6103-6110	Goodyear Kite Balloon
A-6111-6112	Goodyear J Dirigible
A-6113-6192	N.A.F. DH-4B
A-6193-6246	War Department JN-4H
A-6247	Marine Base Paris Island JN-4H
A-6248-6270	Curtiss TS-1
A-6271-6288	War Department JN-4H
A-6289-6299	N.A.F. BS-1 (cancelled)
A-6300-6304	N.A.F. TS-1
A-6305-6315	Curtiss TS-1
A-6316-6325	N.A.F. JN-4 (cancelled)
A-6326-6343	N.A.F. PT-2
A-6344	N.A.F. TG-1
A-6345	N.A.F. TG-2
A-6346	N.A.F. TG-3
A-6347	N.A.F. TG-4

A-6348	N.A.F. TG-5
A-6349-6351	Huff-Daland HN-1
A-6352-6401	War Department DH-4B1
A-6402-6404	Handley-Page HPS-1 (cancelled)
A-6405-6422	Douglas DT-2
A-6423-6428	N.A.F. DT-4
A-6429	Bee Line BR-1
A-6430	Bee Line BR-2
A-6431-6432	N.A.F. NO-1
A-6433	N.A.F. NO-2
A-6434-6435	Caspar U-1
A-6436-6444	N.A.F. VE-7H
A-6445	N.A.F. Free Balloon
A-6446-6447	N.A.F. TS-2
A-6448	N.A.F. TS-3
A-6449	N.A.F. TS-3 (TR-2)
A-6450-6451	N.A.F. NM-1 (6451 cancelled)
A-6452-6454	Martin M2O-1
A-6455-6460	Martin MO-1
A-6461-6464	Vought VE-9H
A-6465-6481	Vought VE-9
A-6482-6499	Vought UF-1 (UO-1)
A-6500-6505	Curtiss CS-1
A-6506	NAS Coco Solo HS-2L
A-6507-6513	N.A.F. HS-2L
A-6514	N.A.F. DH-4B
A-6515-6520	Cox-Klemin XS-1 (6519 to XS-2)
A-6521-6526	Martin MS-1
A-6527	N.A.F. Free Balloon
A-6528-6542	NAS Pensacola N-9
A-6543-6544	Wright NW-1 (NW-2)
A-6545	Marine Base Port au Prince JN-4H
A-6546	N.A.F. UO-2
A-6547-6551	Vought UO-1
A-6552	Dornier "Libelle"
A-6553-6556	NAS San Diego HS-2L
A-6557-6559	NAS Hampton Roads F-5L
A-6560-6562	Huff-Daland HO-1
A-6563-6580	Douglas DT-2
A-6581	Wright-Douglas DT-6
A-6582	Douglas DT-2
A-6583-6602	Lowe-Willard-Fowler DT-2
A-6603-6615	Vought UO-1
A-6616-6617	N.A.F. PN-7
A-6618-6632	NAS Pensacola N-9
A-6633-6662	Martin MO-1
A-6663	Lowe-Willard-Fowler MO-1
A-6664-6688	Lowe-Willard-Fowler MO-1 (cancelled)
A-6689-6690	Curtiss-Hall F4C-1
A-6691-6692	Curtiss R2C-1 (one to R2C-2)
A-6693-6695	N.A.F. N2N-1
A-6696	Larson JL-6
A-6697	NAS San Diego F-5L
A-6698-6700	Goodyear Free Balloon
A-6701-6703	Huff-Daland HN-2
A-6704-6705	Vought VE-9W (cancelled)
A-6706-6729	Vought UO-1
A-6730	Dayton-Wright TW-3
A-6731-6732	Curtiss CS-2
A-6733-6742	NAS Pensacola N-9
A-6743-6744	Wright F2W-1
A-6745-6747	Longren
A-6748	Wright WP-1
A-6749-6768	Boeing NB-1
A-6769-6798	Boeing NB-2

A-6799	N.A.F. PN-8
A-6800	Martin N2M-1
A-6801-6835	Martin SC-1
A-6836-6857	Boeing NB-1
A-6858-6877	Vought UO-1
A-6878	N.A.F. PN-9
A-6879-6880	Loening OL-1
A-6881	Boeing PB-1 (XPB-1)
A-6882-6883	Boeing OB-1 (cancelled)
A-6884-6893	Boeing FB-1
A-6894-6895	Boeing FB-2
A-6896	Boeing FB-4 (FB-6)
A-6897	Boeing FB-3
A-6898-6927	Boeing O2B-1
A-6928-6967	Martin SC-2
A-6968	Curtiss F6C-1 (F6C-4, XF6C-5)
A-6969	Curtiss F6C-1
A-6970	Curtiss F6C-1 (F6C-3)
A-6971	Curtiss F6C-1
A-6972	Curtiss F6C-1 (F6C-3)
A-6973-6974	Curtiss F6C-1 (F6C-2)
A-6975-6976	Curtiss F6C-1
A-6977	Le Pere
A-6978-6979	Curtiss R3C-1 (R3C-2)
A-6980-6983	Loening OL-2
A-6984-7023	Vought UO-1
A-7024	Boeing TB-1 (XTB-1)
A-7025-7026	Boeing TB-1
A-7027	N.A.F. TN-1 (XTN-1)
A-7028-7029	N.A.F. PN-10
A-7030	Loening OL-2
A-7031-7050	Vought UO-1
A-7051-7053	Douglas T2D-1
A-7054	Curtiss R3C-1 (R3C2, R3C-3, R3C-4)
A-7055-7058	Loening OL-3
A-7059-7064	Loening OL-4
A-7065-7088	Martin T3M-1
A-7089-7090	Boeing FB-3
A-7091-7100	NAS Pensacola N-9
A-7101-7127	Boeing FB-5
A-7128-7135	Curtiss F6C-3
A-7136	Curtiss F6C-3 (XF6C-3)
A-7137-7146	Curtiss F6C-3
A-7147	Curtiss F6C-3 (XF6C-6)
A-7148-7162	Curtiss F6C-3
A-7163-7202	Consolidated NY-1
A-7203-7204	Douglas OD-1
A-7205-7220	Consolidated NY-1
A-7221-7222	Vought O2U-1
A-7223	Wright F3W-1 (XF3W-1)
A-7224-7323	Martin T3M-2
A-7324-7334	Loening OL-6
A-7335	Loening OL-6 (XOL-7)
A-7336-7343	Loening OL-6
A-7344	Loening OL-6 (XOL-8)
A-7345-7350	Loening OL-6
A-7351-7360	Consolidated NY-1
A-7361-7380	Vought UO-3 (FU-1)
A-7381	Air Service Kite Balloon
A-7382	Goodyear TC Dirigible
A-7383-7384	N.A.F. PN-10 (PN-12)
A-7385	Boeing F2B-1
A-7386-7389	Goodyear Free Balloon
A-7390-7392	Goodyear Kite Balloon
A-7393	Curtiss F6C-4 (XF6C-4)

A-7394-7402	Curtiss F6C-4
A-7403	Curtiss F6C-4 (XF6C-7)
A-7404-7423	Curtiss F6C-4
A-7424-7455	Boeing F2B-1
A-7456-7525	Consolidated NY-2
A-7526	Ford XJR-1
A-7527	N.A.F. PN-11
A-7528-7560	Vought O2U-1
A-7561-7563	Atlantic TA-1
A-7564	De Havilland XDH-60
A-7565	Romeo Ro.1
A-7566	Martin T4M-1 (XT4M-1)
A-7567-7586	Vought O2U-1
A-7587-7595	Douglas T2D-1
A-7596-7649	Martin T4M-1
A-7650-7652	Curtiss XN2C-1
A-7653	Curtiss XF7C-1
A-7654-7668	Curtiss F7C-1
A-7669	Curtiss XF8C-3
A-7670	Curtiss F7C-1
A-7671	Curtiss XF8C-1
A-7672	Curtiss XOC-3
A-7673	Curtiss XF8C-2
A-7674	Boeing F3B-1 (XF3B-1)
A-7675-7691	Boeing F3B-1
A-7692	Vought XF2U-1
A-7693-7707	Consolidated NY-2
A-7708-7763	Boeing F3B-1
A-7764-7795	Consolidated NY-2
A-7796-7831	Vought O2U-1
A-7832-7851	Loening OL-8
A-7852-7899	Martin T4M-1
A-7900-7940	Vought O2U-1
A-7941-7943	Keystone XNK-1
A-7944	Eberhardt XFG-1 (XF2G-1)
A-7945-7948	Curtiss F8C-1 (OC-1)
A-7949-7951	Curtiss F8C-3 (OC-2)
A-7952-7969	Curtiss OC-2
A-7970-7977	Consolidated NY-2
A-7978	Fairchild XJQ-1 (XJQ-2, XRQ-2)
A-7979-8003	Douglas PD-1
A-8004	Hall-Aluminum XPH-1
A-8005	Sikorsky XPS-1
A-8006	N.A.F. XPN-11
A-8007-8008	Atlantic TA-2
A-8009	Hall-Aluminum XFH-1
A-8010	Boeing XN2B-1
A-8011	Consolidated XPY-1
A-8012	Atlantic XJA-1
A-8013-8017	Consolidated NY-2
A-8018	Atlantic TA-2
A-8019	Consolidated XN2Y-1
A-8020-8050	Curtiss N2C-1
A-8051	Martin XT5M-1
A-8052	N.A.F. XT2N-1
A-8053-8068	Keystone NK-1
A-8069-8088	Loening OL-8A
A-8089-8090	Sikorsky XPS-2
A-8091-8127	Vought O2U-2
A-8128-8156	Boeing F4B-1
A-8157	Atlantic TA-3 (RA-3)
A-8158-8172	Consolidated NY-2A
A-8173-8182	Consolidated NY-1
A-8183-8192	Consolidated NY-2
A-8193-8272	Vought O2U-3

A-8273-8274	Ford JR-2 (RR-2)
A-8275-8276	Loening XHL-1
A-8277-8281	Meadowcraft Free Balloon
A-8282	Aircraft Development Corp. ZMC-2 Dirigible
A-8283	Consolidated XN3Y-1
A-8284-8287	Sikorsky PS-3 (RS-3)
A-8288	Berliner-Joyce XFJ-1 (XFJ-2)
A-8289-8313	Martin PM-1
A-8314	Curtiss XF8C-4
A-8315-8356	Vought O2U-4
A-8357	Keystone XOK-1
A-8358	Martin XP2M-1
A-8359	Berliner-Joyce XOJ-1
A-8360-8400	Consolidated NY-2
A-8401-8410	Consolidated NY-2A
A-8411	Martin XT6M-1
A-8412-8414	Martin P3M-1 (P3M-2)
A-8415-8420	Martin P3M-2
A-8421-8445	Curtiss F8C-4
A-8446-8447	Curtiss XF8C-6
A-8448-8456	Curtiss F8C-5
A-8457	Ford JR-3 (RR-3)
A-8458-8475	Great Lakes TG-1
A-8476	Goodyear Free Balloon
A-8477-8481	Martin PM-1
A-8482	N.A.F. XP4N-1
A-8483-8484	N.A.F. PN-11 (XP4N-2)
A-8485	Bristol Bulldog IIa
A-8486	Fairchild XJQ-2
A-8487-8506	Consolidated NY-3
A-8507-8524	Keystone PK-1
A-8525	Loening XO2L-1
A-8526-8545	Curtiss N2C-2
A-8546	American Motorless Aviation Co. Glider
A-8547-8582	Vought O3U-1
A-8583-8588	New Standard NT-1
A-8589-8597	Curtiss F8C-5 (O2C-1)
A-8598-8599	Ford JR-3 (RR-3)
A-8600-8601	Fleet (Consolidated) N2Y-1
A-8602	Fleet XN2Y-2 to Pennsylvania Aircraft Sydicate for conversion to XOZ-1
A-8603-8605	Fleet (Consolidated) N2Y-1
A-8606	Loening XO2L-2
A-8607	Bristol Bulldog IIa
A-8608-8609	Goodyear C Kite Balloon
A-8610-8612	Goodyear C Free Balloon
A-8613-8639	Boeing F4B-2
A-8640	Boeing XF5B-1
A-8641	Vought XO4U-1 (XO4U-2)
A-8642	Sikorsky XP2S-1
A-8643	N.A.F. XBN-1 (cancelled)
A-8644-8661	Douglas T2D-2 (P2D-1)
A-8662-8686	Martin PM-2
A-8687-8695	Hall-Aluminum PH-1
A-8696	Loening XSL-1 (XSL-2)
A-8697-8628	Detroit Aircraft Corporation TE-1 (Built by Great Lakes as TG-2)
A-8729	Hall-Aluminum XP2H-1
A-8730	Douglas XT3D-1 (XT3D-2)
A-8731	Curtiss XF9C-1
A-8732	Atlantic XFA-1
A-8733-8747	Loening OL-9
A-8748-8790	Curtiss F8C-5 (O2C-1)
A-8791-8809	Boeing F4B-2
A-8810-8839	Vought O3U-1

A-8840	Ford RR-4
A-8841	Atlantic RA-4
A-8842-8844	Sikorsky RS-1
A-8845	Curtiss F8C-7 (XO2C-2, XF8C-7)
A-8846	Curtiss RC-1
A-8847	Curtiss O2C-2 (XF10C-1, XS3C-1)
A-8848-8849	Curtiss XF8C-8 (O2C-2)
A-8850	Pitcairn Autogiro XOP-1 (XOP-2)
A-8851-8871	Vought O3U-1
A-8872-8875	Vought O3U-2 (SU-1)
A-8876	Douglas XRD-1
A-8877	De Havilland XDH-80
A-8878	Grumman XFF-1
A-8879-8890	Martin BM-1
A-8891-8911	Boeing F4B-3
A-8912-8920	Boeing F4B-4
A-8921	Consolidated XBY-1
A-8922-8923	Sikorsky RS-3
A-8924-8927	Goodyear Free Balloon
A-8928-8937	Vought O3U-2 (SU-1)
A-8938	Bellanca XRE-1
A-8939	Consolidated XP2Y-1
A-8940	Grumman XSF-1
A-8941-8970	Curtiss O2C-1
A-8971	Loening XS2L-1
A-8972	Sikorsky XSS-1 (XSS-2)
A-8973	Berliner-Joyce XF2J-1
A-8974	Great Lakes XSG-1
A-8975	Boeing XF6B-1 (XBFB-1)
A-8976-8977	Pitcairn Autogiro XOP-1
A-8978	N.A.F. XFN-1 (cancelled)
A-8979-8985	Loening OL-9
A-8986-9007	Consolidated P2Y-1
A-9008	Consolidated P2Y-1 (XP2Y-2)
A-9009-9053	Boeing F4B-4
A-9054	Lockheed (Detroit) XRO-1
A-9055	Sikorsky RS-3
A-9056-9061	Curtiss F9C-2
A-9062-9076	Vought O3U-2 (SU-1)
A-9077	Vought O3U-4 (SU-2)
A-9078	Vought O3U-4 (XO3U-5)
A-9079-9108	Vought O3U-4 (SU-2)
A-9109	Vought O3U-4 (XSU-4)
A-9110-9121	Vought O3U-4 (SU-2)
A-9122-9141	Vought O3U-4 (SU-3)
A-9142-9169	Vought O3U-3
A-9170-9185	Martin BM-2
A-9186	Bellanca XSE-1 (XSE-2)
A-9187-9195	Berliner-Joyce OJ-2
A-9196	Berliner-Joyce OJ-2 (XOJ-3, OJ-2)
A-9197-9204	Berliner-Joyce OJ-2
9205-9206	Ford RR-5
9207	Bellanca XRE-2
9208-9211	Loening OL-9
9212	Martin XBM-1
9213	Curtiss XF11C-2 (XBFC-2)
9214-9217	Martin BM-1
9218	Grumman XJF-1
9219	Curtiss XF11C-1 (XBFC-1)
9220	Great Lakes XBG-1
9221	Consolidated XB2Y-1
9222	Vought XF3U-1 (XSBU-1)
9223	Douglas XFD-1
9224	Berliner-Joyce XF3J-1

9225	Curtiss XF12C-1 (XS4C-1, XSBC-1, XSBC-2, XSBC-3)
9226-9263	Boeing F4B-4
9264	Curtiss XF9C-2
9265-9268	Curtiss F11C-2 (BFC-2)
9269	Curtiss F11C-2, (XF11C-3, XBF2C-1)
9270-9282	Curtiss F11C-2 (BFC-2)
9283-9329	Vought O3U-3
9330	Vought O3U-3 (XO3U-6)
9331-9340	Curtiss F11C-2 (BFC-2)
9341	Bellanca RE-3 (XRE-3)
9342	Grumman XF2F-1
9343	Curtiss XF13C-1 (XF13C-2, XF13C-3)
9344-9345	Air Cruisers Inc. Kite Balloon
9346	Loening XFL-1 (cancelled)
9347-9349	Douglas RD-2
9350-9376	Grumman FF-1 (FF-2)
9377	Curtiss XS2C-1
9378	Boeing XF7B-1
9379-9398	Vought SU-4
9399	Vought XO5U-1
9400	Northrop XFT-1 (XFT-2)
9401 9402	Franklin XPS-2 Glider
9403-9411	Berliner-Joyce OJ-2
9412	Douglas XO2D-1
9413	Curtiss XO3C-1 (XSOC-1)
9414-9433	Vought SU-4
9434-9455	Grumman JF-1
9456-9458	Consolidated XN4Y-1
9459	Consolidated XP3Y-1 (XPBY-1, PBY-1)
9460-9492	Grumman SF-1
9493	Grumman XSF-2
9494-9520	Great Lakes BG-1
9521-9522	Waco XJW-1
9523-9527	Grumman JF-1
9528-9533	Douglas RD-3
9534-9550	Great Lakes BG-1
9551-9571	Consolidated P2Y-3
9572-9583	Berliner-Joyce OJ-2
9584-9585	Curtiss R4C-1
9586-9612	Curtiss BF2C-1
9613	Douglas XP3D-1 (XP3D-2)
9614-9617	Franklin XPS-2 Glider
9618-9619	Consolidated P2Y-3
9620-9622	Douglas R2D-1
9623-9676	Grumman F2F-1
9677-9717	Stearman NS-1
9718	Stinson XR3Q-1
9719	Marine Base Quantico F4B-4
9720	Douglas XTBD-1
9721	Hall-Aluminum XPTBH-1 (XPTBH-2)
9722	Great Lakes XB2G-1
9723	Great Lakes XTBG-1
9724	Fairchild XSOK-1 (cancelled)
9725	Vought XSB2U-1
9726	Brewster XSBA-1
9727	Grumman XF3F-1
9728	Bellanca XSOE-1
9729-9744	Vought O3U-6
9745	Northrop XBT-1
9746	Vought XF3U-1 (XSBU-1)
9747-9749	Kinner XRK-1
9750-9833	Vought SBU-1
9834	Vought XSB3U-1
9835-9839	Grumman JF-3

9840-9855	Great Lakes BG-1
9856-9990	Curtiss SOC-1
9991	N.A.F. XN3N-1
9992	Air Cruisers Inc. Free Balloon
9993-9994	Douglas R2D-1
9995	Sikorsky XPBS-1
9996	Grumman XSBF-1
9997	Grumman F2F-1
9998	Fairchild XR2K-1
9999	Goodyear G Dirigible
0001-0015	Vought O3U-6
0016	Vought O3U-6 (XOSU-1, O3U-6)
0017-0019	N.A.F. N3N-1
0020	N.A.F. N3N-1 (XN3N-3)
0021-0101	N.A.F. N3N-1
0102	Consolidated XP3Y-1 (XPBY-1, PBY-1)
0103-0161	Consolidated P3Y-1 (PBY-1)
0162-0190	Grumman J2F-1
0191-0210	Stearman NS-1
0211-0264	Grumman F3F-1
0265	N.A.F. XN3N-2
0266	Grumman JF-2
0267	Lockheed XR2O-1
0268-0381	Douglas TBD-1
0382	NAS Norfolk PM-2
0383	Grumman XF4F-1 (XF4F-2, XF4F-3)
0384	Fleet Air Base Coco Solo PM-2 (Built from hull of 8480)
0385	N.A.F. XO2N-1 (XOSN-1)
0386-0425	Curtiss SOC-1 (SOC-2)
0426-0450	N.A.F. N3N-1 (cancelled)
0451	Brewster XF2A-1 (XF2A-2)
0452	Grumman XF3F-2
0453	Consolidated XPB2Y-1
0454-0503	Consolidated PBY-2
0504-0506	Sikorsky JRS-1
0507-0581	Curtiss SBC-3
0582	Curtiss SBC-3 (XSBC-4)
0583-0589	Curtiss SBC-3
0590-0626	Northrop BT-1
0627	Northrop BT-1 (XBT-2)
0628-0643	Northrop BT-1
0644-0723	N.A.F. N3N-1
0724	B.F.W. Me.108b
0725	Caudron C-620
0726-0778	Vought SB2U-1
0779	Vought SB2U-1 (XSB2U-3)
0780-0794	Grumman J2F-2
0795	Bellanca JE-1
0796	Martin XPBM-1
0797-0799	Free balloons (cancelled)
0800	Fairchild JK-1
0801	Beechcraft JB-1
0802-0841	Vought SBU-2
0842-0907	Consolidated PBY-3
0908-0909	Stearman-Hammond JH-1
0910-0948	North American NJ-1
0949	North American NJ-1 (NJ-2, NJ-1)
0950	Curtiss XSO2C-1
0951	Vought XOS2U-1
0952-0966	N.A.F. N3N-1
0967-1030	Grumman F3F-2
1031	Grumman F3F-2 (XF3F-3)
1032-1047	Grumman F3F-2
1048-1051	Lockheed JO-2

1052	Stearman XOSS-1
1053	Lockheed JO-1
1054-1063	Sikorsky JRS-1
1064-1146	Curtiss SOC-3
1147-1190	N.A.F. SON-1
1191-1194	Sikorsky JRS-1
1195-1197	Grumman J2F-2
1198-1206	Grumman J2F-2A
1207-1209	Grumman J2F-2
1210-1211	Goodyear L Dirigible
1212	Society Aeronautica Italiana S-2
1213-1244	Consolidated PBY-4
1245	Consolidated PBY-4 (XPBY-4, XPBY-5A)
1246	Martin PBM-1
1247	Martin PBM-1 (XPBM-2)
1248-1266	Martin PBM-1
1267	Lockheed XJO-3
1268-1325	Curtiss SBC-4
1326-1383	Vought SB2U-2
1384	Grumman XJ3F-1 (JRF-1)
1385	Curtiss XSO3C-1
1386-1396	Brewster F2A-1
1397-1439	Brewster F2A-1 (F2A-2)
1440	Vought XSO2U-1
1441	Lockheed XR4O-1
1442	Grumman XF5F-1
1443	Vought XF4U-1
1444-1470	Grumman F3F-3
1471-1473	Goodyear Balloons
1474-1504	Curtiss SBC-4
1505-1519	Douglas TBD-1
1520	Martin XPB2M-1 (XPB2M-1R)
1521	N.A.F. XN5N-1
1522-1551	N.A.F. SBN-1
1552-1567	North American SNJ-1
1568-1587	Grumman J2F-2 (J2F-3)
1588	Bell XFL-1
1589-1595	Beechcraft GB-1
1596-1631	Douglas BT-2 (SBD-1)
1632	Brewster XSB2A-1
1633-1637	Consolidated PB2Y-2
1638	Consolidated PB2Y-2 (XPB2Y-3)
1639-1670	Grumman J2F-4
1671-1673	Grumman JRF-1 (JRF-1A)
1674-1677	Grumman JRF-1
1678-1679	Grumman JRF-1 (JRF-1A)
1680	Grumman JRF-1
1681-1734	Vought OS2U-1
1735-1755	Douglas BT-2 (SBD-1)
1756-1757	W. L. Maxson Corp. XNR-1
1758	Curtiss XSB2C-1
1759-1808	N.A.F. N3N-3
1809-1843	Curtiss SBC-4
1844-1845	Grumman F4F-3
1846-1847	Grumman F4F-3 (XF4F-5)
1848-1896	Grumman F4F-3
1897	Grumman F4F-3 (XF4F-4)
1898-1900	Beechcraft GB-1
1901-1903	Douglas R3D-1
1904-1907	Douglas R3D-2
1908-2007	N.A.F. N3N-3
2008-2043	North American SNJ-2
2044-2100	Vought SB2U-3
2101	Lockheed XR5O-1
2102-2108	Douglas SBD-2

2109	Douglas SBD-3
2110-2188	Douglas SBD-2
2189-2288	Vought OS2U-2
2289-2455	Consolidated PBY-5
2456-2488	Consolidated PBY-5A
2489-2511	Boeing F4B-4A
2512-2538	Grumman F4F-3
2539-2540	Grumman XTBF-1
2541	Lockheed JO-2
2542	Vought XTBU-1
2543-2547	Beech JRB-1
2548-2572	North American SNJ-2
2573-3072	N.A.F. N3N-3
3073-3130	Vought OS2U-2
3131-3143	Douglas R4D-1
3144	Boeing XPBB-1
3145-3394	Stearman N2S-1
3395-3519	Stearman N2S-3
3520-3644	Stearman N2S-2
3645-3845	Spartan NP-1
3846-3855	Grumman JRF-1 (JRF-4)
3856-3874	Grumman F4F-3
3875-3969	Grumman F4F-3A
3970-4057	Grumman F4F-3
4058-4098	Grumman F4F-4
4099-4198	Ryan NR-1
4199-4248	Curtiss SBC-4
4249-4250	Lockheed R5O-1
4251	Douglas BD-1
4252-4351	Stearman N2S-3
4352-4517	N.A.F. N3N-3
4518-4691	Douglas SBD-3
4692-4706	Douglas R4D-1
4707-4708	Douglas R4D-1 (R4D-2)
4709-4710	Beech JRB-1
4711-4725	Beech JRB-2
4726-4729	Beech JRB-1
4730-4783	Curtiss SO3C-1
4784-4792	Curtiss SO3C-1 (SO3C-2C)
4793-4879	Curtiss SO3C-1
4880-5029	Curtiss SO3C-2
5030-5262	Grumman F4F-4
5263-5283	Grumman F4F-7
5284-5289	Vought OS2U-3
5290-6289	Vought OS2U-3 (cancelled)
6290	Curtiss SNC-1
6291	Curtiss XSNC-1
6292-6439	Curtiss SNC-1
6440-6454	Grumman JRF-1 (JRF-5)
6455	Martin PBM-3 (PBM-3R)
6456	Martin PBM-3 (XPBM-3)
6457-6504	Martin PBM-3 (PBM-3R)
6505-6754	Martin PBM-3 (PBM-3C, some to PBM-S3)
6755-7024	North American SNJ-3
7025-7028	Goodyear K Dirigible
7029-7030	Goodyear L Dirigible
7031	Grumman XF4F-6
7032-7034	Fairchild GK-1
7035-7042	Douglas BD-2
7043-7149	Consolidated PB2Y-3 (various aircraft to PB2Y-3R, PB2Y-4, PB2Y-5, PB2Y-5H, PB2Y-5Z)
7150	Consolidated PB2Y-3 (XPB2Y-5)
7151-7242	Consolidated PB2Y-3 (PB2Y-4, PB2Y-5)
7243-7302	Consolidated PBY-5A
7303	Lockheed R5O-2
7304-9999	Not Assigned

CGAS Port Angeles   *Gordon S. Williams*

APPENDIX C
U. S. COAST GUARD

The beginning of Coast Guard aviation, at least on paper, may be considered to be August 29, 1916, when Congress authorized the establishment and equipment of ten Coast Guard Air Stations in the United States. Before any money had been allotted, however, the U. S. entered World War I and the Coast Guard became part of the Navy. During this period several officers and enlisted men underwent training in naval aviation.

After the armistice the Coast Guard was returned to the Treasury Department and the former Naval Air Station at Morehead City, North Carolina, was made available as a temporary Coast Guard Air Station. The Navy loaned the Coast Guard six surplus HS-2L flying boats, but this station was discontinued due to lack of funds after a year and the airplanes were returned to the Navy.

Coast Guard aviation lay dormant through 1922, 1923 and 1924. In 1925 Lieutenant Commander C. C. von Paulsen, on his own initiative, borrowed a Vought UO-1 from the Navy for a period of one year, and purchased a surplus Army tent hangar for $1.00. The Department of Fisheries allowed von Paulsen to set up a temporary base on a small island which they owned in Gloucester Harbor, Massachusetts. This was the famous "Ten Pound Island" aviation base of the Coast Guard. It too was discontinued a year later, due to lack of funds, and the airplane was returned to the Navy.

Finally, as a result of a Congressional Act of March 3, 1926, appropriations to purchase five new airplanes were received and arrangements made to get them from Army or Navy contracts. Five seaplanes were purchased under Navy inspection and two air stations were opened in 1927. Thus "Coast Guard Number One" became the serial number of a new Loening OL-5. Coast Guard Numbers 1, 2 and 3 were OL-5's; Number 4 and 5 were Vought UO-4's. These five planes flew over 200,000 miles between 1927 and 1930. The OL-5's went out of service by 1933, but the UO-4's lasted through June 1935.

Thus the question of which airplane was the "first" Coast Guard plane seems to be a matter of definition. The HS-2L was the first plane operated by the Coast Guard, whereas the OL-5 was the first plane owned by the Coast Guard.

From 1927 on Coast Guard aviation grew until 1941 when there were nine air stations and 56 aircraft in commission. The Coast Guard became an active part of the Navy again in 1941, and returned to the Treasury Department in 1945.

AIRCRAFT COLORS

The years 1927-1936 were the "blue and silver" period for USCG aircraft markings. From the first OL-5, until the inception of the V Serial System in 1936, all Coast Guard planes had blue fuselages. The top of the wing, and horizontal tail surfaces, was chrome yellow and the underside silver. The underside of the hull, on flying boats, was painted silver. Wing struts were silver, with the FLB wing floats being all silver, and the Dolphin's half silver and half blue.

The entire vertical tail surface of each plane was divided into three sections; one red, one white and one blue. On the flying boats the engine nacelles were silver and the cowls blue. The name U S COAST GUARD was painted in large letters on the side of the fuselage. The letters USCG were painted on the underside of each wing, with the letters US on the top of the left wing, and CG on the top of the right wing.

From 1936 to 1941 all aircraft were an over-all aluminum color. The top of the wing was chrome yellow with no further markings. The remainder of the plane was silver except for the rudder. Starting in late 1935 the top one-third of the rudder was painted Insignia Blue; the bottom two-thirds was divided into five equal vertical stripes, three red and two white. The model designation was placed in white on the blue section of the rudder, the serial number was in black under the words U. S. COAST GUARD on the side of the fuselage. The letters USCG were used on the underside of both wings, and the serial number was painted on the bottom of the hull or fuselage. The USCG emblem was placed on the forward part of the hull or fuselage near the pilot's compartment.

GENERAL NOTES

Supplementary notes to the main text, regarding some special types, are as follows:

The Douglas Dolphins

The reason that such confusion has existed over the correct identification of the various "Dolphin" models used by the Coast Guard is that four different models were in service during a period when the serial numbering system changed twice. The Douglas "RD" PROCYON, the first production Dolphin built, was delivered to the Coast Guard in New York from the factory in February 1931. This plane was a flying boat, not an amphibian, and the wheels that show in photos are beaching gear.

The "RD-129" ADHARA was delivered next, in July 1932, and the RD-1 SIRIUS was delivered third on August 5, 1932. The strange model designation RD-129, painted on the tail of the plane, was a combination of the normal model designation and the individual aircraft serial number.

The first RD-4 was delivered on February 20, 1935, nearly three years later. All four types are externally different in fuselage, engines and tail configuration.

Naval Aircraft Factory PN-12

The Coast Guard borrowed a PN-12 flying boat from the Navy in 1931 for experimental purposes in connection with the proposed design for a new Coast Guard airplane.

Douglas O-38C

This was an Army Air Corps airplane, Serial Number 32-394, purchased for the Coast Guard new on Air Corps Contract AC-4553. It was commissioned by the Coast Guard on December 11, 1931. It was similar to the O-38B but had an engine change to P&W R-1690-C, dual controls similar to the O-38A, and other minor changes. What appears to be a model designation of "CG-9" on the tail in some photos is in fact its serial number as the ninth plane purchased by the USCG.

FBA-17HT4

Coast Guard Number 8, listed only as "seaplane experimental" in the Coast Guard Register, was imported from France and placed in commission on December 16, 1931. This plane was similar to models used in the French Navy at the time and was built by the Hydravions Schreck-F.B.A. Company of Argenteuil, France. The designer was Louis Schreck and many of these were used in Canada where they were known as "Schreck Flying Boats."

In late 1930 the Viking Flying Boat Company of New Haven, Connecticut, was formed to replace the previous Bourdan Aircraft Company, and they acquired the rights to build this plane in the United States. The first model was brought from France and registered NC-792K as a civil demonstrator. Eventually, as a result of experience with No. 8, the Coast Guard ordered six of these flying boats from the Viking Company and they were built and delivered in 1936 as the model OO-1.

General Aviation FLB (PJ-1, PJ-2)

As a result of a design competition entered by eight companies, a contract for five flying boats specifically designed for Coast Guard use was awarded to the General Aviation Company in 1931. These planes were delivered in 1932 and were known for years as the "Flying Life Boats." The serial number appeared on the tail of each as FLB-51, FLB-52, etc., and this was a combination of the name and serial number serving as a model designation. Since the Fokker Company became a subsidiary of General Aviation in 1930 these are generally not called Fokkers, although the company model designation was AF-15 (American Fokker model 15). Later, when General Aviation became North American, the PJ-1 model designation was adopted, but during their early years they were known throughout the service as the FLB's.

The first plane, FLB-51 ANTARES, was completely modified in 1933 to a tractor configuration and remained so until surveyed. The engine nacelles and cowlings were changed, the engine mounts, pilots cockpit, and other sections were modified. This changed the model designation of this one airplane to PJ-2.

Customs Service Aircraft

On March 9, 1934, the Secretary of the Treasury directed that all aviation activities of the Treasury Department be consolidated under one head and so 15 planes of miscellaneous types and their equipment, belonging to the Customs Service, were transferred to the Coast Guard. In addition six Vought O2U-2's were transferred from the Navy to the Coast Guard during the same year.

Coast Guard Number 175

The 1935 contract for six additional Grumman JF-2's was delivered in 1936 with the sixth airplane, Number 175, being traded to the Navy for the Lockheed XR3O-1.

Martin T4M-1

In 1937 the Coast Guard Engine School and Repair Base, Norfolk, Virginia, got a Martin T4M-1 torpedo-bomber from NAS Norfolk to be used for the "detection of engine troubles and ground instruction." This plane did not carry a Coast Guard serial number and was not classed as operational equipment.

SERIAL NUMBER ASSIGNMENT

It is not surprising that so much confusion has existed over Coast Guard aircraft since some pre-war aircraft had as many as three different serial numbers, at three different times, while others had two, and still others had only one.

The "One and Two Digit System," for the lack of a better title, started in 1927 with the first airplane and continued through 1934. There were only 16 planes with these serials, as may be seen by the following tables, but they were broken up into selective groups so that th Dolphins fell into the "20 series" and the FLB's were assigned the "50 series."

In January 1935 the aircraft that were still flying were re-assigned to a new system of Three Digit Serials. These were completely systematized according to a master plan; the 100 Series was reserved for Amphibians; the 200 Series for Flying Boats; the 300 Series for Land Planes; and the 400 Series for Convertible Land-Sea Planes. This system stayed in effect until October 1936.

On October 13, 1936, at 0001 hours, *all* serial numbers were completely re-assigned. This was a sweeping revision that included not only all of the aircraft flying at that time, but for administrative purposes also included every aircraft that the Coast Guard had ever owned regardless of the fact that the plane may have been destroyed prior to 1936. Thus the OL-5, Coast Guard No. 1, became V101 under the new V Serial System. The V Numbers started with V101 so that three digits would be available as a radio call sign. The system was consecutive and complete, with no numbers being left out as had been done with the previous two systems, and it stayed in effect for ten years before the post-war era brought another revision.

Table 1. *One and two Digit Serials, and Three Digit Serials, including a cross reference to the final reclassification under the V System.*

ONE AND TWO DIGIT SERIAL		THREE DIGIT SERIAL		V SERIAL
1	Loening OL-5	None		V101
2	Loening OL-5	None		V102
3	Loening OL-5	None		V103
4	Vought UO-4	404		V104
5	Vought UO-4	405		V105
8	F.B.A. 17HT4	None		V107
9	Douglas O-38C	None		V108
10	Consolidated N4Y-1 (21-A)	310		V110
27	Douglas RD	227		V106
28	Douglas RD-1	128		V109
29	Douglas RD-2	129		V111
51	General Aviation PJ-2 (FLB-51)	251		V116
52	General Aviation PJ-1 (FLB-52)	252		V112
53	General Aviation PJ-1 (FLB-53)	253		V113
54	General Aviation PJ-1 (FLB-54)	254		V114
55	General Aviation PJ-1 (FLB-55)	255		V115
		130	Douglas RD-4	V125
		131	Douglas RD-4	V126
		132	Douglas RD-4	V127
		133	Douglas RD-4	V128
		134	Douglas RD-4	V129
		135	Douglas RD-4	V130
		136	Douglas RD-4	V131
		137	Douglas RD-4	V132
		138	Douglas RD-4	V133
		139	Douglas RD-4	V134
		161	Grumman JF-2	V135
		162	Grumman JF-2	V136
		163	Grumman JF-2	V137
		164	Grumman JF-2	V138
		165	Grumman JF-2	V139
		166	Grumman JF-2	V140
		167	Grumman JF-2	V141
		168	Grumman JF-2	V142
		169	Grumman JF-2	V143
		170	Grumman JF-2	V144
		171	Grumman JF-2	V145
		172	Grumman JF-2	V146
		173	Grumman JF-2	V147
		174	Grumman JF-2	V148
		301	Vought O2U-2	V117
		302	Vought O2U-2	V118
		303	Vought O2U-2	V119
		304	Vought O2U-2	V120
		305	Vought O2U-2	V121
		306	Vought O2U-2	V122
		311	New Standard NT-2	V123
		312	New Standard NT-2	V124
		381	Stinson R3Q-1	V149
		382	Northrop RT-1	V150
		383	Lockheed R3O-1	V151

Table II. *The V Serial Number List. (In effect from 13 October 1936 to 28 December 1945).*

V101	Loening OL-5	V153	Viking OO-1
V102	Loening OL-5	V154	Viking OO-1
V103	Loening OL-5	V155	Viking OO-1
V104	Vought UO-4	V156	Viking OO-1
V105	Vought UO-4	V157	Waco J2W-1
V106	Douglas RD	V158	Waco J2W-1
V107	F.B.A. 17TH4	V159	Waco J2W-1
V108	Douglas O-38C	V160	Fairchild J2K-1
V109	Douglas RD-1	V161	Fairchild J2K-1
V110	Consolidated N4Y-1	V162	Fairchild J2K-2
V111	Douglas RD-2	V163	Fairchild J2K-2
V112	General Aviation PJ-1	V164	Hall Aluminum PH-2
V113	General Aviation PJ-1	V165	Hall Aluminum PH-2
V114	General Aviation PJ-1	V166	Hall Aluminum PH-2
V115	General Aviation PJ-1	V167	Hall Aluminum PH-2
V116	General Aviation PJ-2	V168	Hall Aluminum PH-2
V117	Vought O2U-2	V169	Hall Aluminum PH-2
V118	Vought O2U-2	V170	Hall Aluminum PH-2
V119	Vought O2U-2	V171	Curtiss SOC-4
V120	Vought O2U-2	V172	Curtiss SOC-4
V121	Vought O2U-2	V173	Curtiss SOC-4
V122	Vought O2U-2	V174	Grumman JRF-2
V123	New Standard NT-2	V175	Grumman JRF-2
V124	New Standard NT-2	V176	Grumman JRF-2
V125	Douglas RD-4	V177	Hall Aluminum PH-3
V126	Douglas RD-4	V178	Hall Aluminum PH-3
V127	Douglas RD-4	V179	Hall Aluminum PH-3
V128	Douglas RD-4	V180	Hall Aluminum PH-3
V129	Douglas RD-4	V181	Hall Aluminum PH-3
V130	Douglas RD-4	V182	Hall Aluminum PH-3
V131	Douglas RD-4	V183	Hall Aluminum PH-3
V132	Douglas RD-4	V184	Grumman JRF-2
V133	Douglas RD-4	V185	Grumman JRF-2
V134	Douglas RD-4	V186	Grumman JRF-2
V135	Grumman JF-2	V187	Grumman JRF-2
V136	Grumman JF-2	V188	Lockheed R5O-1
V137	Grumman JF-2	V189	Consolidated PBY-5
V138	Grumman JF-2	V190	Grumman JRF-3
V139	Grumman JF-2	V191	Grumman JRF-3
V140	Grumman JF-2	V192	Grumman JRF-3
V141	Grumman JF-2	V193	N.A.F. N3N-3
V142	Grumman JF-2	V194	N.A.F. N3N-3
V143	Grumman JF-2	V195	N.A.F. N3N-3
V144	Grumman JF-2	V196	N.A.F. N3N-3
V145	Grumman JF-2	V197	Grumman J4F-1
V146	Grumman JF-2	V198	Grumman J4F-1
V147	Grumman JF-2	V199	Grumman J4F-1
V148	Grumman JF-2	V200	Grumman J4F-1
V149	Stinson R3Q-1	V201	Grumman J4F-1
V150	Northrop RT-1	V202	Grumman J4F-1
V151	Lockheed R3O-1	V203	Grumman J4F-1
V152	Viking OO-1	V204	Grumman J4F-1

Table III. *Individual Aircraft Names.*

The Coast Guard, in the 1930's, was able to make use of one of those fascinating peace-time luxuries that are limited to small organizations —the naming of individual aircraft. This usage was so common that many official Coast Guard communications, and nearly all press releases and newspaper stories, referred only to the name of the aircraft.

All flying boats and amphibians were named after stars during the period 1933 to 1936. These names appeared on each side of the nose of the airplane and serve as an accurate means of identification of the individual plane. In photos where the serial number does not show it is often the only means of positive identification.

NAME	TYPE OF AIRCRAFT	3 DIGIT SERIAL
ACAMAR	PJ-1	254
ACRUX	PJ-1	253
ADHARA	RD-2	129
ALDEBARAN	RD-4	135
ALIOTH	RD-4	132
ALTAIR	PJ-1	252
ANTARES	PJ-2	251
ARCTURUS	PJ-1	255
BELLATRIX	RD-4	138
CANOPUS	RD-4	139
CAPELLA	RD-4	137
DENEB	RD-4	134
MIZAR	RD-4	131
PROCYON	RD	227
RIGEL	RD-4	136
SIRIUS	RD-1	128
SPICA	RD-4	130
VEGA	RD-4	133

APPENDIX D

SQUADRON INSIGNIA

Original drawings by William R. McIntyre

Squadron insignia form a basic reference for historical continuity. Wherever the same insignia has been kept through squadron re-numbering and re-designations it provides the only base line upon which one may derive the continuous service of the unit.

The following pages contain all of the insignia that it has been possible to obtain through official and unofficial records. It is fairly certain that there were additional insignias as several units known to have existed are not represented. The squadron lineage given for each insignia is based upon extensive private research of available material and does not constitute an official history of these units.

It has been noted during research on this subject that the exact drawing for each insignia will vary with each artist's rendition. Just as these drawings were done in simplified black and white especially for this book, each presentation will show minor differences.

In addition it should be noted that the "official" insignia, as it is painted on the airplane itself, often changes over the years. Sometimes the difference is one of error in proportion or design; at other times it is a deliberate change in order to bring the insignia into line with squadron re-numbering. An example of the latter is the "Bellerophon" insignia which started with the numeral "5" in the shield, indicating VB-5, and which subsequently changed to a "2" when the squadron was re-designated VB-2.

Excellent color plates for most of these insignias, as well as additional ones for ships and air stations, may be found in the June 1943 issue of *The National Geographic Magazine*.

During the pre-war years the squadrons designed their own insignias and after they had been adopted a copy was sent to the Bureau of Aeronautics to be filed. This informal system is no longer in effect and squadrons today must submit their new insignias, conforming to specific rules, to the Bureau for approval before they may be applied on the aircraft.

Because of the lack of any directive or set of rules governing pre-war unit insignia, the designs seen on the following pages are a mixture of semi-heraldric escutcheons, mythology and comic characters from the Sunday funnies of the time. They form a mixture of violent emotion and broad humor and were a very important part of the traditions of naval aviation at the time.

Fighting Squadron One adopted the High Hat insignia in June 1927. Prior to that time their insignia was a diving eagle (see page 43) which lost favor because of its similarity to a parrot used to advertise chocolate. The idea for a new insignia was suggested when one of the pilots of the squadron appeared in a battered top hat. The "High Hat" emblem immediately became the insignia of VF-1. As someone in the squadron at that time remarked "There was no special reason, it just seemed like a good idea at the time." The fame of the High Hats as a crack outfit has been so great that the insignia has remained through many squadron redesignations to present day use. VF-1B to VF-2B to VB-3 to VB-4 to VS-41.

Fighting Squadron Two was the only squadron in the U.S. Navy to be basically composed of enlisted pilots. To properly describe this organization the insignia pictures the chevron of a chief petty officer which also incorporates the American eagle. The chevron is mounted on a shield with the word "Adorimini," which freely translated means "Up and at 'Em," a battle cry used by Caesar's legions. Colors: Navy blue shield. White eagle and banner. Chevron, red. Wings in top section of chevron, gold. VF-2 1927 through 1941.

Fighting Squadron Three adopted its insignia when its primary mission was dive bombing. This is pictured by Pat Sullivan's "Felix" with a bomb in his hands. Colors: Black and white. VB-2B to VF-6B to VF-3. (This squadron was formerly VF-2 and VF-6B).

Fighting Squadron Four uses a shield of royal blue crossed by a bolt of red lightning, with two red circles in the quarterings. The crest is the head of a wild boar, in recent years claimed to have been taken from the label of a gin bottle. The bolt of lightning, which suggested the squadron's nickname of "The Red Rippers," is a modification of the traditional bend sinister—the mark of illegitimacy. Colors: Lightning, balls and face of boar, red. The rest of the insignia is royal blue except for the teeth and eyes which are white. VF-5S to VB-1B to VF-5B to VF-4 to VF-41.

Fighting Squadron Five used as an insignia a yellow five-pointed star across which an American eagle is diving. The outstretched wings and claws show the eagle ready to strike. The star on the field is taken from the aviation insignia and the eagle represents the plane ready to strike with its machine guns or bombs. Name: The Striking Eagles. Colors: Yellow star imposed on Navy blue field. Black and white eagle. VF-3S to VF-7B to VF-5.

Fighting Squadron Six is personified by a comet blazing a trail across the heavens. The comet or falling star is intended to symbolize speed through the heavens. The field of blue breaks through the tail of the comet to delineate FIGHTING SIX. Colors: Entire comet red; stars white; field of circle royal blue. VF-6. (Before adopting this insignia the squadron was VF-1B and VF-8B).

Bombing Squadron Two has an adaption of the Greek myth of Bellerophon and Pegasus. According to this story, Bellerophon captured the winged stallion Pegasus and set out to slay the three headed Chimera. By diving three times over the monster Bellerophon was able to strike off one of its heads on each attack. Since the primary mission of this squadron was dive bombing the insignia was particularly suitable. The motto which appears over the figures is translated as "First to Attack." It is written in correct Greek of the period in which the story originates. Colors: The figures of Bellerophon and Pegasus are in black. The shield and scarf or plume were painted the color of the section to which the individual airplane was assigned. The figure "5" was placed in the center of the shield originally, and was changed to "2" when the squadron was redesignated. VB-5B to VB-2.

Bombing Squadron Three selected the black panther as its insignia since it embodied the characteristics of the bombing squadron; namely stealth, diving tactics, speed and decisiveness. Colors: Black and white panther; yellow claws, blue eye, teeth and area around the eye yellow, lips red, inside of ear and end of nose pinkish yellow. VB-3B to VB-4 to VB-3.

Bombing Squadron Five used the winged head of Satan, helmeted and goggled, superimposed on a ball of fire. Colors: Face, eye, ball of fire, foremost wing and foremost horn, red; background wing and horn, helmet and beard, black; rim of goggles and goggle strap, grey; teeth, moustache, glass in goggle, white. VB-7B to VB-5.

Bombing Squadron Six adopted the wild goat as its insignia because the characteristics of this animal closely paralleled those of the squadron. "These animals inhabit the most precipitous and inaccessible heights of lofty mountains where they assemble in flocks, sometimes consisting of 10 or 15 animals. During the night they feed in the highest woods, but at sunrise they again ascend the mountains until they have reached the most perilous heights. They are remarkably swift and display amazing agility and dexterity in leaping." Colors: Black and white. VB-6 only.

Scouting Squadron One's insignia dates back to their summer cruise to Honolulu in 1929 when information was received that their landplanes were to be replaced by amphibians. This information was the direct inspiration for the insignia: a very busy looking duck equipped with pontoons and wheels wearing a helmet and goggles. The usual explanation for the duck's pontoons is that the squadron flies so far to sea that even a duck would hesitate to make the trip without floats. Colors: Black and white. VS-1B to VS-41 to VF-42.

The insignia of Scouting Squadron Two was adopted because the duties of a scouting squadron operating with the Fleet require the characteristics natural to the Pointer Dog. It has also been stated that it was adopted to stop the propaganda of certain SARATOGA officers that the VS-2B insignia should be the well known monkey trio, symbolic of see nothing, hear nothing and say nothing. Colors: Black and white. (See page 81 for solid black dog). VS-2B to VS-3.

The original Indian Head used by Scouting Squadron Three was taken from a five dollar gold coin, and was a different face completely within a circle. (See photos on pages 101 and 125). About 1936 the head was changed and the feather headdress extended outside of the encircling border. Colors: Red and black. VS-3B to VS-2.

The insignia of Scouting Four depicts a fabulous winged creature of remarkable attributes. The first mission of the squadron, scouting, is represented by the bird's grim, searching expression and the spyglass hung about its neck; the headphones are indicative of constant reporting of information by radio; the bomb demonstrates offensive readiness; the protective mission (smoke screening) is subtly shown by the cigar clamped in the beak. Colors: Field within oval, red; beak and bomb, yellow; body of bird, silver; eye and dot on beak, red; outline, earphones, cigar, leg, spy-glass and bomb tail, black. VS-4B to VS-42.

This basic insignia was used by four different squadron numbers; VO-3S, VS-5S, VCS-2 and VS-6S. The first use seems to be by VO-3S and was adopted at the time that this squadron was organized because certain characteristics of the planes assigned to them were not conductive to good all-around vision and the pilots thus described them as "blind as bats." This expression led to the adoption of a bat as a squadron insignia. The original insignia of VO-3S had a bat superimposed on a field of red; the body of the bat and veins of the wings were black, the wings yellow. The VS-5 was in black. This insignia with a red background remained when the squadron number changed to VS-5S, VS-5B and VCS-2. The same insignia was also used by VS-6S with a *blue* background. When VS-6B became VCS-3 in 1937 it was abandoned for the Flying Sea Horse insignia.

The new Scouting Squadron Six, an aircraft carrier squadron, adopted a design of a headdress worn by the high priests of the Aztec Indian race during the rites of human sacrifice. The basic design was changed somewhat to set forth the double purpose of the squadron, i.e. the wide-open, alert eyes, significant of scouting, and the bomb in flight, indicative of bombing. Colors: Field of circle, insignia red; wings and inner circle of eyes, yellow; bomb, iris of eyes and outline of wings and circle, black; pupils of eyes and marking on bomb, white. VS-6 only. (Formed as VS-8B for ENTERPRISE).

Scouting Squadron Ten devised an insignia showing a duck taking off from a catapult with a spy-glass in one hand and a bomb in the other. Radio beams are an added description. Since planes equipped to carry out all of these missions at the same time are necessarily compromise types having relatively low speed and performance, hence the small wings and large body of a young duckling. Colors: Beak, feet, hands and wings, yellow; bomb and radio beams, red; water and sleeves, dark blue; field, white; goggles, white; helmet, body, spy-glass, circle and catapult, black. VS-10S to VCS-5.

Scouting Squadron Eleven shows a flying fish. The background is symbolic of the sea, the natural element of the cruiser with its aircraft. The flying fish is one of a few inhabitants of both the sea and the air above it, and there is a resemblance in its graceful flights to the cruiser-based seaplanes. The wings, although differing from those worn by Naval Aviators, bear out such a representation without portraying them in the conventional design. Through its abounding in tropical waters it has become associated with calm green seas, fair weather, and pleasant climes and is frequently regarded by mariners as an omen of good weather and good luck. Colors: Silver fish on a dark green circular background. Edging of wings in black. VS-11S to VCS-6.

The design of the insignia of Scouting Squadron Twelve consists of a white emblematic bird over which there is a standard pair of Navy binoculars. The bird represents flight; the binoculars represent the squadron's scouting and observation mission. Colors: Field of circle, light blue bordered with black; binoculars, black and white; bird, white. VS-12S to VCS-7.

Cruiser Scouting Squadron Three (VCS-3) adopted the "Flying Sea Horse" insignia, depicting force and power, as well as flying and water activities. Colors: Red circle, white field and green sea horse. VCS-3 only.

Cruiser Scouting Squadron Eight shows four dolphins, symbolic of the four planes carried aboard each cruiser, and of the four surface ships of the division. The formation of dolphins is comparable to a formation of aircraft and the similarity of a group of dolphins following a ship to the airplanes carrying out the same maneuver is ever present. Colors: Silver field within a red circle; Dolphins and outline of clouds and sea in black. VS-14S to VCS-8.

Torpedo Squadron One changed its original insignia of wings, torpedoes and bombs, to a "Bombman astride a torpedo" when it received the additional duty of bombing. Colors: Nose of torpedo, yellow; sleeves, stockings and end of fuse, red; eye, gloves and shoes, white; bomb and aft section of torpedo, black. VT-1B to VB-1B to VT-2.

Torpedo Squadron Two shows a fire-breathing flying dragon astride a torpedo. Colors: Red dragon, green spine, yellow claws and tail tip; black torpedo or bomb. VT-2B to VT-3.

Torpedo Squadron Five shows a Valkyrie silhouetted against the setting sun. A Valkyrie was "one of the maidens of Odin, awful and beautiful, who hovered over the field of battle and chose those to be slain . . .". The analogy between the Valkyrie and the torpedo plane is that both are "choosers of the slain." Colors: Outer circle, red; middle circle, white; inner circle plus clouds, light blue; sky background, light orange; horse and Valkyrie, black; hair of Valkyrie and highlights on armor, yellow; wings on cap, white; eyes of horse and Valkyrie, green. VT-5 only.

Torpedo Squadron Six is represented by the Great White Albatross, the largest seabird, capable of prolonged flight over open ocean, and often seen at a great distance from land. The wings of the albatross form a "V," the water spout forms a "T," and the fish in the beak of the albatross forms a "6." Colors: Background, sky blue; water, spout and upper part of water spout, dark greenish blue; albatross and fish, white shaded off to grey-brown. VT-6 only.

Patrol Squadron One adopted the elephant for its representative since that animal has always been noted for his endurance and patience. The elephant of VP-1 stands on a cloud with one eye cocked downward at a target, a bomb securely held by his trunk, awaiting the proper time to make an unerring drop. Colors: Outer circle, red; black and white outline on navy blue field; elephant, grey. VP-1F to VP-21 to VP-101.

Patrol Squadron Two, in line with its name, adopted a patrolman chasing an imaginary enemy. Colors: Black and white, with exception of face and hand which are flesh color; buttons and shield are yellow. VP-2F to VP-31.

Patrol Squadron Three also used the elephant. It was originally pink; the pink, however, soon bleached to white and thus was apropos of the old planes in use. The long glass and bomb held by this wise and long-lived beast typifies the duties of the patrol squadron. VP-3F to VP-32 to VP-52.

The second insignia of Patrol Squadron Four, adopted in place of the rainbow circle, depicted the Griffin, an imaginary creature of Greek mythology with the body and legs of a lion and the wings and beak of an eagle. Figuratively, the Griffin implies a vigilant and repellant guardian. In medieval Latin the word also signifies "a kind of ship." The Griffin is superimposed upon the numeral four. Colors: Griffin, orange and gold. Numeral, white. Field, light blue. VP-4 to VP-22.

The insignia of Patrol Squadron Five consisted of a silhouette of the western hemisphere with a conventional pair of naval aviation wings superimposed, the figures so spaced as to be symmetrically contained inside a compass rose. The insignia is known as "Wings over Panama." Colors: Geographical areas, dark blue; wings, gold; compass rose, red with blue inner ring and black outer circle. VP-5F to VP-33 to VP-32.

Patrol Squadron Six selected a representation of Pegasus as their insignia. Pegasus, a winged horse, was begotten by Poseidon from the gorgon Medusa. Later, by the aid of Athena, he was caught at the spring of Pirene in Corinth by Bellerophon who used him in his conflict with the Chimera and in later wars. A combination of its aerial ability and effectiveness in time of war was considered indicative of VP-6. Colors: Red outer circle; white horse superimposed on blue field; gold wings. VP-6F to VP-23 to VP-11.

Patrol Squadron Seven adopted the great white albatross, for the same reasons as VT-6. Their design was quite different, however, and closely resembles the insignia used by the pre-war aviation unit of the Massachusetts National Guard. Colors: Outer circle, yellow; field within circle, blue; albatross, white with wings tipped with black; beak and talons, brown. VP-7F to VP-11 to VP-21.

Patrol Squadron Eight, in 1933, discarded their old insignia of King Neptune sitting upon a rock in the sea, and in its place substituted the "Flying Eight Ball" inspired by the number of the squadron. In pool, one player strives to pocket balls 1 to 7 before his opponent pockets balls 9 to 15, each player attempting to sink his allotted balls and then the eight ball. If at any time before pocketing all his balls a player should accidentally sink the eight ball, the game is lost to him. The significance is that the eight ball is the last to drop and it is dangerous to fool around with that dreaded number, including a squadron. Colors: Black and white with gold wing. VP-8F to VP-24 to VP-12.

The designating letters of Patrol Squadron Nine are written in the shining sun in this insignia. The wild goose is significant of patrol duties because it is probably the most migratory of all birds, patrolling from the arctic to the temperate climates semi-annually. It travels with unerring judgment to its destination, displaying great endurance and speed; typifying the navigation necessary in patrol duties. It is noted for flying in formation, particularly the "V," analagous to patrol plane activities. Colors: Light blue sky; goose, black and white; VP-9 in orange letters on a yellow field. The designation VP-9 was changed to VP-12 when the squadron was re-designated. VP-9F to VP-12 to VP-24.

The compass rose insignia of Patrol Squadron Ten has superimposed on it the Dipper and Polaris, to show the navigation necessary on long over-water patrols. Because radio is very necessary in sending and receiving information, a group of radio waves is also placed on the insignia. A bomb placed in the center of the design describes the secondary mission of the squadron. Colors: Blue field with white stars. Radio waves and bomb, yellow, with tip of bomb red. VP-10F to VP-25 to VP-23.

The insignia of Patrol Squadron Eleven portrays the Head of Odin, the Chief of Gods in Norse mythology, as well as the God of Wisdom and War. The two ravens shown in the insignia were sent out by Odin each day from his home, Valhalla, to bring him news of the world, thus representing the scouting mission of the squadron. The Anglo-Saxon equivalent of the name Odin is Woden, from which Wednesday (Woden's Day) was derived. The squadron was placed in commission on Wednesday, 1 July 1936. Colors: Shield, light and dark blue; ravens, black with yellow beaks; beard and hair, yellow; eyes, blue; helmet, gold; wings on helmet, orange and gold; headband, orange and black; stars, white. VP-11F to VP-54 to VP-51.

The insignia of Patrol Squadron Twelve is symbolic of the Northwestern United States and Alaska, the normal operating area of the squadron at that time. Mt. Rainier, a prominent and welcome landmark for patrols returning over the fog from seaward, forms the background, while in the foreground is shown the Thunderbird surmounting a totem pole. The Thunderbird was regarded by the Indians as a beneficent spirit. He was further believed to represent the war between light and darkness, and they believed that when the bird turned its head from side to side, as it does when angry, fire darted from its eyes (represented by lightning); that its wings were used for bows from which arrows or knives were shot. The lightning from the eyes (radio), the arrows and thunder from the wings (bombs, guns, etc.), and the legendary battles between the Thunderbird and the whale (submarines) all have a peculiar analogy to patrol plane operations. Colors: Sky, blue; lightning, yellow; snow cap of mountain, white; base of mountain, green; totem pole and Thunderbird, various colors. VP-12F to VP-51 to VP-71.

Patrol Squadron Fifteen used the Kneeling Indian with his hand shading his eyes, looking out to sea. The Indian is representative of areas around Norfolk where the squadron was based. The Indian's attitude is one of "look-see," or patrol. His bow and arrows represent combat or a striking force. Colors: Outer circle is red with a small black border. VP-15 is black, shaded with red. The Indian is copper brown; his mocasins, bow, quiver, headband are yellow. The loin cloth, arrows, tip of feather and warpaint on race are red. The hair and all shadows are black. The background is white. VP-15F to VP-53 to VP-73.

Patrol Squadron Sixteen used the Husky Dog, noted for being a vicious fighter. He is fearless and has more than his share of fighting spirit, with the added attribute of inherent tenacity. The design depicts an eager husky dog licking his lips in anticipation of jumping into an impending fray. Colors: Sky, light blue; hills, purple and mauve; tree, green and white; foreground, white, with the exception of the tongue which is orange and red. VP-16 to VP-41.

Observation Squadron One adopted an escutcheon with a red chevron for its insignia. Three radio waves, for communication, are placed in the upper right corner. The miniature main battery turret of a battleship is placed in the lower left, with the name of the individual ship to which the plane was attached inscribed on the turret in abbreviated form such as TEX for USS TEXAS. The words *"Vide et Dice,"* Latin for "See and Tell," are placed as a motto on the scroll. Colors: Turret and outline of shield, black; field of shield, white; radio waves and chevron, red; scroll, red with white letters; name of ship, white, VO-1 only.

The insignia of Observation Squadron Two was a pelican in flight in front of the rising sun and over the blue sea. The pelican is believed to be symbolic of the squadron equipment and mission because his beak is equipped with a hook similar to the recovery hook of the planes, and because the parallel between the pelican and the planes is undeniably close, to wit: his take-off is made in a shower of spray and a series of bounces; in landing "he poises for an instant and then plunges downward with a splash which may be heard for half a mile and is engulfed in a spray which completely obscures the bird, from which he often emerges tail first." The pelican is keen on spotting his prey and seldom misses the catch when spotted; authorities attribute to the pelican a mild disposition and a wild desire to succeed; they also point out that, although he frequently wanders far from home, he makes a habit of returning. The binoculars denote the principal secondary duty of the squadron officers—that of standing watch aboard ship. Colors: Field within circle, red; beak, yellow; sea, blue; numerals, black; pelican, white. The original insignia had the letters VO on the left horizon where the sun meets the sea, and 2B on the right intersection. VO-2 only, a battleship based squadron.

Observation Squadron Three is represented by "Oswald the Lucky Rabbit" riding a 16-inch shell and directing its course with a pair of reins. "Oswald" is wearing a pair of headphones, denoting a source of information as to where to direct the shell. The insignia is significant of the duty of a battleship observation squadron to corect gunfire. Colors: Shirt, red; pants, blue; the remainder of the insignia is black and white. VO-3 only.

Observation Squadron Four devised an insignia to show its class of aircraft. A battleship, with guns blazing away at the target, is superimposed on a "V" (Heavier-than-air) and the whole is framed by an "O" (Observation). Colors: Red "O"; yellow "V"; blue reflection on water with inner reflection white; black ship and smoke; silver background. VO-4 only.

Patrol Squadron Forty-Two chose the Seal as an appropriate insignia for their squadron because of its historical importance in Alaskan waters, the operational area for VP-42. The seal is balancing a bomb on his nose with precision. Colors: Black and white. VP-17 to VP-42.

Because it spent nearly half of the first year of its commissioning in Alaska, Patrol Squadron Eighty-One chose the Polar Bear standing on Mt. Edgecombe, a volcanic cone outside Sitka Harbor, one of the landmarks of South-eastern Alaska. The area is further denoted by the constellation of Ursa Major pointing to Polaris. Colors: Blue sky, white bear and mountain, black circle. VP-19 to VP-43 to VP-81.

Patrol Squadron Fourteen shows the Eastern coast line of the United States, representing the area in which the squadron operated. Six ducks in flight represent the planes of the squadron. Colors: Sea, light blue; geese, grey-black; land, grey. VP-14F to VP-52 to VP-72.

Patrol Squadron Twenty-One, although based at Seattle, extended its operation area to Alaska. Thick forests of these Sitka Spruce trees grow along the coast from Kodiak Island, Alaska, to California The tree also has an important aviation background as the most important wood used during World War I to manufacture aircraft. Colors: Green tree on white field; black circle. VP-21 to VP-14.

Patrol Squadron 102 (VP-102), the second squadron of Patrol Wing Ten, chose an insignia of Wings Over the Pacific when stationed in Hawaii as VP-26. Colors: Blue sky and plane shadow; yellow sun and right side of globe; white rays and plane; grey shadow. VP-18 to VP-26 to VP-102.

Fighting Squadron 71 formed for the new WASP in 1941 chose Thor, the God of War, with a spiked mace, in front of an ominous black cloud. Colors: Thor and mace, flesh color; cloud, black; ocean waves below, blue. VF-71 (formerly VB-7).

Fighting Squadron 72 chose the Blue Burglar Wasp and added a sailor's white hat and four boxing gloves. Colors: Blue Wasp with white legs and arms; wings and gloves, brown; eye, yellow; hat, white; field of circle, red. VF-7 to VF-72.

Scouting Squadron 71 combined the strength, keenness of vision and power of flight of the eagle with the unyielding strength of the black flint arrowhead. Colors: Eagle's head, golden yellow; eye, white; flint and four speed marks, black. VS-71 only.

Scouting Squadron 72 adopted the Centaur Vampire holding the world with one arm, with an upraised bomb in his right hand, while his tail points to the United States. The Greek mythological centaur, half man and half tiger, is combined with the vampire bat which has remarkable flying ability. Colors: Bat and land masses, blue-grey; globe, yellow; face of centaur, pink.

The new Scouting Squadron Five, formed for the carrier YORKTOWN, adopted the Man-o-War Bird. It is the most aerial of the water birds, never settling on the water, flying throughout the daylight hours from its island home. The seven foot span Christmas Island bird is pictured. Colors: Bird, black with red throat; diamond, red outline with white center.

Patrol Squadron Eight originally adopted an insignia showing King Neptune sitting on a rock, shading his eyes with his right hand as he looks across the sea. This insignia was replaced in 1933 by the Winged 8-Ball. Colors unknown.

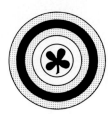

Patrol Squadron Four used, for a time, a series of concentric circles enclosing a clover leaf. Colors: Circles, from the outside towards the center: red, blue, green, yellow; clover leaf is green on a white field.

Utility Squadron One shows a reclining Lion in silhouette in front of the national star aviation insignia. Colors: Lion, letters VJ-1B, EN GARDE and line around blanket all in black; blanket, yellow; insignia, red center, white star, blue field.

Utility Squadron Two adopted the universal sign of utility, the Safety Pin, for its insignia. Colors: A red triangle encloses a red numeral 2, a yellow safety pin (opened), and the black letters UTILITY.

Patrol Squadron Seven chose a version of the Keystone Cop in its early years, replacing it with the Albatross insignia later. Colors: Figure and circle, black on white; orange shading around the hands and face; the letters VP7 are in orange, outlined in black.

Torpedo Squadron One designed an excellent insignia combining its assigned mission with a pair of symbolic wings and the class letters VT. The white wings support two torpedos, while the vertical bomb denotes the squadron's secondary duty. This insignia is painted on the fuselage directly below the pilot's cockpit of the two planes on page 41.

Fighting Squadron Two designed a formal insignia of scroll, shield and crossed machine guns. The colors are unknown but most probably the shield and scroll are red and the guns black. Note how the red plane is in position to down his opponent. This insignia was used by VF-2B and VF-6B, was replaced by Felix-the-Cat when the squadron was re-designated VB-2B.

Observation Squadron Six used a thoughtful design in 1924 (see page 35) consisting of the squadron number enclosed in the class letters VO. Colors unknown. VO-6 lasted three years, from 1924 to 1926, became VO-5S in 1927.

The insignia of the Naval Air Station, Pensacola, is a modification of one used there in 1919. In line with its mission of primary and advanced flight training it chose for its insignia a goose making a stall landing for the following reasons: the goose is generally associated with a certain degree of foolishness and amusement. The silly countenance on this particular goose indicates lack of skill, while the excessive flapping of the underdeveloped wings proves a thorough willingness on the part of the student naval aviators for hard work. The smug expression indicates extreme pleasure at having arrived back on the surface of the water in a single piece. The large beak and mouth of the bird are typical of many of the students, for they make it possible for them to do their best flying while sitting on the ground. The tremendous splash indicates the skidding landing made by most students, while the grotesque position of the goose's feet indicates the helplessness on the part of the students to know what to do with their hands or feet. Colors: Light blue sky; greenish blue water; yellow beak and feet, white body; brown helmet; black outline around lenses of goggles.

APPENDIX E

MANUFACTURERS CODE LETTERS

Manufacturer's letters were first assigned in March 1922 with the establishment of the first system of aircraft model designation. The following list includes all companies that actually built planes for the Navy between 1922 and 1941. Some additional letters, such as Q for Charles Ward Hall, Inc., were assigned but not used.

LETTER	MANUFACTURER
A	Aeromarine Plane and Motor Company
A	Atlantic Aircraft Corporation
A	Brewster Aeronautical Corporation
B	Beech Aircraft Company
B	Boeing Airplane Company
C	Curtiss Aeroplane and Motor Company
D	The Douglas Company
E	Bellanca Aircraft Corporation
E	Detroit Aircraft Corporation
E	G. Elias & Bro., Inc.
F	Fokker (Netherlands)
F	Grumman Aircraft Engineering Corporation
G	Eberhart Aero and Motor Company
G	Great Lakes Aircraft Corporation
H	Hall-Aluminum Aircraft Company
H	Howard Aircraft Company
H	Huff, Daland and Company, Inc.
H	Stearman-Hammond Aircraft Corporation
J	Berliner-Joyce Aircraft Corporation
J	General Aircraft Corporation
J	North American Aviation, Inc.
K	Fairchild Airplane Manufacturing Corporation
K	Keystone Aircraft Corporation
K	Kinner Airplane and Motor Corporation
K	Krieder-Reisner Aircraft Company
L	Bell Aircraft Corporation
L	Loening Aeronautical Engineering Corporation
M	Glenn L. Martin Company
N	Naval Aircraft Factory, U. S. Navy
O	Lockheed Aircraft Company
O	Viking Flying Boat Corporation
P	Pitcairn Autogiro Company
P	Spartan Aircraft Company
Q	Fairchild Aircraft Corporation
Q	Stinson Aircraft Corporation
R	Ford Motor Company
R	Ryan Aeronautical Company
R	W. L. Maxson Company
S	Stearman Aircraft Company (Boeing-Wichita)
S	Sikorsky Manufacturing Corporation
S	Stout Engineering Laboratories
T	New Standard Aircraft Corporation
T	Northrop Aircraft (Douglas-El Segundo)
U	Chance Vought Corporation (Vought-Sikorsky)
V	Vultee Aircraft
W	Waco Aircraft Company
W	Wright Aeronautical Corporation
X	Cox-Klemin Aircraft Company
Y	Consolidated Aircraft Corporation
Z	Pennsylvania Aircraft Syndicate

APPENDIX F

CLASS ASSIGNMENT LETTERS

In order to identify the mission of a squadron or an airplane the Navy established a series of Class letters. These were used for three different and distinct purposes; for squadron designation; for administrative filing and classification, including aircraft description for a table of organization, such as "VB-5B is authorized 18 VF, 1 VSB and 2 VO aircraft"; and for use in the aircraft model designation.

The first official list of the Bureau of Aeronautics was issued as Technical Note 213 of March 29, 1922. This list adopted the already existing classes as set forth in the *Ships Data Book,* adding only Class VA and VM. It also established the first system of combining a manufacturer's code letter with a class symbol and a digit to form an aircraft model designation. Under this system the manufacturer's letter came first and the class second, hence the DT-1, UO-1, etc.

One year later, on March 10, 1923, Technical Note 235 reversed this order and placed the class letter first and manufacturer's letter second. It also dropped the VG and VA Classes and added VN and VJ.

The prefix letter "V," used with class letters for squadron and administrative use, designated Heavier-than-air; the prefix "Z" was used for Lighter-than-air. The "V" was *not* used as a part of the model designation system.

The prefix letter "X," used for model designations, denoted an Experimental aircraft. It will be noted from Table I that it was also used as a squadron letter (VX). A comparison of the following three tables will illustrate the different uses of class letters.

Double class letters were first adopted in 1934 with VBF, VTB, VOS, VSB and VPB being added to the list. The first letter indicated the primary mission for which the plane was designed, and the second letter designated the secondary mission that it was also capable of performing. Some airplanes, such as the F11C-2 and XP3Y-1, were re-designated without any further change in design.

Table I. *Class Letters for Squadron Use. The Heavier-than-air "V" prefix was not painted on the aircraft, but was used for all communications and descriptions of the squadron.*

VB	Bombing
VF	Fighting
VJ	Utility
VM	Miscellaneous
VN	Training
VO	Observation
VP	Patrol
VS	Scouting
VCS	Cruiser-Scouting
VT	Torpedo
VX	Experimental

Table II. *Class letters for Administrative Use. Established by the Navy Filing Code for record keeping, reports, etc. Used for the the classification of aircraft in the "Characteristics and Performance Charts."*

VA	Training (1921 only)
VB	Bombing
VBF	Bombing-Fighting
VF	Fighting
VG	Fleet Plane (1920-1922 only)
VG	Transport, Single-engine
VJ	Utility
VJR	Utility-Transport
VN	Training
VO	Observation
VOS	Observation-Scout
VP	Patrol
VPB	Patrol-Bombing
VR	Transport
VS	Scouting
VSB	Scout-Bombing
VSO	Scout-Observation
VT	Torpedo
VTB	Torpedo-Bombing
—	Special

Table III. *Class Letters for Use in Aircraft Model Designation, 1922-1941.*

LETTER	CLASS	REMARKS
B	Bomber	1931-1941.
BF	Bomber-Fighter	1934-1937.
F	Fighter	1922-1941.
G	Transport, single-engine	1939-1941, GB-1 & GK-1 only.
H	Hospital	1929-1931, XHL-1 only. Also termed Ambulance plane.
J	Transport	1923-1931, to R in 1931.
J	Utility	1931-1941.
JR	Utility-Transport	1937-1941.
M	Marine Expeditionary	1922-1925.
N	Trainer	1923-1941.
O	Observation	1922-1941.
OS	Observation-Scout	1934-1941.
P	Patrol	1922-1941.
PB	Patrol-Bomber	1934-1941.
PT	Patrol-Torpedo	1922, NAF PT-1 & PT-2 only.
PTB	Patrol-Torpedo-Bomber	1937-1938, XPTBH-2 only.
R	Racer	1923-1928.
R	Transport	1931-1941.
S	Scout	1922-1941.
SB	Scout-Bomber	1934-1941.
SN	Scout-Trainer	1939-1941.
SO	Scout-Observation	1936-1941.
T	Transport	1927-1930.
T	Torpedo	1922-1941.
TB	Torpedo-Bomber	1934-1941.

APPENDIX G

RECOMMENDED READING

Naval Aviation by LT W. W. Warlick; United States Naval Institute, Annapolis, Maryland, 1925. A text book for midshipmen at the Naval Academy that contains a great deal of good information on the accepted policy and tactics of the period. The description of the mission and requirements for various classes of naval aircraft is particularly valuable.

The Sky's The Limit by Lieutenant D. W. Tomlinson; Macrae, Smith and Company, Philadelphia, 1930. Fascinating personal account of Navy flying by the famous skipper of Fighting Six and leader of the "Three Sea Hawks" acrobatic team. Filled with caustic, earthy comments on flying and the Navy in 1927-1928. Chapter 12 is a graphic description, with photos, of the end of the PN-11.

Dive Bomber by Ensign Robert A. Winston; Holiday House, New York, 1939. Descriptive autobiography of a pilot with VF-1 and VF-6, but dealing primarily with flight training at Pensacola. This book and *Air Base* are the two most important pre-war books to capture the flavor and feeling of naval aviation as seen by the carrier pilot.

The Ships and Aircraft of The U. S. Fleet by James C. Fahey; Ships and Aircraft, New York City. The first two editions of this respected and authoritative work are invaluable references on pre-war ships and aircraft. The 1939 edition contains the Organization Table for the entire U. S. Fleet, and the 1941 "Two Ocean Fleet Edition" covers all of the ships and aircraft in service in 1941.

Flying Fleets, A Graphic History of U. S. Naval Aviation by S. Paul Johnston; Duell, Sloan and Pearce, Inc., New York, 1941. Contains the greatest number, and best quality, photographs of pre-war Navy aircraft of any book to date. Has very good photo coverage of the pre-World War I period.

Air Base by Boone T. Guyton; McGraw-Hill Book Company, New York, 1941. Excellent autobiography by a pilot in the High Hat squadron who later became a test pilot for Vought-Sikorsky. Well written, detailed description of what it was like to fly from a carrier in the 1937-1940 period. Chapter 12 is a lengthy account of a one day cross-country ferry flight in F3F-3 #1467; from NAS Anacostia to NAS San Diego in 13 hours and 34 minutes flying time.

Navy Wings by LCDR Harold Blaine Miller; Dodd, Mead & Company, New York, 1937. (New and revised edition published 1942). Devoted almost entirely to naval aviation prior to 1922, with the emphasis on the men who flew prior to World War I.

The Flying Guns, Cockpit Record of a Naval Pilot from Pearl Harbor Through Midway by LT Clarence E. Dickinson in collaboration with Boyden Sparkes; Charles Scribner's & Sons, New York, 1942. The first 68 pages of this autobiography deal with Pearl Harbor in December 1941. The author was the pilot of a VS-6 SBD shot down by the Japanese as he flew from the ENTERPRISE to Pearl Harbor on the morning of December 7th.

The National Geographic Magazine, June 1943; The National Geographic Society, Washington, D.C. Pages 721 and 722 show 93 Navy and Marine Corps aviation insignia in full color.

I Took The Sky Road by Commander Norman M. Miller, as told to Hugh B. Cave; Dodd, Mead & Company, New York, 1945. This autobiography of the Commanding Officer of VB-109 is always listed as a World War II book but the first sixty pages all deal with pre-1942 flight training and squadron service—including a description of flying F3B-1's and F4B-4's. The most unique contribution of this book to the period is the complete and detailed description of the XPBS-1. CDR Miller was the "Officer-in-Charge, XPBS-1 Airplane." Pages 60-85 are a graphic, personal description of its flight from San Diego to Soerabaja in February 1942.

The Navy's Air War by The Aviation History Unit, DCNO (Air) and LT A. R. Buchanan; Harper & Brothers, New York, 1946. The official history of naval aviation in World War II, accurate and detailed. Contains considerable material on late 1941 and the Pearl Harbor period.

History of United States Naval Aviation by CAPT Archibald D. Turnbull and LCDR Clifford L. Lord; Yale University Press, New Haven, Connecticut, 1949. The standard reference work on the over-all history of naval aviation from its start, with the emphasis on command policy, economics and individuals. Written by the then Deputy Director of Naval Records and History and the Head of the Naval Aviation History Unit.

Slipstream, The Autobiography of an Aircraftsman by Eugene E. Wilson; McGraw-Hill Book Company, New York, 1950. The first 159 pages of this book, by former President of Hamilton-Standard, Sikorsky and Chance Vought, deal almost entirely with naval aviation from 1924 to 1929. The author was a naval aviator and Chief of Staff for Aircraft Squadrons, Battle Fleet, and writes from first hand experience of such things as war games aboard the SARATOGA. Contains many observations on individuals as well as aircraft development policy.

American Combat Planes by Ray Wagner; Hanover House, Garden City, New York, 1960. Pages 282-428 of this scholarly work cover pre-war Navy combat types, as well as their continuation up to date, so that trends and development over the years may be seen. An excellent, reliable book containing many photographs and much information.

United States Naval Aviation 1910-60 by Adrian O. Van Wyen and Lee M. Pearson; U. S. Government Printing Office, Washington, D.C., 1961. The most valuable single document published to date in the field of naval aviation. It is a reference work of inestimable value because it records chronological information based on directives, orders, authorizations, correspondence, etc., never before available to the civilian reader. Appendix V, "Combat Aircraft Procured," lists aircraft designation, date of contract, first flight, last delivery, number procured, manufacturer, models procured, delivery of production aircraft to operating unit, date and squadron number of first delivery and notes. Available from the Superintendent of Documents for $2.50; Catalog Number D217.2:Av 5.

U.S. MARINE CORPS

AIRCRAFT

1914-1959

On July 28, 1959, Marine Attack Squadron 331 replaced its last AD-6 at Iwakuni, Japan, with a sleek, new A4D-2. Thus ended an era of propeller driven airplanes that started for the United States Marine Corps on January 6, 1914.

In the short span of one lifetime the Marines have advanced from a crude 50 m.p.h. stick and wire pusher, useful for observation only, to the compact A4D jet attack plane capable of delivering more destructive power in one flight than all of the B-17's in World War Two.

This book summarizes in pictorial form this tremendous technological advancement, and although it is limited to USMC equipment it also portrays the broad changes undergone by naval aviation in general. From its inception, up to the present time, Marine Aviation has always been a distinct part of naval aviation. All Marine pilots are Navy trained and designated as Naval Aviators. During the pre-war years it had as one of its functions the training of carrier pilots as an emergency reserve for the Fleet.

The primary job of Marine Aviation, since the establishment of the Fleet Marine Force in 1933, has been that of air support for amphibious landings. This purpose has been the deciding factor in the types of aircraft used by the Marine Corps. Today that role has been expanded even further with the commissioning of the first all-Marine carrier, the CVHA1 Thetis Bay, which carries both the Marine assault troops and transport helicopters to maintain a self-contained landing operation.

Much of the secret behind the skilled and efficient operations of Marine Aviation in World War Two lies in the fact that it was the only one of the services to have the advantage of combat experience, even though on a limited scale, during the peacetime years between the two World Wars. The patrols in China, as well as the jungle fighting in Nicaragua, Haiti and the Dominican Republic which stretched across several years in the 1920's, may not have involved large numbers of casualties or incidents but the very nature of the operations required the constant utilization of all skills and trades. Thus, because of its real and continuing nature, it had a distinct advantage over the periodic war games performed by the Army and Navy.

The date of May 22, 1912, is most often quoted as the birthday of Marine Corps Aviation. It was on this day that Lt. Alfred Austell Cunningham USMC, Naval Aviator No. 5 and Marine Aviator No. 1, first reported for flying training at Annapolis. However, since this book deals with airplanes rather than people, it begins with the date of January 6, 1914. It was at this time that the first two airplanes, as specific pieces of equipment, are known to have been assigned to the Marine Corps.

Our unique form of chronological presentation is the first time that such a method has been used in an aircraft book. It is an attempt to present a graphic documentation of aircraft use in its proper context as contrasted with the normal method of listing aircraft alphabetically by manufacturer's name. The reader should note that each page is dated at the top for easy reference.

It is felt that the alphabetical system does not do justice to the over-all historical picture and that only a complete and systematic presentation year-by-year properly demonstrates the beginning and ending of aircraft types, markings, colors and squadron usage.

A conscientious effort has been made to arrange every illustration as of the date of the photograph, not by the date of construction of the airplane. A careful study of the photos and text will show the full service life of an aircraft type (such as the O2C-1) from the time it is new at the factory, through first line squadron use, to its semi-retirement as a utility hack.

Thus, with very few exceptions, a true visual picture of the service of each type is given and a clear division will be noted at the points where an aircraft type enters and leaves the service and where changes in color and markings take place. Examples of such changes are 1942, when the red center was removed from the star in the national insignia, and 1956 when the midnight blue over-all color was changing to white and gray.

Unfortunately this was not always possible, as with the J2F-5 on page 111, which has 1941 markings but is in the 1943 section. In such cases it was impossible to obtain a proper photograph.

Two conflicting policies were established for this history. One was the importance of using only photos showing actual U. S. Marine Corps aircraft, while the other was the necessity of illustrating every type of aircraft ever operated. Due to the lack of photos of many types in Marine Corps markings, despite a continuous twenty-three year search, it was necessary to substitute photos of Navy aircraft of the same type. Whenever this conflict arose it was decided in favor of illustrating the plane with any available photo rather than eliminate it from the book.

In a few cases it was felt that one photo of a series was adequate as long as no photo existed of the plane in USMC markings. Such a case involves the Howard GH-1, 2 and 3, which are externally indistinguishable, and it was felt that the inclusion of a Navy GH-1 and GH-3 photo would add nothing of value to the GH-2 covered on page 117. In other cases, such as the XSBC-4 and F4F-7, no photograph of any kind has become available.

It should be noted by the reader that the reason some types, such as the AD and F9F, are repeated so often is that one of the goals of this compilation was to include every squadron and every marking for which a photo could be found. Thus the apparent repitition of a given type is actually a presentation of different squadrons or different tail letters. This is not always pointed out in the captions and the reader will gain much additional information by a careful study of the photographs.

Individual aircraft serial numbers have been included whenever known so that pilots can check their log books to see if they have flown the particular plane illustrated. The individual airplane is identified throughout its life by this number which does not change and is not re-assigned.

The pre-war dimensions and performance figures are the most accurate available and are from the official "Characteristics, Weights and Performance of U. S. Navy Airplanes". No such information is available for post-war aircraft and the data presented for these is from Navy and Marine Corps Public Information releases.

In addition to the many individuals and organizations that are acknowledged under each of the photos the author wishes to express his appreciation and gratitude to the following: Robert S. Houston and Francis S. Beise, Air Force Museum, Wright-Patterson AFB; Robert W. Krauskopf and Elbert L. Huber, National Archives and Records Service, General Services Administration; Director of Information, Headquarters, United States Marine Corps; Historical Branch, G-3, Headquarters, United States Marine Corps; CWO Walter Lee Huber, Marine Corps Schools, Quantico; Informational Services Office, MCAAS Beaufort; James C. Fahey and William A. Riley, Jr.

William T. Larkins
August 21, 1959

Curtiss E-1 (A-2)   U. S. Navy
Number two USN plane to USMC 1-6-14. Built 1911. Converted to
O-W-L (Over Water & Land) amphibian, flown by Lt. B. L. Smith.

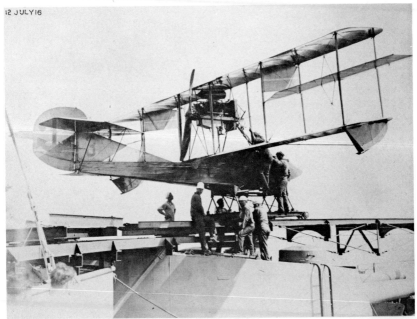

Curtiss C-3 (A-12)   U. S. Navy
Formerly AB-3. Assigned to USMC, with E-1, for USN maneuvers
off Puerto Rico. On catapult of USS North Carolina, July, 1916.

Curtiss R-6 (A-177)   U. S. Navy
One of ten torpedo planes flown on anti-sub patrol in the Azores by
the First Marine Aeronautic Company together with N-9's, HS-2L's.

Burgess N-9 (A-2504)   U. S. Navy
Curtiss seaplane trainer design with rear cockpit machine gun, Hisso
engine. First seaplane ever looped; by Captain Evans, U.S.M.C.

Curtiss JN-4HG-1 (A-4183)   U. S. Navy
At Miami in August 1918, first USMC airfield. JN-4B's, JN-4D's,
as well as double aileron JN-6's, were used by the Marine Corps.

DeHavilland DH-9 (RAF D1651)   Peter M. Bowers
Improved DH-4 design, Siddley B.H.P., 200 hp.   Flown by USMC
pilots operating with RAF Squadrons 217 & 218 in combat, late 1918.

Sopwith "Camel"   Gordon S. Williams
Marine Corps pilots flew a few missions in these planes of R.A.F.
Squadron 213, but none were assigned as U.S.M.C. equipment.

Standard E-1 (Army 33770)   U. S. Marine Corps
100 hp Gnome powered M-1 Defense. Several were flown by the
Marines while in training at Army Fields such as Gerstner, Louisiana.

DH-4B   U. S. Navy
British designed two-place day bomber built in the U. S. by Dayton
Wright, Fisher and Standard.   400 hp Liberty, top speed 124 m.p.h.

Curtiss HS-2L (A-2072)   U. S. Navy
Liberty-powered HS-1L with extra wing panel added. Also built by
Aeromarine and L.W.F.   Used in the Azores, at Miami and Guam.

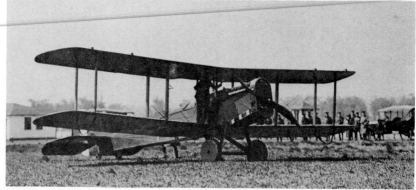

DH-4   U. S. Navy
Marine Corps DH-4's formed the Day Wing of the Northern Bombing
Group in France in World War I, remained in use until 1929.

New Marine Corps Aviation Insignia   U. S. Marine Corps
In August 1920 all U. S. Marine Corps airplanes were ordered to
carry this new insignia. The outer circle was red, the middle blue,
the center white. See DH-4 photo on the top of page 6.

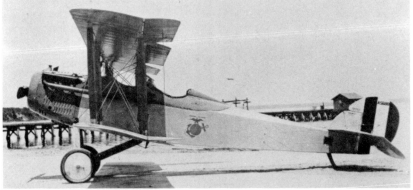

Vought VE-7S (A-5680)   U. S. Navy
At Quantico in May 1921. On December 1, 1922 the USMC emblem
was changed to an insignia red world with yellow continents.

Dayton-Wright DH-4 (A-3280)   U. S. Marine Corps
Fifth plane of Squadron D which arrived at La Frene, France, in
October 1918, completing four squadrons of eighteen planes each.

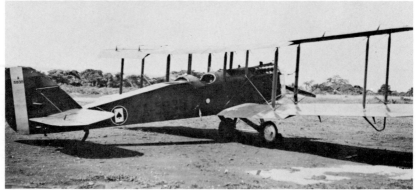

DH-4B (A-5835)   U. S. Navy
At Santo Domingo City, July 1921. First Air Squadron (later VO-1M,
VO-8M, VMS-3, VMSB-231) flew mail, doctors, photo missions.

Thomas-Morse MB-3 (A-6060)   U. S. Navy
Assigned to Flight "F", Third Air Squadron, at Quantico. Eleven
(A6060-6070) were transferred from Army Air Service to Marines.

Thomas-Morse MB-3 (A-6060)   U. S. Navy
1920 fighter with 300 hp Hispano. Weight 1818 lbs, 152 mph maximum
speed, 23,700 foot ceiling. Span 26', length 20', height 8'6".

Fokker D-7 (A-5845)   U. S. Marine Corps
One of six (A5843-5848) unarmed German World War I fighters used
by the Marine Corps for post-war training from 1921 to 1924.

Fokker C-1   Peter M. Bowers
One of three (A5887-5889) two-place D-7 trainers. 243 hp B.M.W.
Weight 2,576 lbs, 112 mph speed, 17,000' ceiling, span 34'10".

Curtiss JN-4 (A-6545)   Lawrence S. Smalley
A "Jenny" built from spare parts by the Marine Base, Port au Prince,
Haiti.   A-6247 was a JN-4H built from spares at Parris Island.

DH-4B (A-5834)   Capt. Francis C. Belcher
M/Sgt B. T. Belcher, first enlisted pilot in USMC, in cockpit of
his plane at Santo Domingo City, 1922. Note covered front cockpit.

Curtiss HS-2L (A-2011)   U. S. Navy
Bringing in the USMC patrol plane at Guam. Operations started as
Flight "L" of Fourth Air Squadron in 1921, became VS-1M, VP-3M.

DH-4B (A-5811)   Lawrence S. Smalley
One of 21 (A5809-5829) DH-4B's purchased from the Army by the
Marine Corps in 1922. The Marines modified two as ambulances,
this one of VO-2M is shown in Haiti; VO-1M had A-5883. Note red
cross insignia on the turtle-back built to house the stretcher. O.I.C.
Colonel Turner flew a two plane DH-4 flight from Washington, D.C.,
to Santo Domingo in 1921. In 1924 VO-2M flew two DH-4B's on the
longest flight in U. S. aviation history - Haiti to San Francisco and
return - 10,953 miles. Six USMC DH-4's took part in the 1921 bombing of USS Iowa off the Virginia Capes. In 1926 M.C.A.S. Quantico
built an experimental DH-4B-3 by replacing the standard Liberty
engine with a Packard 2A-1500 from a Loening OL-6. See Index for
O2B-1 as well as various DH-4 models. The DH-4B weighed 3,786
pounds, did 123.7 miles per hour, had a 15,800 foot ceiling.

Naval Aircraft Factory F-5-L (A-3871)   U. S. Navy
VS-1M had four in 1922 including A-3591 (crashed on a night flight
2-21-22), A-3661 and A-4314. Had 104 foot span, 49 foot 3 inch length.

Elias EM-1 (A-5905)   U. S. Navy
First plane built to Class VM (Marine Expeditionary) specifications
listed by Hq USMC in 1919.   300 hp Hisso engine, 90 mph speed.

Elias EM-2 (A-5906)   U. S. Navy
400 hp Liberty, speed 111 mph. Floats or wheels. Weight 3,916 lbs.
A5906-5911. Span 39 ft. 8 in., length 28 ft. 6 in. Ceiling 19,300 feet.

Naval Aircraft Factory NM-1 (A-6450)   U. S. Navy
All metal with Packard 1A-1237 (325 hp) engine. Design laid down
in 1922, not built until 1925. Span 42 ft., length 31 ft., weight 4190 lbs.

Douglas DT-2 (A-6584)   U. S. Navy
Standard Liberty-powered Navy torpedo bomber of the 1920's with a
50 ft. span, 34 ft. length, maximum speed 103, weight 6,505 pounds.

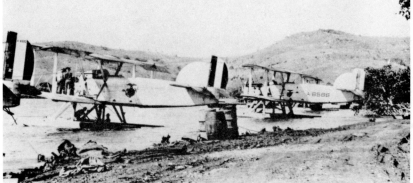

Lowe-Willard-Fowler DT-2 (A-6586, 6592)   I. A. S. Library
Six USMC DT-2's took part in the Winter Maneuvers, February 1924,
at Culebra Island, Puerto Rico.   Both LWF and NAF built DT-2's.

Naval Aircraft Factory VE-7F (A-5692)   Capt. Francis C. Belcher
Single place fighter version of the VE-7 trainer assigned to VO-1M
(Observation One), Santo Domingo, Dominican Republic, 1922.

Loening OL-2 (A-6981)   U. S. Navy
All five (A6980-6983, 7030) eventually were assigned to USMC use.
Inverted Liberty, max speed 121, weight 5016, span 45 ft., length 34 ft.

Martin MBT   U. S. Navy
Twin Liberty powered heavy bomber first flown by Marine Corps in
1921. 71 ft. 5 in. span, 46 ft. 5 in. length, 15 ft. height. Weight 12,078 lbs.

Martin MBT   William T. Larkins
With the new markings of the San Diego based Second Aviation
Group formed in Sept. 1925 from combination of VO-1M & VF-3M.

Naval Aircraft Factory DH-4B (A-6189)   U. S. Marine Corps
Major Brainard's re-modeled DH-4 at Quantico in January 1925.
At that time he was Commanding Officer of the First Aviation Group.

Cox-Klemin XS-1 (A-6515)   U. S. Navy
18 ft. by 18 ft. by 8 ft. sub scout, 60 hp Lawrence L-4, 103 mph, weight
only 974 pounds. One at USMC San Diego January 1926 to August 1927.

Martin MBT (A-5716)   U. S. Navy
It is uncertain how many of these bomber-torpedo planes were flown
by the Marine Corps. 10 were built, 6 known to have been USMC.

Boeing FB-1 (A-6893)   U. S. Navy
Development of Army PW-9 built in December 1925. Wooden wings,
metal fuselage, Curtiss D-12 engine of 410 hp. Weight 2,949 pounds.

Boeing FB-1 (A-6892)   U. S. Navy
Span 32 ft., length 23 ft. 6 in., height 8 ft. 9 in., maximum speed 167 mph.
Ceiling 21,200 feet. A6884-6893 served VF-1M, VF-2M, VF-3M.

Boeing FB-1 (A-6891)   U. S. Navy
At Quantico in April 1926, Note the circle around the letter "F"
to distinguish Marine Fighting Two from Navy Fighting Two.

Boeing FB-1 (A-6888)   U. S. Navy
This photo of Major Ross E. Rowell well illustrates the changing
Marine Corps emblem. Note also the data legend below cockpit.

STATUS OF MARINE CORPS AIRCRAFT
February, 1926

FIRST AVIATION GROUP, QUANTICO
        7 DH-4B-1, 16 O2B-1, 4 MBT, 1 TW-3, 11 VE-7,
        2 VE-7SF, 1 VE-9, 2 NB-2, 6 FB-1, 2 OL-2

SECOND AVIATION GROUPS, SAN DIEGO
        1 DH-4B-2, 9 DH-4B-1, 1 JN, 1 VE-7, 1 VE-7SF,
        2 MBT, 1 XS-1

OBSERVATION SQUADRON TWO, PORT AU PRINCE, HAITI
        3 DH-4B-1, 8 O2B-1, 1 JN

SCOUTING SQUADRON ONE, GUAM
        6 HS-2L, 2 VE-7H

Loening OL-3 (A-7056)   U. S. Navy
Similar to the OL-2 but powered with Inverted Packard 1A-2500
engine of 475 hp. Marines also flew the Liberty powered OL-4.

Boeing O2B-1 (A-6903)   U. S. Marine Corps
One of 30 modernized DH-4B's with metal fuselages (A6898-6927)
as Army DH-4M-1, delivered to First Aviation Group in 1925.

Loening OL-6 (A-7335)   U. S. Navy
A-7332 was used by General Smedley Butler, Third Brigade USMC,
at Hsin Ho, China, in 1927. Power was upped to 525 hp Packard.

Dayton-Wright TW-3 (A-6730)   U. S. Marine Corps
A two-place Trainer Water-Cooled taken over from the Army, the
only one in the Navy or Marine Corps. It was modified in early 1926
by Lt. F. G. Cowie USMC, engineering officer at Quantico, to a
one place duster. A 20-gauge galvanized iron hopper, three feet
high, two feet wide and three feet long was installed forward of the
cockpit over a four foot four inch venturi built under the fuselage.
The average load was 200 pounds per flight at a speed of 65 m.p.h.
The first flights were experimental and conducted over the upper
Chopawamsic Swamp near Quantico on June 21, 1926. A 200 yard
wide swath was laid from a height of 100 feet using one pound of
paris green to three of soapstone per acre. 800 acres were dusted
during the summer of 1926 to control the Anopheles mosquito. The
success of this work lead the Marines to adopt aerial dusting for the
control of malaria. In 1929 Atlantic trimotor #2 at Managua, Nicaragua, was modified for this purpose. See also the USMC Boeing
NB-2 on page 25, and the Martin T4M-1 on page 57.

Vought VE-9   U. S. Navy
Photographed May 12, 1926.   180 hp Wright E-3 gave a maximum
speed of 116 mph, ceiling of 15,250 feet. Weight 2,496 pounds.

Boeing O2B-1 (A-6904)   U. S. Navy
Maintenance funds allowed rebuilding when there was no money for
new purchases, hence the widespread use of the DH-4 in the 1920's.

STATUS OF MARINE CORPS AIRCRAFT
September, 1927

EAST COAST EXPEDITIONARY FORCE, QUANTICO
   VF-8M (VF-1M)* 7 F6C-3
   VF-9M (VF-2M)   3 F6C-1, 3 F6C-4, 1 MBT, 3 VE-7
   VO-6M (VO-3M)   2 NY-1, 1 VE-7, 1 OL-2
   VJ-6M   1 F6C-3, 1 F6C-4, 1 O2B-1, 1 VE-7SF, 1 VE-9,
                 2 NB-2
WEST COAST EXPEDITIONARY FORCE, SAN DIEGO
   VO-8M (VO-1M)   2 DH-4B-1, 1 DH-4B-2, 1 O2B-1, 1 FB-1,
                 2 MBT, 1 NB-1, 2 OD-1, 1 VE-7
USMC EXPEDITIONARY FORCE, NICARAGUA
   VO-7M (VO-4M)   2 DH-4B-1, 6 O2B-1
USMC EXPEDITIONARY FORCE, CHINA
   VF-10M (VF-3M) 9 FB-1
   VO-10M   6 O2B-1, 6 OL-6
FIRST BRIGADE, PORT AU PRINCE, HAITI
   VO-9M (VO-2M)   2 DH-4B-1, 8 O2B-1
MARINE GARRISON, GUAM
   VP-3M (VS-1M)   2 VE-7H
       *Squadron designation prior to 1 July 1927
  (Note: 1 XF6C-5 assigned to VF-9M, November 1927 only)

Curtiss F6C-1 (A-6968)   U. S. Navy
Similar to the Army P-1. Basic design became standard Navy fighter of the late 1920's.   Built in 1925, used by the USMC in 1928.

DH-4B-1 (A-6361)   U. S. Navy
One of a batch (A6352-6401) received from the Army, remodeled
by ten different companies. Had larger fuel tank and wheels.

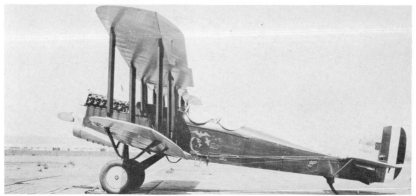

Naval Aircraft Factory DH-4B-2 (A-6134)   William T. Larkins
Navy re-modeled aircraft with all armament removed. A-6134 was
assigned to the Second Aviation Group, San Diego, California.

Curtiss F6C-3   Capt. Francis C. Belcher
Refined version of the F6C-1 as a carrier fighter. Maximum speed
154 mph, ceiling 20,600 ft. Span 31 ft. 6 in., length 22 ft. 7 in., as F6C-1.

STATUS OF MARINE CORPS AIRCRAFT — June 1928
EAST COAST EXPEDITIONARY FORCE, QUANTICO
   VF-8M   6 F6C-3, 1 NY-1
   VF-9M   3 F6C-1, 3 F6C-4, 1 NY-2
   VJ-6M   1 F6C-3, 1 F6C-4, 1 F8C-1, 2 F8C-3, 2 NB-2,
                              1 OL-2, 1 VE-9, 1 DH-4B-2, 1 O2B-1
WEST COAST EXPEDITIONARY FORCE, SAN DIEGO
   VO-8M   1 F8C-1, 7 F8C-3, 1 NB-1, 1 MBT, 2 OD-1
FIRST BRIGADE, HAITI
   VO-9M   1 DH-4B-1, 5 O2B-1, 4 O2U-1
SECOND BRIGADE, NICARAGUA
   VO-6M   3 F8C-1, 3 F8C-3, 3 TA-1, 2 TA-2
   VO-7M   1 OL-4, 1 XOL-8, 3 OL-8, 6 O2U-1
THIRD BRIGADE, CHINA
   VF-10M   9 FB-1, 1 F8C-1, 8 F8C-3
   VO-10M   5 O2B-1, 6 OL-6

Curtiss F8C-1 (A-7945)   U. S. Navy
First of the two-seat fighters to be re-designated as model OC-1.
Photo was taken 3-20-28, two days after its delivery to VO-8M.

Atlantic TA-1 (A-7561)   Peter M. Bowers
First of the Fokker tri-motor transports to serve the Marine Corps.
Built in the United States by Atlantic Aircraft Corp., New Jersey.

Curtiss F6C-4 (A-7395)   U. S. Navy
Major Edward H. Brainard, Officer In Charge USMC Aviation 1925-
1929, in front of his Wasp powered command plane.

Vought VE-7 (A-5676)   William T. Larkins
Standard version, assigned to VO-8M. Photograph taken at San
Francisco April 15, 1928. Note the war surplus JN-4D alongside.

Curtiss F7C-1 (A-7664)   William T. Larkins
Personal plane of Capt. James T. Moore, C. O., Air Service, East
Coast Expeditionary Force, Quantico. Five were rec'd in Jan. 1929.

STATUS OF MARINE CORPS AIRCRAFT
November, 1929

EAST COAST EXPEDITIONARY FORCE, QUANTICO
VF-4M	3 F6C-6, 7 F6C-3, 1 O2U-1
VF-5M	8 F7C-1, 1 JR-2
VO-6M	2 OL-8, 1 UO-1, 1 OC-1, 1 OC-2, 1 O2U-1, 1 NB-2, 1 NY-1B

NICARAGUA
VJ-6M	3 TA-1, 1 TA-2, 3 OL-8
VO-7M	2 OC-1, 3 OC-2, 6 O2U-1

WEST COAST EXPEDITIONARY FORCE, SAN DIEGO
VF-6M	5 FB-1, 6 FB-5
VO-8M	5 OC-2
VO-10M	6 OC-2
VJ-7M	1 OC-1 (2 OD-1 in January)

FIRST BRIGADE, PORT AU PRINCE, HAITI
VO-9M	8 O2U-1 (1 O2B-2, 1 XHL-1 in Jan.)

MARINE GARRISON, GUAM
VP-3M	1 OL-3, 5 OL-6, 3 OL-8

Boeing FB-3 (A-7090)   U. S. Navy
FB-2 with Packard 1A-1500 engine; 3 built. A-7090 was assigned
to VF-6M in 1929, the only year the squadron was thus designated.

Vought O2U-1 (A7568)   Kurt F. E. Schoenfeld
M/Sgt Schoenfeld, USMC Enlisted Pilot No. 8, at Port au Prince,
Haiti. O2U-1's served VO-9M from 1928 to 1933. See photo, page 43.

Atlantic TA-2 (A-8018)   U. S. Navy
VJ-6M transport at Managua, Nicaragua in 1929 with a wing center
section tied under the fuselage. OC-1 down in field was saved.

Boeing FB-5 (A-7104)   U. S. Navy
Production model of FB-3, A7107-7127 built. It was used by both
Navy and Marine fighting squadrons. Two .30 calibre guns in nose.

Boeing FB-5 (A-7104)   U. S. Navy
Top speed 169 mph, stalling 60. Span 32 ft., length 23 ft 2 in. James
C. Mathiesen of California is currently re-building number A-7114.

Boeing FB-1 (A-6885)   Boeing Airplane Company
Rare photo showing VF-6M markings and odd tail stripes. VF-6M
was VF-10M in 1928, became VF-10M again in 1930. See page 27.

Boeing NB-2 (A-6778)   U. S. Navy
VO-6M's modified trainer used for spraying arsenate dust to kill
mosquito larvae in the swamps near Quantico. Note the insignia.

Douglas OD-1 (A-7204)   U. S. Navy
Third design in the VM category. Two (A7103-7104) were built
in 1926. After a short service with VO relegated to Utility duty.

Loening XHL-1 (A-8275)   U. S. Navy
One of two special ambulance planes, the other being assigned to
N.A.S. Hampton Roads. A-8275 crashed on T.O. March 24, 1929.

Curtiss OC-1 (A-7945)   Curtiss-Wright Corporation
Converted Army O-1B design purchased as F8C-1 and re-named
OC-1.   A7945 was fitted by USMC as photo ship. Note tail skid.

Curtiss OC-1 (A-7671)   U. S. Navy
Rare photo of the first XF8C-1. Another (A7672) and four F8C-1's
(A7945-7948) built.   A7672 was modified to XOC-3, see page 35.

Curtiss OC-1 (A-7947)   John C. Mitchell
Span 38 ft., length 28 ft., height 11 ft. 7 in. P & W R-1340 (410 hp). Max
speed 138 mph, stalling speed 59. Weight 3956, ceiling 17,300 feet.

Curtiss OC-2   William T. Larkins
Note twin .30 cal flexible guns, fixed .30's in the lower wings,
ten 17-pound bombs. OC's and O2U-1's fought in Nicaragua.

STATUS OF MARINE CORPS AIRCRAFT
September, 1930

EAST COAST EXPEDITIONARY FORCE, QUANTICO
    VF-8M (VF-4M)* 2 F6C-1, 7 F6C-3, 1 O2U-1, 3 F8C-5
    VF-9M (VF-5M)   7 F7C-1, 1 JR-2
    VO-6M   2 O2U-1, 1 NB-2, 1 XN2B-1
NICARAGUA
    VJ-6M   1 JR-3, 1 TA-2, 1 TA-3, 4 OL-8
    VO-7M   3 OC-1, 3 OC-2, 4 O2U-1
WEST COAST EXPEDITIONARY FORCE, SAN DIEGO
    VF-10M (VF-6M) 8 F6C-4
    VO-8M   4 OC-2
    VO-10M   5 OC-2
    VJ-7M   2 OC-1
FIRST BRIGADE, PORT AU PRINCE, HAITI
    VO-9M   7 O2U-1, 1 OL-8
MARINE GARRISON, GUAM
    VP-3M   1 OL-6, 3 OL-8

*Squadron designation prior to 1 July 1930

Curtiss F6C-3 (A-7146)   U. S. Navy
Quantico based fighter with 1929 markings. The squadron regained
its earlier designation of VF-8M in 1930. See page 27.

Consolidated NY-1B (A-7193)   U. S. Navy
Two-place trainer operated by VO-6M in late 1929 and early 1930.
Widely used as primary trainer by Navy but rare in the Marines.

Ford JR-3 (A-8598)   National Archives
Factory photo taken April 29, 1930. Plane crashed in Nicaragua on
August 4, 1930. These all-metal Tri-Motors did heavy duty work.

Curtiss OC-2's (A-7958, 7959, 7966) U. S. Navy
Two VO-8M and one VO-10M OC-2's flying over San Diego Bay
in October 1930. Note painted wheel covers, noses, top of wings.

Curtiss F6C-3 (A-7147)   U. S. Navy
On May 31, 1930, Captain Arthur H. Page, from Headquarters U.
S.M.C., won the Curtiss Marine Trophy Race held at the Naval Air
Station Anacostia, D.C., by piloting the above plane five times
around a 20-mile course at an average speed of 164 m.p.h. Note
how all openings in the fabric have been carefully taped over to
reduce drag on this specially lightened and modified fighter for
racing purposes. Three Marine F6C-3's participated in the 1929
Curtiss Marine Trophy Race. The F6C-3, as used by the Marine
Corps, was a land plane. The floats are a special fitting for racing only.

Curtiss F6C-4 (A-7394)   U. S. Navy
Switch to air-cooled engines was major policy change of the 1930
period in Naval aviation. Photo shows a surplus aircraft, note paint.

Curtiss OC-2 (A-7954)   Gordon S. Williams
10-O-1 in the field with practice bombs and gun ring. All twenty-one (A7949-7969) went to USMC, originally designated F8C-3.

Boeing XN2B-1 (A-8010)   Boeing Airplane Company
The one and only Caminez-powered XN2B-1 served with VO-6M at Quantico in 1930. Many one only types ended up in the U.S.M.C.

Curtiss F8C-5 (A-8589)   U. S. Navy
The famous "Helldiver" in battle array on 9-10-30. F8C-5's were delivered to VO-6M in late 1930, re-designated O2C-1 in 1931.

Curtiss F8C-5 (A-8589)   Curtiss-Wright Corporation
Showing the special cabin installation for Col. Turner, OIC Marine
Aviation 1929-1931. 5-8-31 photo. Compare with photo on page 31.

STATUS OF MARINE CORPS AIRCRAFT
June, 1931

EAST COAST EXPEDITIONARY FORCE, QUANTICO
    VF-8M   2 F6C-1, 6 F6C-3, 2 O2C-1
    VF-9M   7 F7C-1, 1 XOC-3, 1 RC-1, 1 JR-2, 1 RS-3
    VO-6M   17 O2C-1, 4 F6C-3, 1 NB-2 (1 NT-1 in storage)
NICARAGUA
    VJ-6M   3 RA-3, 2 RR-2, 1 RR-3, 2 OL-8, 3 N2C-2
    VO-7M   9 O2C-1, 3 O2U-1, 2 OC-1, 2 OC-2
WEST COAST EXPEDITIONARY FORCE, SAN DIEGO
    VF-10M   8 F6C-4
    VO-8M   4 OC-2, 1 OL-8
    VO-10M   4 OC-2
    VJ-7M   2 OC-1
PORT AU PRINCE, HAITI
    VO-9M   6 O2U-1, 1 OL-8

Curtiss O2C-1 (A-8589)   William T. Larkins
A8589 with canopy removed and headrest added serving VO-7M as
service type. A8448-8456, 8589-8597, 8748-8756 all to U.S.M.C.

Atlantic RA-4 (A-8841)   U. S. Navy
New plane, shown as of February 1931. Old T/Transport designation
changed at this time to R/Transport.   TA-3 became RA-3, etc.

Atlantic RA-4 (A-8841)   U. S. Navy
The same plane with its nose lengthened 18 in. to improve stability.
3-450 hp Wasps, weight 12,850. Speed 150, span 79 ft., length 50 ft. 7 in.

Curtiss RC-1 (A-8846)   U. S. Navy
The only military "Kingbird" built, as delivered in March, 1931.
It first served VF-9M at Quantico, then VJ-7M at San Diego, Calif.

Sikorsky RS-3 (A-8923)   U. S. Navy
Both A8922 (see page 55) and 8923 served the Marines at Quantico
and in Nicaragua. A civilian amphibian transport known as S-38.

Ford JR-2 (A-8274)   William T. Larkins
Model 4-AT transport used by VJ-6M in Nicaragua. Utility VJ class
for transports was changed to Transport VR, thus it became RR-2.

Atlantic RA-3 (A-8018)   Peter M. Bowers
Rare photo of TA-2 modified. Three only (A8007, 8008, 8018) were
changed. Three Wright R-975 (300 hp), weight 9090, speed 128 mph.

Curtiss XOC-3 (A-7672)   Curtiss-Wright Corporation
XF8C-1 modified by the installation of a Curtiss H-1640 engine.
1 only built. Assigned to VF-9M from December 1930 to June 1931.

New Standard NT-1 (A-8587)   John C. Mitchell
One of these Kinner-powered primary trainers was in and out of
storage and use by VO-6M during 1931 and 1932. Two place plane.

Curtiss F8C-5 (A-8451)   William T. Larkins
Rare photo showing F8C-5 designation and Marine Corps squadron
markings, in use for less than six months. See pages 31 and 32.

Curtiss F6C-4   U. S. Navy
One of VF-10M's eight F6C-4's shown in full markings at San Diego
on August 18, 1931.   Star on underside of top wing is irregular.

Squadron Lineup at San Diego   William T. Larkins
Lineup for inspection at N.A.S. North Island showing the new F4B-4's
of VF-10M and SU-2's of VO-8M.   Note the VJ-7M's N2C-2's.

Curtiss F6C-4   William T. Larkins
Third plane of Marine Fighting Squadron Ten. The F6C-4's were replaced by F4B-4's. Note the winged devil squadron insignia on fin.

STATUS OF MARINE CORPS AIRCRAFT
October, 1932

EAST COAST EXPEDITIONARY FORCE, QUANTICO
    VF-9M   8 F7C-1, 6 F4B-4, 1 RC-1
    VO-6M   13 O2C-1, 1 RA-3, 1 T4M-1, 1 NT-1
NICARAGUA
    VO-7M   9 O2C-1, 7 O2U-1
    VJ-6M   1 RR-2, 1 RR-5, 1 RS-3, 1 OP-1, 4 OL-9,
                        2 N2C-2
WEST COAST EXPEDITIONARY FORCE ,SAN DIEGO
    VF-10M   8 F6C-4
    VO-8M   5 SU-2, 2 OC-1, 5 OC-2
    VJ-7M   2 OC-1, 1 N2C-2
PORT AU PRINCE, HAITI
    VO-9M   8 O2U-1

Ford RR-2 (A-8273)   U. S. Navy
Standing in about the same position as in the photo on the left. It has
the same engines as RA-3. Wt.10,441 lbs., speed 130 mph, span 74 ft.

Curtiss O2C-1 (A-8594)   U. S. Navy
This photo, taken on November 18, 1932, shows the start of the
colorful markings that were to last for the next three years.

Curtiss O2C-1 (A-8848)   William T. Larkins
These red and black tail and cowl markings of VO-6M may have
been initiated for their visit to Canada in August, 1932.

Ford RR-5 (A-9205)   William T. Larkins
This big 5-AT-D was the only one of its kind to serve the U.S.M.C.
Assigned to Utility Squadron Six-M from 1933 through the year 1935.

Vought SU-2's (A-9099, 9102, 9103)   U. S. Marine Corps
Rare June 26, 1933 photo showing Observation Squadron Eight-M
flying its new SU-2 scouts in step formation over San Diego, Calif.
The four other squadrons using SU-2's at this time were VO-9M,
VS-15M and Navy VS-2, VS-3. One SU-2 each was also assigned
to Navy VF-2 and VF-5 as fighter squadron utility planes.

STATUS OF MARINE CORPS AIRCRAFT
February, 1933

EAST COAST EXPEDITIONARY FORCE, QUANTICO
   VF-9M   15 F4B-4, 4 F7C-1, 1 RC-1, 1 T4M-1
   VO-6M   13 O2C-1
   VO-7M   9 O2C-1
   VJ-6M   1 RR-2, 1 RR-5, 1 RS-3, 1 RE-3, 1 OL-9, 1 OP-1

WEST COAST EXPEDITIONARY FORCE, SAN DIEGO
   VF-10M   6 F4B-4
   VO-8M   5 SU-2, 1 OC-1, 5 OC-2
   VJ-7M   1 RR-2, 2 OC-1

PORT AU PRINCE, HAITI
   VO-9M   7 SU-2, 8 O2U-1, 1 OL-8

Boeing F4B-4 (A-9016)   John C. Mitchell
The F4B-4's were first delivered to VF-9M (East Coast), soon to be
followed by delivery to VF-10M (West Coast) in late 1932.

Curtiss N2C-2 (A-8543)   John C. Mitchell
Two-place "Fledgling" trainer assigned to VJ-7M in late 1932 and
early 1933. Three were used in Nicaragua in 1931 with VJ-6M.

Vought SU-2 (A-9101)   U. S. Navy
8-O-3 in flight 2-16-33 showing the flare shields under outboard
wing panels, bomb racks under inboard panels. Formerly O3U-4.

Curtiss OC-1 (A-7945) U. S. Navy
Showing as of 2-16-33 one of two OC-1's transferred to Utility duty,
standard practice as combat aircraft become obsolescent.

Curtiss OC-2 (A-7952) William T. Larkins
7-J-7 illustrating above statement. Note unusual placement of the
Marine Corps emblem far forward on the fuselage, wheel design.

Curtiss F7C-1 (A-7661) William T. Larkins
One of the last F7C-1's, soon to be replaced by more F4B-4's. Note
"M" for Marines under circled class letter. See also page 26.

Pitcairn XOP-1 (A-8976)   U. S. Navy
Rare 11-14-33 photo of the one only USMC autogiro flown by VJ-6M at Quantico and Managua.   280 ft. T.O. run, speed 115, wt 3057.

Sikorsky RS-1 (A-8842)   U. S. Navy
Photo taken 11-25-33 in Haiti. Colonel Turner, OIC Aviation, was killed by turning prop of this plane three days later at Gonaives.

Curtiss F7C-1 (A-7670)   William T. Larkins
Final VF-9M markings for the F7C-1, see photo on page 41. The vertical tail stripes soon disappeared in favor of solid colors.

Curtiss N2C-2 (A-8529)   U. S. Navy
This plane and 6-J-11 (A8530) served VJ-6M in Nicaragua and at
Quantico 1932-1933. Wright R-760-94,   240 hp. Speed 116 m.p.h.

Vought O2U-1 (A-7939)   William T. Larkins
Command type O2U-1 "Corsair" from VO-9M with rear cockpit
machine guns removed and head-rest added as on O2C-1, page 32.

Loening OL-9 (A-8980)   William T. Larkins
450 hp Wasp powered improvement of the OL-8 which saw wide
service with USMC in China, Nicaragua and USA for many years.

Vought O2U-2 (A-8126)   John C. Mitchell
The following four pages show the little known pre-war carrier
operations of VS-14M and VS-15M from Nov. 1931, to Nov. 1934.

Vought O2U-2 (A-8098)   U. S. Navy
VS-14M reported aboard the USS Saratoga on November 2, 1931
with a few O2U-2's, later replaced them with SU-1's and SU-3's.

Vought SU-1 (A-9073)   U. S. Navy
VS-14M's lead plane with red cowl, fuselage band and tail. Its 600
hp R-1690-C upped speed 24 m.p.h. over the O2U-2's 147 m.p.h.

Vought O2U-2's

U. S. Navy

14-S-5, 14-S-4 and 14-S-2 approaching CV-3 Saratoga in a high
landing approach. Note the lowered carrier arresting gear hooks.

Vought O2U-2's

U. S. Navy

Ready for the final landing pattern. Note vertical ID stripe on the
funnel of USS Saratoga. On USS Lexington it was a horizontal stripe.

Vought SU-1 (A-9063)   William T. Larkins
SU-1 had a span of 36 ft., length of 26 ft. 3 in., height of 11 ft. 6 in.,
gross weight 4,622 lbs. Originally ordered as O3U-2, became SU-1.

Vought SU-2 (A-9105)   William T. Larkins
Blue-tailed VS-15M scout from the USS Lexington. This training as
carrier replacements gave 60% of the U.S.M.C. pilots carrier duty.

Vought SU-2 (A-9114)   John C. Mitchell
15-S-6 again but a different airplane, typical of Naval aircraft
mobility and the replacement of damaged aircraft by spares.

Vought SU-1's   U. S. Navy
The six SU-1's of VS-14M flying over San Diego, April 30, 1934.
Bulge on forward fuselage is flotation gear for ditching at sea.

Vought SU-2's and SU-3's   U. S. Navy
Squadron C.O. and five planes from VS-15M. Both units were under
Chief, Naval Operations, thus do not appear in tables on page 39, etc.

Loening OL-8 (A-8087)   U. S. Navy
With VP-3M at Guam, VO-9M in Haiti, VJ-6M in Nicaragua, VO-8M & VJ-7M at San Diego. A7850 crashed Lake Nicaragua 4-13-29.

STATUS OF MARINE CORPS AIRCRAFT
January, 1934

EAST COAST EXPEDITIONARY FORCE, QUANTICO
   VF-9M   23 F4B-4, 1 OL-9
   VO-7M   18 O2C-1
   VJ-6M   2 O2C-1, 1 F3B-1, 1 F4B-4, 1 OL-9, 1 OP-1,
                    1 T4M-1, 1 RR-2, 1 RR-5, 1 RE-3, 1 RS-3,
                    2 O2C-1 (based at Maxwell Field)

WEST COAST EXPEDITIONARY FORCE, SAN DIEGO
   VB-4M   16 F4B-3
   VJ-7M   3 OC-1, 1 OC-2, 1 RC-1, 1 RR-2, 1 OL-9

PORT AU PRINCE, HAITI
   VO-9M   7 SU-2, 2 SU-3, 3 O2U-1, 1 OL-8, 1 RS-1

Curtiss O2C-1 (A-8752)   William T. Larkins
Tank between wheel struts is smoke generator for war maneuvers
and aerial displays. Note tail wheel - another change in the times.

Curtiss O2C-1 (A-8454)   William T. Larkins
The 1934 National Air Races at Cleveland saw the introduction of
these new red-white-blue markings by VO-6M and VO-7M.

Curtiss O2C-1 (A-8589)   William T. Larkins
Colonel Turner's command plane again, this time with VO-6M.
See pages 31 and 32 for previous photos of this same aircraft.

Curtiss O2C-1 (A-8590)   William T. Larkins
7-O-10 being righted after a nose-over landing at Quantico. By
this time VO-7M was operating six three-plane sections.

Curtiss O2C-1 (A-8750)   Peter M. Bowers
The rugged "Helldiver" demonstrated precision dive bombing so well
at the National Air Races that Germany adopted its Stuka tactics.

Curtiss O2C-1 (A-8446)   E. L. Shyrock
One of two F8C-4's converted to XF8C-6, then modified back to
O2C-1 standard and sent to line duty. All F8C-5's became O2C-1's.

Curtiss O2C-1's   U. S. Navy
Beautiful photo of VO-7M's #11, 13, 2, 7, 4 and 8 in line formation
near Quantico.   Top speed of 140 m.p.h., ceiling of 16,050 feet.

Curtiss O2C-1's   U. S. Navy
Span 32 ft., length 26 ft.(longer than the Reserves 22 ft. 2 in. F8C-4),
height 10 ft. 3 in. Gross wt. 4,020 lbs. Endurance 7.6 hours flying time.

Boeing F4B-3 (A-8894)   John C. Mitchell
In the change over from Fighting Ten to Bombing Four this squadron
switched from F4B-4 fighters to F4B-3's for light bombing.

Vought SU-1 (A-9075)   John C. Mitchell
VO-8M was in a state of transition during 1934, absorbing some of
the planes and pilots from disbanded VS-14M and VS-15M.

Boeing F3B-1 (A-7763)   Fred E. Bamberger
Standard Navy carrier fighter, one only operated by the Marines.
It was modified F2B-1 with more h.p., span and weight, less speed.

Boeing F4B-4 (A-9240)   William T. Larkins
VF-9M's 23 F4B-4's appeared at the 1934 National Air Races with
solid colored tails in red, white and blue. Note race pylon in rear.

Boeing F4B-4 (A-9038)   Gordon S. Williams
24 of original order went to USMC, A9009-9010, 9230-9239 to East
Coast;   A9033, 9036-9040, 9240-9245 to West Coast in the year 1933.

Boeing F4B-4 (A-9242)   U. S. Navy
Rare photo of the famous #22 after a rough night landing. The F4B-4
took off in 441 feet, landed at 63 m.p.h., had speed of 184 m.p.h.

Curtiss RC-1 (A-8846)   John C. Mitchell
Well known in the San Diego-Los Angeles area, this odd bird did
a surprising 139.5 m.p.h. with two 300 horsepower Wright R-975's.

Curtiss R4C-1 (A-9585)   U. S. Navy
The big "Condor" airline transport was a welcome addition to
VJ-6M in June of the year 1934, and to VJ-7M in November of 1935.

Bellanca RE-3 (A-9341)   William T. Larkins
A single, civil CH-300 "Pacemaker" purchased by the Navy and
assigned to the Marines in 1933. It served VJ-6M and VMJ-1 at
Quantico through 1938. It operated with an X prefix from 1935 on,
see page 77. A five passenger light transport powered by a Wright
R-975 of 330 hp. Two others served the Navy; A-8938 (XRE-1) and
A-9207 (XRE-2). Photo probably taken at factory prior to delivery.

Sikorsky RS-3 (A-8922)   Steve Bennis
The second RS-3 (see page 34) at Brown Field, Quantico. The
S-38 was used by the Army as C-6, by Navy and civilian airlines.

Stearman C-3B ("A-7939")   John C. Mitchell
Not a USMC plane but an accurate copy for certain flight scenes
in the 1934 Warner Brothers movie entitled "Devil Dogs of the Air".

Vought O2U-1 (A-7939)   John C. Mitchell
The real "Corsair" from which the above Stearman was copied.
Note the accuracy of detail in serial, insignias, squadron markings, etc.

Boeing F4B-4 (A-9014)   William T. Larkins
The F4B-4 had a span of only 30 ft., length 20 ft. 4 in., height 9 ft. 9 in.,
a small, compact, highly maneuverable plane designed for carrier use.

STATUS OF MARINE CORPS AIRCRAFT
June, 1935

AIRCRAFT ONE, FLEET MARINE FORCE, QUANTICO
    VO-7M   12 O2C-1, 12 O3U-6
    VO-9M   2 SU-1, 7 Su-2, 2 Su-3
    VF-9M   23 F4B-4
    VJ-6M   2 JF-1, 1 OL-9, 3 O2C-1, 1 F3B-1, 1 F4B-4,
                        1 T4M-1, 1 XRE-3, 1 RR-5, 1 R2D-1, 1 R4C-1,
                        1 RD-3
AIRCRAFT TWO, FLEET MARINE FORCE, SAN DIEGO
    VO-8M   15 O3U-6
    VB-4M   16 BG-1
    VJ-7M   1 RC-1, 1 OC-2, 1 OL-9, 1 RR-4, 2 JF-1

Vought O3U-6 (A-9729)   Chance-Vought
This factory photo of 2-27-35 shows a new O3U-6 prior to its delivery to the U.S.M.C.   First of block #A9729-9744 for VO-8M.

Martin T4M-1 (A-7633)   U. S. Navy
VJ-6M operated the only T4M-1 torpedo-bomber of the U.S.M.C.
It had a dust bin and hopper for spreading calcium arsenate poison.

Boeing F4B-3's (A-8891, 8896, 8903)   U. S. Navy
Note the special service developed bomb rack between the wheels.
These went out of service in June with the arrival of the BG-1's.

Curtiss O2C-1 (A-8751)   William T. Larkins
The O2C-1's also left combat service in June of 1935 when the
first O3U-6's arrived. Some became Utility hacks such as this one.

Douglas RD-3 (A-9533)   U. S. Navy
The only "Dolphin" amphibian transport of this model used by the
Marines. It has the insignia of Aircraft One, F.M.F., Quantico.

Loening OL-9 (A-8979)   John C. Mitchell
The OL-9 was assigned to VJ-7M in 1934 and 1935 only. It was
replaced by the new Grumman JF-1. See page 85.

Vought O3U-6 (0012)   William T. Larkins
The second batch of these planes, B0001-0016, went to VO-7M.
Note that the "B" is not used on the plane, nor was "A" in 1930's.

Curtiss R4C-1 (A-9584)   William T. Larkins
Workhorse of Aircraft Two, Fleet Marine Force, San Diego, Calif.
Operated by Utility Seven whose insignia appears on the fin.

Vought SU-3 (A-9141)   William T. Larkins
This 1935 National Air Race photo shows the rare "Winged Eye"
insignia of VO-9M used during their one year stay at Quantico.

Great Lakes BG-1 (A-9534)   John C. Mitchell
Sleek, rugged new dive-bomber designed to replace the O2C-1's
and F4B-3's previously used. Delivered to VB-4M in June of 1935.

Douglas R2D-1 (A-9994)   William T. Larkins
Fast, all-metal DC-2 transport. A-9994 had an added fin area as
shown. Marine paratroopers first trained in these, later in R3D-2's.

Ford RR-4 (A-8840)   John C. Mitchell
One of two 5-AT-C types flown by the USMC, this plane was turned
over to VJ-7M by the Navy in 1935. Had three 450 hp Wasp engines.

Great Lakes BG-1 (A-9854)   U. S. Navy
Colonel Roy S. Geiger piloting his new command plane in October,
1936. Note change to small USMC insignia, compare with page 15.

STATUS OF MARINE CORPS AIRCRAFT
February, 1936

AIRCRAFT ONE, FMF, QUANTICO
    VO-7M   14 O3U-6, 3 SU-2, 1 SU-3
    VB-6M   12 BG-1
    VF-9M   19 F4B-4, 1 O3U-6
    VJ-6M   2 BG-1, 2 JF-1, 4 O2C-1, 1 F4B-3, 1 F4B-4,
                      1 T4M-1, 1 OL-9, 2 R2D-1, 1 RR-4, 2 SU-1,
                      1 SU-2, 1 XRE-3
    Service Sqdn   4 F4B-4, 2 BG-1, 3 O2C-1

AIRCRAFT TWO, FMF, SAN DIEGO
    VO-8M   14 O3U-6
    VB-4M   14 BG-1
    VJ-7M   1 BG-1, 1 RC-1, 2 R4C-1, 2 JF-1, 1 O3U-6

ST. THOMAS, VIRGIN ISLANDS
    VO-9M   3 SU-2, SU-3, 1 RD-3, 2 O3U-6

Grumman JF-2 (0266)   U. S. Navy
The only JF-2 to the USMC, all others went to U.S. Coast Guard.
Assigned to VJ-6M at Quantico from November 1935 to June 1939.

Vought SU-1 (A-9067)   Howard Levy
One of two such planes for command and utility use operated by
Marine Utility Squadron Six. Wheel pants have been added extra.

Boeing F4B-3 (A-8911)   U. S. Army Air Corps
The beautiful command plane from Headquarters USMC, Washington,
at Randolph Field 11-1-35.   VJ-6M November 1935 to June 1939.

Great Lakes BG-1 (A-9841)   U. S. Marine Corps
Disbanded for two years, VO-6M became VB-6M with the arrival
of 16 new BG-1's in November 1935. Became VMB-1 in July 1937.

Vought O3U-6 (A-9729)   U. S. Navy
Although the O3U-6 "Corsair" was never operated on floats by the
Marine Corps the first plane was so tested at N.A.S. Anacostia.

Vought O3U-6 (A-9742)   John C. Mitchell
VO-8M Squadron Leader denoted by red 18" wide cowl band and
20" wide fuselage stripe. 8-O-1 is 10" high in 2" thickness letters.

Vought O3U-6 (A-9735)   John C. Mitchell
Note the top of wing and tail are chrome yellow. VO-8M "Ace of
Spades" insignia is 11 inches high. Second section color was white.

Vought SU-4 (A-9432)   John C. Mitchell
Note National Air Race bleachers in background. VO-8M flew
mixed equipment of SU-4's and O3U-6's during transition training.

Vought SU-4 (A-9414)   John C. Mitchell
Running up, ready for squadron take-off. Note 8-O-4 on the left
is an O3U-6. SU-4 was 4 m.p.h. faster than O3U-6's 163 m.p.h.

Vought O3U-6 (0002)   U. S. Marine Corps
Powered by P & W   R-1340-12 of 550 hp, it would take off in 420
feet with no wind. Span 36 ft., length 27 ft. 2 in., height 11 ft. 5 in.

Vought XOSU-1 (0016)   U. S. Navy
The last O3U-6 was modified with full length ailerons, added fin
area, and tested on wheels and floats as XOSU-1 in January 1937.

Boeing F4B-4 (A-9035)   William T. Larkins
VF-9M (VMF-1) flew F4B-4's until June 1938. Rarest plane of all
was A-9719, built from spare parts by the Marine Base at Quantico.

Vought SU-2 (A-9116)   U. S. Marine Corps
Squadron Leader of VO-9M at Bourne Field, St. Thomas, Virgin
Islands. Note non-standard air wheels. Squadron had mixed types.

Vought O3U-6's (0001 etc.)   U. S. Marine Corps
VO-9M got six O3U-6's in November 1935, was down to 2 by Feb
1936. Flew mixture of SU-2, SU-3, RD-2, RD-3, O3U-6 and JF-1.

Douglas RD-3 (A-9533)   U. S. Marine Corps
VO-9M's "Dolphin" from Quantico (see page 58). USMC had one
command RD-2, two utility RD-3's. Both had R-1340-96, 450 h.p.

Vought SU-4 (A-9418)   John C. Mitchell
Rare photo of SU-4 used by Utility Squadron Seven from January to
June 1937 only.   Note VJ-7M insignia on fin, it became MAG-21.

STATUS OF MARINE CORPS AIRCRAFT
January, 1937

AIRCRAFT ONE, FMF, QUANTICO
    VO-7M (VMS-1)* 12 O3U-6
    VB-6M (VMB-1) 12 BG-1 (1 OL-9 added in June)
    VF-9M (VMF-1) 19 F4B-4, 1 SU-3
    VJ- 6M (VMJ-1)   2 R2D-1, 1 RR-4, 2 O3U-1, 2 SU-1, 1 O2C-1,
                    1 F4B-4, 1 XRE-3, 1 O3U-6, 1 JF-1,
                    1 OL-9 (1 XBG-1, 1 JF-2, 1 J2F-1 added in
                    June)
    Commander
        A/C One   1 BG-1 (Hq Wash), 1 BG-1 (A/C One)
    Service Sqdn   2 O3U-1 (VJ-6M), 1 O3U-6 (VO-7M),
    (Aircraft under   1 F4B-3 (Hq Wash), 4 F4B-4 (VF-9M), 1 BG-1
        repair)   (VF-6M), 1 XBG-1 (VJ-6M), 1 XB2G-1
                    (Commander A/C One), 1 T4M-1 (VJ-6M)

AIRCRAFT TWO, FMF, SAN DIEGO
    VO-8M (VMS-2)   1 O3U-1, 8 O3U-6
    VB04M (VMB-2) 11 BG-1, 1 O3U-1
    VF-4M (VMF-2)   6 F3F-1 (Changed in June to 6 F3F-1, 2 F2F-1,
                  1 O3U-1)
    VJ-7M (VMJ-2)   3 JF-1, 1 R4C-1, 1 SU-4
    Commander
        A/C Two   1 O3U-6, 1 BG-1
    Service Sqdn   7 O3U-6 (for VO-8M)

CHARLOTTE AMALIE, ST. THOMAS, V. I.
    VO-9M (VMS-3)   5 SU-2, 1 SU-3, 1 RD-3, 1 JF-1

*Squadron designation change as of 1 July 1937

Great Lakes BG-1 (A-9535)   William T. Larkins
A complete re-designation of squadrons took place 1 July 1937.
Note last use of USMC designating circle around the class letter.

Great Lakes BG-1 (A-9535)   William L. Swisher
The same plane after July 1st. Squadron VB-4M changed to VMB-2.
The letter "M" for Marines was used in place of previous circle.

Great Lakes XBG-1 (A-9220)   William T. Larkins
First BG-1 used as Aircraft One command plane, 1936 to 1938. Note
different aircraft on page 61. BG-1 had a top speed of 188.3 m.p.h.

Grumman F3F-1 (0257)   Gordon S. Williams
Very rare photo showing one of six used by new VF-4M formed in
January 1937.   Became VMF-2 in July 1937 and added 2 F2F-1's.

Vought O3U-6 (A-9733)   William L. Swisher
Leader of third section with blue cowl and fuselage stripe. Frequent
visitor at the old National Guard field, Griffith Park, Los Angeles.

Vought O3U-6 (A-9729)   William T. Larkins
Third plane in Section Four wearing black on the lower half of the
cowl. U. S. MARINES is in four inch high black letters.

STATUS OF MARINE CORPS AIRCRAFT
June, 1938

AIRCRAFT ONE, FMF, QUANTICO

VMS-1	11 O3U-6
VMB-1	13 BG-1
VMF-1	18 F3F-2, 1 SB2U-1, 1 SU-3 (18 F4B-4, 1 SU-3 in February 1938)
VMJ-1	3 SU-1, 3 O3U-1, 1 O2C-1, 1 JF-1, 2 JO-2, 1 JRS-1, 1 BG-1 (Commander Aircraft One), 2 R2D-1, 1 XBG-1, 1 XB2G-1, 1 XRE-3, 1 F4B-3, 1 T4M-1, 1 XF13C-3, 1 SU-4, 1 J2F-1
Service Sqdn	3 O3U-6 (VMS-1), 1 RD-2 (VMS-3), 3 F3F-2 (VMF-2), 1 BG-1, 1 JF-1, 8 F3F-2 (for spares)

AIRCRAFT TWO, FMF, SAN DIEGO

VMS-2	12 O3U-6
VMB-2	13 BG-1, 1 SU-4
VMF-2	17 F3F-2, 2 F2F-1, 1 SBC-3, 1 SU-4
VMJ-2	1 BG-1 (Commander Aircraft Two), 2 JF-1, 1 O3U-6, 1 JO-2, 2 R4C-1
Service Sqdn	1 BG-1 (VMB-2), 1 O3U-6 (VMS-2)

CHARLOTTE AMALIE, ST. THOMAS, V.I.

VMS-3	7 SU-2, 2 SU-3, 1 RD-2, 1 RD-3, 1 JF-1

Grumman F3F-1 (0256)   William T. Larkins
F3F-1's and F2F-1's were used as interim equipment by newly formed VMF-2 while awaiting delivery of its F3F-2's. Speed 231 m.p.h.

Grumman F3F-2's (0973, 0979, 0977)   U. S. Navy
2-MF-4, 10 and 8 in echelon formation over San Diego Bay. Year
1938 saw a major change in equipment of Marine fighter squadrons.

Grumman F3F-2's (0977, 0973, 0979)   U. S. Marine Corps
The same planes in "V" formation. Dash four and eight have camera
guns mounted on top of wing. Note two .30 cal guns in top of cowl.

Grumman F2F-1 (A-9663)   William T. Larkins
Very rare photo of one of two such types used as interim equipment
for a short period. 650 hp R-1535-72 gave a top speed of 231 mph.

Grumman F3F-2 (0972)   William T. Larkins
Note how the big, flat Wright "Cyclone" R-1820-22 engine (850 hp)
changed the basic design from the F2F-1 above. Speed 254.9 mph.

Grumman F3F-2 (0975)   U. S. Navy
Cruising near San Diego. Note machine gun and dive bombing sight
running through the windshield. Canopy is normally closed in flight.

Grumman F3F-2 (1022)   U. S. Navy
Second plane of Section Five with the top half of its cowl painted
Willow Green. Quantico based VMF-1 was formerly VF-9M.

Grumman F3F-2's (1044, 1014, 1020 etc.)   LeRoy McCallum
Aircraft One command plane and VMF-1 fighters at Saint Thomas,
Virgin Islands, during maneuvers. Span 32 ft., length 23 ft., ht. 10 ft. 6 in.

Grumman F3F-2 (0994)   William L. Swisher
Insignia on fin is a dark red diving lion superimposed on a light red
circle. This was changed to include Wake Island in V later.

Grumman F3F-2 (1018)   U. S. Navy
Leader of Section Four with black cowl, fuselage band and inverted
"V" on top wing. Note individual aircraft number in center of "V".

Vought SB2U-1 (0769)   LeRoy McCallum
Each VMF squadron had, in addition to 18 fighters, one utility plane
assigned for tow-target use. Note old Quantico hangar in rear.

Grumman F3F-2 (1009)   Gordon S. Williams
VMF-1's squadron leader. All F3F-2's (0968-1048) went to the
Marine Corps except eighteen for Navy Fighting Squadron Six.

Grumman F3F-2 (1014)   William T. Larkins
At Cleveland for the 1938 National Air Races. VMF-1 did not use
its Bulldog insignia on the aircraft. It became VMF-111 in July '41.

Curtiss SBC-3 (0521)   William T. Larkins
The Marines only SBC-3 which operated as 2-MF-19 until sent to
the Battle Fleet Pool in June 1939. It was a 221 mph dive bomber.

Grumman F3F-2 (1023)   U. S. Navy
1-MF-6 splashed off the USS Ranger. Note how the flotation gear
keeps the nose-heavy plane from sinking, permitting its salvage.

Curtiss R4C-1 (A-9584)   William T. Larkins
Aircraft Two's "Condor" during one of its many visits to N.R.A.B.
Oakland. Span 82 ft., length 49 ft., height 20 ft. 5 in., wt. 17,500 pounds.

Sikorsky JRS-1 (1060)   Harry Thorell
Freshly painted at the factory and awaiting delivery. VMJ-1 was
formerly VJ-6M. Civil S-43, Army YOA-8. Marine Corps had two.

Bellanca XRE-3 (A-9341)   Harry Thorell
Shown after being given its X (Experimental) designation for radio
test work. Note winged Aircraft One squadron insignia. See page 54.

Curtiss XF13C-3 (A-9343)   U. S. Navy
This 232 m.p.h. experimental, rejected fighter was assigned to
VMJ-1 at Quantico from November 1937 to November 1938.

Vought O3U-3 (A-9328)   William L. Swisher
VMS-2 operated two in November 1938, three in 1939 during the
change-over to SOC-3's. Standard shipboard catapult VO type.

Great Lakes XB2G-1 (A-9722)   William T. Larkins
Rejected experimental dive bomber used as command plane for one
year. Major Johnson used it to tour U.S.M.C. reserve bases.

Grumman F3F-2 (1008)   William L. Swisher
VMF-2 plane with individual aircraft number missing. With more
funds available contracts were providing replacement spares.

Vought O3U-1   William T. Larkins
Along with the new equipment the Marines were still flying old types
such as the 1930 O3U-1.   Note the flare tubes on the underside.

Vought O3U-1 (A-8578)   Bern Ederr
Companion to 6-J-11 above. VMJ-1 operated three for the Marine
Corps Schools, Quantico, to June 1938. Both are pre-July photos.

Lockheed JO-2 (1049)   William T. Larkins
All three (1049-1051) of these Lockheed 12-A civil transports went
to the Marines, starting in Feb.1938.This one to USMC Headquarters.

Lockheed JO-2 (1050)   Harry Thorell
Quantico-based VMJ-1's "Baby Electra". VMJ-1 became VMJ-152
in July 1941. Speed was 217 m.p.h.on two 400 horsepower R-985-48's.

Lockheed JO-2 (1051)   William L. Swisher
One Navy JO-2 (1267) was built with a tricycle landing gear and
designated XJO-3. Wartime civil 12A's were bought as R3O-2's.

Lockheed JO-2 (1051)   U. S. Marine Corps
VMJ-252 (old VMJ-2) JO-2 which burned to the ground during the
Japanese bombing of Ewa, Hawaii, airfield on December 7, 1941.

Sikorsky JRS-1 (1061)   U. S. Marine Corps
Powered by two 750 hp R-1690-52's it did 189.6 mph and would
climb to 20,700 feet at 19,096 pounds. Span 86 ft., length 51 ft. 1 in.

Douglas R2D-1   LeRoy McCallum
VMJ-1's two R2D-1's at Saint Thomas, Virgin Islands, during the
1939 maneuvers. Compare insignia on nose with that on page 77.

STATUS OF MARINE CORPS AIRCRAFT
January, 1939

AIRCRAFT ONE, FMF, QUANTICO
    VMS-1   6 BG-1, 10 O3U-6
    VMB-1   14 BG-1
    VMF-1   20 F3F-2, 1 SB2U-1
    VMJ-1   1 SU-1, 3 SU-2, 2 SU-4, 1 F4B-3, 1 BG-1,
                      1 F3F-2, 1 JF-1, 1 JF-2, 1 J2F-1 (at Parris
                      Island), 1 JO-2, 1 JRS-1, 1 RD-2, 2 R2D-1
    Service Sqdn   1 O3U-6, 5 F3F-2, 1 SU-3

AIRCRAFT TWO, FMF, SAN DIEGO
    VMS-2   8 SOC-3, 3 O3U-3
    VMB-2   7 BG-1
    VMF-2   18 F3F-2, 1 SU-4, 1 SBC-3
    VMJ-2   1 BG-1 (Commander Aircraft Two), 2 JF-1,
                      1 O3U-6, 1 JO-2, 2 R4C-1
    Service Sqdn   4 BG-1,14 O3U-6

CHARLOTTE AMALIE, ST. THOMAS, V.I.
    VMS-3   6 SU-2, 1 RD-3, 9 J2F-2, 1 JF-1

Curtiss SOC-3's (1127, 1126)   William L. Swisher
A paratrooper hanging from an R3D-2 was rescued in mid-air by a
VMS-2 SOC-3.   Twelve used by Marines.   Standard catapult scout.

Grumman J2F-2's (1203 etc.)   LeRoy McCallum
Six of VMS-3's nine from batch 1195-1209 lined up on Bourne Field
in the Virgin Islands. 750 hp R-1820-30, speed of 168.5 miles per hr.

Grumman J2F-2A (1204)   LeRoy McCallum
Showing the 1940 Neutrality Patrol Star. "A" suffix on designation
denoted addition of armament, both bomb racks and machine guns.

Vought SU-2 (A-9094)   Howard Levy
Modernized utility ship with controllable pitch propeller and SU-4
rudder. One SU-2 was still at Quantico as late as the middle of 1943.

Vought SU-2 (A-9100)   Howard Levy
Showing the normal dash two rudder as compared with that above.
SU-1/4 had 600 hp R.-690; 36' span, SU-4 20" longer and heavier.

Vought SU-4 (A-9414)   Howard Levy
Ex 8-O-12 (see page 64) all dressed up with added canopy for fast
staff transport. Two were operated at Marine Base, Parris Island.

Grumman JF-1 (A-9439)   William L. Swisher
In 1939 there were four JF-1's with the USMC, one assigned to
VMJ-1, two to VMJ-2 and one to VMS-3. P&W R-1830-62, 710 hp.

Grumman JF-1 (A-9449)   William L. Swisher
VMJ-2's second JF-1. Lightest of the JF series at 5,402 pounds, it
did 168 m.p.h. with a ceiling of 17,800 feet. Span was 39 feet.

Grumman J2F-1 (0186)   Howard Levy
One delivered to VMJ-1 in June 1938. Its 750 h.p. engine moved
its 6,173 pounds along at the same speed as the JF-1. Three place.

Grumman J2F-4 (1656)   William T. Larkins
J2F-1/5 were all 39 ft.span, 34 ft.length, 15 ft.1 in.height. Dash 4
had 790 hp R-1830-30 engine, speed of 171 m.p.h., 900 mile range.

STATUS OF MARINE CORPS AIRCRAFT
January, 1940

FIRST MARINE AIRCRAFT GROUP, QUANTICO
VMS-1	10 BG-1
VMB-1	10 BG-1
VMF-1	20 F3F-2, 1 SBC-4
VMJ-1	1 SU-1, 3 SU-2, 1 SU-3, 2 SU-4, 1 BG-1, 1 F3F-2, 1 JF-1, 1 J2F-1, 4 J2F-4, 1 JO-2, 1 XSBC-4, 1 JRS-1, 1 RD-2, 2 R2D-1, 1 TG-1
BAD-1*	2 O3U-6, 4 F3F-2, 1 SU-2

SECOND MARINE AIRCRAFT GROUP, SAN DIEGO
VMS-2	12 SOC-3
VMB-2	9 BG-1
VMF-2	15 F3F-2, 4 F3F-3, 1 SBC-4, 1 SU-4
VMJ-2	1 BG-1 (Commander, Second Marine Air Group), 1 JRS-1, 3 J2F-4, 1 JO-2, 1 SBC-4
BAD-2	2 JF-1, 7 F3F-2, 8 O3U-6

CHARLOTTE AMALIE, ST. THOMAS, V.I.
VMS-3	9 J2F-2A, 1 JF-1, 1 JRF-1A

*Base Air Detachment, formerly Service Squadron

Curtiss SBC-4 (1287)   William T. Larkins
Production dive bomber serving as a command transport with the new
markings of the First Marine Air Wing. USMC Hq had the XSBC-4.

Grumman F3F-3 (1463)   Howard Levy
Two of these planes served as interim equipment with VMF-2 in
late 1939 and early 1940. It was four m.p.h. faster than the F3F-2.

Douglas SBD-1 (1597)   Douglas Aircraft Company
VMB-2 replaced its BG-1's in late 1940 with the arrival of SBD-1's
Nos. 1597-1602, 1609-1614, 1621-1626 and 1736-1740.

Douglas R3D-2 (1904)   Douglas Aircraft Company
1940 also saw the arrival of the new DC-5 utility transports that were
planned for paratrooper training. Note unusual VMJ-2 markings.

Douglas R3D-2 (1905)   Frank Shertzer
1904-1907 were dash two's for the USMC. 1901-1903 were Navy
R3D-1's, 1901 crashed on factory test flight. Two survived the war.

Curtiss SBC-4 (1312)   William T. Larkins
VMS-8R scout bomber from the original group of 1268-1325 sent
to the Reserve Squadrons. See next three pages for Reserve data.

PRE-WAR MARINE RESERVE SQUADRONS

1930 - 1932

VF-4MR	Squantum (Boston), Massachusetts
VO-7MR	Grosse Isle (Detroit), Michigan
VO-8MR	Seattle, Washington

1933 - 1934

VF-4MR	Squantum (Boston), Massachusetts
VF-4MR	Long Beach, California
VF-5MR	Grosse Isle (Detroit), Michigan
VO-6MR	Brooklyn, New York
VO-7MR	Minneapolis, Minnesota (added 1934)
VO-7MR	Grosse Isle (Detroit), Michigan
VO-8MR	Seattle, Washington
VO-10MR	Oakland, California
VJ-7MR	Anacostia, D. C.

1935 - 1936

VO-1MR	Squantum (Boston), Massachusetts
VO-2MR	Brooklyn, New York
VO-3MR	Anacostia, D. C.
VO-4MR	Miami (Opa Locka), Florida
VO-5MR	Grosse Isle (Detroit), Michigan
VO-6MR	Minneapolis, Minnesota
VO-7MR	Long Beach, California
VO-8MR	Oakland, California
VO-9MR	Seattle, Washington
VO-10MR	Kansas City, Missouri

1937 - 1941

VMS-1R	Squantum (Boston), Massachusetts
VMS-2R	Brooklyn, New York
VMS-3R	Anacostia, D. C.
VMS-4R	Miami (Opa Locka), Florida
VMS-5R	Grosse Isle (Detroit), Michigan
VMS-6R	Minneapolis, Minnesota
VMS-7R	Long Beach, California
VMS-8R	Oakland, California
VMS-9R	Seattle, Washington
VMS-10R	Kansas City, Missouri

Curtiss N2C-1 (A-7652)   William T. Larkins
Used at all Marine Reserve bases except Miami and Kansas City.
N2C-2's were also used, partly for the pilot training program.

Curtiss F8C-4 (A-8436)   Fred E. Bamberger
VMS-2R "Helldiver" in practice dive bombing run. All F8C-4's
(8421-8447) went from the Fleet to the reserves in June of 1931.

Berliner-Joyce OJ-2 (A-9191)   Gordon S. Williams
Seattle-based VMS-9R ship preparing for take-off. The OJ-2's
served all reserve bases after doing shipboard duty at sea.

Grumman SF-1 (A-9471)   Gordon S. Williams
Single-control scout from VMS-9R landing. About half of the Marine Reserve units flew the modified dual-control FF-2 model.

Vought SBU-2 (0837)   William T. Larkins
A much rarer type used only by VMS-1R, VMS-2R and VMS-4R. All aircraft were used jointly by USN and USMC reserve units.

North American SNJ-2 (2009)   North American
New York's freshly painted ship delivered in late 1939. All of the reserve bases had at least one of these for instrument training.

STATUS OF MARINE CORPS AIRCRAFT
October, 1941

COMMANDING GENERAL, FIRST DIVISION,
    FLEET MARINE FORCE
    First Wing   1 JRB-2 (1 SBC-4 in January, 1 JRF-4 in
                    June)

MARINE AIR GROUP ELEVEN, QUANTICO
  VMSB-131 (VMS-1)*19 SB2U-3
  VMSB-132 (VMB-1)19 SBD-1
  VMF-111 (VMF-1)16 F4F-3A, 1 F3F-2, 2 SNJ-3
  VMF-121   18 F4F-3, 2 SNJ-3
  VMJ-152 (VMJ-1) 1 J2F-4, 1 J2F-1, 1 JO-2, 2 R3D-2, 2 SBD-1,
                 1 SB2U-3
  VMO-151 (VMO-1) 11 SBC-4, 2 J2F-4
  BAD-1   7 F4F-3, 2 F3F-2, 7 SB2U-3, 3 SBC-4,
                 4 SBD-1, 1 XSBC-4, 1 FF-2, 2 SU-2,
                 1 J2F-1, 3 SNJ-2, 1 JO-2

COMMANDING GENERAL, SECOND DIVISION,
    FLEET MARINE FORCE
  Second Wing   1 SBC-4, 1 JRF-4

MARINE AIR GROUP TWENTY ONE, EWA,
    TERRITORY OF HAWAII
  VMSB-231 (VMS-2) 24 SB2U-3
  VMSB-232 (VMB-2) 19 SBD-1
  VMF-211 (VMF-2)15 F4F-3, 13 F3F-2, 1 SNJ-3
  VMF-221   3 F2A-2, 11 F2A-3, 1 F4F-3, 1 SNJ-3
  VMJ-252 (VMJ-2) 3 J2F-4, 1 JRS-1, 1 JO-2, 2 R3D-2,
                 2 SBD-1, 1 SB2U-3

CHARLOTTE AMALIE, ST. THOMAS, VIRGIN ISLANDS
  VMS-3   9 J2F-2A, 1 JRF-1A

PARRIS ISLAND, SOUTH CAROLINA
  Air Detachment   1 FF-2, 1 SBC-4, 1 JF-1

MARINE BASE, NAVAL AIR STATION SAN DIEGO
  BAD-2   1 JRB-2, 1 R2D-1

        *Squadron designation prior to 1 July 1941

Schweizer LNS-1 (04385)   U. S. Marine Corps
One of six trainers assigned to Marine Glider Group 71, Page Field,
Parris Island, South Carolina, just before World War II.

Schweizer LNS-1's (04381 etc.)   U. S. Marine Corps
Shown with their N3N-3 tow planes. The Marines also flew ten
LRW-1's (Army CG-4A), LNE-1, XLNR-1, XLNT-1 and XLNP-1.

Douglas SBD-1 (1626)   Douglas Aircraft Company
VMB-2 Squadron Leader. After July the squadron became VMSB-232
(see page 92). Note serial is different from 2-MB-1 on page 87.

Vought SB2U-3 (2044)   United Aircraft Corporation
VMSB-231's change from 12 SOC-3's to 24 SB2U-3's in late 1941
is indicative of the rapid growfh of the U.S.M.C. during that period.

Grumman F4F-3   U. S. Navy
Large numbers of these high performance "Wildcat" fighters replaced the obsolescent F3F-2's in service. This plane is 111-MF-16.

Curtiss SBC-4 (4214)   Peter M. Bowers
Number 2 plane of First M.A.W. but different markings and serial
from 1-MW-2 on page 87. Early SBC-4's were ordered to France.

Grumman JRF-1 (3846)   Frank Shertzer
Command plane for the Commanding General, Second Division,
Fleet Marine Force. It was replaced in 1941 with the newer JRF-4.

Curtiss SBC-4 (4204)   Frank Shertzer
Second of two command planes for the Second Marine Air Wing.
SBC-4's served with Navy VS-3 for a short time in the year 1941.

Grumman FF-2 (A-9356)   William T. Larkins
During 1941 one served with Base Air Detachment One, Quantico,
and one with BAD-2 at San Diego. SF-1 and FF-2 did 206 m.p.h.

Vought SB2U-3   Chance Vought Aircraft Inc.
June 1941 photo showing VMS-1 markings before change to new
designation of VMSB-131. Many SB2U's were lost at Midway Island.

Grumman F3F-2   U. S. Marine Corps
2-MF-16 after a night crash landing. This is a rare photo as the
F3F-2's appeared in warpaint for only a very short time.

Consolidated PBY-5A   Consolidated-Vultee
Seven horizontal red and six white stripes were added in late 1941,
removed in June 1942. Twenty PBY's served Wing Hq, VMO, VMJ.

Brewster F2A-3   Clay Jansson
Improved "Buffalo", maximum speed 321 m.p.h. at 16,500 feet.
Wright R-1820-40 of 1200 hp.   F4F-3 maximum was 331/21, 100.

Brewster F2A-3   Clay Jansson
Camouflaged at Ewa. Cursed and hated victim of exaggerated publicity, it was shot to pieces at Midway Island. Several were exported.

STATUS OF MARINE CORPS AIRCRAFT
30 November 1942

U. S. FLEET MARINE FORCE

MARINE AIRCRAFT WINGS, PACIFIC
Hq Sqdn   1 SNJ-4
Svc Group   1 JRB-2, 1 SNJ-2

FIRST MARINE AIR WING
Hq Sqdn   1 J2F-5, 2 JRB-2, 1 PBY-5A,
              2 SNJ-4, 8 F4F-4, 2 SBD-3,
              5 R4D-1

MARINE AIR GROUP ELEVEN
VMSB-132   6 TBF-1

MARINE AIR GROUP FOURTEEN
Hq Sqdn 14   3 SNJ-4
VMSB-141   3 SBD-1, 48 SBD-3
VMF-121   39 F4F-4, 3 SNJ-4

MARINE AIR GROUP TWENTY-THREE
VMF-212   1 J2F-5, 1 SNJ-3
VMF-223   1 F4F-4
VMF-224   1 J2F-5
VMSB-231   3 SBD-3
VMSB-232   1 SBD-3

MARINE AIR GROUP TWENTY-FIVE
Hq Sqdn 25   1 F4F-4
VMO-251   12 F4F-3, 5 F4F-4, 4 F4F-7, 1 JRB-2,
              1 J2F-5, 3 SNJ-3
VMJ-253   2 J2F-5, 9 R4D-1

SECOND MARINE AIR WING
Hq Sqdn 2   1 JO-2, 9 F4F-4, 4 F4F-7,
             15 F4U-1, 10 R4D-1, 2 SBC-4,
             3 SBD-3

             3 SNJ-4, 1 JRF-4, 9 SBD-4,
             1 TBF-1, 1 J2F-5
ABG-2   2 R3D-2

MARINE AIR GROUP TWELVE
Hq Sqdn 12   3 SNJ-3
VMF-215   5 SNJ-4, 1 F4U-1
VMF-222   6 SNJ-4
VMF-123   1 SNJ-3, 3 F4F-4
VMF-124   3 F4F-3

MARINE AIR GROUP FIFTEEN
```
    Hq Sqdn 15    1 SNJ-3
    VMJ-152       6 R4D-1
    VMJ-153       6 R4D-1
    VMD-154       1 F4F-3, 1 SNJ-3
    VMD-254       3 PB4Y-1, 1 SNJ-3, 1 SNJ-4
```

MARINE AIR GROUP TWENTY-FOUR
```
    Hq Sqdn 24    1 GB-2
    VMSB-143      7 SBD-3
    VMSB-144      7 SBD-3, 3 SB2U-3
    VMSB-243      4 SBD-3, 10 SBD-4, 2 SBC-4
    VMSB-244      8 SBD-4, 5 SBD-3
```

FOURTH MARINE BASE DEFENSE AIR WING
```
    Hq Sqdn 4     2 F4F-4, 2 SBD-4
    VMJ-252       4 R4D-1, 2 J2F-5
    VMF-211       12 F4F-4
    VMF-221       2 F4F-3, 1 F4F-4, 2 SNJ-4
                  (Temporarily detached from
                          MAG-22)
```

MARINE AIR GROUP THIRTEEN
```
    Hq Sqdn 13    1 PBY-5A
    VMF-111       7 F4F-3, 1 J2F-5, 1 SNJ-3
    VMSB-151      11 SBC-4, 1 J2F-5
    VMO-155       9 SBC-4, 1 J2F-5
```

MARINE AIR GROUP TWENTY-ONE
```
    VMSB-131      12 TBF-1
    VMF-213       2 F4F-3, 1 F4F-7, 1 SNJ-3
    VMF-214       5 F4F-3, 1 SNJ-4
    VMSB-234      5 SBD-3
```

MARINE AIR GROUP TWENTY-TWO
```
    Hq Sqdn 22    1 SBD-3
    VMSB-241      1 SBD-2, 18 SBD-3
```

MARINE AIR GROUP FORTY-THREE
```
    VMF(N)-531 2 SNJ-4
```

VMS-3, ST. THOMAS, V. I.
```
    VMS-3         16 OS2N-1, 2 OS2U-3, 4 J2F-5,
                  1 JRF-1A, 1 R4D-1
```

SHORE BASES

MCAS CHERRY POINT, NORTH CAROLINA
```
    B.A.D.        1 BD-2, 1 GB-2, 1 JRF-1, 1 JF-1,
                  1 J2F-3, 1 J2F-5, 1 SB2A-4,
                  4 R4D-1, 2 SNJ-4, 15 SNC-1
```

MCAS EAGLE MT. LAKE, TEXAS
    B.A.D.   1 SNC-1

MCAS EDENTON, NORTH CAROLINA
    B.A.D.   1 SNC-1

MCAS EL CENTRO, CALIFORNIA
    B.A.D.   1 SNC-1

MCAS EL TORO, CALIFORNIA
    B.A.D.   1 SNC-1

MCAS MOJAVE, CALIFORNIA
    B.A.D.   1 SNC-1

MCAS PARRIS ISLAND, SOUTH CAROLINA
    Glider   1 GB-2, 1 JE-1, 3 N3N-3, 1 N2T-1,
    Group 71 1 LNE-1, 6 LNS-1
    Hq Sqdn   1 J2F-2, 2 NE-1, 1 SNC-1, 1 GH-1

MCAS QUANTICO, VIRGINIA
    MCAS One 1 JO-2, 1 GB-2, 1 GH-1, 1 R2D-1,
              1 R4D-1, 4 SNC-1, 1 SNJ-2,
              4 SNJ-3, 1 SNJ-4, 1 SU-2

MCAS SANTA BARBARA, CALIFORNIA
    B.A.D.   1 SNC-1

MCAS ST. THOMAS, VIRGIN ISLANDS
    Hq Sqdn   1 JRF-1A, 4 J2F-5, 1 R4D-1

Vought OS2U-3   U. S. Marine Corps
VMS-3 replaced its J2F-2A's with "Kingfishers", most of which
were Naval Aircraft Factory built OS2N-1 duplicates.

Vought F4U-1   Chance Vought
Although a pre-war design F4U production did not reach the Marine Corps until 1943. Designed around the huge P & W R-2800 engine.

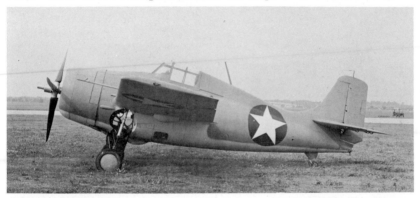

Grumman F4F-3   U. S. Army Air Forces
Rugged, dependable Wildcat that defended Wake Island to the end. Red center was removed from the national insignia in June of 1942.

Consolidated PB4Y-1 (31945)   U. S. Marine Corps
One of VMD-254's photo Liberator's on Henderson Field, Guadalcanal. The U.S.M.C. operated a small number of these B-24's.

Douglas SBD-3's   U. S. Navy
The Marine's war in the Pacific was carried out primarily with only
two planes — the SBD "Dauntless" and the F4U "Corsair".

Curtiss SB2C-1   Curtiss-Wright
Still another "Helldiver" in the long line of Curtiss dive bombers.
Widely used by the Navy, it was used much less by the Marines.

Douglas SBD-5 (10957)   Douglas Aircraft Company
Photo taken 9-18-42 before delivery. Constant refinement in design and production produced six different models of the SBD design.

Douglas R4D-1 (3140)   U. S. Marine Corps
Father J. P. Mannion, first chaplain to join the Paramarines and jump with his men, is shown leaving the open door of a DC-3 plane.

Curtiss SB2C-3   U. S. Navy
The SB2C-3 had one 20mm cannon in each wing in place of two .50 calibre machine guns on the -1, a 1700 hp Wright R-2600-8 engine.

Grumman F4F-3's   U. S. Marine Corps
Four of VMF-211's "Wildcats" parked in a revetment on Palmyra
Island in 1942.   The F4F's entered service in 1941, see page 92.

Grumman F4F-4   Clay Jansson
Normal range 830 miles at 161 m.p.h., ceiling 27,000 feet. The
unarmed, stripped USMC photographic version was model F4F-7.

Douglas SBD-1   Clay Jansson
Under camouflage at Ewa in 1942.   Two-tone gray warpaint replaced the previous aluminum finish in March of the year 1941.

STATUS OF MARINE CORPS AIRCRAFT
31 August 1943

U. S. FLEET MARINE FORCE

MARINE AIRCRAFT WINGS, PACIFIC
   Hq Sqdn   1 R5O-5, 1 SNJ-4

FIRST MARINE AIR WING
   Hq Sqdn 1   2 SNJ, 1 PV-1, 1 PBY-5A, 1 JRB
   VMD-154   6 PB4Y-1, 1 SNJ
   VMF-211   33 F4U-1
   VMF-212   10 F4U-1
   VMJ-252   1 J2F-5, 3 R4D-1, 2 R4D, 1 R4D-5
   VMSB-243   15 SBD-4
   VMSB-244   11 SBD-3, 7 SBD-4
   VMF(N)-531   15 PV-1

MARINE AIR GROUP ELEVEN
   Hq Sqdn 11   2 TBF-1, 6 F4U-1, 1 JRF, 2 SNJ
   Svc Sqdn 11   1 J2F-5, 6 SBD-4, 1 SBD-5,
                        1 JRF, 1 J2F-5, 1 SNJ
   VMF-112   24 F4U-1
   VMF-123   24 F4U-1, 1 J2F-5, 1 NE
   VMF-124   20 F4U-1
   VMF-215   20 F4U-1
   VMSB-132   25 SBD-4, 1 SBD-5
   VMSB-235   31 SBD-4, 1 SBD-5
   VMTB-232   25 TBF-1
   VMTB-233   20 TBF-1

MARINE AIR GROUP TWELVE
   Hq Sqdn 12   1 J2F-5, 1 F4F-7, 1 NE
   VMTB-143   27 TBF-1
   VMSB-234   23 SBD-4

MARINE AIR GROUP TWENTY-ONE
   Hq Sqdn 21   1 F4F-4, 1 J2F-5, 1 J2F-2
   VMF-214   20 F4U-1
   VMF-221   20 F4U-1, 1 F4F-3

MARINE AIR GROUP TWENTY-FIVE
   Hq Sqdn 25   2 R4D, 1 F4F-7, 1 SNJ
   VMJ-152   12 R4D
   VMJ-153   12 R4D
   VMJ-253   10 R4D

SECOND MARINE AIR WING
   Hq Sqdn 2   1 JRB

MARINE AIR GROUP FOURTEEN
  Hq Sqdn 14   18 SBD-3, 9 SBD-4
  VMF-121   19 F4U-1
  VMSB-141   25 SBD-4

THIRD MARINE AIR WING
  Hq Sqdn 3   3 J2F-5, 1 JRF-1A, 1 R4D-1, 1 SNJ-4

MARINE AIR GROUP THIRTY-ONE
  Hq Sqdn 31   11 F4U-1, 1 SBD-5, 1 SNJ-4
                         (Cherry Point & Quantico)
  VMF-311   19 F4U-1, 2 SNJ-4 (Parris Island)
  VMF-321   22 F4U-1, 1 SNJ-4 (Oak Grove)
  VMSB-331   20 SBD-5 (Bogue Field)
  VMSB-341   20 SBD-5 (Atlantic Field)
  VMF-312   11 F4U-1, 1 SNJ-4 (Parris Island)
  VMF-322   10 F4U-1 (Oak Grove)
  VMF-323   9 F4U-1, 7 SNJ-4 (Formed 1 August at
                         MCAS Cherry Point)

MARINE AIR GROUP THIRTY-THREE
  Hq Sqdn 33   1 SBD-4 (Cherry Point)
  VMSB-332   4 SBD-4, 9 SBD-5 (Cherry Point)
  VMSB-333   3 SBD-4, 1 SNJ-4 (Formed 1 August at
                         MCAS Cherry Point)
  VMSB-334   3 SBD-4 (Formed 1 August, Cherry Point)

MARINE AIR GROUP THIRTY-FOUR
  Hq Sqdn 34   3 SBD-4 (Cherry Point)
  VMSB-342   4 SBD-4, 5 SBD-5, 1 J2F-1, 4 SNV-1
                         (Atlantic Field)
  VMSB-343   3 SBD-4, 4 SBD-5 (Formed 1 August at
                         Atlantic Field)

MARINE AIR GROUP THIRTY-FIVE
  Hq Sqdn 35   1 SBD-4 (Cherry Point)
  VMJ-352   6 R4D-5, 1 R5O-6 (Cherry Point)
  VMD-354   1 F4U-1 (Cherry Point)
  VMO-351   1 F4U-1, 3 SNJ-4 (Cherry Point)

MARINE NIGHT FIGHTER GROUP FIFTY-THREE
  VMF(N)-532   12 F4U-2, 5 SB2A-4, 5 SNJ-4
                         (MCAS Cherry Point)

MARINE BOMBER GROUP SIXTY-ONE
  Hq Sqdn 61   24 PBJ (Formed 13 July at MCAS Quantico)
  VMB-413   12 PBJ (Cherry Point)

FOURTH MARINE BASE DEFENSE AIR WING
  Hq Sqdn 4   21 SBD-4, 39 SBD-5, 1 F6F-3, 1 J4F
  VMF-224   33 F4U-1

MARINE AIR GROUP THIRTEEN
    Hq Sqdn 13   2 PBY-5A, 3 J2F-5, 2 R4D, 2 SNJ
    VMF-111   26 F4F-4
    VMF-441   20 F4F-4
    VMSB-151   19 SBD-4
    VMSB-241   21 SBD-4

MARINE AIR GROUP TWENTY-TWO
    Hq Sqdn 22   13 F4U-1
    VMF-222   15 F4U-1
    VMF-223   23 F4U-1
    VMSB-231   11 SBD-3, 7 SBD-4

MARINE AIR GROUP TWENTY-FOUR
    Hq Sqdn 24   2 SBD-4, 1 JRB

MARINE AIR GROUP FIFTEEN
    Hq Sqdn 15   10 R4D-1, 1 JRB-2, 1 PB4Y-1, 1 R4D-3,
                      4 R4D-5 (Camp Kearney)

MARINE AIR GROUP TWENTY-THREE
    Hq Sqdn 23·   3 SBD-5, 1 GB-2, 1 TBF-1, 1 R5O-6,
                      2 SNJ-4 (El Toro)

MARINE BASE DEFENSE AIR GROUP FORTY-ONE
    Hq Sqdn 41   1 R5O-6, 2 SBD-5, 18 SNJ-4, 1 SNJ-3
                      (El Toro)
    VMF-113   21 F4U-1, 3 FG-1, 2 SNJ-4
    VMF-114   19 FM-1, 5 F4F-3, 7 F4F-4, 3 SNJ-4
                      (Formed 1 July, El Toro)
    VMSB-245   14 SBD-4, 14 SBD-5, 2 SNJ-3
                      (Formed 1 July at El Toro)
    VMTB-131   4 SNJ-4 (El Toro)

MARINE BASE DEFENSE AIR GROUP FORTY-TWO
    Hq Sqdn 42   2 SBD-3, 3 SBD-5, 1 J2F-2, 1 R5O-6,
                      2 SNJ-3, 8 SNJ-4 (MCAS Santa Barbara)
    VMF-115   20 FM-1, 2 F4F-3, 2 F4F-4, 3 SNJ-4
                      (Formed 1 July at MCAS Santa Barbara)
    VMF-422   17 F4U-1, 1 FG-1, 5 SNJ-4
    VMTB-134   25 TBF-1, 19 TBM-1, 7 SBD-3

MARINE BASE DEFENSE AIR GROUP FORTY-FOUR
    Hq Sqdn 44   4 SBD-3, 3 SBD-5, 1 JO-2, 2 SNJ-4
                      (MCAS Mojave)
    VMF-218   10 FM-1, 1 F4F-3, 2 SNJ-4, 2 SNJ-5
                      (Formed 1 July, Mojave)
    VMF-225   13 FM-1, 3 F4F-3, 3 F4F-4, 5 F4U-1,
                      9 SNJ-4, 1 SNJ-3
    VMD-254   7 PB4Y-1, 1 F4F-7

VMS-3 ST. THOMAS, V. I.
VMS-3   18 OS2N-1

MARINE OPERATIONAL TRAINING SQUADRON EIGHT
OTS-8   26 PBJ-1, 25 SNB-1, 1 SNJ-3
                (MCAS Edenton)

SHORE BASES

MCAS CHERRY POINT, NORTH CAROLINA
B.A.D.   7 F4U-1, 1 SBD-4, 12 PBJ-1, 1 JRF-1,
                  1 J2F-5, 1 JO-2, 3 R4D-1, 6 R5C-1, 1 JE-1,
                  2 AE-1, 2 GB-2, 3 SNC-1, 1 SNJ-4, 3 SNB-1,
                  15 NE-1.

MCAS EDENTON, NORTH CAROLINA
B.A.D.   11 NE-1, 2 SNC-1

MCAS EL CENTRO, CALIFORNIA
B.A.D.   3 NE-1, 1 GB-2, 1 SNC-1, 1 AE-1

MCAS EL TORO, CALIFORNIA
B.A.D.   2 SNC-1, 1 AE-1, 4 NE-1, 1 SNB-2,
                  26 TDC-2

MCAS MOJAVE, CALIFORNIA
B.A.D.   1 SNC-1, 1 AE-1, 1 NE-1

MCAS QUANTICO, VIRGINIA
B.A.D.   1 SU-2, 1 J2F-1, 1 J2F-4, 2 R4D-1, 1 R5O-4,
                  1 JK-1, 1 AE-1, 1 SNJ-4, 1 GB-1, 1 GB-2,
                  1 GH-1, 5 NE-1, 4 SNC-1, 4 SNJ-2, 4 SNJ-3,
                  8 F4U-1, 1 J2F-5

Assembly &
  Repair   33 F4U-1, 2 F4F-4, 1 SBD-4P, 27 PBJ-1,
                  2 SNJ-1, 2 N3N-3, 2 J2F-3, 2 SNC-1, 2 SNJ-2,
                  1 SNJ-4, 1 JRB-2

MCAS PARRIS ISLAND, SOUTH CAROLINA
B.A.D.   1 AE-1, 1 J2F-2, 1 SNC-1, 2 NE-1

MCAS SANTA BARBARA, CALIFORNIA
B.A.D.   1 GB-2, 1 J2F-3, 2 SNC-1

MCAS ST. THOMAS, VIRGIN ISLANDS
B.A.D.   1 JRF-1A, 1 SNJ-4, 1 NE-1, 3 J2F-5

(B.A.D. - Base Air Detachment)

Vought F4U-1   U. S. Marine Corps
VMF-111"Corsair" decorated for 100 missions against Japanese
atolls in the Gilbert Islands. Note 500-pound bomb under fuselage.

Douglas SBD-6   U. S. Navy
The traditions of France, Santo Domingo, Nicaragua and San Diego
ride with this "Ace of Spades" SBD over Task Force 58 in Pacific.

Curtiss SNC-1 (05229)   U. S. Marine Corps
One of several such advanced trainers used as glider tugs and
liaison planes during the war. This photo was taken in July of 1943.

Douglas SBD-5's   Frank Shertzer
Rear gunner has two .30 flexible guns, two .50's are fixed in the
top of the cowling. Normal load 1,000 lb. bomb; 1,600 lb. possible.

Douglas R4D-1's   U. S. Marine Corps
On the steel landing mat at Henderson Field. They did passenger,
freight and ambulance duty throughout the Solomons Campaign.

Grumman J2F-4   William T. Larkins
Eight versions of the "Duck" were flown by the Marines. Its most
valuable wartime use was rescuing downed pilots during combat.

Grumman J2F-5   U. S. Navy
Another version, wearing 1941 markings. Smooth cowling with the
large air intake on top is one of the distinguishing features of J2F-5.

Columbia J2F-6 (36967)   William T. Larkins
Final version sub-contracted to Columbia Aircraft Corporation. White
bar with red border on star insignia was adopted in June of 1943.

Naval Aircraft Factory N3N-3 (2593)   William T. Larkins
Two-place primary trainer similar to the N2S used by the Marines
in their glider program as well as in the pre-war reserve program.

Vultee SNV-1 (34278)   Gordon S. Williams
One of over 11,000 such basic trainers built, mostly for the Army
as BT-13's and BT-15's. Few with USMC, see VMSB-342, page 106.

General Motors FM-1   U. S. Navy
F4F-4 "Wildcat" built under contract by G. M. Corsairs were built
by Goodyear as FG-1, Brewster as F3A-1. See VMF-225, page 107.

Douglas BD-1   William T. Larkins
Navy version of Army A-20 attack-bomber (BD-2 was A-20A). Few
were used by Marines for high-speed target towing and VJ work.

Grumman J4F-2   William T. Larkins
Small Ranger-engined "Widgeon" amphibian. Two were used by the
USMC, 1 each by Station Operations at Cherry Point and Edenton.

Brewster SB2A-4 (29318)   U. S. Marine Corps
Reclaimed Dutch bombers used as trainers for VMF(N)-531, the
Marines first Night Fighter Squadron, at Cherry Point, July 1943.

Beech GB-1 (1595)　　　　　　　　　　　　　Howard·Levy
Two such model 17's were impressed into USMC service from civilian
life. Red border on white bar was changed to blue in September 1943.

Beech GB-2 (23749)　　　　　　　　　William T. Larkins
Delivered new to El Centro 7-12-44, to El Toro 4-17-45, turned
over to the Navy at San Diego 8-26-46, sold surplus in Feb. of 1947.

Lockheed R5O-5 (12471)　　　　　　　　William T. Larkins
Lockheed 18 transport used as staff and command plane all during
the war by both the Navy and the Marines. Army model was C-60.

Beech SNB-1 (39834)   William T. Larkins
Bombardier trainer, same as Army AT-11, used to train Marine
Corps crews for their new PBJ-1 (B-25) twin-engine bombers.

Beech SNB-2C (23809)   William T. Larkins
Navigation trainer widely used during the later years of the war,
identical to AAF model AT-7C. Many doubled as liaison planes.

North American SNJ-3 (6906)   William T. Larkins
Every model of the SNJ from 1 through 6 was used by the Marines
at one time or another. The SNJ-3 was the same as the AT-6A.

Piper AE-1 (30288)   William T. Larkins
HE-1 ambulance "Cub" re-designated. Rear fuselage half raised
up to admit a litter patient. Powered by Lycoming O-235-2 engine.

Piper NE-1 (26322)   William T. Larkins
Two-place Cub trainer, Army L-4A "Grasshopper". Used for flight
instruction in USMC glider program as well as utility. See page 108.

Lockheed R5O-6 (39617)   William T. Larkins
18-passenger "Loadstar", Army C-60. Two R-1820-87 (1200 hp),
did 253 mph at 13,600 feet, 1180 mile range. Note square door.

Lockheed PV-1   Lockheed Aircraft Company
Modified to become the first USMC night fighter for VMF(N)-531.
First kill was November 1943 near Torokina Point, Solomon Islands.

Fairchild JK-1   William T. Larkins
USMC had one war-impressed civil 24H, either 34112 or 34113.
Ranger engine.   Designation was error, USCG J2K-2 is correct.

Howard GH-2 (32368)   Harry Thorell
"Nightingale" two-litter ambulance similar to the civil DGA-15.
Marines also flew the GH-1 and GH-3 models, minor differences.

Vought F4U-1   U. S. Marine Corps
On the fighter strip at Torokina Point, Bougainville. Note the six
.50 cal machine guns in wings, replaced by cannon in F4U-1C.

North American PBJ-1D (35134)   U. S. Marine Corps
Seven USMC squadrons operated "Mitchell" bombers in World War
Two. First in combat was VMB-413 in the Rabaul area, March 1944.

Douglas R4D-5   U. S. Navy
Lashed down to a bulldozer, truck and road surfacer during two day
typhoon in Palau Islands. Formerly AAF C-47A-30-DO, 43-48178.

F6F-3's and F4U-1's   U. S. Navy
The converted Oiler CVE29 Santee ferrying USMC planes to island
bases in the Pacific. Two F6F-3N's in foreground are #40010, 40062.

Grumman TBF-1C (24343)   U. S. Marine Corps
Taxying through the tropical heat and dust at Bougainville. Grumman
built 2,290 TBF-1's, General Motors built 2,882 as TBM-1's.

General Motors TBM-3E   U. S. Navy
With 8 HVAR rockets on wing racks. The TBM carried 2,000 pounds
of mines or bombs. Five .50 and one .30 m.g. Did 270 at 7,500 ft.

Consolidated PB4Y-2 (59408)   U. S. Marine Corps
Navy modified version of the B-24 with 110 ft. span, 74 ft. 7 in. length.
Speed 237 mph at 13,750 feet. Transport version was RY-3 (p.131).

Curtiss R5C-1's   U. S. Marine Corps
Three C-46A's on an airfield in the Marshall Islands. The increased
air tonnage in mid-war reflected their size and 268 m.p.h. speed.

Grumman F6F-3's U. S. Marine Corps
Hellcats on the captured airfield at Munda, New Georgia. Speed
375 mph. In Dec. 1944, and early Jan. 1945, a Marine night fighter
sqdn flying "Hellcats" out of Leyte shot down 19 planes. Marines
gave close support throughout Philippines campaign. Between Dec.
1943 and Mar. 1944 Marines claimed 816 planes shot down, 198 prob-
ables, 72 destroyed on the ground. In Marshalls their "Corsairs"
and dive bombers dropped 645,325 lbs. of bombs on bypassed atolls in
30 days. "Corsairs" flying off captured Peleliu airfield bombed
Bloody Nose Ridge in strikes only 1,400 yds from take-off to target.

Vought F4U-1 and General Motors TBM-3E U. S. Navy
Both planes are equipped with wing rocket racks, a late war inno-
vation found to be effective against submarines and light shipping.

Douglas SBD-5   William T. Larkins
Showing the perforated split flaps of the SBD in landing position.
During normal 70-degree dive flaps were open both top and bottom.

Consolidated OY-1 (60462)   U. S. Marine Corps
Artillery spotting L-5's of VMO-4 and VMO-5 took a beating at
Iwo Jima. Some OY-1's were experimentally launched from LST's.

Timm N2T-1 (32633)   U. S. Marine Corps
Colonel Gephart, C.O. of ABG-2, flying one of these moulded ply-
wood trainers over San Diego. It did 139 m.p.h., R-760-4, 220 hp.

Stearman N2S-5 (52941)   Boeing Airplane Company
Lycoming powered PT-13D, AAF #42-17560, similar to the better
known Continental powered PT-17. The Marines also flew N2S-3's.

North American SNJ-5 (90879)   U. S. Marine Corps
With MCAS El Toro insignia on the forward fuselage. SNJ-5 was
the counterpart of the AAF AT-6D with a 24-volt electrical system.

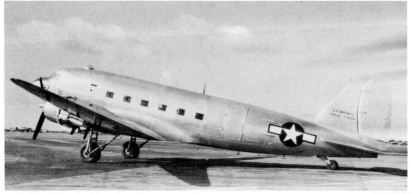

Douglas R4D-5Z (17224)   Peter M. Bowers
Administrative-command version as indicated by the suffix "Z"
adopted in 1945 in place of the former "F". Photo at Shanghai.

Brewster F3A-1 (11076)   U. S. Marine Corps
Late model F4U-1 built by the Brewster Aeronautical Corporation
under sub-contract.   From group 11067-11293.   See also FG-1.

Grumman F6F-5P (77632)   Clay Jansson
One of VMD-354's (Marine Photographic Squadron) modified fighters at Guam in 1945. Lighter, less armament, would do 384 m.p.h.

North American PBJ-1J   Clay Jansson
One of VMB-612's modified B-25J bombers which pioneered USMC
radar directed night rocket attacks on shipping off Saipan.

General Motors TBM-3E's   Clay Jansson
VMTB-232 (pre-war VMB-2) en route to Okinawa in April 1945.
Winged devil in diamond (see page 36) is proudly painted on fin.

Grumman F7F-3N's   U. S. Marine Corps
Three "Tigercats" without their nose radar gear. Developed too
late in the war to enter combat their contracts were cut back.

MARINE CORPS SQUADRON ASSIGNMENT
1 January 1946

Air, Fleet Marine Force, Pacific

Ewa - Hdqtrs. Sq.: MAG-15 - Hdqtrs. Sq. MAG-15 - Hdqtrs. Sq. 15,
SMS-15, VMR-352 and VMR-953. MASG-44 - Hdqtrs. Sq. 44, SMS-
44, and Prov. CAUS-1 (a).
Midway - VMF-322.
USS PUDGET SOUND - Marine CASD-6, VMF-321 and VMTB-454.
USS SAIDOR - Marine CASD-4, VMF-213, and VMTB-623.
USS POINT CRUZ - Marine CASD-8, VMF-217, and VMTB-464.
USS RENDOVA - Marine CASD-7, VMF-216, and VMTB-624.
USS BADOENG STRAIT - Marine CASD-5.

1st Marine Air Wing

Tientsin - Hdqtrs. Sq.-1 and VMO-3.
Tsingtao - MWSS-1.

MAG-12 - Peking

Hdqtrs. Sq.-12	VMF-211
SMS-12	VMF-218
VMF-115	

MAG-24 - Peking

Hdqtrs. Sq.-24	VMF (N)-533
SMS-24	VMF (N)-541
AMS-7	

MAG-25 - Tsingtao

Hdqtrs. Sq.-25	VMR-152
SMS-25	VMR-153

MAG-32 - Tsingtao

Hdqtrs. Sq.-32	VMTB-134
SMS-32	VMSB-224
VMO-6	VMSB-343
AWS-11	

2nd Marine Air Wing

Hdqtrs. Sq.-2, MWSS-2, and VMD-254, all located on Okinawa.
MOG-1 - Hdqtrs. Sq., and VMO-5, at Sasebo; and VMO-2 on Nagasaki.

MAG-14 - Okinawa

Hdqtrs. Sq.-14	VMF-222
SMS-14	VMF-223
VMF-212	

MAG-31 - Yokosuka

Hdqtrs. Sq. -31	VMF-441
SMS-31	VMF (N)-542
VMF-224	VMR-952
VMF-311	

MAG-33 - Okinawa

Hdqtrs. Sq.-33	VMF-323
SMS-33	VMF (N)-543
VMF-312	

MADC-2

Hdqtrs. Sq., AWS-6, and AWS-8, at Okinawa; and AWS-1 at Ie Shima.

4th Marine Air Wing

Hdqtrs. Sq.-4 and MWSS-4 at Guam; and MAB Sq.-1 at Peleliu.

MAG-11 - Peleliu

Hdqtrs. Sq.-11
SMS-11

AWS-2
VMF-122

MAG-21 - Guam

Hdqtrs. Sq.-21
SMS-21
VMO-1
VMJ-2

VMR-252
VMR-253
VMR-353

Aviation (Tactical) Overseas

MAWC - Hdqtrs. Sq., Supply Sq.-5, AWS-12, and VMB-612, at Miramar; and AWS-13, at Santa Barbara.

Personnel Group - Miramar

Hdqtrs. Sq.
Med. Det.
MAC Sq.-1
MAC Sq.-2

MAC Sq.-3
MAC Sq.-4
MAC Sq.-5

MAG-22 - El Toro

Hdqtrs. Sq.-22
SMS-22
VMF-113

VMF-314
VMF-422

MAG-35 - El Centro

Hdqtrs. Sq.-35
SMS-35

VMF (N)-534

MAG-46 - El Toro

Hdqtrs. Sq.-46
SMS-46
MarCASD-3
MarCASD-9
MarCASD-10
MarCASD-11
MarCASD-12
MarCASD-15
MarCASD-16
VMF-124
VMTB-143
VMF-214

VMTB-231
VMTB-233
VMTB-234
VMF-452
VMTB-453
VMF-461
VMTB-473
VMF-511
VMF-512
VMF-513
VMTB-622
VMTB-943

MASG-51 - Santa Barbara

Hdqtrs. Sq.-51
SMS-48
MarCASD-1 (b)
MarCASD-13
MarCASD-14

VMF-114
VMTB-151
VMF-225
VMTB-463

9th Marine Air Wing

Hdqtrs. Sq.08 and MWDD-9 at Cherry Point; and VMD-354 and VMD-954 at Kingston.
1st AWG - Hdqtrs. and Serv. Sq.-1 and AWS-16 at Cherry Point; AWS-17 at Oak Grove; and AWS-18 at Bogue.

MAG-34 - Oak Grove

Hdqtrs. Sq.-34
SMS-34

VMSB-931
VMSB-932

MNF-53 - Eagle Mt. Lake

Hdqtrs. Sq.-53
SMS-53
VMF (N)-531

VMF (N)-532
VMF (N)-544

MAG-91 - Cherry Point

Hdqtrs. Sq.-91
SMS-91
VMF-911

VMF-912
VMF-913
VMF-914

Curtiss SB2C-5   U. S. Navy
Improved version recognizable by the pilots ribless side windows.
VMSB-343 lost six out of twelve in a 1945 storm at Laichow, China.

Douglas R4D-5 (39074)   Peter M. Bowers
With cargo doors open on a Chinese airfield. Center facing wall
bucket seats made simultaneous cargo loading possible in the R4D.

Douglas R4D-3 (06996)   William T. Larkins
Rare C-53 passenger version. 28 only were built, three are believed
to have been used by the Marine Corps. P & W R-1830-92 engines.

Northrop F2T-1   Clay Jansson
One of five P-61 night fighters turned over to the Marine Corps
after the war and used for training at M.C.A.S. Miramar, California.

Grumman JRF-5 (84796)   William T. Larkins
March 1947 photo of a "Goose" amphibian assigned to the USMC
air station at Parris Island, South Carolina. Had 800 mile range.

Martin JM-1 (66749)   William T. Larkins
Orange colored tow target plane which was formerly AAF model
AT-23B-MO, serial number 41-35702, revised B-26C less guns.

Grumman F7F-3 (80524)   William T. Larkins
One-place day fighter with auxiliary belly fuel tank in June, 1946.
Note the small pre-war type USMC insignia on nose, yellow G142.

Grumman F7F-3N (80445)   William T. Larkins
Two-place night fighter version with radar nose at MCAS Miramar
on 5-24-46. Dash 3N version had vertical tail surfaces enlarged.

Grumman F7F-3P (80448)   William T. Larkins
With green and white bands on the cowlings and wings on October
12, 1946.   Two 2,100 hp R-2800-34W.   Equipped with cameras.

Beech JRB-4 (66464)   William T. Larkins
Seven passenger light transport built in 1944, identical to the AAF
UC-45F.   Many lasted ten years, an unusual length of service life.

Consolidated RY-3 (90044)   William T. Larkins
Rare USMC type at Miramar 5-24-46. As AAF C-87C, 22 to Navy.
Span 110 ft., length 75 ft.5 in. Speed 273 m.p.h. at 14,700 feet.

Vought F4U-4 (96879)   Warren M. Bodie
VMF-225's unofficial markings at the 1946 National Air Races showing MARINES and squadron on the plane for the first time since 1941.

Vought F4U-4 (81343)   Leo J. Kohn
Squadrons were assigned identifying tail letters in late 1946 but
the aircraft did not carry the squadron number until the year of 1950.

Grumman F7F-4N (80611)   Harold G. Martin
General Schilt (CG1st MAW) flew an F7F on a Korean combat strike
November 10, 1951 on the 176th birthday of the U. S. Marine Corps.

Goodyear FG-1D   William T. Larkins
NAS Oakland reserve fighter with minute USMC insignia under the
cockpit in May 1947. Goodyear built 3,266 of these F4U-1 planes.

Beech SNB-3Q (51167)   William T. Larkins
Modified transport used as flying classroom to train aircrewmen
in electronic countermeasures missions. The Marine Corps had two.

Grumman F6F-5N (94338)   John C. Mitchell
"Hellcat" night fighter showing the 20mm cannon in the wings and
right wingtip radome. Small USMC insignia decal appears on cowl.

Beech JRB-4 (76776)   Edgar Deigan
Beech 18 transport assigned to Headquarters, U.S.M.C. at the
Naval Air Station, Anacostia, D. C. See JRB-6 on page 138.

Douglas R4D-6 (50748)   William T. Larkins
VMR-252 transport on September 20, 1947. The horizontal red bar
on each side of the star was adopted on May 15, 1947.

Grumman F7F-3P (80391)   William T. Larkins
Note changed cockpit area. F7F-3 day fighter, and its modified
photo version have the radar operator replaced by an extra fuel tank.

Vought F4U-4 (81945)   Peter M. Bowers
VMF-114 "Corsair" from the USS Salerno Bay. Marines began operating from escort carriers in Feb 1945 as Marine Air Service Groups.

Beech JRB-2 (76742)   Warren M. Bodie
Early five passenger transport, built as an AAF C-45A in 1941, at
the 1947 National Air Races with two-star command card on cowl.

Curtiss R5C-1 (50714)   Peter M. Bowers
Command plane in Glossy Sea Blue rather than the standard silver
or camouflage. Also shown at the 1947 National Air Races.

Beech SNB-2 (39265)   Charles N. Trask
AAF model AT-7 navigation trainer from Quantico. 240 of these
were delivered to the Navy in 1942. Many were later re-built.

Piasecki HRP-1   Warren M.Bodie
Original fabric-covered "Flying Banana" with the markings of Marine Helicopter Development Squadron One   (HMX-1),   Quantico.

Sikorsky HO3S-1 (122513)   Warren M. Bodie
This and the HRP-1 were the first two helicopters operated by the
Marine Corps.   450 h.p. P & W Wasp engine. USAF model H-5.

Lockheed TO-1 (33850)   William T. Larkins
F-80C, AAF 47-1397, one of several turned over by the AAF for
Marine jet pilot training. Nov. 1948 photo. Note U.S.M.C. insignia.

McDonnell FH-1 (111788)   U. S. Marine Corps
First jet fighter designed for naval use to be operated by the Marine
Corps. The tail letters "LC" identify squadron VMF-122, and were
formerly "BC" as seen in the photo below. VMF-311 operated 16
TO-1's as armed first-line equipment in 1948, see photo to the left.
Major "Doc" Everton and three pilots from VMF-122 at Cherry Point
formed the stunt team "Marine Phantoms" and toured the United
States doing air shows for two years. 1948 saw the advent of both
jets and helicopters in the USMC   -   the start of a major change.

McDonnell FH-1 (111770)   William T. Larkihs
VMF-122 "Phantom" taxying out to take part in the May 15, 1948
flight demonstration before the Aviation Writers Association meeting.

McDonnell FH-1 (111785)   Warren M. Bodie
Armed with four 20 mm cannon in the nose. Speed 480 mph, range
800 miles. Original designation of FD-1 changed to FH-1 in 1948.

Grumman F7F-3N (80487)   Dave Rankin
A "Tigercat" from VMF-461. This night fighter had a speed of 425
m.p.h. and range of 1,360 miles. Armed with four 20 mm cannon.

Beech JRB-6 (67257)   Warren M. Bodie
One-star command plane from NAS Anacostia. A modernized utility
transport similar to the SNB-5. Two were used by the Marine Corps.

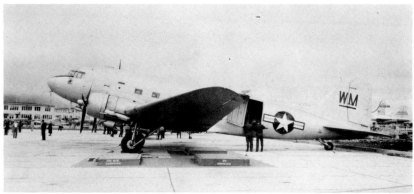

Douglas R4D-6 (50799)   William T. Larkins
From Headquarters Squadron 33. Nose insignia on Marine Corps
planes may be either squadron insignia or USMC emblem, not both.

Vought F4U-4 (81836)   William T. Larkins
Fully armed "Corsair" being demonstrated October 10, 1948. One
"Tiny Tim" rocket, eight 5" wing rockets and one 500 pound bomb.

Vought F4U-4B (62953)   Joe Hardman
Normally armed with six .50 cal machine guns and 2,400 rounds of
ammunition, the F4U-4B mounted 4/20mm cannon. From VMF-312.

Goodyear FG-1D (92371)   Clay Jansson
When two Dallas Marine Reserve squadrons were on summer duty
in August, 1949, one had the "D" circled for quick identification.

Vought F4U-4 (81666)   Harold G. Martin
VMF-211 "Corsair" at the Portrex Maneuvers. The Marines operated
at least two F4U-4P's. The U.S.M.C. had 794 aircraft in use in 1949.

Vought F4U-5N (122184)   Clay Jansson
VMF(N)-513 night fighter at El Toro in 1949, soon to see combat
action in Korea. It could carry two 1,000 lb. bombs or 12" rockets.

New Markings Appear In 1950   U. S. Marine Corps
For the first time since late 1941, when the word MARINES shrank
to one-inch high letters on the fin of aircraft in drab warpaint,
regulations called for identification of the branch of service in letters at least one foot high. These high visibility markings were
adopted February 27, 1950 to facilitate identification on the ground and
at close range. In addition to the large MARINES the squadron
designation was plainly marked for the first time in nine years.

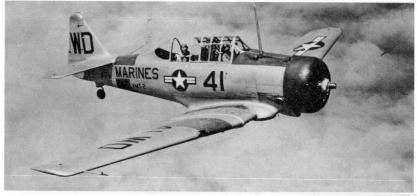

North American SNJ-6 (112129)   U. S. Marine Corps
El Toro based instrument trainer with green fuselage and wing
bands. VMT-2 duplicated other designations, was changed to VMIT-2.

Douglas AD-2 (122224)   Warren M. Bodie
The Marine Corps had only two Attack Squadrons on June 25, 1950
when the Korean War started; it had eleven squadrons two years later.

Grumman F9F-2 (123440)   William T. Larkins
VMF-311 "Panthers" were the first Marine jets to enter combat when
they supported the December 1950 breakout at the Chosin Reservoir.

Grumman F9F-2B (123064)   Harold G. Martin
VMF-115 straight-wing "Panther" at the Portrex Maneuvers, Puerto
Rico, in early 1950. "B" letter suffix denotes wing bomb racks.

Douglas R5D-3 (92003)   U. S. Marine Corps
A former Royal Air Force C-54D returned from Lend-Lease and
then assigned to Marine Corps Transport Squadron 352 at El Toro.

Lockheed TO-2 (124580)   U. S. Marine Corps
Early model T-33A with under-wing tip tanks assigned to Headquarters
Squadron 12, Marine Air Group 12. Painted as HEDRON-12 on plane.

Douglas R4D-5 (17166)   Harold G. Martin
The tail letters "AV" designate Headquarters Squadron 15. Marines
also flew the R4D-4 "Skytrooper", not pictured in this book.

Grumman F7F-3N (80590)   U. S. Marine Corps
VMF(N)-531 "Tigercat" at Cherry Point on April 24, 1950. F7F's
of VMF(N)-542 did night combat duty in Korea Oct to Dec 1950.

Douglas F3D-1 (123761)   Warren M. Bodie
VMF(N)-542 returned to El Toro and received several of these new
"Skyknight" jet fighters as transitional trainers for the F3D-2.

Sikorsky HRS-1 (127785)   Warren M. Bodie
Marine transport helicopter for carrying assault troops, same basic
type as HO4S-1. One 600 hp P & W R-1340-57. 225 mile range.

Bell HTL-4 (128635)   William J. Balogh
Light two-place trainer assigned to HMX-1 at Quantico. This type
later served with VMO-6 in Korea. 176 mile range, speed 92 mph.

Fairchild R4Q-1 (124330)   U. S. Marine Corps
Cherry Point based VMR-252 was the first to get the "Packet", in
early 1950. USAF model C-119C. Huge 3,250 hp R-4360 engines.

Cessna OE-1's   U. S. Marine Corps
Two VMO-2 L-19A artillery spotters. Some were transferred from
the Army to the Marine Corps in Korea. See also on page 155.

Vought F4U-5P (122168)   Clay Jansson
The first USMC aircraft to enter combat in Korea. Two from First
MAW Photo Section flew off USS Valley Forge 7-4-50, one lost.

McDonnell F2H-2P (125687)   Clay Jansson
With 122 photo missions accomplished, some as far up as Yalu river.
VMJ-1 became a photo sqdn in Feb 1952; flew 5,025 combat flights.

Douglas F3D-2 (124620)   Charles N. Trask
VMF(N)-513 "Skyknight" parked on K-2 airstrip, Taegu, Korea in
August 1953. This squadron flew 12,669 combat missions in Korea.

Douglas AD-4 (123810)   Charles N. Trask
VMA-121 Able Dog on K-16 airstrip, Korea. Sqdn set a record by
dropping 156 tons of bombs in one day with 16 AD's in June of 1953.

Grumman F9F-2 (127153)   Clay Jansson
An armed VMF-311 "Panther" parked on K-3 airstrip, Korea.
Note the wing-mounted 500 pound bombs.

General Motors TBM-3R (86143)   Clay Jansson
With turret removed as personnel transport. HEDRON-1, First Marine Air Wing, Korea. Marines also had one or two TBM-3Q's and W's.

Grumman F8F-2 (122617)   Mitch Mayborn
Rare 11-22-52 photo of Marine "Bearcat", one of a few used by the
Marine Corps Schools at Quantico. Powered by 2,500 hp R-2800-34.

Sikorsky HRS-1 (127828)   Gordon S. Williams
HMR-162 transport with its "HS" squadron identification letters.
Weight 7,400 pounds loaded. Capable of carrying 8 armed troops.

Sikorsky HRS-2 (129026)   William J. Balogh
From HMR-361, Helicopter-Marine-Transport Squadron 361, based
at Santa Ana, California. One P & W 600 h.p. R-1340 engine.

Beech SNB-5 (67103)   William T. Larkins
Modernized SNB-2 re-built in August 1951. USAF re-manufactured
a large number of Beech transports as C-45G and H. c/n N790.

Douglas R4D-6R (50816)   Douglas D. Olson
One of a small number of R4D (C-47) types re-built as airline
transports. "R" denotes passenger carrying status. Note the door.

Lockheed P2V-2 (39343)   William J. Balogh
One of two "Neptune" patrol bombers used by the Marine Corps for
airborne electronics aircrew training. The other plane was #39365.

Sikorsky HRS-3 (130261)   Chalmers A. Johnson
Re-engined with Wright R-1300-3 of 600 h.p. It has a wire hoist for rescue or wire laying. Crew of two plus ten passengers. HMR-163.

Douglas R4D-8 (17153)   Charles N. Trask
Two-star command plane assigned to Headquarters Squadron, First Marine Air Wing, at Seoul, Korea, in November of 1953.

Douglas R4D-8 (50782)   Charles N. Trask
VMF(N)-513 developed night close air support by the use of flare planes, even R4D's dropped flares for the fighters. Note the paint.

Vought F4U-4's   U. S. Marine Corps
Red bar in insignia has been removed by the use of a camera filter,
a factor to be evaluated when estimating the date of photographs.

Vought AU-1 (129325)   Gordon S. Williams
Developed for Korean War use as a low altitude air support fighter.
More armor, no supercharger. Some went to French Navy as F4U-7.

McDonnell F2H-2P (125696)   William J. Balogh
VMJ-2 550 m.p.h. "Banshee" at the 1953 National Aircraft Show,
Detroit. Note 3 camera windows in elongated nose. 1,185 mile range.

Douglas AD-2Q (122386)   Clay Jansson
Radar countermeasures "Skyraider" from VMC-1 in Korea. "Q"
versions of AD had two man crew   - pilot and RCM operator.

Douglas AD-4N (126984)   Douglas D. Olson
Carrying air-borne searchlight under the left wing and radar pod
under the right. Note 4/20mm cannon, 12 wing racks. VMC-2.

Douglas AD-4W (126839)   William T. Larkins
VMC-3 "guppy" AD with huge belly radome requiring added tail
fins for stability. 20,000 pound weight, twice that of MBT bomber.

Douglas F3D-2 (127063)   Douglas D. Olson
VMF(N)-531 "Skyknight". Two-place all-weather interceptor with
517 m.p.h. speed. Two Westinghouse J-34's, 3500 lbs. thrust each.

Douglas R4D-5 (17155)   Chalmers A. Johnson
With MAMS-12 (Marine Aircraft Maintenance Squadron) in Japan.
Many R4D-5's were re-built as R4D-8's, see No. 17153 on page 150.

Douglas AD-1 (09226)   William J. Balogh
At least this one AD-1 is known to have been in the Marine Corps.
AD-1 was the redesignated production version of model BT2D-1.

Consolidated-Vultee TN-OY-2 (03963)   Peter M. Bowers
Old VMO-1 "Sentinel" assigned to training duty. VMO squadron does
Utility duty with mixed fixed-wing aircraft and helicopters.

Sikorsky HRS-2 (130144)   Gordon S. Williams
Assigned to HMR-262. Transport helicopters entered the Korean War
on a combat status in September 1951 with the arrival of HMR-161.

Sikorsky HO4S-1 (125506)   Douglas D. Olson
HMX-1. Air Force model H-19, civil S-55. The Marine Corps mission
of assult landings changed the need from Observation to Transport.

Douglas R5D-3 (56498)   Charles N. Trask
VMR-152 transport in Korea. VMR's flew the airlift evacuation out
of Yonpo to Itami, Japan, between December 11th and 16th, 1950.

Cessna OE-1 (136891)   Charles N. Trask
OE-1's directed air strikes, developed night close air support and
did artillery spotting for the First Marine Division in Korea.

Sikorsky HO5S-1 (130123)   Charles N. Trask
VMO-6 did the first night helicopter evacuation of wounded in 1950
at Pusan. The squadron evacuated 7,137 men in three years of war.

Grumman F9F-2 (125152)   Mitch Mayborn
Hawaii-based VMF-451. Navy gave many to city playgrounds in a
nationwide program, some survived only 3 months of kids' curiosity.

Grumman F9F-4 (125919)   Art Krieger
Miami-based VMF-334. Squadron was re-designated VMA-334 (see
page 163) in 1954, back to VMF-334 in 1959 (see page 189).

Grumman F9F-4 (125923)   William T. Larkins
VMF-122 from Cherry Point, North Carolina. The F9F-4 and F9F-5
were identical except for the engine, dash 4 had Allison J33-A-16.

Fairchild R4Q-1 (126736)   Charles N. Trask
VMR-253 "Packet" running up on a snow covered Korean airfield
during the winter of 1953. It can carry 42 troops or cargo.

Fairchild R4Q-1 (128738)   Chalmers A. Johnson
At Itami, Japan, base of VMR-253. The dorsal and ventral fins were
added for flight stability after production was completed on dash one.

Douglas R5D-3 (91995)   Chalmers A. Johnson
Assigned to the Headquarters Squadron, First Marine Air Wing, Japan.
The white top reduces cabin temperature of plane while on the ground.

Douglas AD-3 (122808)   Charles N. Trask
VMA-251 "Blackpatch Squadron" relieved VMF-323 in Korea in
July of 1953. AD could carry more bombs than World War II B-17.

Grumman F9F-5 (125614)   Chalmers A. Johnson
VMF-223 "Panther" with unusual aluminum finish. Several F9F-5's
were used by the Navy in 1953 to test experimental color schemes.

North American FJ-2 (131941)   William J. Balogh
First unpainted, folding-wing USMC version of the USAF F-86
at the press showing, National Aircraft Show, September 1953.

Douglas R4D-5 (39060)   William J. Balogh
New River, Edenton, Beaufort, Atlantic, Wilmington and Washington
are small fields operated under the control of MCAS Cherry Point.

Fairchild R4Q-1 (126575)   William J. Balogh
Station based "Packet". An assault cargo and personnel transport
with clam shell doors at the rear. Gross weight 64,000 pounds.

Fairchild R4Q-2 (131666)   William J. Balogh
Two Wright R-3350 engines of 2,700 h.p. each lift a payload of
12,000 pounds in a 30 ft. by 9 ft. by 8 ft. fuselage compartment.

Douglas AD-5 (132672)   Ships & Aircraft
Multiplex all-purpose version built for twelve different duties. Has
two place side-by-side cockpit seating. Shown at Miami, June 1954.

North American FJ-2's (131990, 131987)   U. S. Marine Corps
Hawaii-based VMF-235 replaced its F4U-4's with FJ-2's in June
of 1954. Note the beginning of the spectacular current markings.

Douglas R4D-6R (50773)   Gordon S. Williams
Command transport from MCAS Cherry Point, North Carolina, which
has the only Overhaul and Repair factory run by the Marine Corps.

Douglas AD-4N (125723)   Charles N. Trask
VMC-1 "Skyraider" on K-16 airstrip, Korea, on 17 February 1954.
FMAW flew 127,496 sorties in Korea, more than all of World War 2.

Grumman F9F-4 (125205)   Gordon S. Williams
VMF-334 "Panther" with Allison J-33A-16 engine of 5,850 pounds
thrust. Shown at 1954 Aviation Writers Association show in Miami.

Grumman F9F-5P (126278)   William J. Balogh
Photo-reconnaissance "Panther" with larger fuselage, higher tail,
longer camera nose and P & W J-48 engine of 6,250 pounds thrust.

Grumman F9F-6P (127492)   Gordon S. Williams
Swept-wing "Cougar" introduced sub-sonic speeds above 650 m.p.h.
A day fighter modified for photographic work, new in late 1954.

McDonnell F2H-4 (127572)   William T. Larkins
VMF(N)-533 "Banshee" at the Dayton Air Show, September 1954.
Note` the folding wings to facilitate carrier storage and handling.

McDonnell F2H-4 (127614)   Clay Jansson
VMF-214 "Banshee" in Hawaii. A twin-jet all weather fighter used
as standard Navy carrier equipment. Some went to reserves in 1958.

Grumman F9F-5's   U. S. Marine Corps
VMA-323 day fighters. F4U-4's of VMF-323 flew off USS Badoeng
Straight, giving close air support for ten days ahead of the Inchon
Landing on September 14, 1950. They also covered the landing and
advance with 500 pound bombs and napalm. VMF-214 did the same
duty flying from the USS Sicily. The operation ended Oct. 7, 1950.

Grumman F9F-4's   U. S. Marine Corps
Four in flight at Miami in 1954. The F9F dive-bombs at an angle of
30 degrees and speed of 552 mph. SBD dove at 70 degrees, 276 mph.

Piasecki HRP-1   Clay Jansson
Early model helicopter practicing water rescue. Helicopters, unlike
fixed wing craft, fly well without any fuselage covering.

Sikorsky HRS-3 (130250)   William T. Larkins
Number 26 airplane of Marine Helicopter Transport Squadron 362
visiting San Francisco in July 1955. Re-engined model HRS-2.

Sikorsky XHR2S-1 (133733)   Gordon S. Williams
31,000 pound twin-engine helicopter designed for U.S.M.C. Fleet
Marine Force support. Two 2,000 hp R-2800's. Two crew, 20 troops.

Vought F7U-3 (128466)   Clay Jansson
Rare photo showing the single "Cutlass" used by the USMC in Feb.
1955 tests for high speed mine laying. A carrier VF, now obsolete.

North American FJ-2 (132055)   Ships & Aircraft
VMA-334 replaced its F9F-4's (see page 163) with unpainted metal
finish "Fury's" as shown in this photograph of May, 1955.

North American FJ-2 (132110)   William J. Balogh
VMF-312 "Checkerboard Squadron" was one of five Marine Corps
units to fly the FJ-2, operated F4U's out of Kimpo early in Korean war.

Lockheed TV-2 (136828)   William J. Balogh
Air Force T-33A two-place trainer, one of many taken over for
instrument training, check flights for transition to flying jets.

Douglas R5D-2 (39113)   Gordon S. Williams
HEDRON, 2nd Marine Air Wing. C-54B, all fuel in wings. VMR-152
had one equipped as a flying Tactical Air Direction Center in Korea.

Cessna OE-2 (140081)   Cessna Aircraft Company
Improved 190 m.p.h. model with self-sealing fuel tanks, armor plate,
flak curtains and six wing rockets. Note wing vanes on test aircraft.

Douglas AD-5 (132654)   Lawrence S. Smalley
The dash 5 model could be modified to serve as a utility plane, basic
attack, photographic, tow-target, passenger, ambulance or radar type.

Douglas AD-5 (133926)   Gordon S. Williams
Rocket armed close air support plane. TBF "Avengers" hit the enemy
75 yards ahead of our troops in the Bougainville landing.

Douglas F3D-2 (127049)   William T. Larkins
VMF(N)-542 in July 1955. "Skyknights" destroyed more enemy
aircraft in Korea than any other Navy or Marine fighter type.

Douglas F3D-2M (125872)   Clay Jansson
With wing racks for the "Sparrow" missile. The gray top with white
undersides was adopted 7-55, with all planes to be so painted by 7-57.

Douglas AD-5W (132791)   Clay Jansson
The AD-5W does not have fuselage dive brakes. The model shown
in this photograph is equipped for Anti-Submarine Warfare.

Kaman HOK-1 (129836)   Clay Jansson
VMO-6 first posted lookouts and patrols on high mountains by helicopter in Korea in 1950.   They strung telephone lines under fire.

Fairchild R4Q-2 (131684)   Robert Stuckey
Re-engined R4Q-1 with Wright R-3350 engines of 2,700 h.p. each.
Armor plate was added to the engines as protection from ground fire.

North American T-28B (140008)   Clay Jansson
Marine Instrument Training Squadron Ten's all-yellow trainer with
green fuselage and wing bands. Note use of USAF model designation.

Kaman HOK-1 (125530)   Kaman Aircraft Corp.
A series of three photos showing a factory demonstration of fire
fighting technique using a helicopter and three man rescue team.

Kaman HOK-1 (125530)   Kaman Aircraft Corp.
Helicopter lands two Ansul Chemical 300-pound dry chemical tanks,
200 feet of hose, rescue tools and 3 firemen near simulated crash.

Kaman HOK-1 (125530)   Kaman Aircraft Corp.
Advancing under the rotor down-wash of the helicopter, which helps
to control the fire, the rescuer removes dummy from burning BT-13.

Kaman HOK-1 (125530)   Kaman Aircraft Corp.
Kaman developed "bear-paws", named after the type of snowshoes
used by Canadian woodsmen, make possible the operation of helicopters from snow, sand and mud by providing a large landing gear
area which will not sink into the soft surfaces. They are small, light
weight and can be carried in the plane for quick field installation.
In early 1956 in-flight hose refueling was demonstrated for the first
time by two HRS's of HMX-1. Later, off Carolina during maneuvers,
HMR-261 and HMR-262 landed 55 combat laden troops on the transport submarine USS Sea Lion. 28 airlifts were made at 5′ intervals.

North American FJ-2 (132111)   William T. Larkins
VMF-232 "Fury". This proven design served with the Air Forces
of Canada, England, Italy, Germany, Turkey, Greece and others.

Douglas AD-5N's   U. S. Marine Corps
VMCJ-3, one of the Composite Reconnaissance Squadrons formed
to replace VMJ. It has 10 photo-recon and 10 electronic planes.

Douglas F4D-1 (134815)   Douglas Aircraft Company
Big delta-wing all-weather interceptor from VMF-115. Note the
airborne starter. The F4D uses the Aero 13F armament control system.

Grumman F9F-5 (125612)   Clay Jansson
Many VMF squadrons flying jet fighters were re-designated as
VMA (Attack) units as the prop-driven AD became obsolescent.

Douglas A4D-1 (137830)   Gordon S. Williams
Early test "Skyhawk" from the Naval Air Special Weapons Facility.
It has two 20 mm cannon in the wing roots, underwing racks for tanks.

Beech SNB-5P (12385)   Kenneth M. Sumney
Re-manufactured SNB-2P photo trainer. The international orange and
white colors were adopted for all the training aircraft in the year 1956.

Douglas AD-5W (135194)   Logan Coombs
The squadron leader from VMC-2. This squadron was re-designated
as VMCJ-2 in 1956. See also the notes under AD-5N on page 172.

Grumman F9F-5P (126287)   Clay Jansson
VMCJ-3 "Cougar" with its tail hook engaged after landing on the
deck of a carrier at sea. Carrier landings are made with hatch open.

Grumman F9F-5P (126277)   Clay Jansson
Showing some of the beautiful individual markings of VMCJ-3 that
distinguished Marine Corps planes before the recent Navy change.

Grumman F9F-6P (128298)   Douglas D. Olson
VMCJ-2 photo plane at the 1956 National Aircraft Show with new
white paint and squadron markings. Compare with AD-5W, page 173.

Grumman F9F-6 (127419)   Clay Jansson
This and the plane below are from VMFT-10, Marine Fighter Training Squadron Ten.   This shows one of the last of the blue "Cougars".

Grumman F9F-8B (141156)   Clay Jansson
700 m.p.h. day fighter powered by P&W J-48 of 7,000 pounds thrust
with aerial re-fueling nose probe. The "Cougar" is now obsolescent.

Grumman F9F-8P (141722)   Clay Jansson
A VMCJ-3 F9F-8P set a record of 204 consecutive aerial refueling
plug-ins in one hour with a VAH-2 AJ-2 over Japan in Nov. 1958.

Grumman F9F-8T (142485)   Clay Jansson
Two-place "Cougar" trainer with the fuselage lengthened 34 inches.
It can exceed Mach 1 in a shallow dive, has nose probe, no guns.

Beech T-34B (144009)   U. S. Marine Corps
A primary trainer for aviation cadet flight indoctrination at Quantico.
The proposed Navy-USAF model designation system was dropped.

Lockheed C-130A-20-LM (USAF 55-46)   U. S. Marine Corps
Loaned by USAF for aerial re-fueling tests in August 1956, resulting
in a contract for GV-1's. Powered by four T-56 4,000 hp turbo-props.

Douglas AD-5 (132401)   Lawrence S. Smalley
Exhaust-streaked "Skyraider" from H&MS-33, Headquarters and Maintenance Squadron 33, which is a characteristic of AD's. See page 167.

Douglas AD-5N (132591)   Clay Jansson
One of the many versions of the multiplex AD-5. Note the radome
under the fuselage and the detachable long range fuel tanks.

Douglas AD-6 (137618)   Clay Jansson
"Skyraider" with the unusual markings of MARS-37, Marine Aircraft
Repair Squadron 37.   2,700 h.p. R-3350, span 50 feet, length 39 feet.

Grumman OF-1 (Mock-up)   Grumman Aircraft Eng. Co.
Two-place VO, 42' length, 42' span. Two Lycoming T-53 turboprop
engines, 300 m.p.h. speed, short take-off. Not purchased by USMC.

Douglas A4D-1 (142168)   U. S. Marine Corps
VMA-224 "Skyhawk" in full trim. Length of 39 feet is greater than
its span of 27 ft. 6 in. It set a sea-level speed record of 695.163 mph.

Douglas F4D-1 (134826)   Clay Jansson
Former Mojave-based VMF-115 (see page 172) re-designated as
VMF(AW)-15, an all-weather fighter squadron.

Vought F8U-1 (140448)   U. S. Marine Corps
The fifth "Crusader" being tested by the Marine Corps at Mojave in
May of 1957. The F8U-1 is now the standard Marine Corps fighter.

Douglas F3D-2-T2 (127084)   William J. Balogh
Training version as evidenced by the suffix letter "T" on the model
designation.   Tail letters are "LP", squadron number is unknown.

Douglas F3D-2Q (125786)   Clay Jansson
Modified for airborne electronics countermeasures mission, they form
half of VMCJ-3's composite squadron. F9F-8P's form the other half.

Sikorsky HUS-1 (143983)   Clay Jansson
HMR-363. The first fully instrumented helicopter. P&W R-1820-84
of 1,425 h.p. Carries 12 troops or 8 litters. Has 56-foot rotor blade.

Sikorsky HRS-3 (137836)   Clay Jansson
HMR-362. Transport helicopters first changed to standard gray-
white paint scheme, then to special USMC green for assault mission.

Vertol HUP-2 (128588)   Clay Jansson
Six place utility helicopter widely used by the Fleet and many Navy and
Marine reserve bases. Piasecki changed its name to Vertol Aircraft.

Douglas R5D-4R (90414)   Clay Jansson
MARS-37 passenger transport. The basic R5D fuselage is empty for
cargo carrying.   "Z" suffix was used for Administrative interior.

Fairchild R4Q-2 (131719)   Clay Jansson
VMR-252 "Packet" with a new radome bulge added to its nose. This
is now standard equipment as a safety feature for all-weather flying.

North American SNJ-4 (27842)   Clay Jansson
One of the very last. From Cherry Point, stored at NAS Litchfield
Park, Phoenix, Arizona, in April 1957. Most were sold as surplus.

Douglas R4D-8 (138820)   Clay Jansson
Rare photo of the re-built "Super DC-3" tested by the USAF as the
YC-129, re-designated as YC-47F, finally turned over to the Navy.

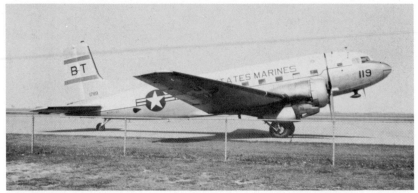

Douglas R4D-8 (17119)   Ralph I. Brown
Serving Marine Training and Replacement Group Twenty. The USAF
bought Convair-Liners so all Super DC-3 production went to the Navy

Douglas R4D-8 (50835)   Clay Jansson
Re-built R4D-6. Each plane was completely re-manufactured as new;
tail, engines and landing gear modified. All kept original serials.

Convair R4Y-1 (140993)   Douglas D. Olson
The first "Convair-Liner" operated by the Marine Corps, assigned
to the flight section of Headquarters U.S.M.C., Washington, D.C.

Convair R4Y-1 (141012)   Douglas D. Olson
A modified civil 340 design with large left hand cargo door serving Air
Fleet Marine Force Atlantic (painted as AIRFMFLANT near tail).

Convair R4Y-1 (141019)   Lawrence S. Smalley
Air Fleet Marine Force Pacific's command job with new weather
radar nose. These were added after the planes had been in service.

North American FJ-3 (136022)   Clay Jansson
Improved FJ-2 wearing the green shamrocks of Miami-based VMF-
333.   Note nose blackened by gunfire and underwing fuel tanks.

Grumman F9F-8 (141204)   U. S. Marine Corps
Last production model of the "Cougar", with nose refueling probe. The
F9F-9 was a major design change and was later re-designated F11F-1.

Douglas AD-5 (133882)   William J. Balogh
Assigned to Marine Aircraft Repair Sqdn 27. Last of the prop driven
USMC combat aircraft; VMA-332 retired its final AD-6 on 7-28-59.

Grumman F9F-8B (141057)   Roger F. Besecker
Late 1958 photo of a VMA-533 "Cougar". Suffix "B" denotes changes
made on the aircraft to carry out loft bombing of atomic stores.

Douglas AD-6 (135399)   William L. Swisher
Heavily armed, improved model of the AD-4 specially designed for
ground support action. Four 20mm cannon. Has fuselage dive brakes.

Hiller XROE-1 (144004)   Harry Gann
One man rotorcycle, weighs 546 pounds, has a 42 h.p. Nelson H59
engine. It can be dropped to downed pilots for self-rescue.

MARINE AIR RESERVE SQUADRONS
Summer 1958

Los Alamitos, Calif. (7L)
VMF-123	F9F-6
VMF-241	F9F-6
VMF-134	F9F-6
VMF-534	F9F-6
HMR-764	HSS/HUP

Oakland, Calif. (7F)
VMF-133	F2H-2
VMF-141	F2H-2
HMR-769	HSS/HUP

Denver, Colorado (7P)
VMF-236	F9F-6

Anacostia, D. C. (6A)
VMF-321	AD-4

Jacksonville, Fla. (6F)
VMF-144	F9F-6

Miami, Florida (5H)
VMF-142	F9F-6
VMA-341	F9F-6
HMR-765	HSS/HUP

Atlanta, Georgia (7B)
VMF-251	AD-4
VMA-243	AD-4

Glenview, Illinois (7V)
VMF-543	F9F-6
VMA-611	F9F-6
HMR-763	HSS

Olathe, Kansas (7K)
VMF-113	F9F-6
VMF-215	F9F-6

New Orleans, La. (7X)
VMF-143	AD-4
HMR-767	HSS/HUP

So. Weymouth, Mass. (7Z)
VMF-217	F9F-6
VMF-322	F9F-6
HMR-711	HSS/HUP

Grosse Isle Mich.(7Y)
VMF-222	AD-4
VMF-231	AD-4

Minneapolis, Minn. (7E)
VMF-213	F9F-5
VMF-234	F9F-5
HMR-766	HUP

Brooklyn, N. Y. (7R)
VMF-131	F9F-6
VMF-132	F9F-6
VMF-313	F9F-6
HMR-768	HRS/HSS

Niagara Falls, N. Y. (7H)
VMF-441	F2H-2

Columbus, Ohio (7C)
VMF-221	FJ-2
VMF-224	FJ-2
HMR-761	HTL/HUP

Willow Grove, Pa. (7W)
VMF-218	F9F-6
VMF-511	F9F-6
HMR-722	HUP

Memphis, Tenn. (6M)
VMF-124	F9F-6

Dallas, Texas (7D)
VMF-111	F9F-6
VMF-112	F9F-6
VMF-413	F9F-6
HMR-762	HTL

Norfolk, Virginia (6S)
VMF-233	F2H-2

Seattle, Washington (7T)
VMF-216	AD-4
VMF-541	AD-4
HMR-770	HSS/HUP

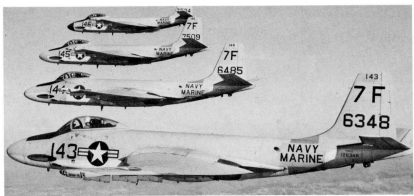

McDonnell F2H-3's (126348 etc.)   U. S. Navy
NAS Oakland "Banshee's" with their orange reserve fuselage bands
and newly authorized NAVY/MARINE for a/c used by both reserves.

Grumman F9F-6 (128139)   Charles N. Trask
Marine Reserve Squadron VMF-132 operates this fighter at Floyd
Bennett Field, Brooklyn, New York. "R" denotes New York base.

North American FJ-3 (135936)   Roger F. Besecker
VMF-511 at Willow Grove, Pennsylvania, replaced their former
F9F-6's with newer FJ-3's in late 1958. Note the trainer colors.

Douglas F3D-2 (125798)   William J. Balogh
VMF(N)-531 (see page 153) was still flying their F3D-2's in 1958
but had changed their squadron designation to VMF(AW)-531.

Douglas AD-4 (123820)   Brian Baker
Surplus at Litchfield Park on 2-28-58, from Marine Attack Training
Sqdn 20. Stored planes proved priceless at outbreak of Korean War.

Lockheed PV-2 (37480)   Brian Baker
At Litchfield Park on 3-14-58. Several versions of the Vega-built
"Harpoon" were used by the Marine Corps during the post-war years.

Vought F8U-1 (143770)   U. S. Marine Corps
Rated at over 1,000 miles per hour, and capable of breaking the
sonic barrier in level flight, Ceiling is over 50,000 feet.

Sikorsky HR2S-1   U. S. Marine Corps
Set a record of 162.7 m.p.h., and for carrying 13,250 pounds to
7,000 feet. Largest helicopter ever operated from an aircraft carrier.

Douglas AD-4B (132307)   Ships & Aircraft
In orange and white trainer colors. From AES-12, the only Aircraft Engineering Squadron in the Marine Corps.

Vought F8U-1 (145430)   U. S. Marine Corps
The "Crusader" has a variable incidence wing to give greater angle
of attack during landing and take-off. See also on page 193.

North American FJ-3M (141393)   U. S. Marine Corps
The fact that wing missile racks are installed on this "Fury" is
shown by the suffix letter "M" added to the model designation.

Vought F8U-1 (143812)   U. S. Marine Corps
Note the cross and shield insignia on the fin repeated in the fuselage
band on this VMF-122 plane. Powered by 10,000 lb/T P&W J-57.

Sikorsky HUS-1's   William T. Larkins
Four green assault helicopters from HMR-361 flying in formation
over Moffett Field on Armed Services Day, May 16, 1959.

North American FJ-3 (135926)   U. S. Marine Corps
The F9F's and FJ's are gradually being replaced by F8U-1's and
A4D-2's. 1959 plans call for the purchase of two-place F4H-1's.

Fairchild R4Q-1 (128736)   Ralph I. Brown
"The People Beater" from MCAS Cherry Point showing the later
improvements such as radar nose and fins added to early aircraft.

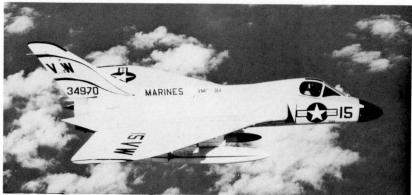

Douglas F4D-1 (134970)   U. S. Marine Corps
The "Skyray", such as this one from VMF(AW)-314, can climb to
10,000 feet in 46 seconds. It weights 25,000 pounds though 1-place.

North American FJ-4B (143516)   U. S. Marine Corps
Attack and dive bomber design with fighter performance and capable
of carrying an atomic bomb. It has a 35-degree swept back wing.

North American FJ-4's (139472, 139475)   U. S. Marine Corps
Two VMF-451 day fighters in formation. Span 39', length 37 feet.
Powered by 7,800 lb/T Wright J65-W-16 engine. Weight 19,500 lbs.

Douglas F3D-2Q's   U. S. Marine Corps
"Skyknights" on a training mission from the Marine Corps Air Station
at Iwakuni, Japan - indicative of the world-wide service of Marine
Corps Aviation over the past forty years. The 2,462 pound, 151 mph
Fokker D-7, considered one of the best fighters of World War I, can
be compared to the 26,000 pound, 1,015 mph F8U-1 of today. The
Marines have kept pace with all aviation advances over the years.

Vought F8U-1 (145432)   U. S. Marine Corps
VMF-235 Squadron Leader with wing in take-off position. Compare
with high speed position shown on page 190. F8U uses titanium alloy.

195

INDEX

INDEX

(Cont.)

INDEX

(Cont.)

INDEX

INDEX

INDEX

INDEX

INDEX

INDEX